T0354527

Books in the series 'The Colonial Economy of NSW 1788-1835'

A Brief Economic History of NSW

The Colonial Economy of NSW 1788-1835–A retrospective

The Government Store is Open for business–
the commissariat operations in NSW 1788-1835

The Enterprising Colonial Economy of NSW 1800-1830–
Government Business Enterprises in operation

Guiding the Colonial Economy–Public Funding in NSW 1800-1835

Financing the Colonial Economy of NSW 1800-1835

Essays on the colonial Economy of NSW 1788-1835

Industries that Formed a Colonial Economy

British Colonial Investment in Colonial N.S.W. 1788-1850

A Population History of Colonial New South Wales

A Population History of Colonial New South Wales

The Economic Growth of a New Colony

Gordon W Beckett

For book orders, email orders@traffordpublishing.com.sg

Most Trafford Singapore titles are also available at major online book retailers.

Printed in Singapore.

ISBN: 978-1-4669-9185-9 (sc)
ISBN: 978-1-4669-9186-6 (hc)
ISBN: 978-1-4669-9187-3 (e)

Trafford rev. 06/18/2013

www.traffordpublishing.com.sg

Singapore
toll-free: 800 101 2656 (Singapore)
Fax: 800 101 2656 (Singapore)

CONTENTS

CHAPTER 1

INTRODUCTION

All research, even that of the most isolated and independent scholar, is collaborative in the sense that it must rest upon and be related to the work of those that came earlier in the field. These words were written by Marjorie Barnard[1] and for this study are quite meaningful. The author is quite isolated and his subject, that of colonial Australia economic history reflected the isolation of this penal settlement.

The purpose of the study is not of a demographic nature, although a section includes reference to the elements of population increase, but more of the economic history of the causes and circumstances of the changing population in the colony. Topics such as the catalysts of economic change and therefore of the growing population are meaningful, and these include, the immigration sponsored by the colonial governors, the exploration that opened up the western plains, and which led to new towns and much speculation from foreign investors, the entrepreneurs that encouraged trade, both export and import, and the pastoralists that risked all by extending the limits of settlement further and further west.

To this end, this study is appreciative of the work by W.D. Borrie, N.G. Butlin and Colin Forster to name just three.

1 Barnard, Marjorie *A History of Australia*

The input of these and similar contributors is to the social and demographic history of this country. Of the economic historians, only Coghlan[2] and Butlin[3] have offered more than cursory attention to the circumstances of population growth. Fletcher, Fitzpatrick and Shann weave the story of the peopling of the colonies into their stories of gold discovery, immigration, and inland transportation. This is not an unreasonable approach to such information; however, the preference in this study is to confirm the factors that gave rise to a steady but often fluctuating population numbers. Many historians such as Barnard &Clark, include their population observations in with immigration; a 'populate or perish' approach to the subject[4]

The Aboriginal **population** may have been as high as 300,000 at the time of British colonization in 1788. Well-intentioned colonial government policies to protect their interests were rarely given practical effect, and the combined impact of introduced diseases, the loss of land, and falling fertility rates accelerated the decline in numbers. By 1860, colonial opinion fatalistically expected the Aborigines to die out within a few decades. In fact there was resurgence of their numbers, if not of their status and economic condition, probably assisted by miscegenation. Government policies shifted toward assimilation by the 1960s. Only then were South Australian Aborigines accorded full citizenship. Aboriginal land rights became an active political issue in the 1970s.

The white population began with large infusions of immigrants, many from the southern parts of England. Australia's population increased fivefold between 1844 and 1855, but the colonies attracted relatively fewer Irish and Scottish than the rest of the immigrating countries. Later waves

---

2 Coghlan, T.A. *Labour & Industry in Australia* Vols 1-4. Coghlan tells his readers that most writers miss the special significance of the question 'to what extent did the convict strain leaven the general population'? (Vol 1 p.561) In 1841, the population of NSW was 130,856, of whom 46,374 were transportees.. In 1828, only 8,725 persons had been born in the colony. In the period between 1828 and 1841, there were 29,427 births, of these 11,832 were to convict mothers and 17,595 to mothers who arrived free. By 1841, convicts had contributed 46% of the whole population.

3 Butlin, N.G. *Forming a Colonial Economy (1810-1850)*

4 Barnard: *A History of Australia* Chapter 21: Clark, *A History of Australia* Vols 1-6

of immigration substantially altered the formerly homogeneous character of the population.

At other times population growth was disappointing. The outflows in the early 1850s could be explained by the returning home of the earlier large influx of gold speculators. Moreover following the return to normalcy after the gold rush, the rates of natural increase generally declined, and birth rates fell below national levels and eventually below the level of net reproduction. It was as if the great development era (that had originated with Macquarie) was coming to an end and steadiness and purposefulness was to govern the socio-economic musings of the population. Mortality rates also have fallen, however, and Australia's infant mortality rate is now among the lowest in the world.

Various writers have different perspectives on Australian history.

N.G. Butlin writes 'the history of Australia is its economic history and the growth of the economic aspects of the country'[5].

Marjorie Barnard records Australian history is seen through the atlas, for 'in the long run geography maketh man'[6].

This study is about the changes that accompanied the growth in the Australian population.

Economic changes foreshadowed population gains; British influences affected population growth; and to a large extent, distance and local geography helped the population numbers. Obviously once in the country, there was very little need or impulse to go back to Britain and many stayed in spite of homesickness or other influences. Distance used to mean isolation. Australia had more than a hundred years to develop in safety, to maintain her racial integrity and by the tolerance and generosity of the Imperial Government, so often and so wrong headedly overlooked, to build and set her house in order according to her own ideas. This distance

5 Butlin, N.G *Forming a Colonial Economy*'

6 Barnard, Marjorie *A History of Australia* p.3

also kept the Australians a small people; it was so much easier to emigrate to America where 'the streets were paved with gold'.[7]

Barnard writes "through millions of years the aborigines adapted themselves to the continent of their adoption as surely and as perfectly as the eucalypts. Except in the far north where they may have had some contact with Papuans and Malays, no outside influence worked upon them". What the aborigines did bring to their new country was an adaptability, which spelt survival and the spiritual inheritance of a dream.[8] A.G.L. Shaw describes them as 'Stone Age people' and 'the only race which could serve as a common ancestor for all mankind'.[9]

The first connection between the white and dark people after Phillip arrived was for economic gain and benefit. Phillip, however, soon found that no advantage was to be reaped from the aboriginal except occasional succour when white men lost themselves in the bush, nor could he estimate their numbers with any accuracy.[10]

Lord Glenelg raises an interesting point in his conveyance of the results of the 1836 (February 9th, 1836) House of Commons Select Committee Report into Aborigines[11].

The aim of the Enquiry was "to secure the aborigines the due observance of justice and the protection of their rights, to promote and spread Christianity among them and to lead them to the peaceful and voluntary reception of the Christian religion . . ."

Glenelg advised, "They (the natives) are to derive the highest possible claim from the Sovereignty which has been assumed over the whole of their ancient possessions. If the rights of the Aborigines as British subjects be fully acknowledged it will follow that, when any of them comes to his death by the hands of the Queen's officers, or persons acting upon their command, an Inquest should be held to ascertain the cause which led to the death. Such

---

7 Barnard, Marjorie *A History of Australia* p.5

8 Barnard *ibid* p.648

9 Shaw, A.G.L. *The Story of Australia*

10 HRA 1:1:29

11 HRA 1:19:48-49

proceeding is important not only as a direct protection to Society against lawless outrage, but to impress on the public the value of any human life". The flaw in this proclamation was that the natives were not Christians, they did not understand the nature of white man law and so 'the treatment of Aborigines remained a matter of grace rather than of justice'.[12]

Dr. H.C. Coombs in his foreword to the N.G. Butlin study of aboriginal population says that Butlin "as been able to speculate about the population of Aboriginal Australia; what its numbers and distribution wee immediately before the arrival of whites; what was the impact of the major events which the contact precipitated on those numbers and their distribution."[13]

Butlin concludes that the pre-contact population of NSW and Victoria regions in 1788 is 250,000 or almost the total generally projected for the country as a whole. This figure is considered by Butlin to be more reliable than the estimate of the national native population by Professor Radcliffe-Brown of 300,000 or Governor Phillip's estimate of one million[14]. Butlin goes on to answer his second query about the Aboriginal peoples. The first question was –What was their population in 1788? The second question was—what was behind the process of Aboriginal depopulation between 1788 and 1850?[15]

Butlin offers a hypothesis to answer the second question. His hypothesis is that

(a) The degree of depopulation was correspondingly larger than previously acknowledged.
(b) The causes of the depopulation may have been significantly different from those previously acknowledged, whether in terms

---

12 Barnard *ibid* p.655

13 Butlin, N.G. *Our Original Aggression* with Foreword by Dr. H.C. Coombs

14 Butlin, N.G. *Close Encounters of the Worst Kind –Modelling Aboriginal Depopulation 1788-1850.* Butlin writes that historians have adopted Radcliffe –Brown's estimate of 300,000 natives for the whole of Australia as the likely pre-contact number. There are no notes as to how that figure was derived and Butlin sets out to model a more exact number, the result being 250,000 for just NSW and Victoria.

15 Butlin *Our Original Aggression* p.5

of black welfare, white killing of blacks or pulmonary or related diseases.

Butlin goes on to examine the effects of white settlement along two lines:

(a) How were natives detached from their resources?
(b) How were resources detached from natives? The word detachment is used by Butlin as a euphemism for ' destruction of the black population'[16]

Butlin, as an economic historian writes in another WPEH "Australia between 1788 and 1815 was at most, a minor though quite expensive irritant to the British"[17]. This is one of two WPEH studies outlining the demography of the colonial period. The second study is WPEH #33 of 1985, in which Forster records that "the first formal census of the modern type in Australia was held in NSW in 1828. It was found, in 1827 the "previous proclamations by the Governor calling free citizens to muster had no legal force, and this latest was authorised by Act of the NSW Legislative Council.[18] It was described as "An Act for ascertaining the number, names, and conditions of the inhabitants of the colony of NSW and the number of cattle, the quantities of located, cleared and cultivated land within the said colony".

Just a short note on two other 'vehicles' of official statistics from 1788 to 1856.

"Up to 1822 attention was directed to a wide range of reports for the British authorities, a large proportion of which came directly from the Governor's office. After 1822 annual Blue Books of statistical information, designed by the Colonial Office, were the most important means of reporting. The third type of official statistic was the census, the first being held in 1828. The colony in this respect was not that far behind the British model. Although Butlin, Statham and Ginswick now question many of the original colonial statistics, it is interesting to note that the

---

16 Butlin *ibid* p.9

17 Butlin, N.G. *White Human Capital in Australia 1788-1850*

18 NSW L.C. *Votes & Proceedings* 1828 p.43

British Statistical Department of the Board of Trade was not formed until 1832. The purpose of this collector of British and Colonial statistics was "to try and collate the incoherent mass of periodical tables then prepared, and for the first time reduce them to orderly and comprehensive returns, accompanied by lucid explanations of the meaning and limitations of the figures".[19]

Any study of the economics of the population growth over a 68-year period will be challenging especially in understanding the factors that encouraged population growth or on the other hand inhibited any growth.

A nation's population can be affected by wars, periods of disease, or starvation. Australia was the 'lucky country' and did not face such catastrophic circumstances. However on the other hand the economic cycles were fairly wild and ranged all the way from boom times to bust, with a wide variety of situations in between. Droughts and floods, locus plagues only seemed to affect the food supply whilst good times attracted migrants; prospects for speculation attracted investors, the wool boom attracted transferee farmers from Britain and the biggest number, next to the natural increase were the transportees of the British Government.

We should be asking at this stage, what were some of the general conditions of success? Why did the settlement achieve success after its early struggles?

Butlin offers a number of 'reasons'[20]

"It may be suggested that the early achievements of the settlement may be seen as the product of seven major conditions:

(a) The early elimination of threats from Aborigines and their almost immediate depopulation.
(b) The early privatisation of the settlement and the firm establishment of private property, private employed labour and market choice in the settlement (a fine balance)

---

[19] Koren, J *The History of Statistics: Their development and Progress*

[20] Butlin, N.G. *Economics of the Dreamtime – A Hypothetical History* p.181

(c) The accession of substantial British support in kind, through the authority to issue bills payable by the British Government, and through the presence of substantial quasi-exports (deployment of natural resources)
(d) The desire for non-tradeables and for goods that could not be readily tradeable
(e) The supply of human capital with skills appropriate to a relatively advanced society
(f) The lack of economics of scale in large areas of non-food production, and
(g) The recovery of property rights in labour time by the majority of convicts

One must ask if the good results from using the techniques identified above were a result of a tightly planned economy or a mixture of planned and under-regulated, or penal and free. It would seem that many of the regimes of success had to have been part of an integrated planning process. For instance, the instruction for Bills to be drawn on the Treasury in London was a better alternative to a penal settlement having an exchequer and a means of exchange, by way of coinage; the competition with and elimination of Aborigines was not British government policy but was an internal struggle for land and hunting rights; the early privatisation of the settlement came about by the failure of government to produce sufficient food locally and the resulting issuing of land grants to the military officers and emancipists who then had the opportunity to either make money or feed themselves and their families adequately; the privatisation of the treasury by King and Macquarie was both a convenience and a display of not really wanting to know the gory details-It was both cheaper and less onerous to the governor not having to account for every penny of this discretionary and illegal revenue to the British Government; British support was necessary because it was a penal settlement rather than a 'slave' market, where convicts would have been sold to settlers and taken off the hands and the 'books' of the British government – this again was a deliberate policy decision by the British authorities; the supply of human capital with skills appropriate to a relatively advanced society may or may not have been deliberate—it is still a matter of conjecture as to whether convicts were selectively chosen in Britain (at the court or even the prison level) for transportation as Phillip and his successors had requested – at least we know from the records that Macquarie attended each arriving ship to select the skilled mechanics that he most needed for government service; the lack of economies of scale was a matter of transition from commissariat policy to import replace and make what could be made locally (and on a timely basis) and then turn it over to private enterprise for convenience. Butlin properly identifies 7 early achievements as if they were 'manor from heaven', but most appear to be policy ideas whose time had come[21].

The study of population growth in Colonial NSW is to be guided by the socio-economic peaks and troughs faced by the convicts and the free settlers –the challenges of learning how to survive in a harsh climate very different to that from when they came; to be acclimatised to small groups of pioneers in many fields – the explorers, the traders, the manipulators, the stoical farmers, the wily public servants, the politicians and the law makers, but mostly the children that would grow into one or other of these categorisations, but mainly the role of being a risk taker in a new colony, a new way of life and a new challenge every day.

The traditional view that the British settlement was intended as an indefinite convict settlement or was a combination of penal colony with pretensions of Imperial strategy and trade interests, when combined with the second view that Aboriginals had no legal 'claim' to the land because they were not 'farmers' in the traditional European sense, have embedded Australian colonial economic history to-date into a narrow perspective. The black armband consensus is that of a concentration on the alleged sordidness of the convict settlements and the deliberate depopulation of the Aboriginal race. The optimists, such as Fletcher and Fitzpatrick claim the settlement was an extraordinarily rapid and successful development of a pastoral Australia between 1788 and 1856.

The rational view should be that the country was an area of very ancient settlement, with the Aboriginal economy being a stably ordered system of decision-making that satisfied the wants of its people. British occupation

21 Butlin, N.G. *Economics of the Dreamtime*

(without deliberate intent) destroyed the Aboriginal economy and society with the accompanying decimation of its population[22]

We obviously don't need to re-write our economic history but it does help to understand the economic setting that gave rise to the rapidly expanding British society in the new settlement, the rapidly declining native population and a developing economy that met the needs of Britain as a source of raw materials for its industry, as an outlet for its trading and the transfer of resources (a takeover) by the new economic managers. This new class, in fact, faced much higher costs, than expected, in achieving 'success'. Their 'success' can only be measured in being able to commandeer these natural resources and transfer them from an ancient society to the newest society This takeover was never the apparent official intent; rather the official intention was to seek a type of merger rather than a takeover. However, the gulf between the two societies was too large to be bridged and British settlement succeeded while the ancient society was destroyed.

Butlin finds a similarity between the 'economic' invasion of Britain by the Romans and the 'takeover' of economic interests in the Great South Land.[23] It is quite a stretch of the imagination but there are certain similarities that given the 1600-year time-span can be identified. Similar strategies learnt from history are probably what Butlin is offering.

"Rome had the essential springboard from Italy to develop a vast network of imperial control[24] extending over much of Europe and the Mediterranean. For 500 years these traditions were injected into England. On one hand Rome delivered a military market, a money economy, organised administration, a villa system of agriculture married to the Celtic farming of Britain, improved agricultural productivity, urban centres, transport systems and extended trade contacts with Europe. On the other hand, it was military control and reflected the hierarchical organisation and exploitation of unfree labour on which the ancient world depended.

---

22 Butlin uses some of these expressions in '*Economics and the Dreamtime*' p.184

23 Butlin *Economics and the Dreamtime* p.187

24 Butlin uses the word 'imperial' often and probably means 'British' rather than royal or monarchist

Butlin acknowledges that these thoughts are derived from Salway in *Roman Britain.*

One can see the similarities between the Roman takeover of early Britain, and the British takeover of New Holland. G. Arnold Wood in his prehistory of Australia makes a similar point but concludes, "It is scarcely conceivable that a transfer of influences corresponding to those of Rome on Britain could have been spread by Asians to Australia".[25]

For all the attribution that we can validly extend to the British for the takeover of Aboriginal economy, many questions remain unanswered. For instance,

- What were the economics of the 'takeover'?
- What were the legalities of the 'takeover'?
- Who were the major players?
- Was disease the main or only component of the Aboriginal depopulation?
- What were the real intentions of Britain in the 'takeover'?

Hopefully these answers will be offered satisfactorily in a later chapter of this study because they do have a particular relevance to this story

Methodology

Developing a population history of the colony requires a methodology, and the following is the approach taken by this writer to the study

a. Assemble statistics of population from 1788-1899 including for each year

    i. Males, Females
    ii. Locally born, migrants, deaths (arrivals, deaths & departures & natural increase)
    iii. Compare official numbers with Manning Clarke numbers

25 G.A. Wood *The Discovery of Australia*

b. Review Coghlan on population drivers and developments
c. 'Introduction' – covers existing studies & reasons for this present study
d. 'Chapter One – review existing records, gaps and new conclusions and goal of what this study is trying to prove

Elements of Increase

i. Natural Increase

The two factors, which contribute to the growth of a population, are the 'natural increase' by excess of births over deaths and the 'net increase' or the excess of arrivals over departures. Particulars of the natural increase can be tracked for each sex. The natural increase for Australia, as a whole, between 1861 to 1935 inclusive wads 4,291,397, consisting of 1,990,920 males and 2,300,477 females and represented 76.53% of the total increase in population. During the 1800s the rate of natural increase grew until it reached a maximum rate of 17.44 per thousand of population.

ii. Net Immigration

This is the excess of arrivals over departures and is subject to greater variations than the 'natural increase' For the 1800s the annual rate of increase averaged 1.68 %, with net migration fluctuating between –0.5 and 0.53.

iii. Influences on population statistics

- Wars & war service
- Depressions
- Overseas economic problems
- 'Home' prosperity
- Seasonal fluctuations – the rate of natural increase is greatest in the quarter ended March, (in the southern states) and in the June quarter for Queensland. The lowest natural increase is in the September quarter.
- Age distribution
- Conjugal condition

- Schooling
- Religion
- Nationality & Race

iv. If the population increases at an average rate of 1.68%, it would have doubled itself in 42 years

Some Thoughts on the social and economic aspects of a Colonial NSW Population History

a. Social History of the Colony

    i. The Convicts
    ii. The Free Settlers
    iii. Education
    iv. Entrepreneurs

b. The Economic History of the Colony

    i. Reasons for the Colony
    ii. Attracting Free Settlers
    iii. Survival
    iv. Government Financial Support in the Colony
    v. English Capital Investment in the Colony
    vi. Growth in the Colony – (a Coghlan Assessment)
    vii. Impact of Governors' Policies on Growth
    viii. Public Finance
    ix. A new Currency
    x. Industry
    xi. Pastoral Development & Land Policy
    xii. Immigration
    xiii. Economic Factors in Growing the Colony.
    xiv. Population Growth and Decentralisation
    xv. Communications, Roads & Rail

Growth of Population

From 1788 when settlement first took place in Australia, until December 1825 when Van Diemen's Land (now Tasmania) became a separate colony, the whole of the British possessions in Australia were regarded as one colony (i.e. New South Wales). The population, during this period increased very slowly, and at the end of 1824 had only reached 48,072.

The period extending from 1825 to 1859 witnessed the birth of the new colonies of Tasmania, Western Australia, South Australia, Victoria and Queensland.

These colonies came into existence as follows:

Tasmania (1825); Western Australia (1829); South Australia (1834); Victoria (1851); and Queensland (1859).

Australia achieved its first million people in 1858, seventy years after the first settlement and assisted by the 'gold rush' during the 1850s.

Influences affecting growth and distribution of population 1788 –1858 included

(P84 ABS1920)

- Mineral Discoveries
- Pastoral Development
- Agricultural Expansion
- Progress of manufacturing industries
- Influence of droughts
- Commercial crises
- Railway development

Special Characteristics of Commonwealth Population

Sex Distribution & 'Masculinity' ii. Age Distribution iii. Race & Nationality

CHAPTER 2

COLONIAL POPULATION STATISTICS & THEIR INTERPRETATION[26]

A. Official Population Numbers from 1788-1858[27]

Year	Total Popln	Year	Total Popln
1788	1024	1824	48072
1789	645	1825	52505
1790	2056	1826	53882
1791	2873	1827	56300
1792	3264	1828	58197
1793	3514	1829	61934
1794	3579	1830	70039
1795	3466	1831	75981
1796	4100	1832	83937
1797	4344	1833	98095

26 A number of commentators have prepared population figures eg Clark, White, Ginswick, but none of them agree with each other and the ABS 'official' population statistics seem to have been well-considered and therefore reliable.

27 Official Year Book of the Commonwealth of Australia No. 13 (1920) *Tables of populations are found from p.83to 300.*

1798	4588	1834	105556
1799	5088	1835	113354
1800	5217	1836	125120
1801	5945	1837	134488
1802	7014	1838	151868
1803	7238	1839	169939
1804	7598	1840	190408
1805	7707	1841	220968
1806	7910	1842	240984
1807	8794	1843	250848
1808	10263	1844	264287
1809	11560	1845	279148
1810	11566	1846	293249
1811	11875	1847	308797
1812	12630	1848	332328
1813	13957	1849	3783362
1814	14086	1850	405356
1815	15063	1851	437665
1816	17553	1852	513796
1817	21192	1853	600992
1818	25859	1854	694917
1819	31472	1855	793260
1820	33543	1856	876729
1821	35492	1857	970287
1822	37364	1858	1050828
1823	40632	1859	1097305

The commentary for those figures in 1920 is as follows:

"From 1788 when settlement first took place in Australia, the whole of the British possessions in Australia were regarded as one colony, viz that of New South Wales. The population during this period increased very slowly and at the end of 1824 had reached only 48,072. The following period 1825-1859 witnessed the birth of the colonies of Tasmania (1825), Western Australia (1829), South Australia (1834), Victoria (1851) and Queensland (1859). The colonies attained their first million in 1858, 70 years after settlement commenced; its second million came nineteen years later in 1877, and its third million twelve years later in 1889; its fourth million came sixteen years later in 1905.[28]

Influences affecting Growth & Distribution of Population[29]

▪ Pastoral Development

Very early in the colonisation of Australia it was recognised that many portions were well adapted for pastoral pursuits, and pastoral developments have led to a considerable distribution of population in various directions. As the numbers engaged in connection therewith, compared with the value of the interests involved, are relatively small, and as pastoral occupancy tends to segregation rather than aggregation of population, the growth of the pastoral industry is only slightly reflected in the population statistics of Australia.[30]

▪ Mineral (Gold) Discoveries

Although outside our period, gold discoveries changed the pattern of population growth. From December 1840 to December 1850 the total increase was 214,948. The rush of people to the goldfield during the next decade caused an increase of 740,229, growing the total population to 1,145,585. The reverse happened in the 1860s when the New Zealand goldfields opened up and the net increase dropped to 22,564, and in fact for the year of 1861, departures exceeded arrivals by 6,283, so the overall gain was due to natural increase

▪ Agricultural Expansion

By the 1850s, the area annually devoted to crops was less than 5 million acres. Also considerable in itself, as a percentage of the land mass of Australia represents less than 1% per head of world population; the area under crop at that time was about 2 acres per head, a fairly high

---

28 Year Book 1920 ibid p.96

29 Year Book 1920 ibid p.84

30 Year Book, *ibid* p.84

amount when consideration it was given over to settlement less than 100 years previously. About 70% of the cropping is devoted to grain, thus the agricultural districts are sparsely populated, though less so than the pastoral areas.[31]

- Progress of Manufacturing Industries

This factor is recognised by the reorientation of manufacturing from the processing of local resources to the more deliberate attempt to replace imported goods especially labour intensive, low cost items such as clothing, footwear and millinery. Factory production averaged (between 1830 and 1860) an annual growth of over 10% whilst population growth averaged less than 5%[32].

- Influence of droughts

Droughts have a marked influence on the distribution of the population. Districts, which in favourable seasons are fairly populous, in times of drought often, become less populated until the return of better conditions. This movement affects the distribution and usually not the total numbers. In some years studies show that natural increase due to drought is low and the excess of births over deaths was abnormally low

- Commercial crises

Such an event affects the migration numbers significantly

- War

External wars in the case of Australia had little effect on pre-1850 population numbers, but did affect the first two decades of the twentieth century.

Two articles prepared by the Commonwealth Statistician and the ABS (Australian Bureau of Statistics) on the development of official statistics

31 Year Book, *ibid* p.85

32 Inge, G.J.R. *Industrial Awakening*

have been reproduced in Appendices A & B for the benefit and interest of readers

The Excitement of the Muster

J.C. Caldwell writes "For the first 40 years of the Australian colonies, our knowledge of population numbers is derived from the musters. Their major deficiencies are that of the omission of the native peoples. Even in 1800 the musters perhaps account for only 1 or 2 percent of the actual population".

Official musters were held in 1799, 1805,1810,1817,1820 and1821. The first full-scale census was held in November 1828.[33]

Most announcements of intentions to account for all persons were generally signed by the Governor of the day and the task assigned to the Commissary officials. Governor John Hunter issued the following General Order.[34]

> *A general muster will be held on Saturday next, the 26th instant at Sydney; on Thursday, the 1st October, at Parramatta and Toongabbie; and on Saturday, the 3rd October, at the settlement at the Hawkesbury – at which places the Commissary will attend for the purpose of obtaining a correct amount of the numbers and distribution of all persons (the military excepted) in the different aforementioned settlements, whether victualled or not (victualled) from the public stores.*

Notice is hereby given to all persons concerned to attend, so that every man be accounted for; and such as neglect complying with this order will be sought after and be either confined in the cells, put to hard labour, or corporally punished.

---

33 J.C. Caldwell introduces Chapter 5 'Population' (Australians: ' Historical Statistics')

34 Government notice *Sydney Gazette*23rd September 1795

The sick may be accounted for by the Principal Surgeon, and officers' servants by their masters

Gathering Population Statistics

As an overview of a main chapter in this study it is necessary to understand how and when the general population was counted. Our study includes reference to records of the day including both 'musters' and the first census and from 1822 the records contained in the 'Blue Books'.

There were four early censuses, which closely followed procedures developed in Britain in 1826 and the recognition of the Statistical Office within the British Board of Trade. The first three colonial census counts occurred in 1828, 1831 and 1836

The Census of1828

Table of Regional NSW Populations – by age & sex groupings—1829

"The first full-scale census of New South Wales was held in November 1828. The total white population was 36598 of whom 15728 were convicts; the free population outnumbered the bond for the first time since 1788. The following table is a summary of the count."[35]

Table taken from *Sydney Gazette* 26th September 1829

	Males	Females
Free		
<12	2561	1565
>12	285	262
Emancipists	5302	1342
Pardoned	835	51
Bond	14155	1573
Born in Colony		
<12	1923	1580

35 Crowley Frank *Colonial Australia – Volume 1* P377

>12	2550	2674
Total	27611	8987
Grand Total	**36598**	

The colony grazed 12479 horses, 262868 cattle and 536391 sheep. The largest grazing area was the Bathurst area."[36]

The census offers us another insight into colonial life in 1828.

The *Sydney Gazette* of December 1828 offers this setting:

"At the end of 1828, Sydney had 1409 houses, 176 cottages, 121 skillings and 67 wooden tenements, making a total of 1773 dwellings. Its urban population was 10815, and the town occupied a large space of ground; if it had been as well fitted with houses as a town of similar size in England, the population would have been eight or ten times as numerous".

The Census of 1833

There was a second census of the white population of NSW (exclusive of the military) on 2nd September 1833, the general result of which ids as follows:

	Male	Female
Free		
<12	17542	8522
>12	5256	4931
Convicts	21845	2698
Total	44643	16151
	60794	

The census of 1836

Frank Crowley writes of the census of 1836. The population was shown to be 77096 of whom 27831 were convicts (only 2577 women); many thousands of others had once been convicts. The greater number lived

36 Crowley, Frank *Colonial Australia – Volume 1* P244

in the County of Cumberland in the vicinity of Sydney (39797) and only 2968 were 'without the boundaries'. This number may have been underestimated because in the same year as the census, the colony exported 3776191 pounds of wool to England, so that the pastoral growth had become quite significant. And probably employed directly and indirectly more than the 2968 persons listed. The spread of grazing on both purchased land and by squatters was extensive and the government had little real knowledge of numbers of people or livestock.[37]

T.A. Coghlan, the leading 19th century statistician and recorder of colonial economic events writes [38] about the early musters or population counts.

'Prior to the 1891 census, only an approximate return was made up of the estimated population on the 31st December in each year' (Coghlan) These estimates were carried out by taking into account the increase caused by the excess of births over deaths, and of arrivals over departures. It is evident, opines Coghlan that if these data could be ascertained exactly, there would be no difficulty in making an accurate estimate of the population, at any time. "Although the machinery of registration of births and deaths ensures a fairly correct return under these heads, it is not so easy to obtain exact particulars respecting arrivals and departures – especially departures. It becomes necessary to make allowance for unrecorded departures.[39] The following estimated population of NSW at the close of 1861 and 1866 is after due allowance has been made for unrecorded departures.

Year	Males	Females	Total
1861	201574	156404	357978
1866	235116	193697	428813

The movement of population between states is subject to great variation between years and between census counts, the increase ranging from 1.73% to 36.26%.

The net increase of population due to immigration also fluctuates widely depending on conditions both at home and at the source of the migration

37 Crowley: Documentary History of Australia p509

38 Coghlan, T.A. ***'Labour & Industry in Australia' – 4 volume set***

39 Coghlan, T.A *Wealth & Progress of NSW 1900-1901*

intake. Between 1181 and 1891, the population of NSW was increased by 162828 persons by immigration, while Victoria showed an increase of 116361. In the ten years from 1891 to 1901, NSW had an increase of immigration to the extent of only 336, whilst Victoria had a net decrease, due to emigration of 111814 persons.

Distribution of sexes also affects population growth. In the census of 1891, males constituted 52.42% and the females 47.58% of the total population. This has undergone little change since 1861, when males were 56.57% and in 1871, males had declined to 54.67%. The excess of males over female population is chiefly at the ages from 30 upwards, and is only what is to be expected in a country the population of which has been largely recruited by immigration. The census of 1891 showed males in their 21st year to be 12785 and females in their 21st year to be 13493. The census also showed that the largest number of any age group is found from 5 to 10 years, whilst the number in the under 5 group is exceeded by both the 5-10 group and the 10-15 group. The cause of this change is the declining birth rate, and as Coghlan insists 'this trend commands the serious consideration of all thoughtful people' [40].

Coghlan also analyses the birthplace of the population in 21891. Of the 1354846 people recorded 1316007 or (97%) were born in Britain or of British ancestry, and although people with the birthplace of Britain were in decline, the Total of British subjects was rising.

Centralisation of the population was another study made by Coghlan. As far back as 1861, when the native-born population amounted to only 45.69%, the number living in Sydney and suburbs formed only 42.13%. Of late (1895), writes Coghlan, there has been a tendency on the part of certain foreign elements to gravitate towards the cities. This is especially noticeable amongst Chinese and Hindu's, as well as Syrians and others from the Levant This trend is markedly different to that of the United States in 1860 through 1890 where the percentage of urban dwellers grew from 16.13% in 1860 to 20.93% in 1870, 22.57% in 1880 and 29.20% in 1890. This trend, opines Coghlan is a sign of the desire of the rural population for an improvement in their circumstances, especially as

40 Coghlan *Wealth & Progress of NSW*

labour gravitates to the market where it will obtain the highest price. Over 57% of the increased population in NSW, due to immigration, between 1881 and 1891, was retained in the metropolis.

Naturalisation may also be a relevant factor in population growth. Between 1849 and 1900, there were only 7519 letters of naturalisation taken out in NSW, although it must be remembered that between these years, the Chinese were prohibited from seeking naturalisation.

Governor King to the Secretary for the Colonies, London

We talk about early musters and the quality of those musters elsewhere, but the muster of 1805 provided some distressing statistics. During the period 1800-1805 there were 617 settlers, 916 free men and 854 free women (most of these were former convicts) but there had also been 468 deaths and 160 marriages, and despite the very high proportion of men in the community, there had been a net increase of 804 children, i.e. exclusive of deaths.[41]

Coghlan writes that Victoria achieved the status of most populous colony in 1854 when the gold rush attracted a great number of people from both interstate and overseas. This trend continued until 1886 when three factors ensured NSW returned to the number one populous state – the natural increase by birth over deaths, the selection of this Colony as a place of settlement by a large number of unassisted immigrants, and the assistance given by the government to persons in the U.K. to make NSW their home.[42]

The largest increase of population in any one year occurred in 1885 when owing to the depression prevailing in the neighbouring colonies, large numbers of adult males flocked to NSW, in search of a livelihood, they could not obtain elsewhere. By coincidence this influx was thwarted by the unfortunate seasonal circumstances in the colony of NSW in 1886, by which many men remained unable to find work.

---

41 HRA 1:7:358 King to

42 Coghlan *Wealth & Progress for 1886-1887*

Since 1860 writes Coghlan, the year following separation from Queensland, the arrivals in the colony of NSW have, in every year, exceeded the departures. Assisted immigration dates from 1832 and has continued to be a policy of the country until its suspension in 1884. The average number of assisted migrants each year between 1860 and 1884 was 3085. Of the 77095 persons assisted 75468 were British born.

The Chinese were the subject of various colonies passing laws restricting their immigration, and prohibiting their landing, except upon the payment of a heavy poll tax. At the census of 1861 there were 12988 Chinese but this number declined through 1871 but then rose until in 1886 they were numbered 213500. This is mostly due to the attraction of Victoria and other colonies as gold producers claiming their interest.[43]

43 Coghlan *Wealth & Progress for 1886-1887*

CHAPTER 3

POPULATION INCREASE, MIGRATION AND INVESTMENT AND ECONOMIC DRIVERS

Sex distribution

Australia has, since the first settlement of the continent in 1788, differed materially from the older countries of the world. Older countries, that are countries having an established civilised population, have, in general, grown by natural increase and their composition usually reflects that fact with the numbers of males and females being approximately equal, with a tendency for females to slightly exceed males. This slight excess arises from a number of causes

Higher rate of mortality amongst males
Greater propensity of males to travel
The effects of war
Employment of males in the armed forces
Preponderance of males amongst emigrants
Masculinity of the Population

"The changing population structure necessarily implied a radical alteration in the size of the male workforce in the total population. The increasing numbers of young males and of all females compelled this change as shown below.

Year	Workforce Males	% of Total Popln
1790	1784	77.7
1795	3692	79.1
1800	4555	74.1
1805	5981	70.7
1810	7100	63.0
1815	9575	61.4
1820	22822	71.1
1825	34565	71.4
1830	47180	69.4

MASCULINITY OF THE NSW POPULATION 1800 to 1855

Year	%
1800	44.91
1805	40.00
1810	31.16
1815	30.76
1820	41.81
1825	53.00
1830	52.06
1835	45.71
1840	34.25
1845	21.05
1850	16.13
1855	11.14

This compares with other countries in various years, which would create a guide and average for base purposes

Canada	1911	6.07
India	1911	2.24
New Zealand	1919	1.15
Australia	1919	1.00
Poland	1914	0.41
Hungary	1912	-0.94

Ireland	1915	-1.36
England	1917	-16.43

Age Distribution

During the first 80 years of settlement, the age distribution of the colonial population has varied considerably. Prior to1856, the distribution averaged as follows:

Males >15	31.4
Males 15-65	67.4
Males <65	1.17
Total	100%
Females >15	43.0
Females 15-65	56.2
Females <65	0.77
Total	100%
Persons>15	36.28
Persons 15-65	62.72
Persons <65	1.0
Total	100%

Sources of Race & Nationality

The primary distribution is between the aboriginal natives and the immigrants, who since 1788 have made the colony their home. Under immigrants would come not only the direct immigrants but also their descendants. For the first 60 years after settlement, the Aboriginal population was in decline (refer also to Chapter 3 of this study – The Aboriginal Economy of 1788). It is of interest to note that in the first census of the aboriginal population in 1911, the Commonwealth statistician made the following reference.[44] "At the census of 1911 the number of full-blood aboriginals who were employed by whites or who lived on the fringe of white settlement was stated to be only 19,939. In Queensland, Western Australia and the Northern Territory, there are considerable numbers of

[44] *Commonwealth Year Book 1901-1919* (1920) p.88

natives still in the 'savage' state, numerical information concerning whom is of a most unreliable nature and can be regarded as little more than the result of guessing".

The academic studies by Dr. Roth, formerly Chief Protector of Aborigines in Queensland puts the number of full-blood aborigines in the 6 colonies at 80,000 in 1919"[45] As a matter of Commonwealth census policy no count was attempted of 'half-castes' as 'no authoritative definition has yet been given.

The predominant race of immigrants and their descendants is British. However, by 1900, the local born population had reached 83%. The figure in 1856 was calculated to be in the 52.5% vicinity. The other main birthplaces included Germany, China, Scandinavia, Polynesia, British India and Japan

From one aspect the total population may be less significant than in respect of the absolute amount than in respect of the density of its distribution. The total land area of the country is 2,974,581 square miles, and at the time of the Constitution of 1901, the country only had a population of 5,347,018 persons, with a density of 1.80. Even today that density is only a little less than 7. The comparative densities are, for the earliest period of statistics maintained (1919 – Statesman's Yearbook), Europe at 122.98, Asia 54.45. Americas 16.87 and Australasia 2.38

Some definitions

Natural Increase

The two factors, which contribute to the growth of a population, are the 'natural increase' by excess of births over deaths and the 'net migration', being the excess of arrivals over departures. In a new country such as the colony of NSW between 1788 and 1856, the 'net migration' occupies an important position as a source of increase of population especially as the early imbalance of sexes and the shortage of females in the colony, allowed for only a relatively small natural increase.

---

45 CYB *ibid* p.89

Net Immigration

The quinquennial period in which the greatest net migration to the Colonies occurred is outside our study period but was that of 1881-85 with a total of 224,040, whilst the period 1901-05 departures exceeded arrivals by 16,793

Total Increase

The total increase of the population is found by the combination of the natural increase with the net immigration

Rate of Increase

The rate of increase in the early colony rose quickly but then steadied as migration took on a smaller 'net ' effect. After 1830 the average rate was only 4% but then declined steadily until by 1901, the rate was only 1.38. NSW always enjoyed the highest rate of increase and averaged over 5% before 1850 declining to 4.83 from 1860. The 1850s were a period of low natural increase and high net migration with the gold fields being the main catalyst.

Urban Population

One of the key features of the distribution of population in Australia is the tendency to accumulate in the capital cities. In every colony the capital city had a greater population than any other town in the colony. It was the hub and as such it carried certain features. The main population area was a port for international shipping. There were adequate fresh water sources servicing the population. In the early days of the colony of NSW the 'urban' population would have been close top 100%, but as Macquarie developed and serviced his regional towns, the urban percentage declined until by 1900, Sydney had only 41.38 % of the colonial population

Aboriginal population

The Commonwealth Year Book of 1901 reminds us that "The Commonwealth Constitution Act makes provision for aboriginal natives to be excluded for all purposes for which statistics of population are made use but the opinion has been given by the Commonwealth Attorney-General that 'in reckoning the population of the Commonwealth, half-castes are not aboriginal natives within the meaning of Section 127 of the Constitution', and should therefore be included in any census count."[46] This is one reason that the ABS (Australian Bureau of Statistics had so much doubt over the number of aborigines in the country – they had not been counted and would not be counted at any time until 1966. The ABS records guesses ranging from 150,000 to as low as 61,705 in 1925[47]

Enumeration

In colonial NSW, the system of 'musters' was the way chosen to count the convicts and the free settlers. The governor would 'gazette' or announce the date and place of the next muster, and usually commissariat officers would officiate at the count. The basis of the count was often widened to include a record of the number and type of livestock, of acres cultivated and would be used to verify the rations receivable by that family 'off the store'. In 1828 the muster system was replaced by the first 'census' where a more detailed record was made of the population demographics including ages, sex and birthplace of each inhabitant and whether 'free' or 'convict'.

Musters

J.C. Caldwell writes in the introduction to the Chapter on 'Population'[48] "For the first 40 years of the Australian colonies, our knowledge of population numbers is derived from the musters. Their major deficiencies are that of the omission of the native peoples. Even in 1800 the musters perhaps account for only 1 or 2 percent of the actual population".

---

46 Commonwealth Year Book #3– W. Ramsey-Smith ' *Special Characteristics of Commonwealth Population*' P.89

47 4The count in each state is estimated at 30th April 1915 by Ramsey Smith as NSW-6,580;Victoria 283; Qld 15,000; SA 4,842; WA 32,000; NT 3,000 for a total of 61,705

48 Australians: Historical Statistics

IMMIGRATION AND INVESTMENT

The economic theory of 19th century British investment

Before we can complete the task of identifying capital formation by the British investor, both public (government) and private investment, let me review a piece by Sir T.H. Farrer (Bart) from his 1887 book *Free Trade versus Fair Trade*. The notation on the front-piece of the book shows the Cobden Club emblem with the words 'free trade, peace, goodwill among nations'. We will discuss Cobden a little later when we review the work of the Australian Senator Edward Pulsford, another outspoken supporter and devotee of the Cobden philosophy, and free trade and open immigration.

> *'The amount of English capital constantly employed abroad in private trade and in permanent investments, including Stock Exchange securities, private advances, property owned abroad by Englishmen, British shipping, British-owned cargoes, and other British earnings abroad, has been estimated by competent statisticians as being between 1,500 and 2,000 million pounds, and is constantly increasing. Taking the lower figure, the interest or profit upon it, at 5 per cent, would be 75 million pounds, and at the higher figure it would be 100 million pound.'*[49]

Farrer equates this income figure to the spread of imports over exports and finds that the two compare. But then he argues there is the question of freights:

> *'A very large proportion of the trade of the United Kingdom is carried in English ships, and these ships carry a large proportion of the trade of other countries not coming to England. This shipping is, in fact, an export of highly-skilled English labour and capital which does not appear in the export returns of the 19th century, and considering that it includes not only the interest on capital but also wages, provisions, coal, port expenses, repairs, depreciation and*

[49] Farrer, T.H *Free Trade or Fair Trade*

> *insurance; and that the value of English shipping employed in the foreign trade is estimated at more than 100 million pound per annum, the amount to be added to our exports on account of English shipping, must be very large.*[50]

He goes further,

> *'. . . add to this the value of ships built for foreigners amounting to over 70,000 ton per annum, worth together several millions, and all these outgoings, with the profits, must either return to this country in the shape of imports, or be invested abroad—I believe £50 million is too low an estimate of the amount of unseen exports. In addition there are the commissions and other charges to agents in this country, connected with the carriage of goods from country to country, but each of these items do not appear in the statistics of exports. I can only assume that we are investing large amounts of our savings in the colonies, such as Australia.*[51]

The Farrer argument in favour of 'free trade' then turns to the 'fair trade' objections to foreign investments. He writes:

> *'When we point to the indebtedness of foreign colonies to England as one reason for the excess of imports, they tell us that we have been paying for our imports by the return to us of foreign securities; and at the same time they complain bitterly that, instead of spending our money at home, our rich men are constantly investing their money abroad, and thus robbing English labour of its rights here.*[52]

But we know that is not the whole story. When British investors transferred capital to the colonies, it was not only in the form of cash (which would come from savings) but it was more often in the form of capital goods. Britain sent iron; the shipbuilders who make the ships to carry the goods

50 Farrer *ibid*

51 Farrer *ibid*

52 Farrer *ibid*

and the sailors who navigated them. What happened when they reached the colonies?. They returned with grain, coal, wool timber making those commodities cheaper in Britain. The investor received interest or profits on the capital invested which would generally be greater than what could have been earned if it had been invested in Britain. That return can be spent on luxury goods, invested locally or re-invested overseas to begin the whole cycle again.

Based on the Farrer argument, it remains true that on the whole the transfer of British capital from an English industry that did not pay to a colonial industry which did pay, was no loss to England generally and caused no diminution in the employment of British labour. However, there are at least two drawbacks to colonial investment by a maritime power; one, in the event of a war, that returns would be open to greater risk, and two; that investors could more easily evade taxation by the British Government.

Obviously, since 1886 when Farrer constructed this argument, the world has changed and investment opportunities have changed. Britain has fallen from its pinnacle as a world power and international commercial leader and the improved collection of statistics now recognises movements of goods and investments on both current account and capital account. However, the concept helped put the Australian colony on the map and attracted enormous amounts of private capital into the colony to make it grow and prosper.

Farrer concludes his argument with this observation.

> *'The desire to make profitable investments, however valuable economically, is not the only motive which governs rich men; it's the love of natural beauty; interest in farming and the outdoor life; personal and local attachments; all of which are quite sure to maintain a much larger expenditure on English land than would be dictated by a desire for gain. Let these other motives have their way, as these investors still contribute to the welfare of the toilers and spinners who produce the goods, and make a good return that in the end makes England wealthier.*[53]

---

53 Farrer *ibid*

Factors affecting British investment in the Colony

A number of factors affected the level of capital investment into the colony – many were ill informed and relied on delayed newspaper reports on activity in the various settlements:

The offer of assisted migration

The failing economic conditions in Britain

Economic expansion for the pastoral industry due to successful exploration in the colony

The settlement at Port Phillip and the eventual separation of Victoria from NSW Wales would promote great investment opportunities

The rise of the squattocracy

The crash of 1827-28 in the colony shakes British Investors

The Bigges' Report of 1823 breathed new life into capital formation especially with Macarthur sponsoring the float of the Australian Agricultural Company

Further along, the good credit rating of the colonies (and there being no defaults on loans) encouraged larger investments and loans into the colonies

Shortage of labour in the colony and the offer of land grants to new settlers became a useful carrot to attract small settlers bringing their own capital by way of cash or goods or livestock with them.

Two other steps had important consequences, one in the colony and the other in Britain. In 1827 Governor Darling began to issue grazing licenses to pastoralists, the terms being set at 2/6d per 100 acres, with liability to quit on one month's notice. From this movement grew, writes Madgwick in *Immigration into Eastern Australia*, the squatting movement and the great pastoral expansion, and the idea of the earlier Governors that NSW should be a Colony of farmers was thus abandoned. The concurrent event was the floating of the Australian Agricultural Company in London. Development by the AAC and the free settlers brought increasing prosperity. Exports tripled between 1826 and 1831.

There is a connection between availability of factors of production and the level of investment. In the early days of the Colony, labour was available, bad labour, convict labour, but still labour. The governors had demanded settlers with capital to employ that labour and develop the land and they proposed to limit land grants in proportion to the means of the settler. Governor Darling declared (HRA ser 1, vol 8) that 'when I am satisfied of the character, respectability and means of the applicant settler in a rural area, he will receive the necessary authority to select a grant of land, proportionate in extent to the means he possesses'.

Let us examine some of these important elements commencing with the Bigge Report into Agriculture and Trade of the Colony.[54]

The Australian Agricultural Company

J.F. Campbell wrote about the first decade of the Australian Agricultural Company 1824-1834 in the proceedings of the 1923 RAHS:

> *'Soon after Commissioner Bigge's report of 1823 became available for public information, several enterprising men concerted with a view to acquire sheep-runs in the interior of this colony, for the production of fine wool.*
>
> *The success which attended the efforts of John Macarthur and a few other New South Wales pastoralists, in the breeding and rearing of fine woolled sheep and stock generally, as verified by Bigge, gave the incentive and led to the inauguration of proceedings which resulted in the formation of the Australian Agricultural Company.*

---

54 Bigge, John Thomas *Commissioners' Report into Agriculture & Trade in NSW – Report No. 1 1823*

The first formal meeting of the promoters took place at Lincoln's Inn, London, (at the offices of John Macarthur, junior).

Earl Bathurst, advised Governor Brisbane in 1824 that.

"His Majesty has been pleased to approve the formation of the Company, from the impression that it affords every reasonable prospect of securing to that part of His Majesty's dominions the essential advantage of the immediate introduction of large capital, and of agricultural skill, as well as the ultimate benefit of the increase of fine wool as a valuable commodity for export."

The chief proposals of the company are:

- *i. The company would be incorporated by Act of Parliament or Letters Patent.*
- *ii. The capital of the company was to be 1 million pound sterling divided into 10,000 shares of 100 pound each*
- *iii. A grant of land of one million acres to be made to the company*
- *iv. That no rival joint stock company to be established in the colony for the next twenty years*
- *v. That the agents of the company would select the situation or the land grants.*
- *vi. The shepherds and labourers would consist of 1,400 convicts, thereby lessening the maintenance of such convicts by an estimated 30,800 pound or 22 pound/per head/ per annum*

The Royal Charter of 1824 forming the company provided for payment of quit-rents over a period of twenty years, or the redemption of the same by paying the capital sum of 20 times the amount of the rent so to be redeemed. These quit-rents were to be waived if the full number of convicts were maintained for a period of five years. No land was to be sold during the five-year period from the date of the grant.'

It was important that the investment be seen to have the support of strong leaders in Britain and democratic governance, and company operated with

A Governor
25 directors
365 stockholders (proprietors)
Leading stockholders included
Robert Campbell
Chief Justice Forbes
Son of Governor King
Rev Samuel Marsden
John Macarthur
Macarthur family members, John jr, Hannibal, James, Charles, Scott and William

John Oxley, the Colonial-Surveyor, had recommended the Port Stephens area as an eligible location for the land grant. The local directors inspected and approved the site but John Macarthur was extremely critical of the selection, the management plan and the extravagance of the first buildings.

This venture was the first major investment into the colony and set the scene for later developments. In 1825 the Van Diemen's Land Company was chartered by the British Parliament and granted land on the northwest corner of the territory. Both the A.A. Coy and the VDL Coy still exist today, after nearly 180 years of continuous operation, a record beaten only by the Hudson Bay Company in Canada.

Macquarie's bank

Nothing quite engenders confidence in an investor like the thought of a new bank opening for business. Less than three months after his arrival in the Colony, Macquarie foreshadowed his plan for a bank on the South African model, as a 'remedy' to:

> *' . . . be speedily applied to this growing evil' of private promissory notes. With some exaggeration he explained that there was 'no other circulating medium in this colony than the notes of hand of private individuals' which, as he said, had 'already been productive of infinite frauds, abuses and litigation'. He accordingly announced his intention to'*

strongly recommend the adoption here of the same system of banking and circulating medium as is now so successfully and beneficially pursued at the Cape of Good Hope.'

By June 1810 Macquarie had developed his plan for 'The New South Wales Loan Bank' as a government institution 'as nearly as possible on the same system and principles as the Government Loan Bank at the Cape of Good Hope'. There, he explained the government issued notes by way of loan on the security of mortgages at 6 per cent per annum. He also pointed out that in England the government borrowed on exchequer bills at 5 %, so that the Cape was 11% better off. 'It appears to me' was his conclusion, 'the most perfect model in all its parts that could be possibly adopted here' By October 1810, he was willing to accept any alternative form of bank which Liverpool (Secretary for the Colonies) might believe to be 'better calculated to effect the desired object.

Obviously a Bank would form the foundation for a monetary policy in the colony, and stop the use of Commissary receipt (store receipts) as an exchange mechanism, promote a currency and an official exchange rate for traders and cease to rely on bills drawn on the British Treasury to pay for goods and services.

The British scene

Circumstances in Britain contributed greatly to the climate of 'greener pastures' over the seas. Conditions were never more favourable for emigration than they were during the 1830s. The decade had opened with rioting in the agricultural districts in the south of England. This was followed by the upheavals of the Reform Bill of 1832, the Factory Act of 1833 and the Corn Laws, which kept wages low and unemployment high. The Poor Law of 1834 withdrew assistance from the poor and re-introduced the workhouse. The Irish rebellion was creating both upheaval and poverty.

These conditions were met by the enthusiastic reports coming from Australia of the progress being made in agriculture, commerce and the pastoral industry.

The assistance granted to emigrants, as a result of Edward Gibbon Wakefield's reforms, made possible the emigration of people who had previously been prevented by the expense. However, it is almost certain that free passage would not have been a sufficient enticement if conditions in Britain had not been unfavourable. It is significant that years of small migration coincided with good conditions in England accompanied by unfavourable reports from the colony.

Creating opportunities in the Colony

The availability of land and labour to yield profit on invested capital is the constant decisive condition and test of material prosperity in any community, and becomes the keystone of an economy as well as defining its national identity. British Government policy for the Australian colonies was formulated and modified from time to time. Policies for the export of British capital and the supply of labour (both convict and free) were adjusted according to British industrial, demographic and other social situations, as well as the capability and capacity of the various colonial settlements to contribute to solving British problems.

By the 1820s there was official encouragement of British investment in Australia by adopting policies for large land grants to persons of capital and for the sale of land and assignment of convict labour to those investors. The reversal of the policy of setting up ex-convicts as small proprietors on small 30 acre plots followed. The hardship demanded by this policy usually meant these convicts and families remained dependent on the commissariat list for support (food and clothing) at a continuing cost to the government. It was much cheaper to assign these convicts to men of property and capital who would support them fully – clothe, house and feed them.

Reasons for the crash of 1827?

a. *The float of the Australian Agricultural Company raised a large amount of capital, mostly from the City of London investment community, and this contributed to speculation and, as noted by Rev John Dunmore Lang, 'sheep and cattle mania instantly seized on all ranks and classes of the inhabitants and brought many families to poverty and ruin'.*
b. *When capital imports cease, the wherewithal to speculate vanished; and speculation perforce stopped; inflated prices fell to a more normal*

level. In his Economic History of Australia, E.O. Shann wrote 'because those formerly too optimistic were now too despairing, and people had to sell goods at any price in order to get money; men who had bought at high prices were ruined, and perforce their creditors fell with them'.

c. *In 1842, it was the same. The influx of capital from oversees, pastoral extension, and large-scale immigration, caused much speculation. The banks, competing for business, advanced too much credit. Loans were made on the security of land and livestock which later became almost worthless; too much discounting was done for merchants (Gipps, HRA Vol 23). In the huge central district on the western slopes, along the Murrumbidgee and the Riverina, the squatters triumphed, as was inevitable. They had the financial resources to buy a run – especially after the long period of drought. Four million acres of Crown Land was sold for nearly £2.5 million. The confidence of British investors was waning. A crisis in the Argentine and the near failure of the large clearinghouse of Baring's made them cautious. Stories of rural and industrial strife in the Colony were not inducements to invest: and timber and metal prices were still falling. Loan raisings in London were under-subscribed and, at the same time, the banks were increasingly reluctant to lend money for land development which was so often unsound.*

Assisted Migration

The dual policy of selling land to people with sufficient capital to cultivate it, and keeping a careful check on the number of free grants was adopted after 1825. 'Yet the Colonial Office', says Madgwick, 'failed to administer land policy with any certainty (R.B. Madgwick Immigration into Eastern Australia). There was no uniform policy adopted to encourage economic development in a systematic and rational way. The Wakefield system found new supporters; the principle had been established that the sale of land was preferred to the old system of grants. The dual system of sales and grants had failed to encourage local (colonial) purchases. They were willing to accept grants or even 'squat' rather than purchase land. Sales to absentee landlords and investors stepped up and this provided extensive revenue to the British Government to promote free and sponsored migration.

The original plans and costs

A letter to Under Secretary Nepean, dated 23rd August 1783, James Maria Matra of Shropshire and London assists us in this regard. It was Matra, who first analysed the opportunity of using the new colony as a penal colony but his estimates were incorrect and ill-founded. He had advised the Government that it would cost less than £3,000 to establish the colony initially, plus a transportation cost at £15 per head and annual maintenance of £20 per head. In fact the transportation was contracted for the Second Fleet at £13/5/—per head and Colonial revenues from 1802 offset annual maintenance.

However, Matra made a significant statement in his letter to Nepean, when he pointed out that the prisoners housed, fed and guarded on the rotting hulks on the Thames River were being contracted for in the annual amount of £26/15/10 per head per annum. He also writes that 'the charge to the public for these convicts has been increasing for the last 7 or 8 years' (Historical Records of NSW—Vol 1 Part 2 Page 7). Adopting this alternative cost (£26/15/10) as a base for comparison purposes, the colony's benefit to Britain over a twenty-year period increased from £140,000,000 to £180,000,000. This calculation assesses the Ground 1 benefit at £84,000,000. Benefit to Britain on Ground 2 is put at £70, 000,000 (again over a 20-year period) which places the value of a convict's labour at £35 per annum. Matra had assessed the value of labour of the hulk prisoners at £35/17/-.

The valuation of convict labour in the new Colony should reflect the fact that convicts were not only used on building sites, but also on road, bridge and wharf construction. This would add (based on £35 per annum) a further £21,000,000.

The Molesworth Committee (a House of Commons Committee investigating transportation) concluded that 'the surplus food production by the convicts would feed the Military people and this, over a period of 10 years, would save £7,000,000 for the British Treasury. The benefits of grants of land to the Military etc can be estimated (based on £1 per acre) at over £5,000,000 before 1810.

From Governor King's Report to Earl Camden dated 15th March 1806 (which, due to a change of office holder, should have been addressed to Viscount Castlereagh as Colonial Secretary) that the convicts engaged in widely diverse work. The Report itself is titled *Public Labour of Convicts maintained by the Crown at Sydney, Parramatta, Hawkesbury, Toongabbie and Castle Hill, for the year 1805*. This work included:

Cultivation—Gathering, husking and shelling maize from 200 acres sowed last year—Breaking up ground and planting 1230 acres of wheat, 100 acre of Barley, 250 acres of Maize, 14 acres of Flax, and 3 acres of potatoes—Hoeing the above maize and threshing wheat.

Stock—Taking care of Government stock as herdsmen, watchmen etc

Buildings—

At Sydney: Building and constructing of stone, a citadel, a stone house, a brick dwelling for the Judge Advocate, a commodious brick house for the main guard, a brick printing office

At Parramatta: Alterations at the Brewery, a brick house as clergyman's residence

At Hawkesbury: completing a public school

A Gaol House with offices, at the expense of the Colony

Boat and Ship Builders: refitting vessels and building row boats

Wheel and Millwrights: making and repairing carts

Manufacturing: sawing, preparing and manufacturing hemp, flax and wool, bricks and tiles

Road Gangs: repairing roads, and building new roads

Other Gangs: loading and unloading boats"

(Historical Records of NSW—Vol 6 P43)

Thus the total benefits from these six items of direct gain to the British amount to well over £174 million, in comparison with Professor N.G. Butlin's proposal that the British 'invested' £5.6 million.

However, one item of direct cash cost born by the British was the transportation of the prisoners to the Colony, their initial food and general well being. Although the British chartered the whole ship, some of the expense was offset by authorising private passengers, 'free settlers' to travel in the same fleet. A second saving was that the authorities had approved 'back-loading' by these vessels of tea from China.

Only limited stores and provisions, tools and implements were sent with Captain Arthur Phillip, the appointed first Governor, and his efforts to delay the fleet until additional tools were ready were met with an order to 'commence the trip forthwith'. This turned out to be a mistake as the new Colony could only rely on minimal farming practices to grow a supply of vegetables and, without the tools to scratch the land and remove the trees and vegetation, little progress was made. This was a potentially big cost to the fledgling Colony.

The Blue Book accounting records, as maintained by Governor Macquarie from 1822 include a reference to 'net revenue and expenses' which suggests an offset of all revenues against all expenses, and including as revenue certain convict maintenance charges, to be reimbursed by the British Treasury. Such reimbursement was accounted for and reported only once, in 1825, when £16,617 'the amount of the parliamentary grant for the charge of defraying the civil establishment' was recorded as a 'receipt in aid of revenue'. Prior to and after that date, there are only reports of payments and outgoings to the civil establishment, military and other personnel, without offset from reimbursement. Other notations in 1825 include revenues from rentals of government assets (Government outsourcing and privatisation obviously started back in 1825) such as:

Ferries	£1,584
Toll gates	£6,554
Gardens	£1,835

Mill	£1,749
Canteen	£910
Church pews	£1,296
Hire of convict 'mechanics'	£6,853
Slaughtering dues	£975
Duty on colonial distillation	£4901
Duty on imported spirits	£178,434
Duty on imported tobacco	£21,817

Even in 1822 the Colony was showing a small operating surplus. This surplus grew through 1828 until, other than for transportation of convicts to the Colony, the charges on account of the British Treasury were less than £100,000 for protecting, feeding and housing nearly 5,000 fully maintained convicts. Against this cost, the charge for housing, feeding and guarding this same number of prisoners in Britain would have been substantially higher since, in addition to the 5,000 fully maintained convicts, there were a further 20,000 being paid for by free settlers and used as supervised labour. Britain surely had found a cheap source of penal servitude for at least 25,000 of its former prisoners, and found a very worthwhile alternative to the American colonies as a destination for its prisoners.

Revenue from Crown Land sales and rents was used to offset Civil (Crown) salaries and expenses. The opportunity cost to the British Treasury includes not only the cost savings but also the lateral savings and benefits produced for England and the British Treasury. Some of the other advantages to Britain include:

- The build-up of trade by the East-India Company
- The advantage of a secure, in-house supply of raw wool, to keep the spinning mills occupied
- The opportunity cost of housing, feeding and guarding prisoners
- The use of convict labour in the new Colony, for such as
  Land clearing, farming, food production
  Road construction
- Building projects such as:
  Public wharves

Barracks
Public Buildings

- Productions of Materials supply eg brick & tile production.
- As unpaid day labour for the pastoral & agricultural industry.

We can assume that land grants in the Colony to men on the military and civil list were a form of 'fringe benefits' and they should be quantified as an alternative to paid remuneration for these people. Even land grants to emancipists were used as an incentive to increase food production.

We can quantify the 'value of direct gain to the British economy' of nearly £140,000,000, compared with the publicly recorded expenditure on transportation, supplies, and military personnel of £5,600,000, between 1788 and 1822. The purposes of trying to quantify these benefits are to challenge to traditional concept that 'the British invested millions of pounds in the Colony of New South Wales'. This is obviously only the case when the outlay is shown and not the on-going benefits for over 50 years, and indeed two hundred years. It is still arguable that the continent of Australia was, in the words of Captain Arthur Phillip 'the best investment Britain will ever make'.

Having established the parameters for studying British (private and public) investment in the Colony of NSW, the question must now be one of who else thinks this investment was of interest and relevance. N.G. Butlin did not complete his manuscript of *Forming a Colonial Economy* because his death in 1991. However his notes to that time were edited and assembled into the book form and we can learn a great deal about the British plans for the colony and its economic development. Butlin writes:

> *'Even though, there may have been other imperial motives behind the British settlement of Australia, there is no doubt that the transportation of convicts to the Antipodes was a convenient solution to social, judicial and budgetary problems in Britain in the 1780s.'*

Butlin further deduces that 'Persons may move between countries (i.e. immigration) when the capitalized value of the differential in expected lifetime earnings abroad as compared with those at home exceeds the transfer and relocation costs'. The good news of free immigration and the capital transfer into the Colony was that between 1788 and 1800 21,302 'free immigrants' arrived. There are nine identified categories of 'immigrants' during this period.

- Military and civil officers and their families
- Former officials returning to the colony
- Convict families
- Indentured labourers
- Assisted immigrants
- Privately supported persons sponsored by colonials
- Free immigrants and their families

Given that Britain provided not only human capital but also fiscal resources to support the people concerned, the volume and, nature of these resources and access to them became interesting. However, it remains the case that Britain, having put into place extensive levels of capital, certainly succeeded in withdrawing a great deal of its early fiscal support and bringing the Commissariat effectively under military control. Obviously another form of 'investment' is public debt, and public borrowing, secured by the full faith and credit of the Colonial government.

The 'works outlay' is another element of 'public investment' and it was not fully accounted for until 1810 when Governor Macquarie arrived. From that date, works outlay (i.e. capital expenditure from the local revenue of the Colony) grew annually from £2,194 in 1810 to £14,700 in 1821. However, this is a small component of total works outlay or capital expenditure since a Mr. Henry Kitchen, in a submission to Commissioner J.T. Bigge, stated that his estimate of building construction under Macquarie was in excess of £900,000.

A table included in *Australians Historical Statistics* titled 'Gross Private Capital Formation at current prices' does not commence until 1861 and later in this study we will try to assemble data on both public and private capital formation from 1800 – based on a separate study of Colonial industrial, building and construction development. This table is derived from Butlin's 'Australian Domestic Product, Investment and Foreign Borrowing 1861-1938'. It appears that no previous studies have been undertaken of private or public Capital Formation between 1788 and 1861.

T.A. Coghlan is generally recognised as a significant contributor to Colonial economic history and he writes in Volume 1 of *Labour and Industry in Australia* of another phase of public investment and its encouragement in the colony, by favourable official policies. Coghlan writes:

> *'Under the Governorship of Macquarie the infant town of Sydney grew considerably. King had been the first Governor to grant leases there (Sydney), but as the leases were only for five years the buildings erected were naturally not of a substantial character. Macquarie granted a number of leases also, but gave permanent grants of land in cases where valuable buildings were to be erected, so that at the end of his term of office Sydney had grown considerably, having the appearance, according to W.C. Wentworth in his Historical and Statistical Account of the Colony, of a town of 20,000 inhabitants though its population, numbered only 7,000; and while the houses were for the most part small one-storied dwellings, it contained buildings, private and public, excellent both in construction and in design, and many stores where goods of all kinds could be bought. The Government Store continued in existence as a shop open to the public until January 1815, when Macquarie, considering that its purpose had been served as a means towards keeping down prices, closed it to all except the military and the convicts in government employment.*[55].

So, having fixed the short-term land lease, Macquarie actively encouraged public and private investment in building and construction. Coghlan provides an insight into another Macquarie step to encourage investment. He writes:

> *'Until Macquarie arrived, the means of communicating between one part of the settlement and another was difficult, as*

---

55 Coghlan, T.A. *Labour & Investment in Australia Vol 1*

> *all roads were poor. Macquarie had a passion for construction, and his roads were excellent. He made a turnpike road from Sydney to the Hawkesbury, completing it in 1811. Now goods and passengers did not have to be carried by boat, as previously was the case. A few years later he constructed the great road over the mountains to the western plains, and also extended his roads in other directions. With the construction of the roads, internal trade and all the industries dependent thereon developed. It took a further time before travelling by road was safe, as many convicts escaped and took to the bush, preying upon defenceless travellers; journeys to any part of the settlement was usually made in company and it was customary to make even the short journey from Sydney to Parramatta about 14 miles in parties.*[56]

If we intend to extend our parameters to further analyse the types and amount of public and private British investment in the Colony of NSW, we will have to now review certain other matters:

- The development of private industries eg boat-building; timber harvesting and processing; agriculture sand pastoral pursuits, whaling and overseas trading – all of which were reasonably capital intensive operations which would have attracted both overseas investors and a local breed of entrepreneurs
- The development of building and construction in the Colony, including reference to the public buildings completed in the period, how much they would have cost and how they were paid for.
- We will try to assemble a table of public and private overseas (British) investment, and establish the background to debt in the Colony from overseas sources.
- We will attempt to recreate the level of investment in the colony by category by first identifying the various sources of both public and private investment and relating value to each one
- We will endeavour to track bank deposits and advances, which until the 1850s were generally in the negative (i.e. advances

[56] Coghlan *ibid*

exceeded deposits and it fell to the local banks to accept British deposits for fixed terms of 1, 2 or 3 years. Banks advanced money by way of pastoralists' overdrafts, on city land and on stocks and shares. Land banks offered mortgages. Banks' liabilities before 1850 by way of term deposits from overseas depositors were almost 40 million pound.

- One gauge of how much money was flowing through the domestic economy is the volume of cheques, bills and drafts passing through the clearing-house. By the 1860s, this amount had risen to almost £6 million each week.
- Coghlan's *Wealth and Progress of NSW* for 1900 reflects on the source and disposition of public capital and can be tabulated as follows:[57]

Source of Funds

Treasury bills and debentures	8,168,554
Transfer from Consolidated Revenue	1,668,640
Sum Available for Expenditure	82,430,777

Use of Funds

Railways	40,450,473
Tramways	2,720,338
Telegraphs	1,255,600
Water supply and sewerage	9,878,833

Catalysts for immigration

Free immigration into the Colony – a new perspective

The need for education in the colony is an interesting pre-emptive to the need for free immigrants. Immigration would help solve numerous gaps in the colony—capital and labour, societal demands and the imbalance of men and women, the demand for a free enterprise economy and 'foreign' investment. The direct association then as now, between education and

[57] Coghlan, T.A. *Wealth & Progress in NSW 1900*

investment, knowledge and growth is unmistakeable. It was largely left to Macquarie to juggle the need for balance in the penal colony, but this was not a high priority and it was passed to Brisbane and then Bourke. Before migration could be practiced, thought Macquarie, I need to rid the streets of the waifs, orphans and unwanted children of a largely immoral society. Bligh had first drawn official attention to the deteriorating social fabric with three times as many 'kept' as married women and the dazzling count of illegitimate children compared with those that numbered in the legitimate category. Education would help, not only with this social dilemma, but also with the rampant illiteracy in the Colony—the three Rs were down to one R and 'riting was largely limited to an X on the spot.

Education, a construction program, local discretionary revenue raising and elimination of spirits as the currency of the day, were Macquarie's top priorities – only then could free immigrants be welcomed. Of course a bank would be helpful in cementing the colony as a land of opportunity. The English thought in terms of symbols even if they were thin. So, understanding the needs for education set the scene for a rational immigration policy.

The economy was at the top of the triangle pointing the way ahead. The fact that the Colony had no treasury was a disincentive to migration but Macquarie believed in balancing finely the needs of a despotic governor with the daily demands on government with the desire for free enterprise. Macquarie had decided that government had the need and responsibility to encourage and sponsor exploration, and it was the crossing of the mountain range west of Sydney town that inspired and commenced the first sustained economic expansion of the Colony. The pastoral movement led the way towards encouraging migration. The financing mechanism for the new policy was the sale of Crown or 'waste' lands and the boom and bust syndrome was set in place by speculators in both land and livestock. The market economy would be in tatters within 20 years of Macquarie's departure.

This is the story of the need for education and a sound economy leading to migration as a catalyst for growth in the 'new' economy.

Immigrants and Free Settlers

On 15th January 1793, Collins records that the *Bellona* transport ship had arrived in Sydney Harbour with a cargo of stores and provisions, 17 female convicts and five settlers, one of whom was a master wheelwright employed by the governor at a salary of £100 per annum. A second was a returning skilled tradesman who had previously been employed as a master blacksmith. All five settlers had brought their families. Collins conjectured that these first five settlers had received free passage, the promise of a land grant and assistance with farming, as incentives for becoming free settlers.

In *A History of Australia*, Manning Clark records that in 1806, 'a dozen families from the Scottish border area arrived as free emigrants and each received 100 acres of land on the banks of the Hawkesbury River in a place they called Ebenezer. They were devout Presbyterians, and were allowed to worship in the colony according to their own lights'. However the authorities were not prepared to tolerate the practice of the Catholic religion, because they saw it 'as an instrument of mental slavery, a threat to higher civilization, and a threat to liberty' (Clark Vol 1)

Developing immigration

Even by the census of 1828, NSW had fewer than 5,000 people who had come out voluntarily out of a population of 36 598. The Colony had attractions unavailable in the USA, free land and convict labour. Settlers were given freehold land for agriculture and pasture but it applied only to men who had immigrated as private citizens, military officers who had decided to stay and pardoned convicts who had been granted land.

In 1831 the British Government, against the opposition of many in the Colony, decided to stop giving away land grants to settlers, choosing instead to 'sell' the land and use some of the proceeds to sponsor migrants to the colony. The initial sale price was 5 shillings an acre. It was a way of inducing poor families to migrate and relieving the labour shortage. Between 1831 and 1840 about 50,000 prisoners were transported and about 65,000 free men and women chose to emigrate.

The balance of the sexes was more equal amongst emigrants than among convicts: but even South Australia, which was wholly an emigrant colony, had only eight females for every 10 males by 1850. In Australia as a whole there were fewer than seven for every 10. The resulting challenge was only partially met by Caroline Chisholm who met every convict and emigrant ship to stress the dangers to young unmarried women. Her main accomplishment was when she convinced the Colonial Office in 1846 to offer free passage to all families of convicts resident in the Colony. Her detractors claimed that the result of her efforts on behalf of convicts and poor emigrating families would be to create in the Colony an imbalance of Catholics In Australia, Catholics were already twice the proportion of the population that they were in England.

'Populate or perish'

The history of Australia is bound tightly into two aspects—the economics of colonisation and the story of immigration.

The first free immigrants who came out on the *Bellona* were given small land grants on Liberty Plains (the Strathfield-Homebush area). The first family to arrive included a millwright who had been on the hulks in Britain for a minor crime and been released. Major Grose, acting as the Administrator after Phillip's departure, observed 'from some dirty tricks he has already attempted, I fear he has not forgotten all he learned as a former prisoner. He is evidently one of those that his country could well do without'.

In his report *The State of the Colony in 1801,* Governor King wrote on the subject of free immigrants:

> *'Settlers are of two classes i.e. those who come free from England and those who were convicts and whose terms of transportation are expired, or who are emancipated. Of the first class, I am sorry their industry and exertions by no means answer the professions they made in England, several of whom are so useless to themselves and everyone about them that they were not only a burden to the public but a very bad example to the industrious. As they brought no other property*

> *than their large families, many have been and will continue an expensive burden on the public, or starve. The settlers are maintained by the crown for eighteen months and have two convicts assigned to each, which is very sufficient to provide against the time of doing for themselves, but that period too often discovers their idleness and incapacity to raise the least article from a fertile and favourable climate, after having occasioned an expense of upwards of 250 pound for each family, exclusive of their passage out The desirable people to be sent here are sober, industrious farmers, carpenters, wheel and mill wrights, who having been used to draw their food from the earth, secure sand manufacture it, would here find how bountifully their labour would be rewarded.'*

It appears that King did not have a very high opinion of the potential for free migration to the Colony.

Phillip's successor – Governor Hunter—was instructed by the Colonial Office to 'encourage free settlers without subjecting the public to expense'. They were to be given larger land grants than the emancipists and as much convict labour as they wanted. Hunter observed in one of his submissions to the Secretary for the Colonies that 'free immigrants would not come to the country whilst the needs of the colony were supplied from Government farms'. Economic factors hit the immigration concept in 1801 when Hunter's successor, Governor King, wrote to the Duke of Portland, as Colonial Secretary, suggesting family immigration. It was declined on the basis that transporting a family would cost £150 and annual maintenance until they were self-supporting would cost £250 (HRNSW).

In 1802, the HRNSW records that free settlers (28 in one group) arrived by the *Perseus* and *Coromandel.* More arrived in the Navy ship *Glatton*, including a person supposedly bearing 'perfect knowledge of Agriculture, having held a very considerable farm in his hands, but which through youthful indiscretion, he found it necessary to relinquish'. The Governor was asked to place him 'above the common class of settlers'. The government, Governor King wrote 'was much imposed on' by these free settlers. The *Glatton* settlers were sent to the Nepean, where they were wrote King 'going on with great spirit and well applied industry'.

In 1804 King reported to Lord Hobart 'there were 543 free settlers supporting 351 wives and 589 children and utilising 463 convicts'. Further free settlers are recorded as arriving in the *William Pitt* in 1805, mainly because land and subsistence was being replaced by the lure of wealth coming from the fine wool being promoted by John Macarthur. This endeavour and attraction of wealth brought a different and probably better class of free settler – the Blaxland brothers arrived on a charter vessel with their families, servants and capital of over 6,000 pound. Again the governor received instructions. 'They are to be allowed 8,000 acres of land and the services of up to 80 convicts for 18 months at the commissary store's expense. Governor Bligh was given similar instructions in reference to a 'lady of quality' – a Mrs Chapman, a widow, Governess and teacher. Bligh was directed to 'afford her due encouragement and assistance'. The next governor, Lachlan Macquarie took a different stance – he discouraged free immigration, probably because the flow of convicts was almost overwhelming his administration. His position is not readily understandable. As a quasi social reformer and developer of free enterprise in the colony, one would have expected Macquarie to welcome free settlers for what social and economic values they could contribute. When the Bigge report was published in London, it raised the interest of men of wealth in the colony and a Lieutenant Vickers, an officer of the East India Company, volunteered to emigrate with 10,000 pound of capital, an unblemished reputation and a purity of private life ' not previously known in any class of society', and in return demanded privileges by way of land grants, livestock and a regular seat at the governor's table. Brisbane, as governor, was directed by Lord Bathurst as Colonial secretary to give Vickers 2,000 acres of land and a house allotment near Newcastle. Brisbane investigated Vickers and found him to be little more than 'an adventurer, a bird of passage, and boycotted by his fellow officers'. Marjorie Barnard concluded, 'Only distance made his deception possible'. Opportunities followed good publicity, and the floating of the Australian Agricultural Company in London in 1823 did much to promote the colony in Britain, and brought another spate of free settlers to the colony.

This then is the early trend in the free settler movement – it had not been seen yet as a government opportunity. But that was about to change. Lord Bathurst came along with an idea, urged by the Wakefield supporters and the rash of economists waging war on the increasing unemployment, poverty and lack of investment opportunities in Britain.

A privately sponsored scheme was funded by a loan to Dr. J.D. Lang by the governor in the amount of 1,500 pound, which brought out 100 selected 'mechanics' (semi-skilled labourers) and their families. Lang used a charter vessel to transport these immigrants, and the understanding was that the immigrants would repay their expenses from future wages. In 1831 this was an inspiring move to privatising a government policy.

Three factors were set to establish an on-going immigration policy. The three factors were bad times in England; shortages of skilled labour of both men and women in the colony; and the cessation of the assignment system.

A commission on Emigration was established in England to select and despatch suitable agricultural labourers. A plan to tax landowners of assigned convicts failed when the difficulty of collection was recognised. There were still 13,400 convicts on assignment in 1831.

The governor agreed that official funds would contribute 20 pound towards each immigrant family and try to recover it after the family settled. The collections were rarely made.

It was left to Governor Bourke to formulate a workable plan. The 'bounty system' relied on sponsored workers funded by government. The government paid 12 pound out of the 17 pound passage money. The Emigrants Friendly Society existed in Sydney to help and protect these sponsored migrants.

A more refined method was needed to select and sponsor these migrants. Glenelg reformed the financial side in 1837. He allocated the revenue from land sales in the colony as a means of affording immigration. The land as well as any revenue derived from its sale, lease or rental, had remained the property of the crown, not the colonial administration. Two-thirds of these funds were to be allocated to migrants by way of grants – 30 pound for a married couple, 15 for an unmarried daughter, 5 and10 pound for children depending on age.

The zenith of immigration success could be seen in the 1830s under Governor Gipps. Land revenue was high, the colony was prosperous and plenty of migrants were on offer and the colony could successfully absorb them. The severe drought at the end of decade (1838) cause land revenue to fall sharply. Gipps proposed a loan to the Land Fund in order to continue the immigration program. He requested of the British Treasury a loan of 1 million pound. The intention of floating the loan would ensure the repayment of the loan. English interest still dwelt on the export of her paupers and her unemployed. The response by Gipps to Lord John Russell's criticism of the Gipps approach to immigration was that the bounty system had caused the depression of the 1842-44 periods and not the reverse.

The Report of the 1837 'Committee on Immigration' opened up for opposition to the traditional White Australia policy.

"This committee was appointed to consider and report their opinion made to the government of New South Wales, for introducing into the colony certain of the Hill Labourers of India; and to consider the terms under which Mechanics and Labourers are now brought from Europe".

Summary

The British trait of pomposity came to the fore during the days of early migration to the colony. 'We are British, we are free, we are pure of spirit and more worthy than the prisoners already shipped' they thought' but we will take or families, our servants, our capital and relocate to the new colony, provided we are treated as privileged persons and given land, livestock and a seat at the governor's table'.

But establishing a class structure was not on the list of plans for Brisbane, Bourke Darling or Gipps. They hands their hands full keeping the economy moving forward and keeping the economy afloat. Although they were guided by an appointed Legislative Council, the governors role was an onerous one – balancing the ever-changing political scene in Britain with the ever-diminishing financial support coming from the British Treasury for colonial operations, and the growing relaxing of isolation of the colony in world events. Trading ships of many nations were daily arrivals into the splendid harbour. The other settlement under the governor's watchful eye was taking more and more time. It was fortunate that Port Phillip settlement was a net contributor to the New South Wales coffers, whilst Morton Bay, and VDL were still being supported out of Sydney. The huge influx of convicts made life difficult in the settlements. Finding places to put these people to gainful employment at little (if any) cost to the Treasury was growing more and more difficult. It was largely 'out of sight, out of mind'. Until they engaged in crime, or the landowners ran into hard times and suddenly the convicts were unwanted and thrown back onto the charity of the government. Free settlers were fine in theory but their growing influence in the political and financial arena of the colony, made both political and economic decisions difficult. The constant pressure to open up new land, build new roads, carry out surveys, create new settlements – was a continuing problem for the governor who kept demanding more and more money to run the colony. That placed pressure on raising more and more revenue, especially for public works, education, migration and government services.

Migrations soon became the life-blood of the colony. They brought their capital, their worldly goods, their ways of life, and over all made a valuable contribution to their new land. They were the basis of attracting new investment from the motherland. But migrants down through the years were always to be attractive in the Australian physic. This was to be a nation of immigrants, but society had to be built around the needs of this new world.

Special Events –Colonial Education & Immigration Policies

Synopsis

As the first of the special events to be examined, we can review the impact of both education and immigration, from the standpoint of the economy, the social framework, the political structure and look at the rocky road that was created by religious bigotry and factions within the colony. Naturally as a bi-product of the immigration policies, the transportation (of convicts) program was its first and most significant contributor. Education was a significant economic tool, as the rate of illiteracy within the colony fell from 75% before 1800 to 25% by 1830. The development of local industry was most dependent then, as it is still today, on a literate and educated workforce. Immigration of free settlers hastened the end of the transportation program and although the mass of people supported and approved of its cessation, the pastoralists, traders and merchants bemoaned the shortage of labour and the high price of skilled labourers arriving from Britain. Naturally the discovery of gold in the early 1850s drove those same prices and shortages even higher, since many in the population looked to find their fortune on the goldfields and gave up regular employment in order to move to the goldfields.

Immigrants and Free Settlers

Collins records that on the 15th January 1793, the Bellona transport ship, arrived in Sydney Harbour with a cargo of stores and provisions, 17 female convicts and five settlers one of whom was a master wheel-wright employed by the governor at a salary of 100 pound per annum. A second was a returning skilled tradesman who had been previously employed as a master blacksmith. All five settlers had brought their families.

Collins conjectures that these first three settlers had received free passage, a promise of a land grant and assistance with farming, as the incentive for becoming the free settlers,

Manning Clark (A History of Australia) records that in 1806, 'a dozen families from the Scottish border area arrived as free emigrants and each received 100 acres of land on the banks of the Hawkesbury River in a place they called Ebenezer. They were devout Presbyterians, and were allowed to worship in the colony according to their own lights'. However the authorities were not prepared to tolerate the practice of the catholic religion, because they saw it 'as an instrument of mental slavery, a threat to higher civilization, and a threat to liberty' (Clark Vol 1)

Developing Immigration

Even by the census of 1828, NSW had fewer than 5,000 people who had come out voluntarily, in a population of 36 598. The colony had the attractions unavailable in the USA, free land and convict labour. Settlers were given land for agriculture and pasture usage. This meant freehold land, and it only applied to men who had immigrated as private citizens, to military officers who had decided to stay and to pardoned convicts who had been granted land.

In 1831, the British Government, against the opposition of many in the colony decided to stop giving away land grants to settlers and chose instead to 'sell' the land and use some of the proceeds to sponsor migrants to the colony. The initial sales price was 5 shillings an acre. It was a way of inducing poor families to leave the country, but as well of relieving the labour shortage. Between 1831 and 1840 about 50,000 prisoners were transported and about 65,000 free men and women chose to emigrate

The battle of the sexes was more equal amongst emigrants than among convicts: but even South Australia, which was wholly an emigrant's colony, had only 8 females for every 10 males by 1850, and in Australia as a whole there was fewer than 7 in every ten. The resulting challenge was only partially met by Caroline Chisholm who met every convict and emigrant ship to stress the dangers to young unmarried women. Her main accomplishment was to convince the Colonial Office, in 1846, to offer free passage to all families of convicts resident in the colony. Her detractors suggested that the result of her efforts towards convict families and emigrating poor families would be to create an imbalance of Catholics in the colony, who were already twice the proportion of the Australian population as they were in England.

'Populate or Perish'

The history of Australia is bound tightly into two aspects—the economics of colonization and the story of immigration.

The first free immigrants came out on the Bellona, and were given small landgrants on Liberty Plains (the Strathfield-Homebush area). The first family to arrive included a millwright who had been on the hulks in Britain for a minor crime and been released. It was Major Grose, acting as the Administrator after the departure of Phillip, who observed ' from some dirty tricks he has already attempted, I fear he has not forgotten all he learned as a former prisoner. He is evidently one of those that his country could well do without'.

Governor King wrote in his report – The State of the Colony in 1801 – on the subject of free immigrants:

"Settlers are of two classes i.e. those who come free from England and those who were convicts and whose terms of transportation are expired, or who are emancipated. Of the first class, I am sorry their industry and exertions by no means answer the professions they made in England, several of whom are so useless to themselves and everyone about them that they were not only a burden to the public but a very bad example to the industrious. As they brought no other property than their large families, many have been and will continue an expensive burden on the public, or starve. The settlers are maintained by the crown for eighteen months and have two convicts assigned to each, which is very sufficient to provide against the time of doing for themselves, but that period too often discovers their idleness and incapacity to raise the least article from a fertile and favourable climate, after having occasioned an expense of upwards of 250 pound for each family, exclusive of their passage out The desirable people to be sent here are sober, industrious farmers, carpenters, wheel and mill wrights, who having been used to draw their food from the earth, secure sand manufacture it, would here find how bountifully their labour would be rewarded".

It appears that King did not have a very high opinion of the potential for free migration to the colony.

Phillip's successor – Governor Hunter—was instructed by the Colonial Office to 'encourage free settlers without subjecting the public to expense'. They were to be given larger land grants than the emancipists and as much convict labour as they wanted. Hunter observed in one of his submissions to the Secretary of the colonies that 'free immigrants would not come to the country whilst the needs of the colony were supplied from Government farms'.

The economic factors hit the immigration concept in 1801 when Governor King, as Hunters successor wrote to the Duke of Portland, as Colonial Secretary and suggested family immigration. It was turned down on the basis that transporting a family would cost 150 pound and annual maintenance until they were self-supporting would cost 250 pound (HRNSW)

In 1802, the HRNSW records that free settlers (28 in one group) arrived by the Perseus and Coromandel. More came in the Navy ship Glatton, including a person supposedly bearing 'perfect knowledge of Agriculture, having held a very considerable farm in his hands, but which through youthful indiscretion, he found it necessary to relinquish'. The governor was asked to place him 'above the common class of settlers'. The government, Governor King wrote 'was much imposed on' by these free settlers. The Glatton settlers were sent to the Nepean, where they were wrote King ' going on with great spirit and well applied industry'

King reported to Lord Hobart in 1804 that 'there were 543 free settlers supporting 351 wives and 589 children and utilising 463 convicts'. Further free settlers are recorded as being in the William Pitt in 1805, mainly because land and subsistence was being replaced by the lure of wealth coming from the fine wool being promoted by John Macarthur. This endeavour and attraction of wealth brought a different and probably better class of free settler – the Blaxland brothers arrived on a charter vessel with their families, servants and capital of over 6,000 pound. Again the governor received instructions. 'They are to be allowed 8,000 acres of land and the services of up to 80 convicts for 18 months at the commissary store's expense. Governor Bligh was given similar instructions in reference to a 'lady of quality' – a Mrs Chapman, a widow, Governess and teacher. Bligh was directed to 'afford her due encouragement and assistance'. The next governor, Lachlan Macquarie took a different stance – he discouraged free immigration, probably because the flow of convicts was almost overwhelming his administration. His position is not readily understandable. As a quasi social reformer and developer of free enterprise in the colony, one would have expected Macquarie to welcome free settlers for what social and economic values they could contribute. When the Bigge report was published in London, it raised the interest of men of wealth in the colony and a Lieutenant Vickers, an officer of the East India Company, volunteered to emigrate with 10,000 pound of capital, an unblemished reputation and a purity of private life ' hitherto known in any class of society', and in return demanded privileges by way of land grants, livestock and a regular seat at the governor's table. Brisbane, as governor, was directed by Lord Bathurst as Colonial secretary to give Vickers 2,000 acres of land and a house allotment near Newcastle. Brisbane investigated Vickers and found him to be little more than 'an adventurer, a bird of passage, and boycotted by his fellow officers'. Marjorie Barnard concluded, 'Only distance made his deception possible'. Opportunities followed good publicity, and the floating of the Australian Agricultural Company in London in 1823 did much to promote the colony in Britain, and brought another spate of free settlers to the colony.

This then is the early trend in the free settler movement – it had not been seen yet as a government opportunity. But that was about to change. Lord Bathurst came along with an idea, urged by the Wakefield supporters and the rash of economists waging war on the increasing unemployment, poverty and lack of investment opportunities in Britain.

A privately sponsored scheme was funded by a loan to Dr. J.D. Lang by the governor in the amount of 1,500 pound, which brought out 100 selected 'mechanics' (semi-skilled labourers) and their families. Land used a charter vessel to transport these immigrants, and the understanding was that the immigrants would repay their expenses from future wages. In 1831 this was an inspiring move to privatising a government policy.

Three factors were set to establish an on-going immigration policy. The three factors were bad times in England; shortages of skilled labour of both men and women in the colony; and the cessation of the assignment system.

A commission on Emigration was established in England to select and despatch suitable agricultural labourers. A plan to tax landowners of assigned convicts failed when the difficulty of collection was recognised. There were still 13,400 convicts on assignment in 1831.

The governor agreed that official funds would contribute 20 pound towards each immigrant family and try to recover it after the family settled. The collections were rarely made.

It was left to Governor Bourke to formulate a workable plan. The 'bounty system' relied on sponsored workers funded by government. The government paid 12 pound out of the 17 pound passage money. The Emigrants Friendly Society existed in Sydney to help and protect these sponsored migrants.

A more refined method was needed to select and sponsor these migrants. Glenelg reformed the financial side in 1837. He allocated the revenue from land sales in the colony as a means of affording immigration. The land as well as any revenue derived from its sale, lease or rental, had remained the property of the crown, not the colonial administration. Two-thirds of these funds were to be allocated to migrants by way of grants – 30 pound for a married couple, 15 for an unmarried daughter, 5 and10 pound for children depending on age.

The zenith of immigration success could be seen in the 1830s under Governor Gipps. Land revenue was high, the colony was prosperous and plenty of migrants were on offer and the colony could successfully absorb them. The severe drought at the end of decade (1838) cause land revenue to fall sharply. Gipps proposed a loan to the Land Fund in order to continue the immigration program. He requested of the British Treasury a loan of 1 million pound. The intention of floating the loan would ensure the repayment of the loan. English interest still dwelt on the export of her paupers and her unemployed. The response by Gipps to Lord John Russell's criticism of the Gipps approach to immigration was that the bounty system had caused the depression of the 1842-44 periods and not the reverse.

The Report of the 1837 'Committee on Immigration' opened up for opposition to the traditional White Australia policy.

"This committee was appointed to consider and report their opinion made to the government of New South Wales, for introducing into the colony certain of the Hill Labourers of India; and to consider the terms under which Mechanics and Labourers are now brought from Europe".

CHAPTER 4

EXPLAINING THE COLONIAL ECONOMIC DRIVERS 1788-1856

In order to understand the growth of the colonial economy, we must understand the economic drivers that underpinned, sustained and supported the colonial economy. There are at least six, if not seven, such economic drivers. They include the factors of (a) population growth, the (b) economic development within the colony, the (c) funding sources such as British Treasury appropriations and the (d) revenues raised from within the local economy (for example, taxes and duties on imports) and (e) foreign investment (both public and private). The traditional concept of growth within the colonial economy comes from (f) the rise of the pastoral industry. A seventh driver would be the all-important Land Board, which played such an important role within the colonial economy The Land Board played an important role in co-ordinating crown land policy, controlling land sales, squatting licenses and speculators, re-setting boundaries of location, establishing set aside lands for future townships and for church and school estates, carrying out the survey of millions of acres of land transferred by grant and sale, and offering terms sales for crown lands and being responsible for the collection of repayments, rents, license fees, quit-rents and depasturing fees. In addition the land board was vested with road reserves for hundreds of miles of unmade roads but important rights-of-way that would well into the future protect access to remote pastoral and farming properties. The main thrust of published material about the Land Board is in conjunction with crown land sales policy, but the Board had a much larger role and the overall Board policies sand performances are what are to be reviewed here.

Although an important factor it is no more important that our other five motivators of the colonial economy between 1802 and 1856. Why have I selected these two specific dates? 1802 was when Governor King first imposed an illegal, but justified and well-intentioned impost on the local free community to build a local gaol to replace one burnt to the ground through a lightening strike but which the British would not replace. The local residents thought a more solid and durable prison was a worthwhile community investment. At the other end, the year of 1856 signalled the first real representative and responsible government in the colony, and although it was not the end of the colonial era, it was certainly the end of Britain's financial support of sand for the colony and as such the colony was expected to stand on its own two feet.

These six factors will be discussed as mechanisms for 'growing the colonial economy between 1802 and 1856'

One consideration that must not be forgotten is the externally enforced pace of colonial expansion, particularly through the organised rather than the market-induced inflow of both convicts and assisted migrants. What this means is that instead of market forces requiring additional labour and human resources, extra labour and resources were imposed on the colony and there was an obligatory process of putting these people to work, in many cases by creating a public works program and pushing development ahead at an artificial pace rather than at a time and rate suited to the local economy. In much the same way, the 'assignment' system in the 1810-1830 period forced landowners to create clearing and development programs in order to utilise the labour available rather than only develop land as demand required.

1. Population growth including immigration of convicts & free settlers

The reason the colonial society did not change very much in the 1820s is that relatively few immigrants arrived. During 1823, Lord Bathurst, Colonial Secretary, sent instructions to Governor Brisbane (Macquarie's successor) altering the administration of the colony of NSW in most of the ways Commissioner Bigge had recommended in his reports.[58] One result of the Bigge Reports was that Macquarie was officially recalled to Britain even though he had canvassed his retirement before Bigge's arrival in 1819. Macquarie was distressed by the Bigge Reports and took very personally the recommendations made for change. Although there were many implied criticisms Macquarie considered that the public perception was that he had not acted properly in his role as Governor. Macquarie set to and compared the circumstances of the colony at the time of his arrival in 1810, with the great achievements he had made through 1821. In hindsight, Macquarie had accomplished much, mostly by means of arrogantly pursuing a series of policies without the pre-approval of the Secretary or the Government in London.

The arrival of only a few immigrants was because Bigge and the Colonial Office believed that only men of capital would emigrate. Labourers and the poor of England should not be encouraged and, as these people rarely had money to pay for the long passage to Sydney, few of them arrived.[59] Although the numbers were small, few of them came unassisted. In 1821 320 free immigrants arrived and this increased each year; 903 in 1826; 1005 in 1829, but slipping to 772 in 1830. Mostly they were family groups with some financial security.

In 1828, the first census (as opposed to musters) of white persons in NSW was taken. 20,930 persons were classified as free and 15,668 were classified as convicts. However, of the free persons, many had arrived as convicts or were born of convicts. In fact, 70% of the population in 1828 had convict associations. However, by 1828, one quarter of the NSW population was native born; 3,500 were over 12 years of age

58 Commissioner J.T. Bigge had been sent by Bathurst to Enquire into the State and Operations of the colony of NSW in 1819; the House of Commons had demanded an inquiry into the colony and had threatened to hold one of its own; Bathurst pre-empted a difficult government situation by appointing Bigge with a very broad and wide-ranging terms of Enquiry. Bigge held two years of investigations in the colony and reported to the Commons in 1823 with the printing of three Reports.

59 Australian History – The occupation of a Continent *Bessant* (Ed)

There was another side to this migration of unregulated souls. Shaw writes" The cost of assistance, the unsuitability of many emigrants, their ill-health, and the numbers of children and paupers that were sent – all these gave the colonists a source of grievance".[60] A large part of the problem was that the English wanted emigration – but those they wished to see emigrate were not welcomed in the colony. A growing opinion in the colony was that free migrants could not work with convicts; the convicts by themselves were too few and with growing expense; therefore transportation must stop and immigration be encouraged. However, immigrants of a good quality were not those the English wanted to send; its preference was for the paupers and the disruptive in the society. To stop transportation would be "attended with the most serious consequences unless there be previous means taken too ensure the introduction of a full supply of free labour". [61] In the next five years, the number of free immigrants increased so much that transportation could be stopped with little political backlash. Between 1835 and 1840, the colony was quite prosperous (it was a case of boom and bust—the great depression came in 1841); sales of crown land were large, and consequently the funds available for assisting immigrants were plentiful.[62]

In 1838, land revenue was over £150,000 and assisted migrants numbered 7,400; in 1839, land revenue was £200,000 and assisted migrants 10,000; in 1840 revenue was over £500,000 and assisted migrants 22,500.

Between 1832 and 1842, over 50,000 assisted and 15,000 unassisted migrants arrived in NSW; or they might have arrived as convicts, and over 3,000 arrived that way each year. Thus between 1830 and 1840 the population of the whole of Australia increased from 70,000 to 190,000, with 130,000 of those in 1840 being in NSW. Of these 87000 were men

60 Shaw, A.G.L. *The economic development of Australia* p.44

61 HRA Bourke to Colonial Secretary *Governor's despatches* 1835

62 The British Treasury had agreed to put 50% of land sale proceeds into assisting immigrants with shipping costs; a further 15% into assisting Aborigines' and the balance was for discretionary use by the crown. These percentages changed in 1840 when all sale proceeds were spent on immigration but the land fund still ran out of funds in 1842 and no further assistance was made to immigrants other than by the colonial government borrowing funds in the London market through its own credit.

and 43000 were women; 30,000 had been born in the colony; 50,000 were free settlers, 20,000 were emancipists and 30,000 were convicts.[63]

2. Foreign Private Investment

We need to make the distinction between foreign public investment, and foreign private investment. The British Treasury appropriated specific funds for infrastructure programs in the colony, such as public buildings, churches, gaols, roads etc.

One reason that local colonial taxes and duties were imposed on the colony was to give the governor the funding source for discretionary expenditures in order to improve his administration. There were many instances of expenditures which could not be covered by the British funds, such as a bounty to recapture runaway convicts, building fences around the cemeteries and whitewashing the walls of public buildings (for instance barracks) in the settlement. The British Treasury would have considered such items of expense as being unnecessary. Road repair and maintenance was intended to be covered from toll receipts but they were never sufficient to make necessary repairs. Governors Hunter and Bligh did little to improve public and community buildings, roads and bridges and by the time Macquarie arrived in the colony in 1810, there was a major backlog of building work and maintenance to be undertaken. Macquarie expanded the local revenue tax base in order to give himself more flexibility in pursuing improved conditions for the settlers and the population at large.

Although Macquarie did not specifically seek new free immigrants for the colony, word of mouth circulated that the colony was in a growth stage and worthy of being considered for either immigration or investment. Usually one accompanied the other. The first private investment came with the immigrants. Free settlers would either cash up in England or transfer their possessions to the colony, and this small level of private investment was the start of a major item of capital transfers to the colony.

---

63 Shaw *ibid*

However, private capital formation took many forms; the early settlers, bought or built houses, they built or bought furnishings; they had carriages and often employed water conservation.

As the system of land grants was expanded and farming was encouraged the spread of settlement required a combination of public and private investment.

The government had to provide roads and townships, and the settlers had to provide pastoral investment. This pastoral capital formation consisted of five main types of assets:

> Buildings – residence, outbuildings, wool shed or grain storage
> Fences – stockyards, posts and rails
> Water conservation – dams, tanks, wells
> Plant – cultivators, tools
> Stocks – food, clothing, household items, materials for animal care and general repairs—livestock

Stephen Roberts offers an interesting insight into the colony of 1835.[64]

"It did not need much prescience to foresee the whole of the country united by settlement – so much had it outgrown the coastal stage of Sydney town. It was a new Australia – a land of free settlement and progressive occupation – that was there, and the old convict days were ending.

Both human and monetary capital were pouring into the various colonies and transforming the nature of their population and problems. Convicts no longer set the tone; even autocratic governors belonged to a day that was passing, and instead, the country was in the grip of a strangely buoyant, and equally optimistic, race of free men".

As part of our private capital formation, we must remember the growth of human capital and the needs for specific labour. Capital requires labour with a specific role. The establishment and expansion of farming meant more than shepherding and ploughing. There was a considerable demand

---

64 Roberts, S.H *The Squatting Age in Australia 1835-1847 (published 1935)*

for building skills, for construction and maintenance of equipment such as drays and carts, harness making and repair, tool-making etc. It became important, in order to support and sustain capital growth and economic development to be able to employ labour with multi-skills. This was a new phenomenon for the colony, especially since Britain did not develop these types of broad skills and self-motivation in its criminal class. The Rev. J.D. Lang sought a temporary answer by specifically recruiting 'mechanics' in Scotland as immigrant for the colony.

3. British Public Funding transfers

Public Capital formation is obviously different to private capital formation. I have given an example of rural-based private capital formation elsewhere in this study and will do so again here, in order to demonstrate both types of capital investment.

Private capital formation took many forms; the early settlers, bought or built houses, they built or bought furnishings; they had carriages and often employed water conservation techniques, which included tanks or earthen dams.

As the system of land grants was expanded and farming was encouraged the spread of settlement required a combination of public and private investment.

The government had to provide roads and townships, and the settlers had to provide pastoral investment. This pastoral (rural-based) capital formation usually consisted of five main types of assets:

Buildings – residence, outbuildings, wool shed or grain storage
Fences – stockyards, posts and rails
Water conservation – dams, tanks, wells
Plant – cultivators, tools
Stocks – food, clothing, household items, materials for animal care and general repairs—livestock

Public capital on the other hand was a socio-economic based government asset, and included:

Roads, bridges, crossings, drainage, excavation and embanking, retaining walls

Hospital, storehouses, military barracks, convict barracks, Court-house, police posts, government office buildings

Market house, burial ground, Church, tollhouse, military magazines.

Obviously the list can go on and on.

Major Public Works in NSW 1817-1821

Roads
Sydney to Botany Bay
Sydney to South Head
Parramatta to Richmond
Liverpool to Bringelly, the Nepean and Appin
Buildings
Sydney
A military hospital; military barracks; convict barracks; carters barracks; Hyde Park
Toll-house; residences for the Supreme Court Judge, the Chaplain and the
Superintendent of Police; an asylum; a fort and powder magazines; stables for
Government House; a market house; a market wharf; a burial ground; St. James
Church
Parramatta
All Saint's church spire; a hospital; a parsonage; military and convict barracks; a
Factory; stables and coach-house at Government House; a reservoir
Windsor
St. Matthew's Church; military barracks; convict barracks
Liverpool
St. Luke's church; a gaol; a wharf; convict barracks

4. Economic Development

K. Dallas in an article on *Transportation and Colonial Income* writes, "The history of economic development in Australia is concerned with the transplanting of British economic life into a unique and novel environment. All colonial societies resemble each other in the problems of transplanting, but only in Australia was there no indigenous communal life vigorous enough to influence the course of future development"[65]

Dallas in the same article declares, "The economic effects of the transportation system are usually misunderstood. The real development of Australia begins with the pastoral industry and the export of wool in the 1820s. Until then, penal settlements were a base fore whalers, and made the pastoral possibilities known to English capitalist sheep farmers earlier than they would otherwise have known."[66]

Since this is such a major point on which much disagreement exists, an analysis of its merits is required. No less authority than N.G. Butlin, J.Ginswick and Pamela Statham disagree and they record in their introduction to 'The economy before 1850 "the history books are preoccupied with the pastoral expansion in NSW. It is reasonably certain from the musters that a great many complex activities developed and Sydney soon became not merely a port town but a community providing many craft products and services to the expanding settlement".[67]

The next section of this study outlines the remarkable contribution of Governor Macquarie between 1810 and 1821, most of the physical development taking place before the arrival of Commissioner J.T. Bigge in 1819. The table of infrastructure and public building development below confirms that the greatest period of economic development in the colonial economy took place under the Macquarie Administration and did not wait until the spread of settlement and the rise in the pastoral industry (which brought with it so many economic problems) in the late 1820s and 1830s.

---

65 Dallas, Keith *Transportation & Colonial Income* Historical Studies ANZ Vol 3 October 1944-February 1949

66 Dallas *ibid*

67 The Australians: Statistics Chapter 7 'The economy before 1850'

IMPACT OF THE COLONIAL ISOLATION DURING THE 1800S

The question of isolation was of positive benefit to the British authorities because the concept of creating a '*dumping ground for human garbage*' was synonymous with finding a '*penal wasteland that was out of sight and out of mind*'.

However the disadvantages to the Colonial authorities were numerous

There was the tyranny of distance—the huge risks, of frightening transportation by sailing ship to a land hitherto unknown, uncharted and unexplored, promising huge risks and great loss of life.

Food preservation during the voyage and in the Colony was a challenge with no refrigeration or ice. The only preservatives being salt and pickling.

Communications between Sydney and London made exchange of correspondence, obtaining decisions and permission tiresomely long. It often occurred that the Colonial Governor wrote to a Colonial Secretary, who during the twelve months of round trip, had been replaced with another person.

Laws and justice, in the Colony, were to be based on British law, but in reality, local laws became a mix of common sense and personal philosophies eg Lt Governor Collins, as Advocate-General in the Colony desperately needed law books to practice, but they were never sent. Bligh, as Governor, ruled virtually as a despot and tyrannical dictator, knowing that a sea trip of seven months was between him and any admonishment or complaints being heard.

Factors Affecting British Investment in the Colony

A number of factors affected the level of capital investment into the colony – many were ill informed and relied on delayed newspaper reports on activity in the various settlements.

a. The offer of assisted migration

b. The failing economic conditions in Britain
c. Economic expansion for the pastoral industry due to successful exploration in the colony
d. The settlement at Port Phillip and the eventual separation of Victoria from New South Wales would promote great investment opportunities
e. The rise of the squattocracy
f. The crash of 1827-28 in the colony shakes British Investors
g. The Bigge's' Report of 1823 breathed new life into capital formation especially with Macarthur sponsoring the float of the Australian Agricultural Company
h. Further along, the good credit rating of the colonies (and there being no defaults on loans) encouraged larger investments and loans into the colonies
i. Shortage of Labour in the colony and the offer of land grants to new settlers became a useful carrot to attract small settlers bringing their own capital by way of cash or goods or livestock with them.
j. Two other steps had important consequences, one in the colony and the other in Britain. In 1827 Governor Darling began to issue grazing licenses to pastoralists, and the terms were set at 2/6d per hundred acres, with liability to quit on one month's notice. From this movement grew, writes Madgwick in Immigration into Eastern Australia, the squatting movement and the great pastoral expansion, and the idea of the earlier Governors that the colony of New South Wales should be a colony of farmers was thus abandoned. The concurrent event was the floating of the Australian Agricultural Company in London. Development by the AAC and by the free settlers brought increasing prosperity. Exports tripled between 1826 and 1831.
k. There is a connection between availability of factors of production and the level of investment. In the early days of the colony, labour was present—bad labour, convict labour, but still labour. The governors had demanded settlers with capital to employ that labour and develop the land. They proposed to limit land grants in proportion to the means of the settler. Governor Darling declared (HRA ser 1, vol 8) that 'when I am satisfied of the character, respectability and means of the applicant settler in a rural area,

> he will receive the necessary authority to select a grant of land, proportionate in extent to the means he possesses.

Under Macquarie the colony had boomed with new buildings, new settlements, new investment and lots of convicts. Under Brisbane the needs for economic consolidation and new infrastructure would be addressed, together with an appeal for free settlers.

Some significant events took place during the Brisbane guardianship

The British were intent on accessing every available trading opportunity with the colony, and formed in Scotland *The Australia Company*

A road was built to connect the Windsor settlement to the new settlement at Maitland. This decision opened up the Hunter River district to new farming opportunities

The responsibility for convicts was transferred from the Superintendent of Convicts to the Colonial Secretary, although this move was to be reversed within the next decade

The first documented discovery of gold was made. It was hushed in the colony lest convicts run off to find their fortunes

In Bigge's third and final report, he recommended extra colonial import duties and less British duty on imported timber and tanning bark

The most significant event of all was the confidence placed in Bigge's favourable opinion of the potential of the colonial economy by the London Investment community and the resulting subscription of one million pound for the Australian Agricultural Company. The subscription was accompanied by a grant of one million acres of land around Port Stephens and the allocation of 5,000 convicts, but also brought inflation to livestock prices and availability throughout the colony.

J.F. Campbell wrote about the first decade of the Australian Agricultural Company 1824-1834 in the proceedings of the 1923 RAHS.

"Soon after Commissioner Bigge's report of 1823 became available for public information, several enterprising men concerted with a view to acquire sheep-runs in the interior of this colony, for the production of fine wool.

The success which attended the efforts of John Macarthur and a few other New South Wales pastoralists, in the breeding and rearing of fine wool sheep and stock generally, as verified by Bigge, gave the incentive and led to the inauguration of proceedings which resulted in the formation of the Australian Agricultural Company.

The first formal meeting of the promoters took place at Lincoln's Inn, London, (at the offices of John Macarthur, junior).

Earl Bathurst, advised Governor Brisbane in 1824 that . . . .

His Majesty has been pleased to approve the formation of the Company, from the impression that it affords every reasonable prospect of securing to that part of His Majesty's dominions the essential advantage of the immediate introduction of large capital, and of agricultural skill, as well as the ultimate benefit of the increase of fine wool as a valuable commodity for export.

The chief proposals of the company are:

The company was to be incorporated by Act of Parliament or Letters Patent.

The capital of the company was to be 1 million pound sterling divided into 10,000 shares of 100 pound each

A grant of land of one million acres to be made to the company

That no rival joint stock company to be established in the colony for the next twenty years

That agents of the company would select the situation or the land grants.

The shepherds and labourers would consist of 1,400 convicts, thereby lessening the maintenance of such convicts by an estimated 30,800 pound or 22 pound/per head/ per annum.

The Royal Charter of 1824 forming the company provided for payment of quit-rents over a period of twenty years, or the redemption of the same by paying the capital sum of 20 times the amount of the rent so to be redeemed. These quit-rents were to be waived if the full number of convicts were maintained for a period of five years. No land was to be sold during the five-year period from the date of the grant".

Being important that the investment be seen to have the support of strong leaders in Britain, and democratic governance, the company operated with· One Governor; · 25 directors; and 365 stockholders (proprietors). The old English structure was retained, that of, Governor and his Court, with the directors being the members of the Court whilst the Governor was the Chairman of the Board or Court

Leading stockholders included

- Robert Campbell
- Chief Justice Forbes
- Son of Governor King
- Rev'd Samuel Marsden
- John MacArthur
- Each Macarthur son, John Jr, Hannibal, James, Charles, Scott & William John Oxley. The Colonial-Surveyor (Oxley) had recommended the area of Port Stephens as an eligible spot for the land grant. The local directors inspected and approved the site but John Macarthur was extremely critical of the selection, the management plan and the extravagance of the first buildings.

This venture was the first major investment into the colony and set the scene for later developments. In 1825 the Van Diemen's Land Company was chartered by the British Parliament and granted land on the northwest corner of the territory.

Both the A.A. Coy and the VDL Coy still operate today after nearly 180 years of continuous operation, a record beaten only by the operation of the Hudson Bay Company in Canada.

Sir Timothy Coghlan was the colonial statistician whilst he was involved in preparing the series 'The Wealth and Progress of New South Wales 1900-01'. He was later appointed as Agent-General in London before compiling the 4-volume set of 'Labour and Industry in Australia'.

Circumstances in Britain contributed greatly to the climate of 'greener pastures' over the seas.

Conditions were never more favourable for emigration than they were during the 1830s. The decade had opened with rioting in the agricultural districts in the south of England. This was followed by the upheavals of the Reform Bill of 1832, the Factory Act of 1833 and the Corn Laws, which kept wages low and unemployment high. The Poor Law of 1834 withdrew assistance from the poor and re-introduced the workhouse. The Irish rebellion was creating both upheaval and poverty

These conditions were met by the enthusiastic reports coming from Australia of the progress being made in agriculture, commerce and the pastoral industry. The assistance granted to emigrants as a result of Edward Gibbon Wakefield's reforms made possible the emigration of people who had previously been prevented by the expense. It is almost certain that free passage would not have been a sufficient enticement if conditions in Britain had not been unfavourable. It is significant that years of small migration coincided with good conditions in England accompanied by unfavourable reports from the colony.

4. Creating Opportunities in the Colony

Availability of land and labour to yield profit on invested capital is the constant decisive condition and test of material prosperity in any community, and becomes the keystone of an economy as well as defining its national identity.

British Government policy for the Australian colonies was formulated and modified from time to time. Policies for the export of British capital and the supply of labour (both convict and free) were adjusted according to British industrial and demographic and other social situations, as well as the capability and capacity of the various colonial settlements top contribute to solving British problems.

By the 1820s there was official encouragement of British Investment in Australia by adopting policies for large land grants to persons of capital and for the sale of land and assignment of convict labour to those investors. Then followed the reversal of the policy of setting up ex-convicts on small 30 acre plots as small proprietors. The hardship demanded by this policy usually meant these convicts and families remained on the commissary list for support (food and clothing) at a continuing cost to the government. It was much cheaper to assign these convicts to men of property and capital who would support them fully – clothe, house and feed them.

We can ask, what led directly to the crash of 1827?

a. Firstly, the float of the Australian Agricultural Company raised a large amount of capital, mostly from the City of London investment community, and this contributed to speculation and 'sheep and cattle mania instantly seized on all ranks and classes of the inhabitants' (written by Rev'd John Dunmore Lang) 'and brought many families to poverty and ruin'.
b. When capital imports cease, the wherewithal to speculate vanished; speculation perforce stopped; inflated prices fell to a more normal level, and wrote E.O. Shann in Economic History of Australia 'because those formerly too optimistic were now too despairing, and people had to sell goods at any price in order to get money; men who had bought at high prices were ruined, and perforce their creditors fell with them'.
c. In 1842, it was the same. The influx of capital from oversees, pastoral extension, and large-scale immigration, caused much speculation. The banks, competing for business, advanced too much credit. Loans were made on the security of land and livestock, which later became almost worthless; too much discounting was done for merchants. (Gipps, HRA Vol 23) In the huge central

district on the western slopes, along the Murrumbidgee and the Riverina, the squatters triumphed, as was inevitable. He had the financial resources to buy his run – especially after the long period of drought. Four million acres of crown land was sold for nearly 2.5 million pound. The confidence of British investors was waning. A crisis in the Argentine and the near failure of the large clearinghouse of Baring's made them cautious. Stories of rural and industrial strife in the colony were not inducements to invest: and wood and metal prices were still falling Loan applications being raised in London were under-subscribed, at the same time, the banks were increasingly reluctant to lend money for land development, which was so often unsound.

5. Assisted Migration

The dual policy of selling land to people with sufficient capital to cultivate it, and keeping a careful check on the number of free grants was adopted after 1825. 'Yet the Colonial Office', says Madgwick, 'failed to administer land policy with any certainty (R.B. Madgwick 'Immigration into Eastern Australia'). There was no uniform policy adopted to encourage economic development in a systematic and rational way. The Wakefield system found new supporters. The principle had been established that the sale of land was preferred to the old system of grants. The dual system of sales and grants had failed to encourage local (colonial) purchases. They were willing to accept grants or even 'squat' rather than purchase land. Sales to absentee landlords and investors stepped up, and as can be seen from the following table, provided extensive revenue to the British Government to promote free and sponsored migration.

6. Successful exploration promotes new interest in the Colony

A period of rapid expansion followed the change in economic policy. Wool exports by 1831 were 15 times as great as they had been only 10 years earlier (in 1821). The increase in the number of sheep led to a rapid opening of new territories for grazing. It was the search for new land with economic value that underpinned most of the explorations. Settlers and sheep-men quickly followed exploration, and growth fanned out in all directions from Sydney town.

However, exploration was not the only catalyst for growth.

a. The growing determination to exclude other powers from the continent stimulated official interest in long-distance exploration by sea and by land and in the opening of new settlements. For instance, J.M. Ward in his work ' The Triumph of the Pastoral Economy 1821-1851' writes that Melville and Bathurst Islands, were annexed and settled between 1824 and 1827, whilst Westernport and Albany were settled in order to clinch British claims to the whole of Australia
b. When Governor Brisbane opened the settlement at Moreton Bay in 1824, it was to establish a place for punishment of unruly convicts and a step towards further economic development, and of extending the settlements for the sake of attracting new investment

7. Colonial Failures fuel loss of Confidence

The collapse of British Investment can be traced to one or two causes, or indeed both.

I. The British crisis of 1839 reflected the availability of capital for expansion by the Australian banks of that day – The Bank of Australasia and the Union Bank. These banks, three mortgage companies and the Royal Bank went into a slump due to shortage of available funds and deferred the raising of new funds until after the crisis. Stringency in the English Capital market had a serious impact on the capital raising opportunities in the colonies.
II. The second possibility is that the sharp decline was initiated by bad news of returns in the colonies, and that its role accentuated a slump with the dire consequences experienced in 1842-43. Recovery was delayed and made more difficult as there was 'no surplus labour in the colony'

It would be dangerous to imply or decide that every slump in Australia could be explained as being caused by economic events. British investment was independent then, as it is now, and so the more valid explanation of the downturn in British investment in this period is that negative reports from the colonies disappointed and discouraged investors with capital to place.

Most facts about public finance in New South Wales lead to the conclusion that it was disappointed expectations that caused the turn down in the transfer of funds. At this same time Governor Gipps (Sir George Gipps) was being pushed by bankers and merchants to withdraw government deposits from the banks and thus this action caused a contraction in lending by the banks which in turn caused a slow down of colonial economic activity. The attached statistics of land sales, registered mortgages and liens on wool and livestock reflects the strong downturn in the agricultural economy, which naturally flowed on to the economy as a whole.

CHAPTER 5

THE ABORIGINAL ECONOMY IN 1788

There was an economy in operation in New Holland at the time of the arrival of the first white settlers in 1788.

Early Aborigines were the first discoverers and occupiers of the Australian continent, the first to establish functioning societies and economies, and the first to make the large-scale adaptations required to use almost every type of ecological condition in Australia. The arrival of the First Fleet did not mean merely 'contact' with Aborigines, but the destruction of Aboriginal society and populations and the transfer of their resources *to the benefit of both the new arrivals and those who remained in Britain.*[68] What settlement meant in this case was the cheap acquisition of Aboriginal resources, just as it did in the Americas. In other cases, overt conquest, which led to comparatively little settlement, provided a mechanism for imperial access to resources without such an overt asset transfer. It improved the terms of trade for the conquerors, opened up opportunities for imperial development and to some extent ameliorated the imperial process by a sharing of the benefits of such development. In the process it recognised property rights, but this option did not apply in the Americas or Australia[69]

---

68 Butlin, N.G. *Economics of the Dreamtime – A hypothetical history* p.2 (Butlin's italics)

69 Butlin *ibid* p.3

The Cambridge Economic History of Europe explains economic development in the industrial nations of Europe in terms of the growth of inputs of land, labour and capital, plus technology. If we extend this concept to Britain, should we not also recognise that its new acquisitions did not merely imply food but included all natural resources, such as wealth under the surface?[70]

Butlin has specialised in the statistics of the Aboriginal economy in and after 1788.

Here are some observations made by Butlin:[71] Butlin's three works each record some varying aspects, at differing times of the Aboriginal population movement between 1788 and 1850 and the Aboriginal Economy.

He approaches the Aboriginal Economy through a system of time budgeting.[72]

"On that basis, it is possible to order Aboriginal time allocation in terms of a range of categories along the lines of:

Food collection
Environment management and adaptation
Food preparation and distribution
Clothing, bedding and household utensils
Production Planning, including decisions to relocate
Travel and transport
Housing
Equipment production and maintenance
Education
Law and Order
Defence
Religious Observance
Ritual ceremonies
Art, and

---

70 Cambridge Economic History of Europe

71 Butlin, N.G *Our Original Aggression, Economics of the Dreamtime & Forming a Colonial Economy*

72 Butlin, N.G *Our Original Aggression*

Recreation and
Entertainment.

Such a list may, adds Butlin, be considered common to both the white and Black society, although Aboriginals were more inclined to pooling of resources and to sharing, even though in the penal society the definition of 'convict rations' and 'board and lodging' brings the two societies closer together than first thought.[73]

Butlin models the Aboriginal populations at the time of white arrival, and suggests the NSW/Vic population was 250,000 aborigines, with a total Australian aboriginal population at one million (of which only 10,000 were located in VDL). So obviously the Qld, NT, WA & SA populations were in excess of 740,000

As with the Governors before him, Governor Darling's instructions regarding Aborigines, stressed the need to protect the natives, both "in their persons, and in the free enjoyment of their possessions".[74] The Governor had also been instructed to co-operate with the Archdeacon in providing the means by which the Aborigines could be converted to Christianity and 'advanced in civilisation'. In response to Thomas Brisbane declaring martial law in Bathurst, Lord Bathurst informed Darling (Brisbane's successor) that it was his duty "when the aborigines made 'hostile incursions for the purpose of plunder' and only when 'less vigorous measures' had failed, 'to oppose force by force, and to repel such aggression in the same manner, as if they proceeded from subjects of any accredited state".[75]

Attempts by Archdeacon Scott and Bishop Broughton produced reports the need for substantial expenditure on education and general welfare reform. Darling's response was that the expense and the difficulty of finding suitably qualified people posed formidable problems. Darling admitted that his response was more to economy than to any lack of interest in aboriginal welfare. He admitted he had little understanding of their culture or way of life. 'Those who he saw in an urban setting

---

73 Butlin *Economic & the Dreamtime*

74 Governors despatches 1826 HRA 1:12:125

75 Brisbane to Bathurst 1824 HRA 1:11:409; Bathurst to Darling 1825 HRA 1:12:21

depressed him, as the appearance of the natives about Sydney is extremely disgusting, due to the frequent and excessive use of spirits. Tribes living in the interior were not exposed to this evil and appeared to be a much finer race'.[76] Darling was critical of the language problem and the fact that different tribes could not converse with each other.

It would appear that very few of Darling's predecessors or even his successors took the time or interest to understand the Aboriginal economy or society, in order to make informed judgements and policies about a diminishing but still aggravating problem Darling was largely pre-occupied with skirmishes (and massacres) between the white settlers and the Aborigines. But neither legislation nor regulation seemed to be the answer to the hostilities and deaths and anger and retaliation.

Perceptions prevailed, as a basis of policy decision-making on behalf of Aborigines. David Day claims 'Officers of the First Fleet of British invaders believed they were stepping ashore on a continent that had not felt the heel of civilised man".[77] Such perceptions of uneducated stone-age peoples unfamiliar with any white man or white man's ways, persisted until the Gipps Administration, and so not much got changed to improve their way of life, or their economy. Even Manning Clark perpetuated the myths and false perceptions when he introduces Volume 1 with the thought 'Civilisation did not begin in Australia until the last quarter of the eighteenth century'[78] The implications of that sentence served to justify the continued dispossession of the Aborigines who, Clark argued, had lived for 'millennia in a state of barbarism'[79]

Our conception and perception of civilisation has a European orientation to it, but the Aborigines lived with some form of deliberativeness.

Butlin is concerned with implication not motives of the Aborigine as an 'economic man'. However, the main questions we need to ask relate to:

Was Aboriginal economic behaviour rational or not?

---

[76] Fletch, Brian, *Ralph Darling: a Governor maligned*

[77] Day, David *Claiming a continent – A New History of Australia* p.3

[78] Clark, C.M.H. *A History of Australia* Vol 1

[79] Clark, *ibid*

Did the population change with production (mainly climatic) setbacks or did they adapt to known technologies or change their tastes, technology, methods of production and allocation of labour?

Butlin explains "the Aboriginal economy in Australia was established over thousands of years by the successfully arriving migrants from South-East Asia and by their locally born descendents. If we accept prevalent views of very low rates of natural increase amongst hunter-gathers, it would follow that any population build-up to occupy the entire Australian continent even within a time-span of several millennia is explicable primarily by immigration inflow It is not plausible to approach the study of the Aboriginal economy in terms of a static structure and function. The dynamism may be summed up in the proposition that Aboriginals evolved in Australia from hunter-gatherers to resource managers and 'improvers'."[80]

The Aboriginal economy is structured into many segments and activities:

- Food gathering
- Food technology
- Aboriginal culture and society (this is integral to the economic understanding & interpretation
- Inter-group associations
- Property rights in land (individual, centralised or communal)
- Marriage customs
- Property in ritual
- Economic decision-making

This aspect of the pre-history of Australia is still being written.[81]

Becker suggests that hunter-gatherers had a scarce resource, which was time and that the Aboriginal economy could be better considered in this light.[82]

---

80 Butlin *Forming a Colonial Economy* p.56

81 Lourandos, Harry *Continent of Hunter-Gatherers—New Perspectives in Australian Prehistory*

82 Becker, G.S. *A Theory of the Allocation of Time*', The Economic Journal, September 1965

Mulvaney discusses some features of their life-style. He identifies many plants and animals that were common to South-East Asia and Australia in the distant past, as well as the continuous landmass between New Guinea and Tasmania with the mainland.[83] The emergence of two large lakes, one in the Gulf of Carpentaria the other in Bass Strait, provided a large food resource of fish, fowl and habitation for native animals as well as humans. With water being a prime consideration to human and animal (food) habitation, Mulvaney concludes that 60,000 years ago both the Murray and Darling Rivers were much broader than they are today and shows the existence of the active Lake Eyre and Lake Frome in south-central Australia – conditions which deteriorated after 60,000 BP.

David Day puts it in a similar way." It could even be argued that Aborigines were more sophisticated than Europeans have proved to be in Australia. While the Aborigines lived for hundreds of centuries in Australia, changing their lifestyles in reaction to gradual changes in the environment and sometimes even shaping that environment to maximise their returns from it, just two centuries of European occupation have seen almost irreparable harm done to the environment through greed or ignorance. There has been a recent return to Aboriginal methods of land management to take care of national parks and to live successfully in arid areas".[84]

Early attempts at understanding the natives was not left only to Government officials, the churchmen in the colony were assigned the tasks of 'civilising' this race, and the Rev. J.D. Lang records:

"Their wanderings are circumscribed by certain well-defined limits, beyond which they seldom pass, except for purposes of war or festivity. In short, every tribe has its own district, the boundaries of which are well known to the natives generally . . ."[85]

Some characteristics of the Aboriginal economy in Australia

- Omnivorous diet

---

83 Mulvaney, D.J. & Golson, J (eds). *Aboriginal Man and Environment in Australia*

84 Day *Claiming a continent* p.7

85 Lang, John Dunmore *An Historical & Statistical Account of NSW* 1833

- Limited inter-group trade (usually exchange)
- A marked division of labour by gender
- Education – learning by doing
- Limited storage capacity
- Communal sharing rules
- Communal property rights
- Population control
- Complex kin relationships
- Formal non-literacy
- Limited formal government
- Recognised as 'grass farmers'
- Native animals and sea-food recognised as 'valuable'

CHAPTER 6

TRACKING THE ECONOMIC CYCLES IN THE COLONY 1788-1856

As an introduction to the question of economic cycles, it should be noted that the British expenditures in the colony were large and significant. However, local revenues, which had commenced in 1802 and which ran until 1819 without being validated or legitimised, became equally significant. Butlin[86] records "British fiscal outlays dominated until the early 1830s. But, almost from the beginning, an obscure local Australian *fisc* emerged and was soon formalised, growing rapidly from 1810. By the mid-thirties, local revenue raising and public spending had risen to match public outlays of Britain and exceeded the latter during the second half of the decade"[87] Prior to the introduction of income tax in 1799, British domestic revenue was made up of half in excise and one quarter each from Customs and Land Taxation. Colonial revenues commenced in 1802 (by Governor King) and were both excise and administrative taxes. The impost of harbour dues (collected by the Chief Naval Officer) for mooring ships, for wharfage, for provisioning, were the main revenues, but then excise on spirits took over as the prime revenue component.

---

86 What a Way to run an Empire, Fiscally (WPEH #35-1985), N.G. Butlin

87 Butlin, *ibid,* page 1

Another point of difference in Britain and the colonies was that most excise revenue raised in Britain was done so by salaried officials, whereas in the colony this was a highly privatised process with the Naval Officer earning a commission on his collections and the 'treasurers' of the two 'funds' receiving and then disbursing the funds were private citizens – Rev. Samuel Marsden and Darcy Wentworth. The statute 1 Geo III, c.1 of 1760 surrendered the rights of the Crown to collect British revenue to the Parliamentary system and an appropriation of expenditures to the Crown and to public organisations, including the operation of governance, including parliamentary provision for salaried officials in the British treasury.

British Government spending in the colony was spread amongst several bodies – the Victualling, Navy & Transport Boards paid for transporting convicts to the colony and maintaining them en route; the Paymasters (Army & Navy) paid salaries for military and civil officials, as appropriated by the Westminster Parliament; the Commissariat was responsible for the supply, storage and distribution of provisions and rations for the operation of government and convict maintenance, as well as tools of trade for the convict workers, and all the materials used on government work sites. In addition the Commissariat between 1791 and 1813 filled the role of treasury by issuing a negotiable 'store receipt', allowing bartering and making advances The Commissariat also assumed responsibility for paying supplementary allowances to local officials, for compensating persons for performing public services for which no British appropriation existed or for totally funding some other public services.

However honourable the intentions of the senior officials in the colonial governance may be, there was great potential for conduct benefiting private rather than public interest. For example, John Palmer became a wealthy Commissary-General, (and more so when his brother-in-law, Robert Campbell secured trading access to the Commissariat stores, and then both Marsden and Wentworth rapidly accumulated great wealth after their appointments as treasurers of the Police & Gaol Fund (Wentworth) and the Orphan Fund (Marsden).

Governor King identified a few examples of such self-interest such as beneficial pricing, kickbacks and fraudulent recording.[88] Graft was not limited to the Commissariat officials, but was found in the early Banks, the Naval Officer, and remotely located government officials (Windsor & Liverpool). Even Captain William Bligh, as Governor, was extremely generous to himself in the supply of convicts, rations and equipment for his farming ventures

Land grants were extensive in the colony until the early 1820s (Macquarie alone made grants of over 550,000 acres). The policy originated under Governor Phillip as a means of keeping emancipists on small acreage and trying to supplement the meagre official rations by becoming self-supporting and even contributing any surplus to the Commissariat. Once the expansion of settlement under Macquarie crossed the Blue Mountains, more extensive acres were released in order to encourage large-scale livestock grazing and broad acre grain production.

With the colony, until 1815, mainly penal in nature and operation, British expenditures during this time averaged about two-thirds of total requirements with the balance coming from local revenues. Butlin equates this as "British budgetary expenditures, during this period as just on two-thirds of local NSW gross domestic product"[89] The British Treasury channelled most of their funding through the commissariat, and therefore underpinned even further the role of the commissariat as a colonial treasury, at least until 1817 when the Bank of NSW was established and coinage and currency was regularised.

The advent of the Land Fund in 1833 redirected British expenditures even further. By being 'legally' British, the land sales revenues by replacing the transportation of convicts to the colony by sponsored immigration, mainly unwanted and poor Britishers[90]

Official expenditures were rendered unreliable by the use of convicts in public employment. A great deal of convict labour was engaged in farming

---

88 HRA 1:3:474

89 Butlin, *ibid* Page 19

90 Madgwick, R.B. *Immigration into Eastern Australia 1788-1850*

and public construction works. Even the 'assignment' system, a supposedly neutral cost policy, fell into the category of commissariat expenditures for rations, clothing and blankets. Thew use of convicts as public clerks was accepted because they were cheap and their charge was loaded onto the British expenditure.

Thirdly, the production and output of convict labour was never recorded, as an offset to official expenditure and often the revenue resulting from convict work was never accounted for. Convicts extracted coal and limestone which was sold publicly; convict labour produced grain a, fruit and vegetables for Commissariat use and for resale to the public; convict labour operated the ferry service across the Harbour and up the Parramatta River; convict labour raised livestock which was slaughtered and sold publicly; and convict labour produced materials in the Lumber Yard and Timber Yard, which was later sold publicly; convict labour cut timber for export to Britain, and resale within Britain. There was no account for the sale of convict production, and no accounting for convict work undertaken for private benefit. Convicts were often used to unload private cargoes arriving in the colony

Such activities were not of great concern in the colony. Such standards were considered acceptable to the times, the circumstances and the prevailing concepts of right and wrong.

Colonial Economic Cycles[91]

1810-1813 commercial crisis
1814-1815 livestock price pressures
1841-1843 Depression
1826 Depression
1827-1828 Depression
1810-1820 Great economic activity
1830s Rapid expansion due to wool

91 Butlin *Forming a colonial Economy* P.224

The Growth of Government Resources

A later chapter of this study will analyse "the growth of government resources in the colony, and will work within the two periods (1) 1786-1822, when government was the dominant provider of financial and labour resources; (2) 1822-1856, a period which saw Britain's financial disengagement from the colonies. These two periods also conform to stages of colonial development identified by other economic historians and are also tied loosely to the main constitutional changes affecting the colony" [92]

First Period—Period 1786-1822

By approving the new penal settlement in Botany Bay, British foreign and economic policy entered a new and irreversible phase. The Government had committed itself to a major public investment in building public infrastructure and creating an economically viable economy, even if it was naturally limited to self-sustenance and the export of suitable raw materials back to England. The new economic policy was further resourced with the significant change of policy from the previous sale of convicts in North America, to planters, and where the sale price formed an important part of the contractor's remuneration and profit. Thus the British Government took little interest in the convicts once they had been delivered to the contractor.

The Government was now agreeing, under its new policy, to take direct responsibility for establishing and maintaining a prison colony and for the transportation and subsequent care of the convicts.

The enigma facing the first governor, Captain Arthur Phillip, was that as well as the almost 1,000 convicts, he was accompanied by over 300 persons, who formed the basis of a free settlement. So Phillip had split responsibilities, he required criminal laws and regulations to administer the penal settlement, but he needed a civil code to administer not only the initial free settlers, but also the expected additions coming from the ranks of emancipists.

---

92 H.M. Boot *Government & The Australian Economies* AEHR Vol 38, No 1 Page 77

The highlight of the Phillip Administration must have been the failure of the government farms to produce suitable quantities of food, and as a result of that failure the colony remained incapable of feeding itself or surviving without continued financial, and other, support from the British Government. This liability was to exist in the main for the next thirty years, through the transfer of peoples, goods, equipment and funds to sustain the settlement. This scenario had been anticipated by the House of Commons Committee on Transportation of 1784, when it reported: an unprecedented role for Government in any new convict settlement and regarded the prospective profit of the settlement as a condition for the resumption of transportation[93]. The more likely discussion in that committee was not the economic consequences of the reactivation of the transportation program, but the social assessment of the overcrowded prisons and hulks so close to London.

An early significant policy change by colonial governors was to be less reliant on government farms and food production and to turn this challenge over to the private sector even at the cost of land grants and assigning convicts. This conversion of public resources to private individuals was a theme to be maintained frequently by governors from Governor King forward. As we have seen with the using of convicts as clerical labour as a means of diverting expenditures, from the "earliest years, governors had an interest in passing the burden of colonial expenditure on to Britain".[94] Local procedures made the task of limiting or lessening expenditures (as directed by the British Treasury) quite difficult to track. With a privatised accounting system in use in the colony and the commissariat outside the direct accounting control of the governor, there was no mechanism to track expenditures let alone control them. Budgeting was unknown in the colony before 1822 and not officially recognised until 1834, when Governor Bourke introduced the first Appropriation. Other distractions, such as Governor King allowing the Commissariat to issue bills on London without the governor's signature also made tracking difficult. This failure to monitor expenditure ensured that the burden of colonial support fell heavily on Britain, allowing colonial imports and living standards to rise far above levels that could have been financed by the unaided efforts of the

---

93 Clark *A History of Australia* Vol 1 Page 50-53

94 Boot *ibid* p.79

convicts and free colonists. On the other hand, opportunities to privatise government resources raised the prospects of fortunes to be made from farming or trade and encouraged the exertions of many in the military who might otherwise have remained idle. On the contrary, weak British controls allowed the development and imposition of local revenues (recognised by Macquarie as discretionary revenues for the governor's pleasure) to remain in place illegally from 1802 to 1819. It was in 1802 that Governor King, imposed a series of levies to fund the rebuilding of the Sydney Gaol, and it was in 1819 that a ratification Act was passed through the Westminster Parliament, legitimising the illegal tax charged by three successive governors and a series of interim administrators.

If the arrival of Macquarie signalled an end to the period of British neglect and many of the earlier abuses, then it also signalled the greatest surge of public investment in the colony's history. Soon after Macquarie's arrival, the flow of convicts to the colony began to increase. The arrival of so many transportees in need of active work and the increase in British support payments on behalf of these convicts and the vigour with which Macquarie went about putting these people to work, and its accompanying expenditures helped to concentrate an enormous economic growth into the decade of 1810-1820. Another feature of the Macquarie Administration was the infrastructure planning; by way of the laying out of new towns and settlements, exploration and the building of schools, churches and hospitals. All of these were essentials supports for the high rate of economic growth. Macquarie wanted to portray the presence of an emerging free society.

Bigge, in his Report on the State of the Colony, took the opportunity to portray those same developments as evidence of the extravagance of the Macquarie administration.

Macquarie's recall in 1822 marked an important turning point in relations between the British Government and the colonial economy.

Second Period—Period 1822-1850

It appeared to be the changing British policy that some form, even a half-hearted attempt at self-administration for the colony would further rein in the need for continuing British expenditures there. This interim and first small step took place in 1822-1823 with the establishment of a Legislative Council advising the new Governor, Sir Thomas Brisbane

Butlin records "The Australian economy expanded rapidly in the 1830s, with the frenetic pace of growth reflecting an emphasis by British investors, the colonial born and new settlers developing the pastoral industry.[95]

Fitzpatrick notes: "The Australian economy, hitched to a wool wagon moved forward at a rate which would not be exceeded between 1840 and the early gold period a dozen years later.[96]

The boom times of the 1830s were soon followed by the depression of the 1840s. The depression of the 1840s was the first experience the colonies had of a slowdown to a long-run expansionary period. The decade of the 1830s had stimulated a very rapid growth in the colonial economy mainly due to the stimulation of immigration using revenues from the sale of crown lands. In addition, wool on which the boom was based was strong enough to carry the results of the immigration boost. The wool cheques in 1834 were four times as great as in 1831. In 1840 they were seven times as great[97]. A decade of depression then ensued, with rapid expansion returning with the 'gold rush' in the early 1850s[98].

Boot claims that British financial commitments began to narrow after 1823 and ceased for the civil establishment in 1827[99]. It was really more of a strategic redirection and the assignment of public infrastructure development to the private sector. For instance the British Government wanted the proposed railway system to be privately funded from the very first (as was the case in Britain), but local resistance decided that only government ownership and development was possible.

British expenditure in the colony after 1830 focused narrowly on penal and defence matters, whilst grant-in-aid and commissariat expenditures

---

95 Butlin *Forming a Colonial Economy* p225

96 Fitzpatrick, B.C. *The British Empire in Australia: An economic history p.33*

97 Fitzpatrick, *ibid p.34*

98 Butlin, N.G *Forming A Colonial Economy P225*

99 Boot *ibid* p.83

continued elsewhere in the colony. This change caused local revenues raised in the colony to rise significantly and remain in the 8-10% range until 1840.

Butlin points out that the Colonial Governments never completely filled the gap left by the reduction in British spending, with the result "that publicly provided services lagged increasingly behind the private economy, especially during the rapid pastoral advances of the 1830s".[100] The major economic crisis of the 1841-1843 periods caused the NSW Legislative Council to seek even further financial cuts and economies than those imposed by Britain. The 1840s was a period of marked slowdown in the colonial economy. This trend, remarks Boot, was similar to that in an earlier period. Boot suggests "The reduced British contribution to total spending in the colonies may have been a slowing influence in the 1820s and 1830s, though its effect at this time was outweighed by other expansive influences." Large fluctuations in British commissariat spending in the 1830s added an element of instability to colonial NSW in the period whilst the reduced spending on immigration subsidies (the crown land sales had dropped to almost zero and the Immigration Fund was unfunded), and the slowdown in transportation (just prior to its termination in the early 1840s) added a further deflationary aspect to an already depressed economy.

Darling's Administration contributed to a better functioning and more efficient public service[101]. McMartin reports "Darling successfully established a salaried and professional public service twice the size of that he had inherited from Governor Brisbane. With the assistance of William Lithgow (the Colonial Auditor-General) Darling reorganised departments, giving them better defined responsibilities and authority and thus allowing for more effective co-ordination of interdepartmental and political relationships; Darling also reformed the colony's financial system and 'checking' procedures, and commenced a modern budgetary program"[102]. This whole process was able to provide the important

---

100 Butlin *ibid p. 174*

101 McMartin, A *Public Servants and Patronage: foundation and rise 1788-1859*

102 McMartin *ibid*

continuity between the British financial disengagement and the future full financial autonomy by the colonial administration.

Boot and Butlin both conclude, "The Bigge report and the Darling reforms were the colonial complement to reforms already achieved in imperial administration.[103] The result was that colonial affairs were more effectively monitored from London and were exposed to contemporary currents of British legislative opinion requiring the colonies to conform more closely to colonial policy[104]".

The end of transportation and the desire of the British government to terminate on-going costs of maintaining the remaining convict population brought a deliberate move by the NSW Legislative Council to have more control over the colony's affairs[105]. The efforts of the Legislative Council to balance its books between 1839 and 1856, saw a stagnant spending on education (in spite of a steady rise in the number of children in the colony; the surveyor-general's department was impoverished and unable to complete its obligations; the police force was diminished and unready to fill the needs during the gold rushes in the early 1850s; shortage of funds meant the colonial public service was unable to recruit staff, and the previously hoped for continuity during the transition period from British rule to self-government was waning.[106]. The statistics show that government spending was already a declining portion of the GDP as far back as 1822 (it had naturally, but only temporarily turned around during the Macquarie Administration), but by the 1840, the figure was at an all time low.

Boot makes an interesting observation as a conclusion to his study, which in effect contradicts his earlier point to the effect that British Government withdrew financial support from the colony without any real planning or policy direction. He now makes the point "many of these financial strictures and changes arose as by-products of the British Government's desire to put its own financial affairs in order rather than from any belief

---

103 Butlin, *ibid*

104 Boot *ibid* p85

105 Melbourne, A.C.V. *Early Constitutional History of Australia*

106 Epitome of Official History of NSW (1888)

in the positive benefits or active intervention in government in colonial development.

Economic Drivers of the Colonial Economy

THE COLONIAL ECONOMIC DRIVERS 1788-1856

In order to understand the growth of the colonial economy, we must understand the economic drivers that underpinned, sustained and supported the colonial economy. There are at least six, if not seven, such economic drivers. They include the factors of (a) population growth, the (b) economic development within the colony, the (c) funding sources such as British Treasury appropriations and the (d) revenues raised from within the local economy (for example, taxes and duties on imports) and (e) foreign investment (both public and private). The traditional concept of growth within the colonial economy comes from (f) the rise of the pastoral industry. A seventh driver would be the all-important Land Board, which played such an important role within the colonial economy The Land Board played an important role in co-ordinating crown land policy, controlling land sales, squatting licenses and speculators, re-setting boundaries of location, establishing set aside lands for future townships and for church and school estates, carrying out the survey of millions of acres of land transferred by grant and sale, and offering terms sales for crown lands and being responsible for the collection of repayments, rents, license fees, quit-rents and depasturing fees. In addition the land board was vested with road reserves for hundreds of miles of unmade roads but important rights-of-way that would well into the future protect access to remote pastoral and farming properties. The main thrust of published material about the Land Board is in conjunction with crown land sales policy, but the Board had a much larger role and the overall Board policies sand performances are what are to be reviewed here.

Although an important factor it is no more important that our other five motivators of the colonial economy between 1802 and 1856. Why have I selected these two specific dates? 1802 was when Governor King first imposed an illegal, but justified and well-intentioned impost on the local free community to build a local gaol to replace one burnt to the ground through a lightening strike but which the British would not replace. The local residents thought a more solid and durable prison was a worthwhile community investment. At the other end, the year of 1856 signalled the first real representative and responsible government in the colony, and although it was not the end of the colonial era, it was certainly the end of Britain's financial support of sand for the colony and as such the colony was expected to stand on its own two feet.

These six factors will be discussed as mechanisms for 'growing the colonial economy between 1802 and 1856'

One consideration that must not be forgotten is the externally enforced pace of colonial expansion, particularly through the organised rather than the market-induced inflow of both convicts and assisted migrants. What this means is that instead of market forces requiring additional labour and human resources, extra labour and resources were imposed on the colony and there was an obligatory process of putting these people to work, in many cases by creating a public works program and pushing development ahead at an artificial pace rather than at a time and rate suited to the local economy. In much the same way, the 'assignment' system in the 1810-1830 period forced landowners to create clearing and development programs in order to utilise the labour available rather than only develop land as demand required.

1. Population growth including immigration of convicts & free settlers

The reason the colonial society did not change very much in the 1820s is that relatively few immigrants arrived. During 1823, Lord Bathurst, Colonial Secretary, sent instructions to Governor Brisbane (Macquarie's successor) altering the administration of the colony of NSW in most of the ways Commissioner Bigge had recommended in his reports.[107] One

[107] Commissioner J.T. Bigge had been sent by Bathurst to Enquire into the State and Operations of the colony of NSW in 1819; the House of Commons had demanded an inquiry into the colony and had threatened to hold one of its own; Bathurst pre-empted a difficult government situation by appointing Bigge with a very broad and wide-ranging terms of Enquiry. Bigge held two years of investigations in the colony and reported to the Commons in 1823 with the printing of three Reports.

result of the Bigge Reports was that Macquarie was officially recalled to Britain even though he had canvassed his retirement before Bigge's arrival in 1819. Macquarie was distressed by the Bigge Reports and took very personally the recommendations made for change. Although there were many implied criticisms Macquarie considered that the public perception was that he had not acted properly in his role as Governor. Macquarie set to and compared the circumstances of the colony at the time of his arrival in 1810, with the great achievements he had made through 1821. In hindsight, Macquarie had accomplished much, mostly by means of arrogantly pursuing a series of policies without the pre-approval of the Secretary or the Government in London.

The arrival of only a few immigrants was because Bigge and the Colonial Office believed that only men of capital would emigrate. Labourers and the poor of England should not be encouraged and, as these people rarely had money to pay for the long passage to Sydney, few of them arrived.[108] Although the numbers were small, few of them came unassisted. In 1821 320 free immigrants arrived and this increased each year; 903 in 1826; 1005 in 1829, but slipping to 772 in 1830. Mostly they were family groups with some financial security.

In 1828, the first census (as opposed to musters) of white persons in NSW was taken. 20,930 persons were classified as free and 15,668 were classified as convicts. However, of the free persons, many had arrived as convicts or were born of convicts. In fact, 70% of the population in 1828 had convict associations. However, by 1828, one quarter of the NSW population was native born; 3,500 were over 12 years of age

There was another side to this migration of unregulated souls. Shaw writes" The cost of assistance, the unsuitability of many emigrants, their ill-health, and the numbers of children and paupers that were sent – all these gave the colonists a source of grievance".[109] A large part of the problem was that the English wanted emigration – but those they wished to see emigrate were not welcomed in the colony. A growing opinion in the colony was that free migrants could not work with convicts; the convicts by themselves

---

108 Australian History – The occupation of a Continent *Bessant* (Ed)

109 Shaw, A.G.L. *The economic development of Australia* p.44

were too few and with growing expense; therefore transportation must stop and immigration be encouraged. However, immigrants of a good quality were not those the English wanted to send; its preference was for the paupers and the disruptive in the society. To stop transportation would be "attended with the most serious consequences unless there be previous means taken too ensure the introduction of a full supply of free labour". [110] In the next five years, the number of free immigrants increased so much that transportation could be stopped with little political backlash. Between 1835 and 1840, the colony was quite prosperous (it was a case of boom and bust—the great depression came in 1841); sales of crown land were large, and consequently the funds available for assisting immigrants were plentiful.[111]

In 1838, land revenue was over £150,000 and assisted migrants numbered 7,400; in 1839, land revenue was £200,000 and assisted migrants 10,000; in 1840 revenue was over £500,000 and assisted migrants 22,500.

Between 1832 and 1842, over 50,000 assisted and 15,000 unassisted migrants arrived in NSW; or they might have arrived as convicts, and over 3,000 arrived that way each year. Thus between 1830 and 1840 the population of the whole of Australia increased from 70,000 to 190,000, with 130,000 of those in 1840 being in NSW. Of these 87000 were men and 43000 were women; 30,000 had been born in the colony; 50,000 were free settlers, 20,000 were emancipists and 30,000 were convicts.[112]

2. Foreign Private Investment

We need to make the distinction between foreign public investment, and foreign private investment. The British Treasury appropriated specific

---

110 HRA Bourke to Colonial Secretary *Governor's despatches* 1835

111 The British Treasury had agreed to put 50% of land sale proceeds into assisting immigrants with shipping costs; a further 15% into assisting Aborigines' and the balance was for discretionary use by the crown. These percentages changed in 1840 when all sale proceeds were spent on immigration but the land fund still ran out of funds in 1842 and no further assistance was made to immigrants other than by the colonial government borrowing funds in the London market through its own credit.

112 Shaw *ibid*

funds for infrastructure programs in the colony, such as public buildings, churches, gaols, roads etc.

One reason that local colonial taxes and duties were imposed on the colony was to give the governor the funding source for discretionary expenditures in order to improve his administration. There were many instances of expenditures which could not be covered by the British funds, such as a bounty to recapture runaway convicts, building fences around the cemeteries and whitewashing the walls of public buildings (for instance barracks) in the settlement. The British Treasury would have considered such items of expense as being unnecessary. Road repair and maintenance was intended to be covered from toll receipts but they were never sufficient to make necessary repairs. Governors Hunter and Bligh did little to improve public and community buildings, roads and bridges and by the time Macquarie arrived in the colony in 1810, there was a major backlog of building work and maintenance to be undertaken. Macquarie expanded the local revenue tax base in order to give himself more flexibility in pursuing improved conditions for the settlers and the population at large.

Although Macquarie did not specifically seek new free immigrants for the colony, word of mouth circulated that the colony was in a growth stage and worthy of being considered for either immigration or investment. Usually one accompanied the other. The first private investment came with the immigrants. Free settlers would either cash up in England or transfer their possessions to the colony, and this small level of private investment was the start of a major item of capital transfers to the colony.

However, private capital formation took many forms; the early settlers, bought or built houses, they built or bought furnishings; they had carriages and often employed water conservation.

As the system of land grants was expanded and farming was encouraged the spread of settlement required a combination of public and private investment.

The government had to provide roads and townships, and the settlers had to provide pastoral investment. This pastoral capital formation consisted of five main types of assets:

Buildings – residence, outbuildings, wool shed or grain storage
Fences – stockyards, posts and rails
Water conservation – dams, tanks, wells
Plant – cultivators, tools
Stocks – food, clothing, household items, materials for animal care and general repairs—livestock

Stephen Roberts offers an interesting insight into the colony of 1835.[113]

"It did not need much prescience to foresee the whole of the country united by settlement – so much had it outgrown the coastal stage of Sydney town. It was a new Australia – a land of free settlement and progressive occupation – that was there, and the old convict days were ending.

Both human and monetary capital were pouring into the various colonies and transforming the nature of their population and problems. Convicts no longer set the tone; even autocratic governors belonged to a day that was passing, and instead, the country was in the grip of a strangely buoyant, and equally optimistic, race of free men".

As part of our private capital formation, we must remember the growth of human capital and the needs for specific labour. Capital requires labour with a specific role. The establishment and expansion of farming meant more than shepherding and ploughing. There was a considerable demand for building skills, for construction and maintenance of equipment such as drays and carts, harness making and repair, tool-making etc. It became important, in order to support and sustain capital growth and economic development to be able to employ labour with multi-skills. This was a new phenomenon for the colony, especially since Britain did not develop these types of broad skills and self-motivation in its criminal class. The Rev. J.D. Lang sought a temporary answer by specifically recruiting 'mechanics' in Scotland as immigrant for the colony.

---

[113] Roberts, S.H *The Squatting Age in Australia 1835-1847 (published 1935)*

3. British Public Funding transfers

Public Capital formation is obviously different to private capital formation. I have given an example of rural-based private capital formation elsewhere in this study and will do so again here, in order to demonstrate both types of capital investment.

Private capital formation took many forms; the early settlers, bought or built houses, they built or bought furnishings; they had carriages and often employed water conservation techniques, which included tanks or earthen dams.

As the system of land grants was expanded and farming was encouraged the spread of settlement required a combination of public and private investment.

The government had to provide roads and townships, and the settlers had to provide pastoral investment. This pastoral (rural-based) capital formation usually consisted of five main types of assets:

Buildings – residence, outbuildings, wool shed or grain storage
Fences – stockyards, posts and rails
Water conservation – dams, tanks, wells
Plant – cultivators, tools
Stocks – food, clothing, household items, materials for animal care and general repairs—livestock

Public capital on the other hand was a socio-economic based government asset, and included:

Roads, bridges, crossings, drainage, excavation and embanking, retaining walls

Hospital, storehouses, military barracks, convict barracks, Court-house, police posts, government office buildings

Market house, burial ground, Church, tollhouse, military magazines.

Obviously the list can go on and on.

Major Public Works in NSW 1817-1821

Roads
Sydney to Botany Bay
Sydney to South Head
Parramatta to Richmond
Liverpool to Bringelly, the Nepean and Appin
Buildings
Sydney
A military hospital; military barracks; convict barracks; carters barracks; Hyde Park
Toll-house; residences for the Supreme Court Judge, the Chaplain and the
Superintendent of Police; an asylum; a fort and powder magazines; stables for
Government House; a market house; a market wharf; a burial ground; St. James
Church
Parramatta
All Saint's church spire; a hospital; a parsonage; military and convict barracks; a
Factory; stables and coach-house at Government House; a reservoir
Windsor
St. Matthew's Church; military barracks; convict barracks
Liverpool
St. Luke's church; a gaol; a wharf; convict barracks

4. Economic Development

K. Dallas in an article on *Transportation and Colonial Income* writes, "The history of economic development in Australia is concerned with the transplanting of British economic life into a unique and novel environment. All colonial societies resemble each other in the problems of transplanting, but only in Australia was there no indigenous communal life vigorous enough to influence the course of future development"[114]

[114] Dallas, Keith *Transportation & Colonial Income* Historical Studies ANZ Vol 3 October 1944-February 1949

Dallas in the same article declares, "The economic effects of the transportation system are usually misunderstood. The real development of Australia begins with the pastoral industry and the export of wool in the 1820s. Until then, penal settlements were a base fore whalers, and made the pastoral possibilities known to English capitalist sheep farmers earlier than they would otherwise have known."[115]

Since this is such a major point on which much disagreement exists, an analysis of its merits is required. No less an authority than N.G. Butlin, J.Ginswick and Pamela Statham disagree, and they record in their introduction to 'The economy before 1850 "the history books are preoccupied with the pastoral expansion in NSW. It is reasonably certain from the musters that a great many complex activities developed and Sydney soon became not merely a port town but a community providing many craft products and services to the expanding settlement".[116]

The next section of this study outlines the remarkable contribution of Governor Macquarie between 1810 and 1821, most of the physical development taking place before the arrival of Commissioner J.T. Bigge in 1819. The table of infrastructure and public building development below confirms that the greatest period of economic development in the colonial economy took place under the Macquarie Administration and did not wait until the spread of settlement and the rise in the pastoral industry (which brought with it so many economic problems) in the late 1820s and 1830s.

Economic Growth during the Macquarie Administration

Governor Macquarie arrived in the colony in December 1809 and commenced his administration on 1st January 1810

In 1812 a select committee of the House of Commons was appointed to enquire into the colony of NSW. The circumstances related mainly to the disposition of former Governor Bligh and the many complaints received in England regarding the hardships caused by the monopoly of the favoured

---

115 Dallas *ibid*

116 The Australians: Statistics Chapter 7 'The economy before 1850'

class".[1] A new Charter of Justice was conferred on the colony as a result of the committee report in 1813[2]. The Governor's Court was a 'modification of the previously existing tribunal'[3]. The Supreme Court was to consist of a judge, appointed by the Governor – the first Judge Jeffrey Hart Bent arrived in July 1814 but following a dispute with Governor Macquarie, Bent was recalled by Earl Bathurst and replaced by Mr. Barron Field, an English Barrister who arrived in 1817.

Macquarie oversaw a period of agricultural expansion and a series of explorations in order to open up new grazing areas in the inland

In 1813, the first crossing of the Blue Mountains took place and the Bathurst Plains were discovered. This search for new, more fertile land was made necessary because of the repeated droughts and the unsuitability of the coastal plains for agriculture or pastoral purposes. The three explorers Wentworth, Blaxland and Lawson "affected a passage across a chain of mountains clothed with dense timber and brushwood, and intersected by a succession of ravines, which presented extraordinary difficulties – not so much from their height as from their precipitous character".[4] Within fifteen months from the discovery, Governor Macquarie ('with characteristic promptitude'[5]) caused a road to be made; sand many new settlers quickly transferred their flocks and herds to the newly discovered country.

In 1817, Captain P.P. King (son of former governor King) sailed from Sydney to survey the east coast to Cape York. In the same year Surveyor-general John Oxley explored the Lachlan River following it for more than 400 miles. During his return he came across an extensive and fine pastoral country, which he named Wellington Plains and he finally reached the Macquarie River. The following year Oxley traced the Macquarie River and reached the Liverpool Plains and discovered the Hastings and Manning Rivers.

In 1818 Hume discovered the pastoral district of the Monaro of which Goulburn is now the centre. In the following year Hume traced the Murrumbidgee River, and the Riverina district.

With these discoveries, the known area of the colony grew by twenty times its former extent, and "the new sources of wealth, of incalculable amount, were thrown open to the industry and enterprise of its inhabitants".[6]

With the new agricultural lands had to come a new agricultural policy and this came in the form of minimum prices for produce purchased by the Commissariat. But the colony was experiencing a new lease of life as was expressed by a correspondent to the *Morning Chronicle*, printed in September 1825. The nom-de-plume of 'Austral-Asiaticus' supposedly belonged to Lt. G.T.W.B. Boyes, who had been appointed during the Macquarie administration to head up the Commissary accounting and audit systems.

The letter was a response to printed criticisms of Macquarie policies, and the incredible deterioration since the resignation of Macquarie and read in part "Under Macquarie's judicious administration, commerce and agriculture flourished, because they received from the Executive Government that fostering protection and encouragement which, in turn, in the infant state of the colony, were indispensable for their growth. The farmer received for his corn, the grazier for his cattle, such a fair equitable price from the Commissariat, for the large purchases made on account of government (namely 10/—per bushel for wheat and seven-pence per pound for beef) as enabled them respectively to support a state of decent mediocrity, suitable to their sphere of life and encouraged increasing industry and perseverance in their pursuits. The merchant was not embarrassed in his commercial speculations by the difficulty of making his remittances, but could, at all times obtain Treasury Bills for that purpose without paying, as at present, a premium of from £15 to £20 per centum for the accommodation. Under the change of system, introduced on the accession of the present governor, an entire and distressing alteration of affairs took place . . ."[7]

However successful Macquarie was with his encouragement of exploration and his agricultural policy, the most remarkable feature of Governor Macquarie's administration was the number of public buildings erected, the total reaching 250. His roads policy almost must also be noted for the benefits it produced.

Commissioner Bigge had been directed by Earl Bathurst to "examine all the laws, regulations and usages of the territory and its dependencies, and into every other matter or thing in any way connected to the administration of the civil government, the state of the judicial, civil, and ecclesiastical establishments, revenue, trade and resources".[8]

Macquarie did little to defend his administration other than writing an extremely long letter to Bathurst which commenced" I found the colony barely emerging from infantile imbecility and suffering from various privations and disabilities; the country was impenetrable beyond 40 miles from Sydney; agriculture was in a languishing state; commerce in its early dawn; revenue unknown; threatened with famine; distracted by faction; the public buildings in a state of dilapidation and mouldering to decay; the population in general depressed by poverty; no public credit nor private confidence; the morals of the great mass of the population in the lowest state of debasement and the religious worship almost totally neglected – Such was the state of the colony when I took charge in 1810. When I left the colony it had reaped incalculable advantage from my extensive and important discoveries. In all directions, including the supposed insurmountable barrier called the Blue Mountains to the westward of which are situated the fertile plains of Bathurst; and in all respects enjoying a state of private comfort and public prosperity"[9]

5. Colonial revenues and expenditures

Local Colonial Revenues 1810-1820

The summary financial statements[10] show that Macquarie used a significant proportion of local revenues for road making and maintenance and public building construction and their maintenance. Although there was a 'tacet' agreement between Bathurst and Macquarie that the British government would fund military and the main church buildings, the colonial revenue would be used for infrastructure and most 'public' use buildings

The point being made here is that although the British Treasury was burdened with nearly £100,000 of colonial expenditure per annum[11], the local community, by having to pay higher prices for its imports was carrying about 50% of the British expenditures which include much that rightly should have been paid by the home government. In addition to British ownership of the public buildings, colonial government departments and divisions were paying 'rent' for the use of those buildings. The local commissary was paying £200 per annum rent for the use of the 'bonded' store—a building that cost only three times that when it was built in 1818 by convict labour and local materials. A loan by the Colonial Fund to the Commissary account of £19,000 is never shown as being repaid, so the British government was being directly subsidised by the people of Sydney Town.

It was left to Brisbane (Macquarie's successor) to recommend construction only through the tender process. It had been Macquarie's submission to Bathurst that the tender process would be expensive to the colony and add unnecessary costs to buildings. As Lithgow was to later recommend that no building under an outlay of£200 should need any British approval, thus obviating the time-consuming preparation of plans, estimates and waiting 18 months for project approval. (HRA 1:11:386)

The Report of Major Ovens and William Lithgow[12] in reform of convict work organisation offers a principalled insight into the obligation of convicts to work for the government and the various trade's roles entered into by convicts. A sub-enclosure to the report lays out the expenditures on maintaining convicts, being £12.8s 2d on rations per annum, plus an amount of £7.8s3d for 'indulgences' to convicts, offset by 'contra' of the value of 'production' or output per convict. Ovens concludes that convicts 'pay their way' provided they are made to work and be productive. Thus if each convict were only paid 3/—per day, the cost would be £46.16s 0d per annum. Against this is the cost of £20 for their maintenance, justifying the loss of 50% productivity that Oven's envisages by convicts not committed to their work.

A wide range of Macquarie era statistics is available to demonstrate economic growth during the period 1810-1821

Macquarie encouraged exploration in a practical way, by using government funds and government stores to support a practical program of exploration. By 1815, cattle were being moved across the Nepean, Bathurst was a settlement, grain and vegetables were being grown on the Bathurst Plains,

Blaxland, Lawson and Wentworth were enjoying the governor's plaudits while each were receiving a thousand acres of land, but only Lawson chose to have his land across the ranges. The road to Bathurst of 191 miles in length was completed and travellers were using it daily, together with bushrangers, and aboriginals. The Lachlan River and the Liverpool Plains region were being opened up and Oxley was exploring north to Morton Bay. Even Bathurst was amazed when he heard of the discovery of the Macquarie River – he did not expect 'after the fruitless attempt by Captain Flinders to discover any considerable river, to expect that such a river as the Macquarie would be found in the interior of the continent flowing so far westward'. Bathurst ordered further exploration along the stream to verify if 'a few hundred miles beyond the penetration of the continent, the Lachlan and Macquarie Rivers ran into the western sea'.

Macquarie took to heart the need for town planning, improved roads and a better image for the still young colony. New roads, even before the major 191-mile road over the Mountains to Bathurst, were being built by soldier labour to South Head and the colony's first turnpike to Green Hills on the Hawkesbury had reached Parramatta. The two bridges in Sydney had been widened at the cost of much good liquor currency. Everywhere were to be seen the evidence of the Macquarie ability to contribute to the 'ornament and regularity of the town of Sydney, as well as to the convenience and safety of the inhabitants thereof'[117]; these monuments included the new stone wharf at Sydney Cove, the improved wastes of Brickfield Hill, the completion of Macquarie Place and the houses of Sydney not to be built unless approved by the governor; they were not to encroach on the street, less they be forced to move back into line. Each house was to be numbered at the cost of 6d to the owner. Neat frontal palings of 4 feet high must guard all dwellings; wood must not be cut in the public parks, and shirts were no longer to be washed in the Tank Stream.

Macquarie needed to convince the majority of settlers in both the towns and the rural areas of the need for 'ornamental' improvement in the colony. These were the poor, uneducated people, many emancipists and ticket of leave people, married or de facto with children to protect and look after. Already under previous administrations, differences of opinions between

---

117 HRA 1:7:427 Macquarie to Bathurst

these people and the propertied segment had developed, and the local newspapers even with their small circulation were quite influential and persuasive not only of government but have public opinion as well.

Summary Revenue of the Police Fund 1810-1821[118]

Year	Beckett's figures[119]	Ginswick figures[120]
1810	6489	3272
1811	11359	10939
1812	11347	13494
1813	23109	14621
1814	8378	13325

118 The Police Fund was first commenced in 1802, under the name the Gaol Fund. Governor King intended to replace the original Sydney Town Gaol constructed of woods but which burnt in 1801 with a new gaol, built with British Government funds; the British Treasury declined to approve the funding so the governor sought voluntary community funding to finance the building but this appeal fell short so he used Treasury funding with the understanding it would be replaced by local revenues. He imposed a duty on spirits and liquor coming into the colony, until Macquarie decided in 1810 to use this source as discretionary revenue to supplement the funding for his building program. The revenue growth within the colony was embarrassing to Macquarie's predecessors and King decided to introduce an Orphan Fund and share the revenue, initially 3:1 but then changed the role of each fund and shared the revenue 7/8ths to 1/8th. The Police fund paid for road repairs, fencing, wood for heating public buildings, building repairs and often civil salaries, when other funds were not available. The quarterly results for both funds were published in the *Sydney Gazette,* after 'auditing by the Lt-governor. Darcy Wentworth was treasurer of the Police Fund and Samuel Marsden was Treasurer of the Orphan Fund, whose monies were used for building the Female Orphanage in Parramatta and sponsoring schools and teachers in the colony.

119 The author has prepared his own financial summary of both the Orphan and Police Funds from quarterly reports in the *Sydney Gazette.* The purpose of reporting these figures is the highlight the unexplainable differences between the Beckett figures and the Ginswick figures. No trace can be made of the Ginswick figures since no copy of the MS remains in the public domain, so the Ginswick source cannot be verified for accuracy.

120 Jules Ginswick was an economic historian who specialised in statistics from the cpre-1850 period and whose Ms was quoted extensively by N.G. Butlin

1815	16544	17994
1816	18076	17782
1817	23709	24706
1818	28996	31006
1819	38684	40844
1820	40389	42968
1821	45338	44507
Total	**272418**	**275460**

James Thomson writes,[121] "The imposition of customs duties and other taxes in support of the public revenue was left entirely to the discretion of the governor of the colony. Tariff and duty rates set by Brisbane remained in force until new rates (slightly increased) were proclaimed by Governor Darling on 16th October 1828.

In the tears between 1824 and 1840(16 years), the customs revenue had increased at the rate of 578%. In 1824, the population of the colony was 32,702 and customs revenue was 17s 7d per head. In 1840, population was 129,463 and duty was at £1.10.11/2d per head. By 1875, writes Thomson, with population at 606,652, customs revenue per head was still at only £1.12.11/2d per head.

Customs Revenues received in NSW 1824-1841

64929	Amount—£	Year	Amount—£
1824	28763	1834	124501
1825	48437	1835	140424
1826	47733	1836	153682
1827	49472	1837	163286
1828	65116	1838	145330
1829	74731	1839	158232
1830	78657	1840	195080
1831	87803	1841	223845
1832	93864	1842	215253
1833	108466	1843	64929

121 *Financial Statements by the Treasurers of NSW 1855-1881* with explanatory notes by James Thomson p.490

6. The Growth of the Pastoral Industry

An important step in growing the pastoral industry was taken by Governor Darling in 1827, when he began issuing grazing licenses to pastoralists. After a brief experiment, the terms were fixed in 1828; the Land Board charged an annual rent of 2/6 per hundred acres, with liability to quit on one month's notice.

Shaw claims "from this small beginning grew the squatting movement and the great pastoral expansion and thus the policy of the early colonial governors that the colony would be a country of farmers was definitely abandoned.

Events before the squatting policy helped the governor make his decision.

The Blue Mountains had been crossed in 1813; Macquarie had opened the settlement in Bathurst and built a road over the mountains linking Sydney, Parramatta and Bathurst; In 1825 the Australian Agricultural Company was given a grant of land by way of a Royal Charter, and in exchange for one million pound of capital, received one million acres and a large number of convicts. The initial selection took much of the rural acres around Port Stephens area on the east coast of NSW, but it was not long before the company exchanged this land for more fertile lands but a similar quantity on the Liverpool Plains, away from the coastal plains, although the company kept 2,000 acres of coal bearing land in the Newcastle area.

Governor Darling, probably unwittingly took British Government transportation policy full circle when, in 1827 he received a message from Lord Bathurst, with a reminder of the background to the transportation program implemented.

In the early days of the colony, there were lots of convicts, free labour, but little work for them and many costs associated with their maintenance. The governors had demanded settlers with capital to employ the labour and develop the land. It was then proposed to limit land grants in proportion to the means (the capital) of the settlers. The colony received settlers, some with capital but many without. Those without had been kept largely off the land in the selection process. When the governor shall be satisfied of the character and respectability of the applicant, and the amount of capital he can command, and intends to immediately apply for agricultural purposes, has been duly ascertained, he will receive the necessary authority to select a grant of land proportionate in extent to the means e possesses".[122]

The system of grants laid down by Brisbane was that every grantee was bound to receive and maintain 1 convict for every 100 acres of land or every 40 acres of cultivated land. Because of this policy, there was a great demand for convicts and 'so much competition exists amongst the settlers to obtain convict labour that it is no longer necessary to hold out any premium to ensure convicts were assigned and taken off the hands of the colonial government'.[123]

So settlers had been demanded to use the convict labour, land was granted with the use of convicts but in 1827, the colony had run out of convicts to assign and there was no apparent need for more settlers, being enticed by a land grant. Thus, there was to be a return to the policy of immigrant workers who would be the poor and the social outcastes of Britain, who usually had no capital to bring with them. The new policy declared the *Sydney Gazette* was to be; Land is reserved for capitalists but the capital thee settlement needed was 'capital in labour' to feed the need for more labour that accompanied the transfer of capital assets.

7. THE LAND BOARD

As an economic driver of the colonial economy, the Land Board played an important role in co-ordinating crown land policy, controlling land sales, squatting licenses and speculators, re-setting boundaries of location, establishing set aside lands for future townships and for church and school estates, carrying out the survey of millions of acres of land transferred by grant and sale, and offering terms sales for crown lands

---

122 HRA 1:14:376 Darling to Under-Secretary Hay on 'terms upon which land is granted to settlers in NSW

123 HRA 1:13:221

and being responsible for the collection of repayments, rents, license fees, quit-rents and depasturing fees. In addition the land board was vested with road reserves for hundreds of miles of unmade roads but important rights-of-way that would well into the future protect access to remote pastoral and farming properties. The main thrust of published material about the Land Board is in conjunction with crown land sales policy, but the Board had a much larger role and the overall Board policies and performances are what are to be reviewed here.

The main economic drivers supported by the Land board, would include generating land sales and manipulating the use of the land sales revenues for direct economic gain through a successful migration program; the opening up of new counties parishes and townships, led directly to the successful pastoral industry revolution in the colony; and the surveying and funding of public roads developed the communication and transportation infrastructure to support and sustain rural growth;

Background

Coghlan[124] records that "the first regulations dealing with crown land sales were published in 1823 but it took some time before a plan could be developed that would achieve a fair price for land suitable for encouraging settlement and not interfering with the assignment of convicts. This regulation notified the settlers "it was intended that persons who wished to purchase land would be permitted to do so, after receiving the governor's assent to their written application, but no individual was allowed to purchase more than 4,000 acres, nor any family more than 5,000 acres. The usual price was 5s per acre, but land in the Sydney Region (County of Cumberland), the price was fixed by Lord Bathurst at 7/6 to 10/—per acre.

In 1824, the Colonial Office, viewing the need for a complete change in the law, indicated that Commissioners would be appointed to divide the colony into counties, and parishes, and make a valuation of all the land in the territory with the view to fixing an average price at which all disposable land would be sold. Matters moved quickly from this point.

---

124 Coghlan, T.A. *Labour & Industry in Australia 1917* Vol 1 p.232

Commissioners were appointed in January 1826, and in September 1826, the (now called) Land Commissioners placed values on available lands in certain districts. These lands were then put up for sale and it was open to anyone to apply by sealed tender for those lands with the minimum (government) price to be recognised by buyers. This tender system did not last long, and did not provide many land sales, and so in September 1828, public auctions were introduced. All sales were to be published for two months beforehand but no one was admitted that did not have the Governor's permission to bid.

Neither system was successful and very little land was sold in this way. In NSW, only 13,672 acres were sold between 1823 and 1831. The second problem was that 'payment was evaded for much of the land that was purchased', due to administrative failures.[125]

The regulations drawn up for the sale of crown land was not only aimed at setting a fair price for the sale of the land, and the qualifications of the buyer, but also of promoting the cultivation of the soil. Until 1831, none of these objectives was attained. The regulations provided that 'grants should be only given to persons who possessed capital available for the cultivation of the land granted, equivalent to half its value. Enquiry was made of each applicant, and reviewed by a board of officials (the Land Board). However, what constituted capital and how should it be valued? Material, plant and stock, as well as money, would constitute capital for the purposes of the grant but placing a value on it was found to be difficult by the Board. A resumption after seven years was imposed, if certain development had not taken place in the interim.

Edward Gibbon Wakefield appeared on the scene and proposed a whole series of changes to the system including displays of surveyed land maps, a 10% deposit and some guarantees of future development with penalties for failure to deliver.

One explanation for the low number of acres sold in the colony is that the large number of land grants had diminished the demand for land purchases – the demand for land had been fairly well satisfied by the grants

[125] Coghlan *ibid* p.233

already made. A second explanation is that the colonial government was unprepared for the demands of mapping and surveying that was required for the sales program. A third explanation is the reluctance of the buying public to accept the system of sale by auction for cash as a final settlement of the government crown land sales program.

In 1832 and 1833, the land disposed of was quite small in acres sold, but from 1834, a significant movement (sales picked up rapidly) occurred, which was to deliver great difficulties to the colony and its government.

Land Sales in NSW 1832-1840[126] (in Acres)

Year	Grants	Sales	**Year**	Grants	Sales
1832	15	20860	**1837**	200298	370376
1833	70117	29025	**1838**	179929	316160
1834	84408	91399	**1839**	310250	272619
1835	160137	271947	**1840**	225742	189787
1836	47633	389546	**1841**	101726	203884

These tables show that whilst land sales were raising revenue for the Crown, the governor was issuing large grants without a capital charge, but with the land carrying an annual quit-rent.

Town lands were of a very different nature. Until 1829, the usual dealing with town lots was by lease, although Macquarie had made a few grants of town lands in fee simple. The usual lease rates were 1d and 2d per rod in country townships.[127]

When quit rents were abolished in 1831, the town lots were priced for sale at between £2 and £20 per acre, with most parts of Sydney being priced at £50 per acre. Coghlan reports that prime sites in George Street, Sydney sold at £18,150 per acre (Cnr. George & Bridge Street in 1834) and £27,928 per acre (Cnr. George & King Street in 1835)

126 Ginswick *Manuscript* (as quoted by N.G. Butlin in *Forming a Colonial Economy)*

127 Coghlan *ibid* p.241

The Government took another significant step in October 1829, when it proclaimed 'the limits of location' – the government was setting outside boundaries for the colony – a person may go outside these limits but not purchase lands or grazing rights thereto, to the exclusion of anyone else. It would not be until 1836 that the squatter's rights would be recognised on land outside the limits of location of the nineteen counties—in 1836, the first licenses were issued 'to depasture the vacant crown lands beyond the limits of location'.

The future Land Board was confronted with a huge backlog of surveying and mapping works – From 1788 to 1823 the amount of land grants in the colony was 520,077 acres; from 1823 to 1831 the area of land granted and sold was 3,557,321 acres; but in this last figure is included the grant to the Australian Agricultural Company in 1825 of 1,048,960 acres and various lands reserved by Governor Brisbane for church and school purposes, amounting to 454,050 acres; from 1831 to 1838 sales amounted to 1,450,508 acres, so that in total the Crown had parted with 5,981,956 acres all within the boundaries of location. The original mapping of the nineteen counties included 24,669,000 acres much of which was mountainous and unusable.

Development of farmland, under Brisbane and Darling, in NSW was slow. When Macquarie departed from the colony, in 1822, he was proud to advise Bathurst that 32,000 acres were cleared and cultivated. However, 12 years later, even though a further 3,500,000 acres had passed into private hands, the amount of cultivated acres was still showing at only 60,000[128].

The *Votes & Proceedings* of the NSW Legislative Council for 1833, records that in July the Governor (Richard Bourke) presented a Bill to regulate the affairs of the Church & Schools Land Corporation. The Bill passed all stages and transferred ownership of all lands previously belonging to the corporation to the Crown, through an agent with specific, but limited, powers to deal with these lands.[129]

---

128 Epitome of Official History of NSW (1887) p.235

129 Epitome of Official History of NSW (1887) p.56

No final resolution to the legality of either this transfer (or the original transfer to the corporation) was made until The *Imperial Land Sales Act of 1842* (5 & 6 Vic, c.36-1842) was passed, and in which statute was "reserved to the Crown the power of disposing of all waste lands for any purpose 'of public safety, convenience, health and enjoyment'.[130] Two other local acts assisted in clarifying the Crown Lands debacle – The Crown Lands Alienation Act and The Crown Lands Occupation Act, both passed in 1861, and which permitted anyone, of any age or sex to select between 40 and 320 acres of Crown land anywhere in the colony for £1 per acre, whilst the auction system (with a reserve of £1 per acre) was re-instituted; a terms payment system was authorised, with a deposit of 25% in cash and the balance within 3 years. Nominally, the selector had to live on his land but no policing was undertaken of this requirement. These acts became known as the Robertson Acts after John Robertson, the NSW Minister for Lands.[131]

S.J. Butlin is the only economic historian (other than T.A. Coghlan) that has a word to say about the Land Board activities, but he only records a plan to broaden the economic role of the Board in 1841, which the Governor disallowed.[132]

"It was a member of the NSW Legislative Council[133], who in constructing a plan to extricate NSW from the major slump of 1841-43, recommended that the Land Board be empowered to buy up mortgages in exchange for deferred Land Board notes or certificates, bearing 7% interest. The council passed a Bill incorporating the Holt plan in spite of Sir George Gipps having threatened to withhold Royal assent".[134]

Although this would have been an important step in strengthening the role of the Land Board and of limiting the damaging economic impact of the depression of 1841, Governor, Sir George Gipps refused to support the Bill and it lapsed, and what could have become an important mechanism for alleviating pastoral failures was lost. Obviously Butlin refers to this

---

130 Epitome *ibid* p.358

131 Epitome *ibid* p.358

132 Butlin, S.J *Foundations of the Australian Monetary System* p.331

133 Thomas Holt

134 HRA 1:23:231 Gipps to Stanley; *Sydney Herald* 6th December 1843

Holt plan as a means of evidencing the negative role Gipps played in not acting positively to minimise the effect of the depression.

How and Why the Land Board was formed

The first step in the formation of the Land Board was the appointment of Land commissioners in 1823 by Governor Brisbane.[135] The first 1825 despatch from Bathurst to Brisbane was date 1st January 1825 and detailed the problems surrounding the granting and settling of crown wastelands[136]. Bathurst directed that "a general division of the whole territory of NSW be made into Counties, hundreds and Parishes". Bathurst also made the point that this arrangement would be created by an Imperial statute and that the NSW Legislative Council "will not be required to enact any law for the purpose". This reference by Bathurst would have been an unwelcome revelation by the Legislative Council, which had only been formed two years previously and was very protective of its rights and responsibilities. Its appointed members had hoped, together with Brisbane, that there would have been more local debate and public discussion on such an important issue—the land issue affected the future of local government, the future direction of the limits of location, and the regulated spread of settlement for the pastoral industry.[137]

Bathurst in the fifth paragraph of his despatch directed that to meet and implement these policy decisions, a Commission should be established and a survey made of the whole colony. [138] Bathurst directed that each county be 40 square miles, so that each county could conveniently be re-ordered into hundreds (a 100 square miles) and parishes (25 square miles). This despatch consists of 30 HRA typed pages and so would have

---

[135] HRA 1:11:925-30 Bathurst to Brisbane

[136] Bathurst terms them 'waste Lands of the Crown' HRA 1:11:434

[137] In the third Bigge report on Agriculture and Trade, the recommendation was "that the country intended to be settled be laid out and surveyed, and subdivided into farms in suitable sizes for land grants and that each district be no more than 36 square miles. (1823 Report p.49)

[138] By 1825, 5 counties had already been established in the colony (Cumberland, Westmoreland, Camden, Argyle). Bathurst was proposing a further 14 counties as stage 1 and then the rest of the territory as settlement spread from Sydney. (Note 103 p930 HRA 1:11)

been 200 + of handwritten pages, also included a proposal to establish a corporation for holding church and school lands (to be called estates, suggests the despatch in para.18); also a direction that all lands be valued (the instructions for valuing were that an average be struck for each parish, taking into consideration the topography of the lands and the fertility of the soils-para.15); a statement that all future sales will be settled only using 'ready money' (Para. 16) and instructions for the reservation of lands for public purposes (para.17).

Bathurst set the maximum amount of land for any one purchase at 9,000 acres, and reserved the right to collect a 'quit-rent' at the rate of £5 per cent upon the average value. Such payment could be lump summed at 20 times the annual amount, thus pre-paying 20 years of such rents. As an offset, each convict that was fully maintained (at no expense to the government) would be allowed 32/—per annum.

Bathurst stresses that the success of the overall plan depended on the survey and valuation being completed as a priority move and within the survey to set aside public lands and future townships. Bathurst attached to the despatch a draft charter of incorporation of the Church and School estates, and a summary of Rules for Emigrants going to New South Wales. It was later challenged in the Supreme Court of NSW as to whether Crown Lands could legally be transferred to a separate corporation and that is why the ratifying legislation was passed in 1842.[139]

The three commissioners appointed in June 1825 were John Oxley, William Cordeaux and J.T. Campbell[140]. Brisbane also advised Bathurst

[139] This situation is not unlike the taxes and duties imposed on imports to the colony from 1802, and which were shown to be illegal and it took until 1819 for a ratifying statute to be passed by the House of Commons

[140] John Oxley was the Surveyor-General and an explorer of note; Cordeaux was a military officer who had accompanied Oxley on some explorations; and accompanied Commissioner J.T. Bigge and Oxley on an inspection trip to Bathurst in 1819. Cordeaux also operated the commissariat store in Liverpool; John Thomas Campbell had been official secretary to Macquarie, helped found the Bank of NSW, and Brisbane recommended he be appointed to the NSW Legislative Council and Darling appointed him Collector of Customs to replace John Piper

in the despatch that Oxley had declined to accept the £500 per annum emolument offered.[141] Following the appointment of the three Land Commissioners, Bathurst refined his proposal and directed the formation and structure of a Board of Commissioners to be known as the Land Board.

In his despatch dated July 1825, Bathurst recommended to Darling (Brisbane's successor) that in the "exercise of the powers granted to you by your commission and Instructions, for the sale and granting of Waste Lands of the Crown within your government, it will be found convenient to establish a Land Board.[142] for . . . reviewing applications for grants and from whom you can receive reports on the claims of the different applicants. You are authorised to constitute a Board of this nature to consist of not more than three persons, who must permanently reside in Sydney. Gentlemen engaged in public office, should be given preference. They can be granted remuneration for these services not exceeding £100 per annum. You will lay down guidelines for them, for the despatch of their business. The establishment of the Board should not be made unless it improves Public benefit. As soon as the division of the territory into counties is completed, you will name a commissioner of the peace in each county and they will act as a magistrate".[143]

Darling advised Bathurst on 5th May 1826 that he had formed the Land Board and made suitable appointments.[144]

"The members of the Land board are Colonel Stewart, the Lieutenant-Governor; William Lithgow, Colonial Auditor-General; J.T. Campbell, formerly Secretary to Governor Macquarie"

---

141 HRA 1:11:680 (note 199, p.948 confirms the named commissioners) Oxley was not being as generous as may be first thought. He was in receipt of a civil salary as surveyor-general. He also received a percentage of the survey fees which usually amounted to £1,500 per annum extra for Oxley, so declining a £500 honorarium, was quite self-serving and protecting his positions.

142 HRA1: 12:21 Bathurst to Darling

143 HRA 1:12:21 Bathurst to Darling

144 HRA 1: 12:266 Darling to Bathurst

Darling claimed that it was an opportune moment to establish the board, at a time when new arrangements were being made for the "disposing and granting of land. Stewart is a competent man of business and Lithgow is invaluable from his perfect knowledge of business and information on all points connected with official details".

Darling added, "I should state to your Lordship that the total disorganisation of the departments and indeed every branch of government, when I assumed the administration, encouraged me to form an advisory board – the Board of General Purposes – which gives me advice and recommendations on any particular points which may require investigation".[145] It appeared to be important to Darling that he establishes his Land Board along sound principles lest he be thought of as being a lax administrator.

Another important despatch by Darling to Bathurst dated March 1826, takes 80 pages in the HRA, so it was probably several hundred handwritten pages.[146]

The main contents were government orders relating to 'gratuities' for convicts employed by government[147]; a Report by the Board of General Purposes[148]; a Report by the Land Board and minutes of the Executive Council.

The Land Board reported to the newly arrived Governor Darling on 26th January 1826, providing a background briefing by the Surveyor-General's office that informed the Governor that between 1788 and 1810, successive

145 HRA 1: 12:266 Darling to Bathurst

146 HRA 1:12:363-444

147 "Gratuities" were to be paid to convicts employed as Overseers, storekeepers, clerks or in any other capacity, at the rate of 1s6d per day or £22/16/3 per annum, plus an allowance for clothing and rations, with each gratuity conditioned upon the good conduct and responsibility of the convict.

148 Darling had established the Board of General Purposes, at no cost to the government, or with any remuneration to the participants in order to advise him on solutions to specific situations. He had surrounded himself with eight advisers, knowledgeable and experienced in a variety of areas, and organised them into various sub-committees to consider a specific problem and report back to Darling with a solution.

governors had extended grants to individuals (mainly to convict settlers and averaging less than 100 acres each) amounting to 117,500 acres; and over 12,000 acres had been set aside for use by Churches and schools in Sydney and Parramatta (including the Female Orphan School in Parramatta); that Governor Macquarie, between 1810 and 1821 had granted lands in excess of 400,000 acres, much of which was selected at large (i.e. uncontrolled) and remained unsurveyed at the time of his departure).

John Oxley, as Surveyor-General, had directed the survey of the colony and "divided the territory into Counties, Townships and sections of a square mile, reserving in each township, four square miles or 2,560 acres in the most suitable situations for future villages etc. However, the reservation of land for Church and school estates had not been ordered nor completed at that time. Governor Brisbane, the report confirmed, had made appropriations of over 1,068,000 acres, of which 200,000 acres were to be Crown reserves and 334,000 acres contracted to be sold to individual settlers, with the balance of land being by grants. Oxley revealed that his was a difficult task of surveying properties that were scattered over "an extent of country of nearly 250 miles in length by 140 miles in width".[149]

The Land Board noted in its second report to Darling that the quit rent had been increased from £5 per centum to 15s. per 100 acres, with the prospect that this increase would stall the sale of crown lands. The report also noted for Darling's information that there were four types of land grants:

Lands granted by Macquarie but not yet approved under seal – meaning that they could still be disallowed
Lands granted on condition of permanently maintaining a certain number of convicts
Lands on which a quit rent of 15/—per hundred acres is imposed; and
Purchased lands

Upwards of 1,800,000 acres of land had been appropriated in NSW under any one of the above methods, and these were located in one or more of

[149] Oxley to Darling 1826 HRA 1:12:380

eight counties and over 80 parishes covering 35,000 square miles –for which the boundaries (of these counties and parishes) were still undefined in 1826.

The reservation in each parish for future roads initially caused concern, as they could not be vested in other than the crown, because the existing statute did not allow those reserves to be vested in any other authority. It was later decided to vest them temporarily in the Land Board, until active roads were developed within these reserves.

The land board proposed to Darling that by following the instructions issued by Bathurst and former governor Brisbane, the probable average price of the 2,000,000 acres of mixed description lands suitable for settlers would be only 3/—per acre. Obviously, this figure had been influenced by the new increased quit rent of 15s per 100 acres, in order to maintain the quit-rent to value ration at about a 5% level. However the Board noted that 'if, as directed, the average of the whole parish was to be taken as a value, then the price could not exceed 1s 6d per acre.

This land board report demonstrates that the Secretary of State's office in London had little understanding of the practicalities of life in the colony of NSW and was intent on making policy in an absurd vacuum, including such acts as selecting people for government appointment in London, and setting land prices and regulations in isolation without regard for local conditions or demands. This was further reflected in the disappointing volume of Colonial land sales, where only a cash settlement was allowed at the time of sale and there was insufficient means in the colony to make such settlement. The Board concluded that only the opulent man could make such payment arrangements and this would cause the most valuable property to be purchased by speculators and land jobbers. "These unprofitable occupants (absentee landlords) would be enabled to maintain a decided advantage over the free immigrant settler, who receives his land with interest terms, and then has to pay for the improvements". Such land for free immigrant settlers will be what land did not sell on the open market (so the Land Board advised Darling), so it may not be fertile land and there may not be any means for expansion since most of the sold land is held by speculators and non-residents who will ask any price for their holding.

This second report also drew attention to the enormous task of surveying all crown lands and the shortage of people to carry out the work. This was to be a continuing problem for the Land Board for many years, especially the mechanics of verifying that land sale conditions were being met. For instance, Colonial Secretary (Frederick Goulburn) had issued instructions in November 1823 placing conditions on grants by Governor Brisbane that of each 30 acres granted at least 10 acres would have to be cultivated or buildings, fences or other improvements made (to a value of £50), within five years, or the grant would lapse and revert to the Lands Board. The Lands Department, the commissioners or the Board never verified these conditions, before new regulations were issued in 1827.

The Board recommended to the Governor in late 1826 that town lots in Parramatta, be offered on a leasehold basis rather than remain unsold and undeveloped. At least, stated the Board, the government would be receiving rent as revenue. The Board was quite critical of a government notice informing settlers that they are offered "an additional grant of 100 acres of land for every convict maintained by the settler free of expense of the Crown for one complete year". The Board pointed out that this arrangement was unauthorised and that the original Secretary of State proposal was to be a 'credit' of 32s to be allowed to settlers for every convict employed. The computations show that for each 100 acres at 3/—per acre or £15, and then offering an additional 100 acres of land is equal to almost 10 times what the original allowance would be. The Board also recommended the cancellation of all tickets of occupation (i.e. squatting licenses)

Later in 1826, and in another briefing paper to the new governor, Ralph Darling, the Board stated that the survey work was still very much incomplete from both the days of Macquarie and Brisbane grants; the Board could not set a land price for unappropriated lands and could not establish suitable set aside areas for Church and school establishments. 'Since', they wrote, 'the Board could not carry out the required actions of the Secretary of State, but they appear to be very urgent, we have deemed it necessary to ask your Excellency to decide on a solution with the least possible delay". William Lithgow, J.T. Campbell and William Stewart signed this report for the Land board.[150]

The Land Board in Operation

This section highlights the participation in the Land Board of William Lithgow, the Colonial Auditor-General who had also been appointed a Commissioner of the Land Board. Such appointment was probably a potential conflict of interest situation since Lithgow was a large pastoral landowner, who obtained grazing licenses on large tracts just outside the limits of location, before any survey work had been completed and on the back of exploration by Oxley (a fellow commissioner) and Hamilton Hume (a close friend).

The land board had been created in response to the decision to slow the staggering rate of land grants, and commence the sale of crown lands. It was designed to be an overseeing and monitoring body, with the authority, to enforce the collection of fees and quit-rents associated with grants of crown land.

William Lithgow had been appointed a member of the Board in 1826 by Governor Darling with his expectations that the very large job of surveying crown lands, both granted and sold, would soon become current and continue to meet on-going demands for surveys of new townships, and the large pastoral lands that needed to have boundaries surveyed for identification purposes.

Lithgow as a member of the Land Board officially wrote to Governor Darling on 11th March 1826 concerning the delay in surveying land granted during the past 5 years. The letter recites: "The surveyor-General (John Oxley) states in his report 'that the principal portion of 400,000 acres, granted by the late Governor Macquarie remained unsurveyed at the time of his departure, and that out of 1,068,000 acres appropriated by Governor Sir Thomas Brisbane by grant or sale, or as Crown reserves, the boundary lines of at least half remain unascertained". The letter urged

150 HRA 1:12:413 Land Board Report attached to despatch from Darling to Bathurst, July 1826

Darling into action to recruit more qualified surveyors from England. The letter also responded to Darling's instructions ordering the division of the country into counties, hundreds and parishes. The Land Board explained that the policy could be implemented only if further manpower was provided.

We can see Lithgow's concerns in a further letter from the Land Board to Darling dated 29th March 1826. The submission recommends that the Surveyor-General's Office was far too busy with boundary identification to be collecting quit rents. Instead, Lithgow and other members of the Board (including J.T. Campbell and William Stewart) recommended that the position of Collector of Land Revenue be located within the office of the Colonial Treasurer.

The Land board was required to handle many disputes, and the report of one such dispute was handed to the Governor on 25th December 1826 along with a stinging rebuke on a flawed policy:

"The board recommends that the governor does not grant further lands to applicants who *do not even intimate any intention ever to become resident in the colony,* which will reduce the great abuse in the future distribution of crown land in the colony" [151] Lithgow also recommended that locals residents not be allowed to act as 'agents' for absentee landlords, especially those who used their influence in England to gain an unfair advantage.

The Land Board remained in existence until the Robertson Acts installed a Board with broader powers in 1858.

The House of Commons passed The Sale of Waste Land Act of 1828, and this statute raised the minimum reserve price of crown land to one pound per acre, except that large acreage of land in remote areas could be sold at a lower price, and it established a formula for the use of the land revenue; fifty percent was to be spent on immigration, the rest was to be expended by the Governor in accordance with British Government directives from time to time[152]. The Governor was to continue to have power to issue

---

151 Government Despatches – *Land Board*)

152 Epitome of Official History of NSW

depasturing licences and to make regulations for the use and occupancy of unsold lands, but the existence of the Sale of Waste Lands Act placed an important restriction on the colony by implying a continuing prohibition against the Legislative Council legislating on these matters. The first directive on how the Governor was to spend a portion of the fund, enjoined the Governor to spend a proportion on Aboriginal protection and another on the roads; he was left free to hand any surplus over to the Council for appropriation; but it was made clear that the whole of the second fifty percent was to be considered as an emergency reserve for Britain, if the Council proved difficult". McMinn sheds some further light on the Crown Lands mystery but there still remains the question of whether, year after year, these funds were fully used or just included as a contribution to general revenue. It would appear that somewhere there is a firm directive from the British Treasury that the revenues from Crown Lands sale was to be used to 'offset' some of the British costs of maintaining the Colony. The 'Blue Book' is evidence that as general revenues, these land funds were already being used to pay for the costs of feeding, clothing, and housing convicts, and we know they were specifically used to pay for 'sponsored immigrants', aboriginal 'protection', and new roads. The costs of the military establishment were charged against general revenues so in the quite large 'pot', nearly all Colonial expenditures were subsidised or offset by revenues from the Sale of Crown Land. Britain it seems, offered to pay only for the shipping and supplies costs of getting their prisoners to the Colony. After 1828, we know that convict production—both agricultural and mineral—went a long way to paying their expenses, so perhaps the British Treasury did in fact get off very lightly indeed, especially for the benefits it derived.

Two financial statements (being summaries of the Blue Books) for 1827 and 1828 place further doubt on the application of funds derived from crown land sales.[153]

[153] HRA1: 13:541 and 689

Public Department and Establishment Costs [154]

Establishment	£ for 1827	£ For 1828
Governor's office	4825	5000
Col. Secretary's Office	6125	6000
Legislative Council	800	800
Collector of Customs	5530	5670
Coll'r of Internal Revenue	670	800
Surveyor-General	4550	6000
Land Board	2700	2800
Colonial Treasurer	1570	1600
Colonial Auditor	1300	1400
Other	21000	20000
Supreme Court	11200	12000
Police and Gaols	14500	15000
Civil Engineer	2435	2000
Church & Schools	4000	4100
Total	82095	81400

The HRA does not offer a detailed breakdown of government expenses by establishment for 1828, but rather offers 29 categories of estimated costs, which would today be similar to a budget appropriation. These estimates have been used for comparison purposes.

ABSTRACT OF COLONIAL REVENUES

Revenue Item	1827	1828
Duties on Spirits	41429	
Ad valorem Duty	9000	
Wharfage & Light House duty	5000	
Sale of Newcastle coals	1254	
License fees	4530	
Tolls & ferries	3450	
Fines collected	771	

154 Costs which form a charge on the Colonial Revenue of NSW to meet annual expense of several public departments and establishments

Government fees	2900	
Sale of gov livestock	3236	
Total Revenues	74470	
1/8th portion to C & S estate	-5595	-5800
Colonial Revenue	68874.11.9	73509.13.8

The question of Crown Land's revenues remains. It is apparent from the 'Blue Book' notations that this revenue was initially 'reserved' for specific allocation by the Crown and remained in the Colony as an offset against British Government fiscal obligations (eg Civil List salaries) until self-government in 1855. A relevant quotation from the 1887 Financial Statements of the Colonial Treasurer of New South Wales follows:

"Prior to the passing of the Constitution Act, the Territorial Revenues of the Colony belonged to the Crown, but upon that coming into operation in 1855, they were placed at the disposal of the local Parliament, and together with the taxes, imposts, rates and duties were formed into one fund, under the title of the Consolidated Revenue Fund. In lieu of the Crown Revenues thus given up to the Colony, an annual Civil List of 64,300 pound was made payable to Her Majesty out of the Consolidated Revenues of the Colony." What this means is that the British Treasury allowed the offset of all direct British payments made on account of the Colony against revenues raised by the sale, rent or lease of Crown lands, until 1838 when the decision was made to allocate a 50% portion of Crown Land Revenues towards subsidising immigration to the colony, and a further 15% towards the support of 'natives' in the colony, and the balance was to be made discretionary, although Britain chose to use most of the excess for administrative (eg civil salaries) purposes.

The Blue Books for 1828 include a *Statement of Outstanding Debts,* due to the Governor. The relevance of this statement is that whilst revenue from land sales started as general revenue it was re-allocated to the Land Fund, but the debts to the government from mostly land sales sources are showing to be part of the Consolidated Revenue Funds. These mixed signals require clarification.

STATEMENT OF OUTSTANDING DEBTS PAYABLE TO THE GOVERNMENT

Type of Debt	Amount of Debt
Promissory Note on land sale	42760[3]
PN for sale of livestock	10543
PN for sale of other Gov. Property	1782
Rent of lands in arrears	396
Quit Rents in arrears	5765
Tolls & Ferry Lettings	1919
Market Dues	125
Auction Duties	1025
Coals Sold	52
Fees & Fines from Courts	685
Rent on Gov. Buildings	175
Loans with interest	498
Service of Gov stallions	918
Due to Lumber Yard	30
Cattle sold from Gov herds	14
Cows on Loan	2495
TOTAL	69189

The Land Board became a department of state in 18 and changed its name to the Lands Department. The Lands Department and the Public Works Department were merged in 1856. I have referred earlier to the new activity of 'jobbing' in land. This 'land banking' by individuals or speculating by buying key sites was abhorrent to Governor Darling, and he proposed[156] that original purchasers of land be not allowed to resell for a period of 7(seven) years from the date of purchase lest any sale be declared illegal. Darling also considered that the impost of quit-rents was an alternative to ordinary taxes and sufficient quit-rents should be collected to meet the ordinary needs of Government.

---

155 Governor Darling had supported the 1827 recommendation by John Oxley that terms sales should be allowed with a nominal interest charged on outstanding amounts. The initial interest rate was set at 5%pa.

156 HRA1: 14:294 Darling to Huskisson August 1828

The Land Board struggled with the question of preparing an average value of land in each parish. Their concerns, as expressed to Darling,[157] was 'should the different quality of land within a parish reflect in the average price. The Board kept quoting the earlier direction from Bathurst, which was impractical and had caused all the delays and confusion (refer Page 5 this study). A second concern was that the quit-rents to be collected were an ongoing charge against the land and would, in effect, drive down the sale price of the land by the equivalent of the capitalised quit-rents[158].

THE LAND FUND

Coghlan writes about the Land Fund[159]

"When in 1831 it was decided to abolish the system of free land grants, and to dispose of the public estate by auction in lieu of private tender, it was also decided that the proceeds of land sales should be paid into what was called the Land Fund, from which were to be paid the charges incidental to the introduction of immigrants; and it was from the inability of the Land Fund to meet these charges that the public debt of NSW first had its rise. From 1831 to 1834 the Land Fund was sufficient, but in 1841 the engagements for immigration purposes were so heavy that it became necessary to supplement the fund in some way and it was decided to borrow against the security of the Land Revenue. On 28th December 1841 a debenture loan of 49,000 pound was offered in the colony through the Sydney Gazette, the first loan raised in any colony.

THE MILITARY CHEST & THE LAND FUND

The military chest, as an account style for the colonial treasury was identified in the financial statements contained in the 'Blue Books', and we can readily identify the revenues credited to that account as well as the expenditures charged against the military chest.

157 HRA1: 14:294 Land Board to Darling August 1828

158 HRA 1:14:298 *Commissioner of Survey to governor Darling*

159 Coghlan in 'Wealth & Progress of NSW' (P837)

However the Land Fund is without mention in the 'Blue Books' at least through the end of 1838, and the origin of this nomenclature must be accepted as 'untraceable' without proper basic evidence. We know only of its existence in firstly, the Australians: Historical Statistics P112, and then its mention in the works of economic historian, S.J. Butlin.

That assumption must be as follows:

A. If the military chest is accepted as a predecessor to the 'Land Fund' then its purpose must have been essentially the same. The military chest took its revenue from the proceeds of sale of crown lands, sale of stores sent from England, sale of produce from the Convict Establishments and sale of crown livestock. In other words, only material items possessed by the crown; and that is most probably why the notations on the Blue Books changed from 'Receipts in Aid of Revenue' to 'Revenue of the Crown'. This important change occurred in the 1834 financial statements.
B. Obviously the Land Fund was so designated either officially or by Australian Economic Historians to be the account into which official 'crown' revenue is deposited and from which crown reserved expenditures are drawn. The crown reserved its use of portion of the funds for conveying selected immigrants into the country, and for (15%) aboriginal welfare. We will return to the official sanctioning of these funds later.
C. S.J. Butlin in his masterwork "makes several passing references to the 'Land Fund' without fully identifying its source or use.[160]

S.J. Butlin writes that "in February 1838, William Rucker, a Melbourne storekeeper, announced the opening of a Derwent Bank agency, to 'receive deposits and discount bills and orders for account and under the responsibility of the Derwent Bank Company in Hobart. He fixed the discount rate at 20%, letting it be known that Hobart rates would apply when a court was established in which debts might be recovered. Attempts were made, with what success it is not clear, to secure the accounts of the Customs Officer and of the Land Fund for the agency. But the agency met with considerable difficulty."

---

160 Butlin, S.J. Foundations of the Australian Monetary System 1788-1851

In 1846 there was a squabble between Stuart Donaldson, NSW Treasurer, Murray MHR and Dr. Bland MLC as to where certain colonial debentures were to be funded. Donaldson wanted the subscription to come from the public; George Murray thought the Trust and Loan Bank should do the funding, but "Dr Bland wanted the loans to come from the Land Fund"

"Because of its late settlement and mining boom, land purchase in South Australia was heavy in the late 'forties and the local accumulations in the Land Fund were more than the local commissariat required. The practice developed, with English blessing, that any surplus in the Fund was paid to the commissariat which shipped the specie to other colonial commissariats in need, especially that in New Zealand, the amount being credited to the colony's account with the Land and Emigration Commissioners in London"[161]

Grey, in South Australia, decided to use, contrary to official directions from London, to use any bank he chose for Government business, and he used the Bank of South Australia. Being contrary to official direction, this action permitted a penalty. The Land Fund, which was a transient deposit remitted to England for immigration payments, was divided between the Australasia and the South Australia, but all other government business was given to the Australasia."[162]

"In 1851, the SA Treasury decided to require banks to hold cash at least equal to the government deposit, and to insist on this for the Land Fund."

Some of these references throw doubt on the strict governmental use of the Land Fund.[163]

"It was Lord John Russell's opinion in 1840 that the general revenue ought to provide for the general expenditure, leaving the Land Fund, apart from 15 percent to be used for expenditure on Aborigines, free for immigration purposes as originally intended"[164]

---

161 Butlin *ibid* p.490

162 Butlin *ibid* p.539

163 Butlin *ibid* p.540

164 'Historical Records of Victoria—Volume 7 –Public Finance p.35

Coghlan in his extensive work helps place some of these matters in relation to sale of crown land & immigration into perspective.[165]

"It was upon emigration from England at the cost of the land revenue that the colonial authorities finally placed their confidence. They offered in 1822 to set aside 10,000 pound from the Land Fund for emigration purposes; of this sum they desired that about two-thirds should be devoted to promoting the emigration of unmarried women, as the proportion of men in the colony was excessive, and that about one-third should be used in loans for the emigration of mechanics. The colonial office objected vigorously but the British Treasury agreed to the proposal with the proviso that no further sum should be expended upon immigration until the money received from the sale of land had reached 10,000 pound."[166]

"It had been Edward Gibbon Wakefield's philosophy that the idea of land disposition in the colonies was adopted . . . . If the land was sold, the proceeds of the sale might aptly be applied to transferring labour from Britain to the colony without which labour the land would be of very little value. In 1831 the English Government resolved to alter the land system of Australia with the view of throwing open the country more freely to settlement, and thereby increasing immigration."[167]

In the first four months of 1832, 103 mechanics reached the colony but were disappointed to find pay rates considerably less than those promised in England. The female emigrants all found ready employment, chiefly as domestic servants.[168]

"Considering its resources, the colony went into the immigration business in a big way. The estimated expenditure of 1838 was 120,000 pound of which 80,000 was spent in chartering 26 ships, and 40,000 expended on bounty immigrants."[169]

---

[165] Coghlan, T.A. "Labour & Industry in Australia "—Vol 1, p.220
[166] Historical Records of Victoria—Volume 7 –Public Finance p.35
[167] Historical Records of Victoria—Volume 7 –Public Finance p.218
[168] Historical Records of Victoria—Volume 7 –Public Finance p.222
[169] Historical Records of Victoria—Volume 7 –Public Finance p.226

"With the overall success of the program it was decided that the whole of the rapidly increasing land revenue of New South Wales should be devoted to immigration and in 1837. 3093 immigrants arrived of whom 2688 were sponsored and 405 arrived under the bounty regulation of the colonial government."[170]

Land Fund 1833-1850[171]

	Revenue '000			Expenditure '000[172]		
Year	Land	Other	Total	Immign	Other	Total
1833[173]	26.1	0.1	26.2	9.0	17.2	26.2
1834	48.2	42.9	60.8	7.9	52.9	60.8
1835	88.9	121.3	131.9	10.7	121.2	131.9
1836	131.4	121.1	263.3	11.8	251.5	263.3
1837	123.6	202.6	254.9	44.4	210.5	254.9
1838	120.2	185.8	353.8	108.0	245.8	353.8
1839	160.8	148.8	321.8	158.3	163.5	321.8
1840	325.3	283.6	480.0	148.0	332.0	480.0
1841	105.8	21.4	386.5	331.6	54.9	386.5
1842	44.1	51.7	117.2	112.0	19.7	131.7
1843	29.3	49.3	56.5	11.6	44.9	56.5
1844	16.9	126.0	127.5	69.0	58.5	127.5
1845	38.0	131.0	127.9	20.0	107.9	127.9
1846	38.8	153.5	146.5	1.2	145.3	146.5
1847	51.7	109.7	212.3	1.0	232.6	233.6
1848	51.7	109.7	212.3	113.8	98.5	212.3
1849	109.0	237.4	296.0	138.5	157.5	296.0
1850	158.5	104.8	373.1	166.2	206.9	373.1

170 Historical Records of Victoria—Volume 7 –Public Finance p.227

171 This table extracted from Historical Statistics can only be verified by reference back to the Blue Book Financial statements for those years, provided we make a generous assumption.

172 These figures are in thousands of pounds (£)

173 Receipts in aid of Revenue (i.e. paid into military chest - no record of land sales)

A Practical Dilemma

One can imagine the first 'carving up' of the colony into Counties, Parishes and townships, that the surveyor's task was not an easy one.

For a start the surveyor was looking for 'natural' barriers or identifiable separators, to distinguish counties. A mountain rage, a river or a coastline would make an easily identifiable and recordable boundary. Sometimes a main road might suffice, but mostly they wanted something more than a tree line or a fence post and fence line, which could be dismantled or moved to be a boundary. So establishing boundaries for each division was an important first step.

By 1834, Major Thomas Mitchell (who had arrived in 1827 to become deputy surveyor-General, but upon the death, shortly thereafter, of John Oxley, was to become the Surveyor-General) had prepared a map based on a triangulation approach[174] covering the nineteen counties then existing around Sydney. This map was published in three sheets in 1834 at the scale of 8.6 miles to 1 inch and entitled *Map of the Colony of NSW.* It is sometimes called *The Map of the Nineteen Counties.* This stood as the largest, though not the first topographic map to be produced in Australia in the nineteenth century.

However the pressures of land settlement did not permit any further topographic mapping of the country for a further 60 years. It was recognised that the need for topographic intelligence was a necessary adjunct to land management.[175]

The dilemma facing these early 'town planners' was how to create a road network serving the remote townships. The major roads linking inland towns to Sydney town were mostly toll roads, so there was a funding mechanism to create and repair these major links. Secondary roads were of importance only to the local land owners, and the government took the

---

174 Theodolites and circumferentors were used for angle measurement, baselines were measured on the shores of Botany bay and Lake George near Canberra, and the survey was connected to the astronomic observatory then at Parramatta

175 Lines, John D. *Australia on Paper – The story of Australian Mapping*

decision to create 'reserves' for future secondary roads and to wait for local landowners (usually those adjoining the reserve) to create a cart track, rather than spending any public monies on this huge network of parish and county (secondary) roads.

John Oxley addressed this dilemma in a memorandum to Governor Darling dated 20th September 1827.[176]

"A clause was inserted in the planning for (land) grants (and the grants themselves) reserving to the Crown the right of making roads etc through the lands of the respective proprietors, but does not seem to be understood, probably in consequence of the nature and description of the settled country not being sufficiently known.

The road reserve is a right to take such land as may be necessary for a public or parochial road through lands granted[177], without paying for the lands taken. A solution would be to cause lines of these roads to be so marked so that they may, most advantageously for the district, communicate with the public or turnpike roads, leading to the towns and settled parts of the country is all that is required of the government, for with the exception of a few slight bridges over hollows and wet places, nature has effected the rest, by affording in most cases a clear and excellent road. The trees stand wide apart and do not impede or slow the passage of carts and travellers. Remote roads are chiefly used by stock and light travelling carts, and it would be useless to specifically plan a road alignment at this time until more use is undertaken.

The cost of construction of the public main roads is at present constructed by the convicts and defrayed by the Crown. There remains the question of cost associated with roads leading to farms not bordering on the great public roads, or those on which the principal towns and villages are situated. These roads, by, by way of distinction, may be termed Cross or Parish Roads. They require little or no formation, as the upper crust of the

---

176 HRA 1:14:303 *Surveyor-General Oxley to Governor Darling.*

177 The problem had arisen that landowners claimed control over these reserves and often refused to give up the land for planned roads. The dilemma became that the government legality of the reserve and who the reserve land was vested in became the subject of a legal challenge.

natural soil will remain passable for years without having the least labour bestowed upon them. There is not much cart traffic on such roads, but a toll may be levied sufficient to defray a portion of the expense of making them.

Oxley also spelled out for the Governor the problem of construction of roads through improved lands.

This was a problem not easily resolved until road reserves were dedicated to a statutory authority, the literacy rate improved so land owners could read and understand their contracts, surveys were brought up-to-date and properly showed road reserves, and

A system of deed recording was invoked for the colony.

CHAPTER 7

THE ECONOMIC SETTING FOR THE COLONY

Some Special Economic Events

A number of 'special' events have influenced the course of the early economy and impacted on the extent and rate of economic growth and these have been nominated for further outline. The list of events is not extensive but indicative of sometimes more obscure events which can affect economic growth eg education.

Although it may be suggested that the Report by Commissioner Bigge did not largely influence the Colonial economy, it must be stated that his recommendations to continue with the new Bank of New South Wales, which had been chartered incorrectly by Governor Macquarie, moved the economy along, as did his support for the continuation of the transportation of convicts to the Colony. His lack of support for land grants and early release of convicts may have slowed the economic growth until the consequences of his recommendation that the sale of Crown land be made, was considered in London. After the decision was made in , to replace the system of land grants with its outright sale, the revenue from the Sale of Crown land became considerable and kept the economy afloat, even if it was being badly managed in terms of food production ,until 1810, and the arrival of Macquarie.

Other special events fed on each other. Exploration across the mountains and uncovering the mystery of the rivers opened up huge pastoral areas and fostered the growth of the sheep and wool industries. The continued growth of the pastoral industries all through the 1800s was eclipsed as the prime exporting commodity only upon the 'official' discovery of gold. The discovery of gold once again filled the Colonial coffers and set into motion the most remarkable of special events , the expansion of the rail system across the Colony of New South Wales and between the Colonies. Instead of relying on sea transport, the very reason that the major cities were initially located on harbours and bays, the cities were now connected by rail. The senior colony of New South Wales, could now diversify its population, move livestock and produce from Tamworth and Albury to the populace of Sydney. The most powerful benefit of the advent of the rail system is the most simplistic one. The Colonial labour-force learned how to engineer bridges (the Hawkesbury); how to construct gradients (crossing the Blue Mountains); and engineer the iron horses themselves for local conditions. This new knowledge led directly to the coming engineering shops and the likes of business adventurers such as Thomas Mort, whose remarkable drive, ingenuity and entrepreneurial ability led to the formation and operation of The Mort Dry Dock & Engineering complex in Balmain; The NSW Fresh Food & Ice Company, the development of refrigeration and the opening of abattoirs in remote locations rather than in Sydney town. Neither can we overlook the value of education in and to a largely illiterate economy. Finally the growth of the free trade movement brought to the fore the likes of Parkes, Reid, Wise and Pulsford—politicians who stood for a sound forward-looking, progressive party, whose policy suited the peoples of the Colony and led to the formation of the first 'party' ticket in the country. Federation took centre stage in the second half of the century and again changed the face of the country and whilst our analysis of the fiscal considerations of Federation and the post-Federation relations between the Commonwealth and the States will set the stage for review as to whether the Federation movement was successful.

There may well be more 'special events' than those discussed but it seems that these interlinking events boosted the Colonial economy in a remarkable way:

- the crown land policy and reform
- the growth of education
- the Report by Commissioner Bigge
- exploration
- pastoral expansion
- the expansion of the rail system
- the Fiscal impact of Federation
- Commonwealth-State Financial Relations

The results of all these events, led to a growing population, increased productivity and production; an amazing increase in both exports and imports, leading to an improved quality of life for all and the climate to keep the momentum going in the right direction.

The transportation of convicts seemed to have settled into a workable routine by the time of the arrival of Governor Lachlan Macquarie as Governor Bligh's replacement. The Report of the Select Committee on Transportation of 1812—records that

'The convicts who were distributed amongst the settlers, were clothed, supported and housed by them; they either work by the task or for the same number of hours as the Government convicts; and when their set labour is finished, they are allowed to work on their own account. The master has no power of corporal punishment over them as this can only be inflicted by the interference of a magistrate. The convict, if he feels abused by his master, can complain to a magistrate who, if justified, can deprive the master of his servant.

It is to be found in the written evidence of Mr Commissary Palmer to this inquiry that the expense of each convict in the service of the Government was about 40 pound per annum, made up of food—about 24 pound; clothing—about 10 pound and the equivalent value of rental accommodation at 6 pound, and that a free labourer at Sydney could be hired for about 70 per year, but would do twice as much work. Palmer reports the annual expense of a convict is 30 pound(24 + 6—with clothing being furnished by the Commissary, compared with the cost of holding them in a prison hulk on the Thames at 24 pound, and with the value of their work being about 8 pound or 1/3rd of the cost of keeping them."

The system was fundamentally changed in 1836, and the 2nd Select Committee of Inquiry into Transportation in 1837-38 recorded that "All applications for convicts are now made to an officer—'Commissioner for assignment of Convict Servants' who is guided by Government Regulations. Settlers to whom convicts are assigned, are now bound to send for them within a certain period and pay the sum of 1 pound per head for their clothing and bedding.

Each assigned convict is entitled to a fixed amount of food and clothing—in NSW of 12 lb of wheat, or equivalent in flour and maize meal, 7 lb of mutton or beef or 4 ½ lb of salt pork, 2 oz of salt and 2 oz of soap each week. 2 frocks or jackets, three shirts two pair trousers, 3 pair shoes and a hat or cap, annually. Plus one good blanket, a palliasse or wool mattress which remain the property of the master. Obviously they are well fed, well clothed and receive wages of between 10 to 15 pound per annum."

The 2nd Select Committee also heard evidence on convicts who have been emancipated or their sentence has expired.

"These people find no difficulty in obtaining work at high wages; and having acquired experience in the Colony are generally preferred to new arrivals. They fill many positions of trust for instance as constables, overseers of pastoral properties and road or building gangs, as superintendents of estates , clerks to bankers, lawyers and shopkeepers, and even as tutors in private families. Some have married free women and have become prosperous."

Introduction

The discovery of gold on the mainland, in all states, had so powerful an effect that a special analysis of its benefits, must be made. We observe that the main bonuses to the Colonies was population and wealth. By-products became an increase in exports, offset by an increase in consumption goods, all designed to improve the quality of life, the dramatic growth of the railways system which brought with it extensive overseas borrowing, additional employment and new skills.

This section will review each of these benefits and explore the race problems that arose in the Colonies and the Commonwealth (originating with the gold rush), and see if this was limited to politician's minds or if it pervaded the lives of the peoples. Edward Pulsford claimed, as a rabid open-immigration supporter that the people of Australia supported the right of the Chinese and the Japanese to migrate to this country, the same as the majority of them had, not too many years previously.

Another by-product became the exploration for other minerals such as silver, copper and silver-lead, which became important export items from 1884.

Background

An extract from an address to the New South Wales Legislative Council by Governor Fitzroy on 11th May, 1853 gives an interesting insight into one aspect of the discovery of gold in the Colony and the improvement in the prosperity of its settlers.

"I desire first to acknowledge, with gratitude to Divine Providence, the general prosperity presently enjoyed by all classes of the community. At no former period of the existence of the colony has the material condition of its inhabitants been in a more satisfactory or progressive state. Although the prices of the necessities of life have been very considerably advanced, I am happy to say that they still continue abundant; whilst the increased means at the disposal of the people generally have enabled them without difficulty or inconvenience to meet the additional expenditure to which they are subjected. I must except from this satisfactory state of things, the paid servants of the crown, whose incomes, fixed with reference to former prices, now prove inadequate to their proper position and reasonable support. It will be my duty to invite your concurrence in such an advance in their present remuneration as the altered circumstances of the Colony may appear to render just and expedient.

Whilst in the enjoyment of so large a measure of material prosperity, we must not forget the duty which devolves on this Legislature to make some corresponding provision for promoting the intellectual and moral advancement of the community. Measures are being prepared for augmenting the amount allotted for education, with a view to extension of primary schools, as well as the encouragement of institutions destined to promote the higher branches of literature and science"

The British Colonial Secretary commissioned a report on the subject of the effects of gold discovery in 1852, and the report noted:

"assuming there are 30,000 men engaged at the gold mines in Victoria alone, then 15,000 of that number have been diverted from their previous occupations in that province, along with a further 5,000 from South Australia. To supply the places of these 20,000 , there would be required, under the regulations of the commissioners, 100,000 persons and these would only restore the labouring population to the state it was before the discovery of gold. Thus the immediate need is for a regular and uninterrupted supply of labouring immigrants, because every careful servant soon becomes an employer".'

In real terms, most of the gold was 'sold' overseas, rather than treated in the Colony.

In what well may be the first legislative statement of fiscal and monetary management in the Colonies, the South Australian Bullion Assay Act of 1852 heralded significant changes in the currency management of the Colonies. The Act enabled rates of exchange to be fixed, which prevented further speculation of gold in Adelaide, it stopped the drain on the Banks of coinage, encouraged former South Australian Colonists to return 'home' from the Victorian gold-fields, with their gains, and enabled the three banks of the day to survive the panic, namely The South Australian Bank, Bank of Australasia and the Union Bank of Australia. These banks were formed following the success of the Bank of New South Wales (founded in 1817 for the purpose of keeping the public account).

The discovery of Gold was kept secret whilst convict transfers were still being undertaken, lest the 'dream' of great wealth became stronger than the requirement to work out a penal service.

The discovery of large tracts of good grazing land and its associated export development of wool, and the discovery of large gold deposits rapidly boosted the fortunes of the Colony.

Gold Production & Value

The Wealth and Progress of New South Wales, published by the Colonial Statistician (Mr T. A. Coghlan) in 1900 records the value of gold produced in the Colony between the years 1851 and 1901, as being close to 50 million pounds. For the Australia wide production, this figure becomes close to 450 million pound, with the largest value being attributed to the State of Victoria at 210 million pound or close to half the total Australasian value of production.

Another side effect of the discovery of gold in the eastern states was the emigration of population from South Australia to the eastern states. In January 1852, the South Australian Parliament passed 'The South Australian Bullion Act' with the major background speech by the Premier observing "Throughout 1851 and 1852, South Australia has rapidly lost population to the adjacent Victorian goldfields. Worried bankers ,merchants and shopkeepers wonder what they ought to do about the situation, as it looked as if they might all be heading towards bankruptcy. The Burra Burra copper miners had been amongst the first to leave for the El Dorado, and soon most of the towns in the country districts were nearly cleared of their menfolk. There has been a general depreciation of land and property values. Every emigrant took whatever money he had in gold, thereby reducing specie to the banks, but diggers who returned with gold could not find buyers for it. The Chamber of Commerce and the Bank Managers conferred, and in January 1852, George Tinline, the Manager of the Bank of South Australia, had the idea of assaying gold into stamped ingots and then allowing it to pass as legal tender.

A hurried meeting of the S. A. Legislative Council was called and a special act was passed on January 28, 1852 to 'provide for the assaying of uncoined gold and to make banknotes, under certain conditions, a legal tender for the next twelve months' .

Owners of the ingots were authorised to convert the gold for bank notes at the rate of 3 pounds 11 shillings per ounce. The Bullion Act should not have been assented to by the SA Governor as it interfered with currency but the Act restored confidence in trade, and helped save the Colony of South Australia from insolvency, and it led to the importation of 1,500 million pound of gold from Victoria.

Population Growth

The statistician's figures of population on the goldfields are probably not very reliable because of the difficulty in collecting such information but the estimates for December 1861 shows there were over 17,000 miner's rights and business licenses on issue and an estimated working population of over 28,000. This compares to an estimated working population in the Victorian goldfields in April 1854 of 67,000 (there were 40,000 licenses on issue in 1852), including approx 2,000 Chinese. The Ballarat District had 17,000 workers, The Bendigo/Sandhurst District had 16,000 workers, and the Castlemaine district had over 23,000 workers. There was estimated to be, in total, nearly 7,000 itinerant travellers at any one time in the 5 goldmining districts in Victoria.

Government Revenue

MAIN SOURCE OF GOVERNMENT MINING REVENUE—(1885) '000

Year 1885

Mineral Leases	20,750
Mineral Licenses	2,311
Miners Rights	4,143
Leases of Mining Lands	4,510
TOTAL REVENUES—MINING	31,714

This compares with Revenue from General Fines and forfeitures of 20,171 pounds for 1885.

Dr. G. L. Buxton (The Riverina 1861-1891) submitted that ,

"influx of population during the gold-rush years would, as a result of natural increase, have generated substantial pressure on existing resources, including land, and that this may have inevitably led to a struggle for redistribution of wealth."

But that is when he then goes on to say

"recently N. G. Butlin has suggested in 'Investment in Australian Economic Development" that the selector-squatter struggle has been over-emphasised by historians, but an adequate knowledge of this struggle is necessary for any real understanding of the course of pastoral investment in New South Wales and the development of Australian rural society and its politics."

That the British overlorded the Colony for the first 112 years and imposed their own ways, standards and conditions, might well be considered another significant step in our economic history, and then the growth of the rural economy and the definite boost thereto from the coming of the railway system should be another .

Customs revenues peaked in 1842 at 182 thousand pound, at a time when, for the first time, the Colony's total revenue leapt to 700 million pound. These spikes were on account of the gold discovery and the importation of goods and the inflow of people to the gold fields.

The discovery of gold and the burgeoning wealth of the Colony prompted the Legislative Council in 1852 to seek the British Government's acceptance of an offset arrangement whereby the Colony of New South Wales would accept responsibility for all civil (ie official) salaries, provided the British Government surrendered all Colonial revenues to the discretion (under a proposed new constitution) of the Legislature.

The verification that the British authorities accepted Colonial funds, raised from the earliest sale and lease of Crown Land, and to be used for the funding of 'free immigration' to the Colony.

a. The concurrent Napoleonic wars being undertaken by the British, as well as the ongoing American War of Independence placed a substantial burden on the public purse, and the British Treasury was seeking every opportunity to limit, defray or offset expenses relating to the Colony in the Great South Land.

N. G. Butlin in the introduction to Chapter 7 of Historical Australian Records—Statistics—'The Economy before 1850', suggests there is a great deal of statistical data available on the new settlement before the discovery of gold. 'It represents some indication of the nature of the workforce of the settlements, the arrivals of convicts and free settlers, the economic activities they developed to support themselves and the heavy expenditure by the British Government to make the settlement a success. The Colony was supposed to support itself, increasingly so as pressures for public economy grew in post-Napoleonic Britain. The tables on Colonial Fund and Land Fund Revenues show this increasing shift to local self-support'. Butlin, by implication, is suggesting the financial pressures on Britain by the Colony would have caused the use of Crown Land sales to become a relief in the homeland Budgets.

The gold 'rush' brought great wealth not only to many individuals but also to each of the Colonies of Victoria, New South Wales, Queensland and Western Australia. A great leveling followed also immediately when the depression of 1890-3 came about.

The use of all this gold extracted in such a relatively short-period is interesting, and the Colonial Statistician records that ' Gold is coined only at the Sydney mint, and the weight of gold sent for coining in the period 1885 to 1886 was 15,005,884 ounces, and valued at 56 million 880 thousand pound(56,880,142); but of this amount New South Wales produced only 6,994,135 ounces or 26,716,196 pound. Queensland was the second largest contributor followed by New Zealand and then Victoria. The greater part of the gold extracted in New South Wales, Queensland and New Zealand came to Sydney for coinage, but by far the largest portion of the balance of gold extracted goes to Melbourne. Of the total gold extracted, some 317,312,707 pounds value, nearly 18 percent passed through the mint of the Colony, being sovereigns and half-sovereigns.'

Gold produced in the Colony of New South Wales peaked in 1862 at 620 thousand ounces but fell away consistently until in 1886 less than 100 thousand ounces was produced. This decrease is explained by the Colonial Statistician's office as being:

"the fact that the rich alluvial deposits discovered in the early days had been exhausted, and other resources of a more permanent nature are being developed. These ventures offer more regular employment to the labouring classes, perhaps without the chance of accumulating rapid fortunes but with more security against loss. The key New South Wales gold production areas were Bathurst, Mudgee districts, Tumut and Adelong, Temora, New England District. In the early days many mines were abandoned by reason of the want of proper appliances for the saving of gold. Now these mines have been re-opened and a revival of mining in these various districts is being seen. However the dry weather over the last few years has had an important influence on alluvial gold-mining, and large areas of payable ground are now deserted, owing to the want of water for sluicing purposes.

The economy was strengthened because it added gold to the powerful list of woollen exports. Wool temporarily lost its number one export title to gold from 1856 to 1870 but then returned to the top of the list.

The discovery of gold strengthened the Australian demands for the introduction of responsible government. By the end of 1852 the British Government had accepted these arguments, and invited the members of the legislatures of New South Wales, Victoria, Tasmania and South Australia to draft new constitutions. This request drew two events to the fore. Firstly a split occurred in Australian politics between the conservative constitutionalists and the liberal constitutionalists. Secondly, responsible government became the architect of chronic instability of governments that followed. The Australian delegation to London had accepted uncritically that responsible government—governing for one's own people—was the one way of ensuring control over domestic questions. But it was soon learnt that responsible government assumes two main parties, and to have two main political parties you need groups with clearly defined principles and interests. 'Between 1856 and 1878 it was found that there were differences of 'interest' but no serious differences of principle' (Clark—Select Documents in Australian History Vol 2 P.321)

The rest of the world watched change take place over centuries whilst Australia abbreviated all those same changes into less than 100 years. During that time Australia grew in monetary, population and self reliant terms. The changes in Australia were compressed into a shorter period but driven by the need to catch the rest of the world and make a mark.

At the time of the first gold rush in 1851, only 4 out 10 children attended school. By 1861, education was free, compulsory, secular and schools were well attended.

At the time gold was discovered, license fees and duties on exports of gold and duties on the domestic conversion of gold were applied and this revenue helped fill the Treasury coffers.

A short time before had come the first Appropriation Bills and 'Ways and Means' through the Legislative Assembly in 1832 under Governor Bourke. This was a major step forward in Government economic planning, as was the limited deficit budgeting that commenced at this time. The improvement in Government economic planning simplified the analysis of and planning for the dramatic increase in revenues and thus availability of funds for improving social infrastructure such as railways, roads, new inland settlements, schools, law courts, mechanics institutes and libraries, cottage hospitals. Government played a different role in those early days, when development of government and community assets was a much higher priority than maintenance of those assets, as is the case today. The Treasurers of the 1850s were in demand to understand and carefully formulate priorities that served their colony, rather than the select few.

Effects of Gold Discovery

A number of immediate results came from the discovery of gold:

a. it assisted in terminating transportation
b. it assisted in bringing responsible government forward
c. land and political reforms came about as a result of the digger's demands for such reforms
d. a general consequence was a rise in prices, wages, rents and charges
e. A shortage of general labour supply.

Self-Government

It is pointed out above that the discovery of gold was hidden and suppressed for many years. It was recorded in 1896 by the Colonial Statistician that the existence of gold had been known to the authorities during the early days, when the Colony was a convict settlement, but for obvious reasons of State, the matter remained secret. The first authenticated discovery of gold is contained in the field notes of Assistant Surveyor McBrian bearing the date of 16th February, 1823, with the reference being to a location on the Fish River just out of Bathurst, where Edward Hargraves made his big and public find twenty-eight years later. In 1839, Count Strezlecki , the namer of Mount Kosciusko, found gold in the Goulburn area, and was asked by Governor Gipps to keep the matter secret. The Rev. Clarke found gold in 1841 in the Macquarie Valley and expressed his belief publicly that 'the precious metal would be found abundantly dispersed throughout the Colony'. Edward Hargrave's discovery in 1851 was the first officially recognised find and led to the 'Gold Rush'.

Finding a Place for Gold

Gold occupies a foremost place in the country, both on account of the quantity found and the influence which the discovery had on the settlement of the country.

Coghlan, T. A. (Wealth & Progress of NSW-1900-1901) expresses a concern over the actual discovery date.

"The date of the discovery of gold in New South Wales was, for a long time, the theme of much controversy, and the question as to the original discoverer was long disputed. It is now agreed, that the existence of gold was known to the authorities during the early days when the state was a convict settlement, but for obvious official reasons the matter remained secret. As set out previously, the first authentic record of its discovery is contained in an extract from Assistant-Surveyor McBrian's Field-book, bearing date 126th February, 1823, in which the following note appears.—'At 8 chains 50 links to river, and marked gum-tree—at this place I found numerous particles of gold in the sand and in the hills convenient to the river.' The river referred to is the Fish River, at about 15 miles from Bathurst, not far from the spot to which the first gold rush was made twenty-eight years afterwards. "

In 1839, Count Strzelwcki found gold in Clwydd and communicated the discovery to Governor Gipps, but was requested to keep the matter secret, lest the existence of gold should 'imperil the safety and discipline of the Colony' (Coghlan P371). The Rev'd W.B. Clarke found gold in 1841 in the Macquarie Valley, but it was not until 1851 (the last convict had been shipped to the Colony some years previously in 1840, and by 1850 most had been released) that payable deposits were proved, by Edward Hargraves, a British immigrant and a recent traveller from California, in the area of Bathurst, on the banks of the Macquarie River. Only a few weeks later, deposits were found in Ballarat and Sandhurst (Bendigo) and Mount Alexander, all in the Colony of Victoria. For his find and public announcement in the SMH of 15th May, 1851, Hargraves was awarded 10,000 pound and appointed a Commissioner for Crown Lands.

The finds were all located in easily worked alluvial deposits, and therefore without costly diggings or appliances. Coghlan suggests "Rich they may be (and thus attracting the greater number of miners), alluvial deposits are very soon worked out, their area generally being of limited extent."

In July 1851 a 'mass' of gold was found in the Maitland area gold-fields which weighed 106 lb or 1,272 oz. Coghlan clarifies the description and says although called a 'nugget, it was really a piece of reef gold.' Another nugget in 1858 was found near Orange, which was melted at the Sydney mint and weighed 1,182 oz with a value of 4,389 pound 8 shillings and 10 pence. Numerous other large nuggets were found around the Colony, including Temora, Maitland, Mudgee, Hargraves and Delegate (via Cooma).

From 1851 to 1901, a quantity of 13,475,633 ounces was produced in New South Wales with a value of 49,661,815 Pound. Values increased during this period and although 1862 produced the most quantity (640,622 oz worth 2467,780), 1899 exceeded the value of any other year (496,196 oz worth 11,751,815).

The quantity of gold produced in 1901 fell from 345,650 to 267,061 whilst the number of miners employed dropped 5,894 for that period.

The Gold Dredging Act validated all leases and applications until 1899, and authorised a system of sluicing and dredging which has 'awaked considerable activity in certain districts where gold is being saved from the beds of rivers and creeks, as well as from wetlands which the ordinary miner experienced considerable difficulty in working.' (V & P NSW LA 1899)

Coghlan comments on the irregularity of gold-mining (P376)—"It is a well known fact that in years of prosperity, when employment of all kinds is easily obtainable, people are attracted from gold-mining to other pursuits, which, while offering smaller chances of rapidly acquiring wealth, nevertheless gives steady employment, and when working in steady occupations is scarce, these persons again give their attention to gold-mining. The depression in trade experienced during the last few years had the effect, therefore, of largely increasing the seekers after gold, many of the unemployed being supplied with Miner's Rights and with railway passes to take them to likely spots where a living could be made by fossicking, on the condition that the cost could afterwards be refunded, when the men were in a position to repay the money." Another benefit to the Colony of this process was that, in addition to the miner's right, the government hoped many men, and their families would take up residency in the area, on the gold-fields. The benevolence of the state was masterful in its manipulation for the betterment of all!

When the names of the districts where alluvial ,quartz and gold were found in the late 1800s is listed, one finds the areas where new population growth was taking place at increased rates.

Armidale, Bathurst, Orange, Parkes, Wyalong, Cobar, Peak Hill, Gundagai, Wellington, Forbes, Nowra, Gulgong, Temora and the Lachlan District. Discoveries covered much of the State, and even as late as 1894, the discovery of riches in the Lachlan District attracted more than 10,000 men of whom 4,600 were still there in 1901. However much gold was discovered, the average gold won per miner was 17.24 ounces, valued at 62.1.10 pound.

There were growing factors, other than just the population. There were 318 steam engines used in mining in 1899, 1762 crushing machines and 1,986 stamp heads. All this equipment was made in the Colony and valued at 975,000 pound. It also required skilled workers to maintain and operate the equipment.

Coghlan records (P381) that "from the date of the first discovery of payable gold, in 1851, to the end of the year 1900, the quantity of gold produced in the Commonwealth and New Zealand represents a total of 443,550,310 pound, extracted in the short space of 49 years. The share of each state is as follows:"

State	Value	%
NSW	48,740,533	11.0
Victoria	257,386,448	58.0
Queensland	50,209,783	11.3
South Australia	2,294,975	0.5
Western Australia	22,914,059	5.2
Tasmania	4,598,412	1.0
Commonwealth	386,144,210	87.0
New Zealand	57,406,100	13.0
Australasia	443,550,310	100.0

Compared to the world's production of gold, the Commonwealth of Australia only produced, in 1900 about 26% with NSW only being 2.3% and Victoria being 12%.

Population of Gold Towns in 1900

Armidale	4,249	Bathurst	,9,223
Orange,	6,331	Parkes	3,181
Wyalong,	1,510	Cobar,	3,374
Peak Hill,	1,107	Gundagai	1,487
Wellington,	2,984	Forbes	4,294
Nowra,	1,904	Gulgong	1,579
Temora	1,603	the Lachlan District	10,000

The Chinese Problem

Timothy Coghlan, a close friend and admirer of our Federation Senator Edward Pulsford, made a controversial observation on the Chinese question.

He wrote "The unanimity with which the Australian states have passed laws restricting the immigration of Chinese may be taken as some evidence of the un-desirability of the race as colonists. At the census of 1861 there were , in New South Wales, 12,988 Chinese. In November , 1861 , a duty of 10 pound per head was imposed upon Chinese male immigrants. This continued until November 1967, and led to a decline in the number of Chinese in the State to 7,220. By 1881 the number had risen to 10,205 and to 15,445 at the end of 1888. Numerous departures followed and only 12,156 were found in 1891 and less than 11,000 in 1901. For many years New South Wales offered little inducement to the Chinese as a place of settlement, the superior attractiveness of Victoria and other States as gold producers claimed their attention. During the riots at Lambing Flat in 1860, large numbers of Chinese came across the border from NSW and established themselves in Victoria, their strength being constantly supported by new arrivals, but they did not remain in NSW as is shown above. The violent anti-Chinese attack on the Burrangong goldfield near Young NSW ('Lambing Flat')on 30th June, 1860, by 3,000 diggers led to many Chinese being beaten and their camps destroyed. Tensions were reduced by the departure of many of the Chinese and the passing of the Chinese immigration restriction bill in November 1861.

From 1878 to 1888 over 27,000 Chinese arrived in New South Wales whilst 16,000 departed."

This second rush in 1878 caused the introduction of the 'Influx of Chinese Restriction Act' in 1881, re-imposing the poll tax of 10 pound. The next measure by the Parliament followed a meeting of all state representatives where it was agreed that they were witnessing a 'growing danger'. The new Act came into force on 11th July 1888 and prohibited any vessels from carrying into the State more than 1 Chinese passenger to every 300 ton of cargo, and each Chinese landed are required to pay a poll-tax of 100 pound; they were not to engage in mining except with the permission of the Minister for Mining, nor were they permitted to take advantage of the Naturalisation Act. Any Chinese that come as British subjects (from Hong Kong) had to pass the educational test prescribed by the Immigration Restriction Act of 1898.

The penalty for breach of the Chines Restriction Act was 500 pound. The Act had greatly reduced Chinese immigration, but it was believed that a large number of Chinese found their way into NSW through the other States.

The 'History of the Australian Gold Rushes' edited by Nancy Keesing records an extract of an unpublished manuscript by the Manager of the Robe branch of the Bank of South Australia (Thomas Drury Smeaton) written in 1865.

"in 1858 there were 33,000 Chinese on the Victorian gold-fields, whilst in 1853 there were fewer than 2,000. The Chinese coolies were highly unpopular among the miners often for reasons based on ignorance and prejudice. In 1855, Victoria passed an Act imposing a poll-tax of ten pound on each Chinese immigrant and forbidding ships to carry more than one Chinese passenger for every ten tons of the vessel's tonnage. The shipping masters promptly evaded the tax by landing coolies at South Australian ports, from which they travelled overlands to the goldfields. The town of Robe on Guichen Bay in South Australia was a favoured port. In all about 16,500 Chinese passed through Robe on their way to the diggings. Of this large number all were males"

Conclusion

Our goal was to determine the quantity and value of gold extracts in the Colony of New South Wales and the country as a whole. Another purpose was to determine which areas of the State were most influenced and how the proceeds were utilised. What labour was involved and what by-products were advantaged?

In summary then we learnt that New South Wales produced 12,862,922 ounces of gold valued at 48,740,533 pound, whilst the Commonwealth produced 63,464,717 ounces valued at 443,550,310 pound. Of this amount 96,676,500 pound was put into circulation as coinage and over 2 million ounces were exported, valued at about 16 million pound.

Over One million pounds worth of equipment was employed, including the steam engines valued at 970,000 pound.

New businesses flourished on the gold-fields—sale of stores and provisions, prostitution, tent-makers, log houses, basic furniture, firewood cutting and sale, tool making, Cobb & Co. coaches—and gold escort services, sly grog production (officially alcohol was not allowed onto the gold fields), policing, licensing and clothing makers.

The biggest benefit of the gold discoveries was the move by the British Government to provide responsible government to each of the Colonies.

Edward Pulsford in 'Trade and Commerce in New South Wales' (1892) writes

"The most important event which occurred in the decade 1850-1860 was the discovery of gold, which will for ever stamp 1851 as the most remarkable year in the commercial history of New South Wales, from the foundation of the Colony to the present. Volumes could be written to record the successes and failures of gold-mining, the way in which new towns are settled, and development both retarded and promoted.

On 22nd May, 1851 the Governor of New South Wales had proclaimed the Government's right solely to sell all gold removed from the Colony's diggings. And then provided that a license fee of 30 shillings per month was to be paid to dig on Crown lands. From the first find, the Government had been determined to have a two-way control over the gold successes, so that the Government received its share.

Frank Crowley in Colonial History—Volume 2, 1841-1874 records(P206) a detailed report, dated 10th October, 1851 by Lieutenant-Governor Latrobe to the Colonial Secretary (Earl Grey) in London :-

"The immediate effect of the gold discoveries were a sudden increase in the size of the population in Eastern Australia and the export of large quantities of gold bullion to Britain. At first, wool growing and cattle raising suffered from loss of workmen, but squatters quickly adapted to the new situation. There was a large meat-market on every goldfield, and mass production of cheap galvanised fencing wire enabled a small number of boundary riders to replace the army of shepherds. Freight costs were greatly reduced by the keen competition between shipowners, at a time when wool prices were steadily rising. Farming was at first disturbed and then stimulated by the rising population and the increased demand for food. Many small industries in and around Sydney were adversely affected by the shortage of labour, rising wages and competition from the flood of cheap imported goods from Britain. Every ship that brought immigrants and gold-finders had its holds jammed tight with pots and pans, picks, shovels, shop clothing, lanterns and cheap furniture. The commercial boom in Sydney and Melbourne lasted until 1855 and the sudden increase in capital available for investment and speculation resulted in a building bonanza, especially in Melbourne City and the towns centred around the goldfields such as Bendigo and Ballarat. "

The associated boom in trade and commerce also brought fortunes to Melbourne merchants as well as to the farmers and squatters who were close to the diggings. Store keepers on the fields made a great deal of profit from their buying and selling. Flour resold at 3 d per pound, mutton at 3.5 d per lb., sugar was 2s 6 d per lb.; tea was 4 shillings/lb, boots 2 pound; blankets 2 pound.

The Sydney Morning Herald of 4th August, 1852 announced 'Steam Communication with England at last' and reported that steam powered ships were now running between Britain and Australia on a frequent basis.

In the middle of 1852 the diggings at Bendigo held about the same number of workers as did the Ballarat diggings—30—40,000 people at each. It was reported that about 2,000 carts and drays were on the road from Melbourne at any time of the day.

An ex-convict writing in the Melbourne Argus questioned the acceptance of the ill-effects of the gold fever—the increase in crime, the high price of labour, the stopping of the public works, in particular the unfinished sewerage system in Melbourne and other burdens of the 'root of all evil'

Another less obvious problem with the gold-fever came from the society ladies of Sydney, who claimed that' the town had gone downhill rapidly during the last two years, mainly because of the extortionate prices being charged and the scarcity of domestic servants'. (SMH 10.7.1853)

Because of the local shortage of coins in Sydney, and fluctuations in the price of raw gold and in thew exchange rate between Australia and Britain, the Royal Mint was invited to and accepted the opening of a mint in Sydney on 14th May, 1855.

The goldfields , concludes Crowley (Vol 2, P404) in a very short time contributed a major economic boost to the Australian Colonies that had only received sixty years of Imperial Expenditure from the convict system.

The Albury Border Post of 22nd February, 1860 waxed poetic in its article on the value of the goldfields.

"The traffic from Sydney to Melbourne will bring a population to the fine port and district of Twofold Bay. In this manner are the gold discoveries utilising themselves, and we imagine that each unoccupied portion of this vast continent will in its turn be visited by the wave of population, the flowing and ebbing of which will leave there a deposit, turning the wilderness into a fertile valley, and bidding the desert to bloom as the rose."

So we conclude with the recognition of some of the essential gains from the discovery of gold and can say that the country was much better off having discovered the riches under the ground, and transferred some of them to the top of the ground.

RAILWAYS and ECONOMIC GROWTH IN THE AUSTRALIAN COLONIES

Introduction

It would be considered natural that one of the key factors contributing to economic growth in a new country would be the creation of a railway network to service the rural and regional areas of that country. That an investment of 34 million pound and the creation of up to an estimated 50,000 jobs would assist as well, is unquestionable. But what other benefits could follow? A settlement system of towns developed because of the railways, and the infrastructure for those towns developed quickly and the railways rapidly attracted additional population.

Most assuredly the railways provided alternative transport to the bullock teams and horse drawn drays that were in common use and were so slow. The fact that steam engines relied on coal and that the tracks were laid on wooden sleepers cut from the forests contributed to the growth of these primary industries?

The wool industry had reached the stage when sheep numbers were growing rapidly, the yield of wool per sheep grew and the mills of England were still starved for wool. Here again the railway movement of both wool and livestock was an important task.

But what else might have resulted from an investment of 34 million pound starting just as the gold fields were at full operation? Did the overseas borrowing help or hurt the colony? Would the rail system, passengers and freight be able to service the debt? Or would the interest become a burden on the Colonial finances?

Railway growth in New South Wales

Boundary changes in the Colony of New South Wales were completed with the transfer of the Queensland region in 1859. The Colony of Victoria had been formally transferred in 1855. Self-government in New South Wales was achieved in 1856 and from that time the Colony became more a master of its own destiny than at any time previously.

The topography of New South Wales is not naturally conducive to a network of rail links throughout the Colony, since much of the coastal area is bordered by a mountain range and traversed with sizeable rivers which would need to be to be bridged. The State can, in fact, be divided into three distinct zones each differing widely in character and physical aspect with The Great Dividing Range providing a clear demarcation between the coastal zone and the Great Plains. So there were and are natural limitations when planning a railway system.

The first part of a 'network' was one of meeting the principal aims of constructing a railway—a network must link towns to the city, and to the ports. Rail communication—the revolution of steam that had already transformed so much of England and Europe , had also brought great wealth and growth to the United States, and it was expected the same benefits would accrue in Australia.

In 1846, the Government agreed to carry out a survey, and if found to be feasible, it was decided to construct a line between Sydney and the city of Goulburn. Two years later, the Sydney Railroad and Tramway Company was formed, with a capital of 100,000 pound, and an object of construction of rail-lines from Sydney to Parramatta and Liverpool, with extensions to Bathurst and Goulburn. On July 3rd, 1850 the daughter of Governor Sir Charles Fitzroy (Mrs Keith Stewart) turned the sod of the first railway in Australia. The private company did not succeed and the Government took over the works. A second private company, formed to complete a rail-link between Newcastle and Maitland suffered the same fate and so the Government quickly owned two potential rail services. The Government saw a solid future in completing the rail service and went to work on construction with such vigour that the Parramatta line was declared open on 26th September 1855 and the Goulburn line was opened on 27th May, 1869. If we were planning the same exercise today, the variety of considerations would still include the following facts:-

- Parramatta was still an out-of-Sydney location with 12,500 people (in 1855)
- Wollongong was a growing area with 3,500 people but access from Bulli and Nowra was extremely difficult because of the terrain and steep mountain passes.

- Newcastle was already a significant area with 13,000 people but traversing the Hawkesbury would be both difficult and expensive.
- Dubbo and Orange were attractive areas but the Blue Mountains were again the impasse with a high cost and a major engineering challenge—crossing the Mountains and handling the extreme gradients.
- That left Goulburn (10,600) and Wagga (5,100) as the two areas with a growing population that were penetrable by rail.

For ease of access and the lowest cost of laying the line and serving a good population with potential passenger and freight traffic, a line to Parramatta and a main southern line to Goulburn, which could be linked to a interstate line and branches to Wagga, Hay etc was the most practical decision.

However, further progress over the next twenty years was very slow and in 1875 the length of the line had only reached 435 miles. However from 1875 to 1889 much progress was made and by 1889 a further 1,748 miles was completed. This work was being carried out at the average rate of 125 miles per year. In 1899 the Berrigan to Finley line was opened (14 miles). In the next two years, the Tamworth to Manilla and the Moree to Inverell lines were both opened and in the following year the Broken Hill to Tarrawingee line became the property of the Government. The privately built Broken Hill—Silverton Rail line was to remain in private hands but was open to all freight and passenger movement for 5 years before reverting to Government ownership. It was to be become (because of the quantity of ore being shipped) the potentially most profitable line in the Commonwealth. The amount of rail line under construction by the end of 1901 was a further 540 mile.

Table A

RAILWAY CONSTRUCTION 1855—1901

Year	Miles Opened	Total Opened	Year	Miles Opened	Total Opened
1855	16	16	1879	45	733
1856	9	25	1880	115	848

1857	17	42	1881	148	996
1858	15	57	1882	282	1278
1859	0	57	1883	52	1330
1860	13	70	1884	301	1631
1861	4	75	1885	114	1745
1862	24	98	1886	162	1907
1863	27	125	1887	151	2058
1864	20	145	1888	68	2126
1865	0	145	1889	57	2183
1866	0	145	1890	10	2193
1867	60	205	1891	1	2194
1868	44	249	1892	3	2197
1869	70	319	1893	154	2351
1870	21	340	1894	150	2501
1871	19	359	1895	30	2531
1872	38	397	1896	0	2531
1873	5	402	1897	108	2639
1874	0	402	1898	52	2691
1875	33	435	1899	15	2706
1876	73	508	1900	105	2811
1877	90	598	1901	34	2845
1878	90	688			

Because exact figures are not available, we can only speculate on the number of men employed on construction, and of the total people including women and children who made a contribution to life on the construction projects.

We still can hear stories today of grandparents living in tents beside the tracks, where the men worked on the line and the women were paid cooks and providers. Permanent railway settlements at crossings, signal boxes and railway terminals started many small rural towns, created employment and were soon to be serviced by schools, stores and churches

Table B

POPULATION PER MILE

Year	Popln to each mile of line	No. of train miles run	No. of train miles per hd of popln
1860	4979	174,249	0.5
1865	2822	483,466	1.2
1870	1467	901,139	1.8
1875	1366	1,472,204	2.5
1880	882	3,239,462	4.4
1885	544	6,638,399	7.2
1890	502	8,008,826	7.4
1891	521	8,410,421	7.5
1892	538	8,356,096	7.2
1893	515	7,505,310	6.3
1894	495	7,169,785	5.9
1895	501	7,594,281	6.1
1896	510	7,719,618	6.1
1897	497	8,130,405	6.4
1898	492	8,340,338	6.4
1899	497	8,806,647	6.7
1900	464	8,894,352	6.6
1901	466	10,763,697	7.9

TABLE C

COLONIAL RAILWAY LINES CONSTRUCTED AS OF 1901

State	Gov't Lines open	Private Lines	Total Lines Open
NSW	2,845	85	2,930
Victoria	3,238	0	3,238
Queensland	2,801	55	2,856
Sth Australia	1,882	19	1,901
West Australia	1,355	623	1,978
Tasmania	446	148	594
Commonwealth	12,567	930	13,497
New Zealand	2,212	88	2,300
Australasia	14,779	1,018	15,797

These tables are sourced from 'The Wealth and Progress of New South Wales 1990-1901' by T.A. Coghlan (P472-3-4)

Coghlan makes one final comparison between the railway systems of the old world and the new world and for brief illustration we will review the length of lines, the population per mile of line, and the area per mile of line in selected countries. The latter measurement is just for comparison purposes and like many of the Coghlan statistics was used to show the superiority in many areas (but mainly New South Wales) over Victoria.

Table D

INTERNATIONAL COMPARISON OF INSTALLED RAIL SERVICE LINKS

Country	Length of Railway	Popln per mile of Line	Area per mile of Line
NSW	2930	466	106
Victoria	3238	370	27
Argentine	10595	432	105
Austria-Hungary	22147	2,030	11
Britain	21,700	1,885	6
USA	190,833	396	18
Sweden	6649	767	26
Japan	3481	12571	42

Edward Pulsford (the leader of the Free Trade movement within Australia) and a Federationist, wrote in his 1892 tract—'Trade & Commerce in New South Wales' (P45):-

"In 1871 the number of miles of railway open was 358; by 1881 this had been increased to about 1,000 and by 1887 to 2,000. Since then the pace has moderated, and the aggregate is now about 2,200 miles. A small number in comparison with the United States aggregate, yet in proportion to the population it is not a bad exhibit. The railways consist almost wholly of main lines. A line from the Queensland border, in the north, to the Victorian border, in the south, passing through Sydney on the way, is the principal one—the total length being 869 miles. The second in importance runs from Sydney in a north-westerly direction to Bourke, on the River Darling, its length being 503 miles. Railway development has also proceeded rapidly in the other colonies, and it is now possible to journey by train from Adelaide, the capital of South Australia, to Melbourne, the capital of Victoria, 509 miles; on from Melbourne to Sydney, the capital of New South Wales, a further 576 miles, then on from Sydney to Brisbane, the capital of Queensland, 723 miles more. Making in all 1,808 miles of what is practically one railway line. The total mileage throughout Australasia is about 12,000 (in 1892)."

Our task is to examine the associated development that came with the railway system, to try to ascertain the number of direct and indirect employees working on the railway system, show the benefits of population growth coming with the gains of decentralisation and the general improvement in the rural quality of life.

The three distinct rail systems provide the basis for the potential growth and development that would follow the opening of the railway lines

a. The southern system, including the principal line in the State, (through Goulburn to Cootamundra) ,branches at Junee and places the important district of Riverina, as far as Hay in one direction and Finley in another, in direct communication with Sydney from which they are distant 454 and 448 miles respectively (756 & 746 Km).Several other branches connect onto this south-western line, connecting other important districts with Sydney. Culcairn connects with Corowa, on the Murray; and Culcairn to Wagga via The Rock; from Cootamundra to Gundagai; and Cootamundra to Temora. A line between Murrumburrah to Blayney connects the Western and Southern systems. The connection allows the direct shipment of western livestock to the markets in Victoria. A branch from Cooma to Goulburn connects the rich Monaro grazing district to the Sydney markets.
b. The North-South Main line passed through, by 1901, the most thickly populated districts in NSW and places Brisbane, Newcastle, Sydney, Melbourne and Adelaide in direct communication. The first sleeping cars were used in 1901 in New South Wales at Albury and provided for the comfort of passengers. European and British

mails are landed in Adelaide (in 1900) by ship and transported 1,085 miles overland to all parts of Victoria, New South Wales and Queensland. A branch line connected the Illawarra on the South Coast to Sydney and Nowra.

c. The western system extends from Sydney towards the Blue Mountains and onto Mudgee through the Bathurst Plains and connects the rich agricultural lands of Bathurst, Orange, Wellington, Dubbo and Bourke (on the Darling River) to the all-important Sydney markets. A branch line from Orange connects to Parkes, Condobolin, Warren and Nyngan. Another branch connects the mining town of Cobar to the Sydney port (for mineral exports) and agricultural market (for rural products). This line is extended to Broken Hill and connects onto the South Australian system.

d. The Northern System, commences in Newcastle, with connections to Sydney through Strathfield, making Sydney the Hub of all rail services in New South Wales by July 1901. This northern line accesses the great coal centres and on through the rich Hunter Valley into the New England areas and towns such as Maitland, Tamworth, Armidale, Glenn Innes and Tenterfield. The wide Hawkesbury River was finally bridged in 1889 by the Union Bridge Company of America. Its construction was hazardous and spectacular. It was the largest structure of its kind in the southern hemisphere. Its total length was almost 3,000 feet. Five piers had to be sunk to a depth of up to 160 feet below high-water level in swift-running currents, a record achievement at that time.

The Hawkesbury River was crossed by this iron bridge at a cost of 327,000 pound, thus completed the connection from Adelaide, Melbourne, Sydney and Brisbane a total end-to-end distance of 1,808 miles, but between Oodnadatta in South Australia and Cunnamulla in Queensland there is a continuous line of 3,100 miles opening up and inter-linking these four key states. The earliest development of the Colonies had depended on the port systems, creating inter-Colonial trade by sea, but the rail system had developed a two-fold benefit, the opening of the inland areas to markets, new towns with people migration to the rural areas, as well as creating an inter-state rail system.

A number of engineering feats accompanied the construction of the overall system. There were difficult gradients in all three systems with over 2,807 miles involved with a gradient, especially through the Illawarra, Blue Mountains and Hawkesbury areas. From the beginning, Australia's railways were modelled on British lines and then modified to suit local conditions. English-type rails were used at first, later to be replaced by lighter ones. All rails were imported until 1906 because the New South Wales Government had wanted to wait until the new Commonwealth Government imposed import duties in 1901, to confirm that protection would be offered to a local industry making iron rails, without the State having to guarantee either a minimum quantity to buy or accept an inflated price. In any case the State lost an important industry because by the time the tariff was announced most rail lines in the country had been installed.

As in the USA, rails were spiked to the sleepers rather than chaired as they were in Britain, and wood fuel was used as an alternative fuel when coal was not available. It fell to NSW to inaugurate the first government-owned railway in the country and in fact, in the British Empire. It was this methodology of spiking that essentially restricts the use of existing rail lines for the planned VFT (very fast train) in NSW in the year 2000.

Expenditure, population served and revenues

The first major benefit to the Colony of New South Wales was the investment in the Rail system at a total cost 38,932,781 pound or 13,682 pound per mile. This cost included 4,677,001 pound for rolling-stock; 340,657 pound on machinery; 638,698 on workshops and 10,036 pound on furniture for a total, of 5,666,392 pound for ancillary equipment, plus the rail laying cost 33,266,389 pound. The benefits of constructing rail rolling stock in NSW created great employment opportunities for newly emerging engineering industries, including Mort's Dock (employing over 1,000 men) and the Government-owned rolling stock workshops (employing over 4,000 men) .

Of the 38,932,781 pound 903,565 was provided from Consolidated Revenue of the State, with the balance being raised by the issue of debentures and other stock. These long-term low interest bonds yielded their investors about 4.5% on average and were almost self-servicing from year one in 1856 because of the passenger and produce traffic they handled.

The net revenue for the year ended June, 1901, after paying for working expenses, was 1,530,578 pound or a return of 3.94 % on the total outlay or 4.24% on the borrowed funds. Based on the early years of full operations, only a good rate of growth could be expected in the future years of operation. The Parliament had also allocated 1,000,000 pound for extending and improving the metropolitan lines and by 1901 75% of this amount had been repaid from revenue. In spite of the extensive gradients and obstacles the cost per mile of line compared favourably with international costs but topped the costs within Australasia.

From humble beginnings in 1855, when the first lines attracted only 350,000 passengers for the year, by June 1901, the number of passengers numbered 29,261,324. An even more dramatic growth can be seen from the tonnage of goods carried. From 2,469 tons in 1855, this grew to 6,398,227 tons in 1901, a growth of 2,591 times the original tonnage. It was not until the line crossed the Blue Mountains and serviced the far interior that goods traffic became a major source of revenue for the railways.

It was recognised that there were numerous unprofitable lines and the Government of the day (in 1901) agreed to review all lines and branches for local benefit rather than on strict terms of profit before making any closures. This consideration was based on the cyclical nature of freight and passenger movements and the imposition of the then current drought effecting the movements. The June 1901 results showed that there was 1,368 miles of line, originally costing 14,545,000 pound that was losing an average of 320,000 pound per annum. The Railways Commissioners suggested in 1901 that surplus crown land on either side of the line be sold with proceeds going to the Railway Capital Fund.

So, at this point, we can start to see the full impact of the railway investment of nearly 40,000,000 pound in the Colony of New South Wales.

Employment was created in laying the line; building the rolling stock; maintaining the lines and rolling stock; servicing and operation staff such as drivers, signalmen and station staff; and many rural towns built family living accommodation for rail-staff in remote areas and this population growth assisted schools, townships, local building jobs; and, in addition, there was the furthering of coal extraction to power the steam locomotives.

Other benefits included the provision of skilled workmen who now had the capabilities of completing other major projects of a similar dimension, including ship construction at Mort's Dock & Shipbuilding in Sydney.

For the less populous states, Labour came from inter-state as well as overseas to work with the railways.

"Many of the navvies who built Queensland's first railways were Irish migrants and were known as 'Jordan's Lambs' after Henry Jordan, Queensland's immigration agent in London. These 'lambs ' were early agitators for the 8-hour working day. They were to suffer when economic depression forced the Queensland Government to suspend public works. A great many skilled railwaymen were thus lost to Queensland, when they moved south in search of work." (Illustrated History of Australia—Hamlyn P574) .

A big labour problem came about due to the low population of the western states (mainly Western Australia) which were vast in size and grossly-underpopulated and was being slowed down by a shortage of workmen in its construction program.

It is interesting to analyse the expenditures on operating costs:

From 1891 through 1901, working or operating expenses as a percentage to gross earnings averaged 59 percent.

In 1901 operating expenses broke down as follows:

Line and easement maintenance	10.81 d
Locomotive powering	16.98 d

Repairs & renewals	3.89 d
Traffic expenses	11.98 d
Compensation	0.25 d
General expenses	1.65 d
TOTAL	45.56 d

Again in 1901, the statistics on intra-state travel in NSW also shows an interesting picture:-

Total passenger journeys	25,489,985 passengers
Number of miles travelled	150,956,272 miles
ave. miles per passenger	5.93 miles
gross receipts from passengers	315,723 pound
Ave. receipts per mile, per passenger	0.50 d
Ave. operating cost per mile	0.4556d
Ave. receipts per head	20s 3.8 d

The goods traffic has risen to 4.7 tons per head of population in 1901 which compared favourably to Victoria at 2.8, Queensland at 3.1, South Australia at 4.5 and Western Australia at 9.5. These figures reflect the importance of the rail system to the economy in each State.

From 1855, when tonnage and goods freight revenue in New South Wales stood at 140 (tons) for 156 (pound), these figures had grown to 6,398,227 (tons) and 2,203,249 (pound revenue), in 1901.

The largest commodity categories in the goods freight being carried in 1901 were:-

*	Coal, coke and shale	3,956,033 ton
*	Firewood	218,058
*	Grain, flour	504,880
*	Hay, straw and chaff	154,403
*	Wool	99,164
*	Livestock	200,339
*	'A' and 'B' class goods	398,402
*	All other goods	867,000
	TOTAL TONS	6,398,227 Tons

Before we move along to review population growth in the larger towns, we can summarise some of the direct and tangible benefits from the railways. The direct employment numbers used in construction and operating of the railroads is not provided by Coghlan's Wealth and Progress of New South Wales but by interpolation of the average pay rates in 1901, we can conclude that approx 50 man years was used to complete an average mile of preparing and laying track. Other employment numbers can be derived in the same manner.

Direct Employment (using ave. pay rate assumptions)

Per mile construction	50 man years
For total track laid	140,000 man years
	(+/-3,800 men per year employed)
Construction of rolling stock	8,000 man years
	(+/-1,000 men employed per year)
Maintenance and Operations	10,000 men
Repairs on rolling stock	4,000 men

These figures show that a substantial amount of available labour was used on the construction and operating duties of the railways. Part verification comes from Manning Clark who states in 'Select Documents in Australian History' that

"by 1890, the NSW Railway workshop alone employed over 4,000 men, which was about one-third of the total number of workers employed on the railways in that Colony. Furthermore, the need for carriages, goods wagons and locomotives provided an expanding market for the products of Australian foundries and general engineering shops. "

Each Colonial Government established big repair and maintenance workshops in their colony, and these expanded rapidly with the railway boom of the 1880s.

The volume of goods being transported by rail is indicative of the importance of the rail system to the rural sector and the ability to move goods to market and to port for export quickly and economically.

The main goods to benefit from the rail system are:

Minerals
Wood
Wool
Coal
Grains
Livestock.

An intangible benefit was the engineering skills developed during construction of iron bridges (Hawkesbury), tunnelling (Blue Mountains), gradient engineering and management and manufacture and design of rolling stock (Sydney Workshops). The hardwood sleepers for the tracks were easily obtained from the eucalypt forests of the coastal region, and wood fuel was used to fire the boilers when coal was not available.

The slow bullock wagons were the only means of transporting wool to the ocean and sometimes, as in the Victorian gold-rush, even these wagons disappeared, leaving stations not only without an outlet for their wool but also without vital supplies. So the rail system was a major boost for the pastoralist as well as the agriculturalists, who wanted to ship fresh produce to the markets.

For many years, Echuca (serviced by a line by the Victorian Railways through Bendigo from Melbourne) boomed with anything up to 5000 bales of wool a day being transferred from steamers and barges on the Murray to freight trains. The wool came from as far away as Bourke in NSW and had been humped by camels across the wide open plains to the Darling River. To shippers in Melbourne and Sydney that wool was most valuable. Transportation within Australia was being diversified. Paddle steamers, coaches, bullock trains, steam trains and ocean vessels all played an important part.

Another service provided by the railway was its special 'starving livestock' program whereby livestock was moved from drought conditions in one area to fresh feed in other areas. Likewise the program encouraged the moving of hay and packaged feed from grower to the livestock and this benefited many pastoralists who were able to maintain stock in good condition. Both programs were heavily subsidised (a 30% discount) by the State Government.

It was more than coincidence that following the gold rush with its enormous claim to workers rushing to the fields to find their fortune, and once the easy 'surface' gold was depleted, the workers wanted earned income for stability. These workers were largely put to work on the railway system in rural areas and so the potential huge unemployment problem was tempered by the attraction of hard but regular work, building a railway system throughout the State.

The gold rush had , in other ways, provided a powerful impetus for the building of the railways that had contributed so much to conquer the inland of the vast continent. The discovery of gold created general prosperity and a scarcity of labour, and so the available workers became more independent and employers were forced to make valuable concessions.

Workers returning from the gold-fields also brought with them a strong attitude of militancy. In May 1856, the eight-hour day had been achieved in the building industry in NSW—and without any reduction in daily wages. The movement then spread to workers in the 'indoor' trades in Melbourne such as cabinet-makers, coach-builders and iron trade craftsmen.

But, the eight-hour day was a misnomer. They were really fighting for a 48-hour week, and as work ended early on Saturdays, the standard hours on other working days were about 8.75 (8 ¾) c. Confusion caused by the Railway Gauge Conflict

An extract from The Illustrated History of Australia shows the way confusion came about over the rail gauges in the mainland states.

The NSW Board of Railway Commissioners recommended to Earl Grey (the Colonial Secretary) in 1848 that the English standard 4' 8 ½" be adopted throughout Australia. Since Victoria was not separated at that time, that area, as well as Queensland was covered under this proposal.

"Two years later, an Irish Engineer, F.W. Shields, joined the Railway in NSW, and even though the Irish railways gauge was a broad one (5 ft 3 inches), and thus more expensive to lay and maintain, he persuaded the Legislative Council of NSW to use that gauge instead of the planned English gauge. The authorities in Britain did not see anything wrong with the idea, or perhaps they just did not care. Shields resigned soon after during a pay dispute and his successor changed back to the 4 ft 8 ½ inch. Victoria and South Australia, both of whom had ordered rolling stock from overseas continued to use the broad gauge and could not change, whilst Queensland and Western Australia, for reasons of economy adopted the narrow 3 foot 6 inch gauge. The Trans-continental railway opened by Commonwealth Railways in 1917 used the 4 foot 8 ½ inch gauge and brought Western Australian isolation to an end. The west became joined to the east for the first time.

d. Population Growth in Selected Areas

It is not a surprising result to find that the great cities of Australia, like their counter-parts in all other parts of the world, accumulated the majority of the population and achieved the highest growth rates. One of the results of the industrial revolution that improved farm productivity, was that rural population commenced to decrease. Farm workers were attracted to the cities by electricity, schools for their families, stable employment and for a while, a better quality of life. That trend is still taking place but may be at a turning point for the very same reasons that the population once used as justification for moving away from rural areas.

In 1861 the native-born population amounted to only 46% of the total Colonial population and the native-born population of the Sydney metropolitan population was only 42%. The British born residents generally preferred the city living whilst the non-British residents generally preferred the rural districts. The growing Chinese population also preferred the city life.

The metropolitan trend grew as follows, along with the Sydney residents:-

1861	26.70%	95,596
1871	26.73	136,483
1881	30.34	237,300
1891	34.47	308,270
1901	35.90	400,650

Coghlan explained this trend in a thoughtful work, following the 1899 census of the Colony.

"The growth of the Australian cities is due mainly to the physical configuration of the continent, which makes no other mode of development possible—for there are no great rivers with leagues of navigable waterway stretching into the heart of the country far remote from seaports. To some extent the growth of cities has also been favoured by the commercial development of the states. For many years wool-growing has been the staple industry of the country; and while the actual tending of flocks needs few hands, and those widely scattered, the handling of bales of wool at a convenient place of shipment demands all the resources of a great commercial centre. Also, gold-digging, to which the state owe so much, is not an industry likely to promote permanent settlement in the interior. The miner of the past was in every respect a nomad: if successful in his quest after the precious metal, he became an emigrant to the Old World or a sojourner in an Australian capital."

The growing population in the city and the country can be seen from the following:-

Year	City	Country
1870	134,578	364,081
1880	223,886	524,064
1890	380,048	741,820
1900	590,630	873,960
1901(census)	487,900	871,233

The railways provided the much needed access to markets for rural and agricultural output. The railways boomed and caused the Railway Department to place more orders for rolling stock and engines and commenced building more branch lines. The Government started again to borrow from overseas to pay for the capital improvements and with the import of capital came immigrants and labour. In the period just prior to World War One, there was a large inflow of migrants and they helped to expand the market and the work force. Agricultural expansion stimulated manufacturing, especially of agricultural implements and machinery Manufacturing made a rapid growth and diversified, and shared a growing proportion of the national product rising to about 14% in 1913. This growth was also due to the growing average income for each working family, the protectionist policy under Deakin and the Labour Party, and the population increases. Family income was supported by a rise of women in the workplace. The number of men employed in NSW manufacturing increased by 78 % between 1900 and 1914 but the number of women employed rose by 158%. Sydney was included in the building boom of the 1907-1912 period, and in 1911 the NSW Statistician wrote 'The city of Sydney is undergoing a process of rebuilding, and inferior buildings are giving way to superior factories and premises'.

Three selected inland towns make an interesting study for population and economic growth

Town	Population 1901	Population 2000
Goulburn	10,612	22,500
Dubbo	3,409	30,000
Orange	3,990	30,000
Tamworth	5,799	32,500
Wagga	5,108	58,200
Broken Hill	27.500	25,000

The development of Goulburn is typical of most of these inland towns.

The stockade (in Goulburn) became the principal penal establishment in the southern district and was noted for its harsh discipline. There were usually 250 convicts hutted there. They slept on bare boards with a blanket apiece. 10 men to a box or cell.

The first school and church opened in 1839 and the Goulburn Herald was established in 1848. It was later incorporated into the 'Post' which is still published today.

The settlement began to expand after 1850 due to a number of factors.

a. the pastoral industry had expanded
b. gold was discovered in Braidwood in the early 1850s (a local labour shortage was the immediate result)

c. settlers began to arrive from the 1860s
d. the railway arrived in 1869, facilitating access to the Sydney markets. The town remained the southern railhead until 1875.

As a result, Goulburn became the first inland city in 1863 after being gazetted as a municipality in 1859.

The railway was especially crucial as a catalyst for the town's boom period in the 1870s and 1880s when industries such as coach-building, iron foundries and saddlery-making began to develop. A dairy factory was set up in 1901 and woollen mills in 1922. The town has been a major wool sales centre since 1930.

Another contributor to economic growth was the closer settlement program that broke up huge pastoral holdings into smaller family holdings which saw the early addition of fruit-growing and dairying to the local agricultural production.

Electricity did not arrive until 1922. Bushrangers added adventure to the local area and kept the civilian prisons busy.

The story of Wagga, Dubbo, Orange and Tamworth follow much the same pattern. A slow start, discovery of gold, a growing settlement, building of schools and churches, the coming of the railway, and each major town having a huge edifice of a rail station to recognise the importance of the rail service to the town and closer settlement, small engineering shops, retailing of farm machinery, manufacturing and servicing standard farm machines, diversification of agriculture, growing wealth, electricity, retail stores, surfaced roads, wagons, Cobb & Co coaches, quicker rail access to the City, war service and with it a rural male population in decline. The Railway Commissioners assisted, perhaps unwittingly, in directing growth by selecting certain rural towns as transfer hubs, where trains would be 'parked' overnight, and goods re-assigned to another train, and the location for rail families to take up permanent residence.

An economic profile of Goulburn today can be compiled, for analysis, from the ABS Regional Statistics for 1999.

When Goulburn was proclaimed a municipality in 1859, its area of potential township as laid out by the Surveyor-General's office was approx 30 square miles. Those geographic and statistical boundaries remain today.

The population has remained relatively stable during the 1990s at 21,000, whilst its age distribution , like much of rural NSW has aged overall with post-school leavers moving away from the City. Today's population age grouping is :-

0-4 years	1,573
5-14 years	3,222
15-19 years	1,746
20-54 years	10,182
55-64 years	1,803
65 years and over	2,779

It is noteworthy that in 1996-97 there was a positive gain in population numbers with births (304) exceeding deaths (198)

Driving through the main street of Goulburn today, one does not appear to see many (if any) vacant shops but the building rate in 1997-98 was a record $7,092,000 made up of shops ($635m), factories ($180m) offices ($205m) and other ($6,072,000—accounted for by a new shopping centre). Housing generated $7,183,000 in new dwellings (73) thus averaging a little less than $100,000 each in estimated construction costs.

Obviously little farming is carried on in such a small geographic area and this is confirmed by there being only 27 farm units totalling 5633 hectares with an output of $1,2386,000. This was essentially sheep with lamb production numbering 15,563 and only 1,531 head of cattle.

The main activity within the city boundaries was manufacturing production, estimated to be $161 million from 40 manufacturing units, employing 1,083 people.

The 12 motels and hotels could accommodate 984 bed nights and employ 144 people. The city sponsors a number of annual events including

The Lilac Festival, the Music Jamboree, a Blues Music Festival and the Goulburn Rodeo. The Goulburn Show and Rose Festival in March is also a major drawcard for tourists. The motor racing on most weekends, reverses the norm of high occupancy rates during the week and empty rooms of a weekend. In Goulburn, it is very difficult to find a room on a weekend but there are some vacancy's during week nights.

Being the centre of renewed interest in rural activities Goulburn is naturally poised to enjoy major growth as a tourist town. Like many inland cities, it has still not found its real competitive edge but is actively seeking any industry that may be looking to relocate. The concept of cluster industry development has not been adopted as it is considered too restrictive, narrow and limiting rather than bringing any and all industries to town and let them shake out to see who and what holds together. Goulburn has become the regional hub, where for many decades a wealthy pastoral setting known in the region for the strong wool merino in Gunning and the ideal lambing conditions around the Marulan area. Goulburn, for over 150 years, was the mainstay for the wool and pastoral industry and remains so today. The original railway brought much progress to the town and the idea of a VFT passing through and possibly stopping in Goulburn has made the City campaign to be the location for the second Sydney airport, the focus of a community project. The next 'railway' phenomenon has been witnessed on the horizon.

Dr. G. L. Buxton , as Lecturer in Economic History at Adelaide University published his doctoral work 'The Riverina 1861-1891' in 1967, and makes references to the effect of the railways coming to the region in the late 1800s.[178]

"From the time that New South Wales had ignored the instruction that the Murrumbidgee was to be the inter-colonial boundary and had fixed it at the Murray—and on the south bank at that—Victorian Governments had cast covetous eyes at the Riverina. The whole of the area as far north-east as Wagga, lies nearer Melbourne than Sydney. Its economic ties were with Melbourne, and Victorian Governments said that they would continue tapping the area and if possible annex it. In 1863 a Victorian Select

[178] Buxton, G.L. The Riverina 1861-1891'

Committee on the Riverine District had been appointed specifically 'to take evidence and report on the best method of securing to the Victorian Railways the Trade of the River in the districts of Murray, Murrumbidgee and Darling Rivers. Partly on the basis of the report the Victorian railway had been extended in 1864 to Echuca, 120 miles from Melbourne and only forty-five from Deniliquin. Two years later petitioners were urging the New South Wales Government that the railway should be extended to Deniliquin. By 1870 the Deniliquin and Moama Railway Company had been formed and in 1876 the Victorian-gauge line was thus extended by private enterprise to Deniliquin."[179]

(P209)"The Railway Commissioners were to be informed of the hardship under which farmers laboured, under existing railway tariffs and the rates were to be revised; millers were to return bags to the producers of cereal, or reimburse them with two-thirds of the original cost; the government was to be urged so as to have the statistics of farm produce collected as to form reliable records of the cereal products of the colony, and finally, the union advocated the advisability of farmers cooperating with the object of building grain sheds for the purpose of storing their grain. By 1891, closer settlement, under the Robertson's Act, had given the selectors their land; railway extensions and differential rates were giving them access to metropolitan markets, and cooperation was breaking the political and commercial monopolies of the labour unions. But it was in fact the very land sales revenue which selectors had helped to boost which had saved New South Wales governments from having to resort to an extensive protective tariff system like Victoria. It is true that the southern Riverina declined earlier as a result of the general movement of population in a north-westerly direction. Selectors selling out to squatters or their fellows and accompanying rationalisation of holdings caused depopulation of the southern towns; as did the progressive outward movement of casual workers and contractors, including Chinese, engaged in fencing, dam sinking and ringbarking; while teamsters and those employed in coaching and the river-steamer traffic continually retreated before the advancing railways."[180]

---

179 Buxton, G.L. The Riverina 1861-1891'

180 Buxton, G.L. The Riverina 1861-1891'

If the several hundred temporary residents engaged in building railways and associated works at Albury are excluded, and some allowance made for Wagga having become a Municipality with consequent boundary extensions between 1861 and 1871, the growth rates of Albury and Wagga are parallel. Both grew rapidly in the seventies but were required to share with other towns which developed as rural service centres the prosperity resulting from closer settlement. Deniliquin grew rapidly with the fat stock market of the late fifties, declining as that traffic did in the sixties. Growth recovered during the seventies, with rising prosperity from family selection and a further boost from the private railway link with Melbourne. The extension of the New South Wales government railways to the area in the early eighties, partly in answer to Victorian economic aggression, effectively reduced Deniliquin's economic hinterland, while movement of selectors out of the district further decreased the need for services. A combined flour mill and brewery, a wool scour, soap factory and the railway marked the limits of local industrial enterprise. The seasonal wool traffic to the railhead provided Deniliquin's major annual economic activity, with livestock movements of less importance as the Victorian protective tariff increased. Brick-works and saw mills, as in other towns, operated according to the demands of the building trade. In southern Riverina, building activity generally declined during the period, Between 1881 and 1891 the number of houses in Narrandera increased from 248 to 370 and in Wagga from 594 to 921. By contrast the number of houses in Albury rose only from 1,051 to 1,097 and in Deniliquin from 545 to 549."[181]

"The railways to Hay and Jerilderie ended the domination of Deniliquin in the western Riverina, both of these towns growing at Deniliquin's expense. Within a year of the railway reaching Jerilderie a flour-mill had been built. During the seventies Hay had grown in importance as a transport centre for teamsters, Cobb & Co. coaches, and river steamers loaded with wool or station supplies, including fencing wire. Thousands of tons of copper ore brought by teams from Mount Hope, 160 miles north, and the Araunah mine in Nymagee, 220 miles north, were loaded on to steamers at Hay for smelting in Adelaide, and machinery passed back along the same route. Until the railway reached Hay in 1882 the bridge was opened for as

[181] Buxton, G.L. The Riverina 1861-1891'

many as six steamers a day, but in the whole of the following year only six passed through. Some squatters, accustomed to dealing with Melbourne, continued to send wool by steamer to Echuca when the river was high, but the differential rates netted an increasing amount of this traffic for Sydney, while the existence of the railhead enabled Hay's prosperity as the centre of the outback transport system to be maintained."

Narrandera and Corowa both grew as a result of selection activity, the need for services increasing as the district was more closely settled. Corowa's agricultural and pastoral hinterland gave rise to flour-mills and a wool scour; saw-mills cut red gum and pine; and in 1892 the completion of the Culcairn—Corowa railway link to Sydney assured further growth. By 1891, Narrandera, on a population basis, was the most highly industrialised town in the Riverina. Besides being a railway junction for the Hay and Jerilderie lines, and before that a steamer port, Narrandera was the centre of an extensive timber trade which drew on the surrounding natural pine forests. Timber from its several sawmills was sent all over the Riverina and as far as the upper Darling. A coach factory, a brewery and cordial factory, flour-mill(1884), wool scour(1886), and meat freezing works (1890)—in which rabbits increasingly replaced sheep—all contributed to the towns stability; while earlier gold had been mined. Narrandera's most rapid growth had been from 1871 to 1881, from a population of 142 to 1,142 . The 1871 census return included only twenty-two householders—the rest were recorded as 'persons sleeping on premises'.[182]

Amongst the more general changes were the westward and northward movement of the 'selection frontier' and the 'ringbarking and fencing frontier'. The first followed available land, the second the spread of improvement techniques to an ever increasing area. Both led to a movement of land seekers and casual labour to areas progressively 'further out'. Similarly as the railway fan opened out, a further outward migration followed; that of the teamsters and those engaged in coaching and river traffic. All too often the program of railway development in eastern Australia was directed by inter-colonial rivalry, as the use of different (rail) gauges and differential rates indicates. The line to Hay effectively cut off Deniliquin's northern hinterland; that to Jerilderie severed it from the

182 Buxton, G.L. The Riverina 1861-1891'

east.. This was the New South Wales Government's eventual answer to the Victorian policy off tapping the Riverina at a series of points along the Murray. Thereafter Deniliquin' linked with Melbourne rather than Sydney, though on a more limited scale than previously because of its reduced hinterland. Socially it made less difference. Even in the eighties it was said of the residents of Hay that they wore Melbourne clothes, read the Melbourne newspapers and drank Melbourne beer; and in the four southern Riverina counties, half the population were Victorian born. At the same time the extension of railways contributed to the growth of a number of small service centres, particularly in the wheat belt nearer Wagga and Albury. These railway towns, scattered at regular intervals, along the line formed focal points for the activities of farming communities. Often the extension of the railway was the result of successful closer settlement in the more favoured areas of the Riverina. However even today the largest towns remain those on the major permanent rivers."[183]

Considerable changes had also taken place in the carriage of wool. Stations with a frontage to navigable rivers preferred to load wool direct on to steamers or barges by which it travelled to Echuca and thence by rail to Melbourne. From other stations it was carted by dray to the nearest railway. With the advent of the rail to Echuca , Wodonga, and Deniliquin, Wagga, Albury, Narrandera, Hay and Jerilderie, and the introduction of differential rates, river traffic declined. Inevitably wool-growers sold to the highest bidder—in this case, the colony offering the cheapest access to the sea-ports. Except for 1890, when the shearer's strike held up 10,000 Melbourne-bound bales of wool at Wodonga, there had been no difficulties in transporting wool, the quality of which had been continually improving, as had the yield per sheep.

The movement of livestock was another matter. Victorian protection, ministering to the commercial interests of Melbourne, had avoided a tariff on wool. But protection for meat-producers led to ever-increasing duties on livestock imports. In the late 1870s, despite the 1s. per head tax on sheep, as many as 12,000 per week were railed to Melbourne via Moama(on the NSW side of the Murray River at Echuca). Until 1891 it was reckoned that 75% of the cattle marketed in Melbourne came from Queensland

[183] Buxton, G.L. The Riverina 1861-1891'

and New South Wales, but in 1892, with protection an election issue, tariffs became prohibitive—rising from 5s to One pound per head on cattle—and smuggling was rife. Some of the problems of moving livestock cheaply and efficiently were avoided by the introduction of meat freezing and chilling works at Narrandera. By 1891 meetings had been held in other towns to encourage the building of freezing works there.

A typical pattern of development in the regions saw a rapid increase in town population in the seventies, relative decline with waning opportunities in the eighties as the selector frontier moved further north-west, and some recovery in the nineties. The migrations of the seventies resulted, in spite of the general slow down of growth and economic activity in the sixties, and with natural increase, the Riverina had seen a six-fold growth of population in thirty years, much of the increase being in the numbers of women and children. This growth in the respectable urban and farming communities and the vastly increased number of schools and churches took much of the roughness from the pastoral society typical of the fifties.

Conclusion

The answer to the question as to what benefits came with the railways investment can now be summarised.

What resulted, from investment in the Railways system for the colony of NSW, was the employing of many men returning from the gold fields and looking for permanent steady work, the development of railway towns, transfer hubs, and workshops; all these were developed as part of the growth of the railway system, and these operational and maintenance facilities also put many thousands of men, and women to permanent long-term employment. Railway towns were established and commenced with small settlements, all to be serviced with stores, schools, churches, roads and buildings.

The engineering work provided skills in bridging, tunnelling, gradient management, and these skills were then used all over Australia and New Zealand.

The associated construction involved major railway stations throughout the Sydney area and in every country town. Many large construction jobs were undertaken in the bigger towns such as Orange, Goulburn, Albury and Wagga, where huge station terminals and complexes were built.

Many railway towns sprung up with the Railway Commissioners funding the cost of houses for railway families.

Transfer hubs were built at junctions where undercover workshops for cleaning and maintenance and storage buildings were constructed, and many employees engaged. Train crews were generally housed and maintained in these hubs.

Workshops were built in the Sydney area to meet manufacturing, maintenance and cleaning obligations.

At the peak in 1885 over 12,000 men were employed by the Railway system in New South Wales alone. This was replicated in each Colony but, with the exception of Victoria, on a smaller scale.

Immediate associated development took place in the coal industry in New South Wales where production increased steadily to meet the needs of steam generation for the railway systems in New South Wales and Victoria. Victoria accepted shipment of over 160,000 tons of coal to keep its trains operating.

Other development occurred in the hubs by new industries starting such as, coach building, woollen mills, iron foundries, fencing contractors, Cobb & Co coaches, meat works with refrigeration and freezers (all of which needed installing and servicing). Electricity was being distributed through rural towns by the late 1910s, and larger mining operations were opening up because of the ability to transport the ore to refineries and ports.

The investment of under £40,000,000 in the Colony of New South Wales achieved great results. It created huge employment opportunities, opened up the inland areas for new towns and served the rural economies by providing fast and cheaper access to the markets and ports than previously available. But most importantly the capital came from overseas which meant that many new arrivals followed the importation of capital, and that the capital was serviced from operational revenues was unique. The Government of New South Wales, as opposed to the Governments of the other colonies did not have to burden itself with meeting debt or interest payment from current revenues.

This gain meant that other services in the Colony could grow as planned without the colony losing revenue. The economic growth continued with the on-going development of electricity to both town and country people and the growth of the telegraph system that would eventually link all the colonies to each other and overseas.

The gap created by the tyranny of distance was swiftly closing.

LAND REFORM IN AUSTRALIA

The Problem

By 1860, the need for new land legislation in the eastern colonies became urgent because the leases of the squatters issued under the authority of the Order in Council of 1847, expired in 1861.

The attempt to pass new land legislation was one of the immediate causes of conflict between the Legislative Assemblies and the Legislative Councils of the colony of New South Wales.

The two New South Wales Acts did provide for other forms of land tenure, other than 'conditional purchase' and 'leasehold' eg there was purchase by auction, purchase of timber reserves, stock reserves, etc However these acts dealt exclusively with the disposal of crown lands, and did not affect private sales of land.

The author of the Alienation and Occupations Bill (leading to the above mentioned Acts) in NSW, John Robertson, insisted that the interests of the squatters and selectors be safeguarded. The Bill made ample provision for the obtainment of lands by those who really desired to settle upon the land and improve it, whatever might be attempted to be done for the advancement of the masses of the people, the squatter's interests were by no means overlooked.

An editorial in the SMH of 8th October 1860 sets out the record of the crown lands

"the origin and basis for our colonial prosperity has been pastoral occupation of the waste (Crown) lands. For a time it was the only thing possible, and it answered excellently its purpose of creating a valuable export, and spreading civilisation over the interior. But the growth of society requires modification to the system. Experience seems to point out that the advantages it has offered are too much confined to a particular class—that the scope offered to the agriculturalist and the small squatter is too limited, and a demand has arisen that greater freedom and opportunity should be given to those who are willing to invest their industry and their savings in rural pursuits. It is natural that those who feel, and who have perhaps felt for some time, the pressure of restrictions, should be prompted to advocate rather violent rearrangements—to sweep away, not only without compunction, but with a certain grim satisfaction, all the vested interests that have grown up, without sufficient considering the evils that would result even to themselves and their friends from such an iconoclastic policy. "

The SMH of 10th October, 1860 had reported some of the speeches in the Legislative Assembly:

"The moral argument for the squatters was presented by, Mr O'Shanassy(himself a squatter): ' Within a few days of the end of the year, would it be thought fair to say ' Here, you pastoral tenants, whose rights have been recognised under law for the past twenty years,—you who opened up the wilderness, risked all your invested capital—and after all your pains and trouble, you are within fourteen days of losing your tenure. Go about your business!. No man in the community would deal in this way with slaves, let alone men of character and respectability.'

Some further background

A Member of the NSW Legislative Assembly—Mr Jenkins—spoke during the debate:

' It has been said that the produce of the pastoral districts did not stand so high on the list of exports as those of the gold districts. Now I do not wish to deprecate that interest, but I can show that a mistake was make in those statements, for the pastoral exports are far greater over a period than those of gold (the amount of gold dust exported annually is between 2 & 3 million pound; whilst the pastoral exports are between 3 & 4 million pound. But which industry employs the most labour. The amount of grain imported into the Colony has practically declined to zero, whilst the local production was fast overtaking demand.'

Alternatives

Following the earlier acts, an inquiry into 'Public Lands' was completed by Messrs. Morris and Rankin, who roundly condemned the entire system and concluded that the 'most noteworthy matter that has come to light, and the most ominous for the future well-being of the Colony (of NSW), is the class contest for the possession of its lands which has covered five-sixths of the surface. The huge area of 86 million acres has provided a field on which every form of abuse has been carried out in defiance of the public interest. It needs little argument to prove the vice of a policy which of its very essence divides the rural population into two hostile camps; and it would be superfluous to state that the personal virtues of veracity and honourable dealing have been tarnished by the daily habit of intrigue, and the practice of evading the law and by declaration in defiance of fact universally made. '

The most radical solution to the Land Reform Movement was adopted in New South Wales, where it was called ' Free selection before survey'. The essential feature of this system of selling Crown land, was not the sale price of the land, but its immediate release to homesteaders; they paid one-quarter of the price as a deposit, and received their title deeds after three years and completion of the payment. John Robertson successfully piloted two Bills through both Chambers incorporating these principles., after a political crisis involving strong opposition from squatters with seats in the Upper House. The Two Acts gave adequate protection to squatters by granting them long leases of Crown Land in pastoral areas, but allowed selectors to take up Crown land in agricultural or mixed farming and grazing areas with the minimum of delays and with only a low deposit. They could then begin cultivation immediately, and wait for the government surveyor to arrive later. However, they could get their freehold only if they made improvements.

The new system worked!

A Brief History of Crown Land Disposal

The practice of recording money derived from the sale of crown land as a separate entry to which only the British Treasury was entitled (refer 'The Land Fund") was common to all colonies and formed one of the largest items of their annual income. Auction sales raised significant income before being suspended in 1883, when 'it became evident that this indiscriminate sale of the public estate and its alienation was threatening to endanger the true interests of the country" (Wealth & Progress of NSW 1886-87—P385). This alienation was due to rivalry between the two principal classes of settlers—the pastoral tenants and the free selectors, and the fact that the sales were concluded without conditions relating to use, improvement or settlement. Sales were temporarily suspended by auction and it was decided to sell only limited area during any one year.

Under the Crown Lands Act of 1861, the Governor was empowered to sell crown leasehold lands (upon which improvements had been made) to the owners of the improvements, without competitive bids, at a price determined by valuation, the minimum price being fixed at One pound sterling per acre. The area of land able to be purchased in this way was increased from 320 acres to 640 acres. This privilege of purchasing, without competition, Crown Lands held under lease did not extend merely to the pastoral tenant of the crown but to leaseholders in general including goldfield leases. Broad acre Pastoral leases could also be freeholded in lumps of 25 square miles. All conversions of crown land generated revenues of two hundred and ten thousand in 1871 and two hundred and sixty thousand pounds in 1886. The Government entered into 'conditional' or terms sales which in 1862 amounted to twenty-five million acres and generated a total of eleven million five hundred thousand pounds. Interest accrued on such terms transactions and in 1886 amounted to two million 605 thousand pounds.

Full details of annual sales and lease of crown land and revenue there from can be found in the Statistics section of this volume.

Pastoral leases generated generous revenues but a significant element of default occurred. In 1886 revenue obtained from these leases amounted to only 374 thousand pounds, but lease payments in default amounted to over 500 thousand pounds.

Revenue from Government services was the largest sector of overall Government revenue.

In 1886, the percentage breakdown was as follows:

Services	40.7
Taxation	34.4
Land sales etc	21.6
miscellaneous	3.3

CHAPTER 8

EXPLORATION TRAVELS WITH JOHN OXLEY

Probably Colonial Surveyor-General John Oxley carried out the most important exploration work in Colonial NSW. Oxley was responsible for opening up much of the vast inland grassland and plains of NSW, and his survey work in these new areas created small townships as well as opening the way to land selection and development by the Australian Agricultural Company in the Port Stephens region of the colony and later the Liverpool Plains region, in 1824

John Oxley solved the challenge put before him by Governor Lachlan Macquarie to solve the puzzle of the rivers. The challenge was to find their source and where they emptied and to establish whether or not there was a large inland body of water with greatly fertile lands surrounding it which contributed to the river system of the Colony of New South Wales.

Oxley had arrived in the Colony in 1803 and in 1814 was appointed Surveyor-General of the Colony.

In 1816, Macquarie requested Oxley to head up an expedition to follow the trail of the recently returned Blaxland, Lawson and Wentworth over the Blue Mountains. Macquarie had a number of reasons for this request Firstly he had been doubtful of the full truth of the Wentworth expedition and wanted independent verification; secondly, Oxley was a reticent 'explorer' and Macquarie wanted to see him gain both confidence and experience in discovering the new challenge of surveying in the unknown; and thirdly, Macquarie needed to open up new areas for the pastoral industry which, with over 1 million sheep and a hundred thousand cattle, desperately needed new open grazing lands.

Oxley left , accompanied by Lieutenant Evans, a sound , reliable engineer and architect in early 1817, and upon his return on the 30th August, 1817 wrote to Macquarie reporting the highlights of his journey. The Oxley Journal is hundreds of pages but his letter highlights the essential aspects of the journey and is recorded in full in W.C. Wentworth's volume (1814) 'A Statistical Account of the Colony of New South Wales'. Oxley wrote his account from Bathurst which, after the Wentworth journey over the mountains, became the base camp for future expeditions and the start of a township and watering point for squatters and pastoralists taking up new land in the west.

"I proceeded down the Lachlan in company with the boats until the 12th May, 1817, the country rapidly descending until the waters of the river rose to a level with it, and then dividing into numerous branches , inundated the country to the west and north-west, and prevented any further progress by boat, the river being lost in marshes.

We then proceeded with the horses, in a course towards the coast to determine if there were any intersecting streams that might come into the Lachlan.

I continued this course until the 9th of June , when having lost two horses through fatigue and want, and the others in a deplorable condition, I changed our course to north, along a range of lofty hills, running in that direction, as they afforded the only means of procuring water until we should fall in with some running stream. On this course I continued until the 23rd June, when we again fell in with a stream, which we had at first some difficulty to recognise as the Lachlan, it being little larger than one of the marshes of it, where it was quitted on the 17th of May.

I was unwilling to have the slightest doubt that any navigable waters falling westward into the sea, between the limits pointed out in my instructions. I continued along the banks of the stream until the 8th of July, it having taken during this period a westerly direction, and passing through a perfectly level country, barren in the extreme, and being evidently at periods entirely under water. We were a full five hundred miles west of Sydney, and nearly in its latitude; and it had taken us ten weeks of unremitted exertion to proceed so far. We had demonstrated beyond the shadow of a doubt, that no river whatever could fall into the sea, between Cape Otway and Spencer's Gulf.

It now became my duty to make our remaining resources as extensively useful to the colony as our circumstances would allow: these were much diminished: an accident to one of the boats, at the outset of the expedition, had deprived us of one-third of our dry provisions, of which we had originally but eighteen weeks; and we had been in consequence for some time on a reduced ration of two quarts of flour per man, per week. To return to the depot by the route we had come, would have been as useless as impossible.

It was my intention to take a north-east course, to intersect the country, and if possible ascertain what had become of the Macquarie river, which it was clear had never joined the Lachlan. On the 7th of August we were now quitting the area of the Lachlan and had passed to the north-east of the high range of hills, which on this parallel bounds the low country to the north of that river. This renewed our hopes of soon falling in with the Macquarie, and we continued upon the same course, occasionally inclining to the eastward, until the 19th passing through a fine luxuriant country, well watered, crossing in that space of time nine streams, having a northerly course through rich valleys; the country in every direction being moderately high and open, and as generally as fine as can be imagined.

An accident let us down this stream about a mile, when we were surprised by its junction with a river coming from the south, of such width and magnitude, as to dispel all doubts as to this last being the river we had so long anxiously looked for. Short as our resources were, we could not resist the temptation this beautiful country offered us, to remain two days on that junction of the river, for the purpose of examining the vicinity to as great an extent as possible . . . . as far as the eye could see in every direction, a rich and picturesque country extended, abounding in limestone, slate, good timber, and every other requisite that could render an uncultivated country desirable. The soil cannot be excelled, whilst a noble river of the first magnitude affords the means of conveying its productions from one part to the other.

It appeared to me that the Macquarie had taken a north-west course from Bathurst, and that it must have received immense accessions of water in its course from that place. We viewed it at a period best calculated to form an accurate judgement of its importance, when it was neither swelled by floods beyond its natural and usual height, nor contracted within its limits by summer droughts; from the boldness and height of the country, I presume, must be at least as many, some idea may be formed, when at this point it exceeded in breadth and apparent depth, the Hawkesbury at Windsor. Many of the branches were of grander and more extended proportion than the admired one on the Nepean River from the Warragambia to Emu Plains. On the 22nd we proceeded up the river and between the point quitted and Bathurst, crossed the sources of numberless streams, all running into the Macquarie; two of them were nearly as large as that river itself at Bathurst. The country from whence all these streams derive their source, was mountainous and irregular, and appeared equally so on the east side of the Macquarie. This description of country extended to the immediate vicinity of Bathurst; but to the west of those lofty ranges, the country was broken into low grassy hills, and fine valleys watered by rivulets rising on the west side of the mountains, which on their eastern side pour their waters directly into the Macquarie.

I shall hasten to lay before your Excellency the journals, charts and drawings, explanatory of the various occurrences of our diversified route; infinitely gratified if our exertions should appear to your Excellency commensurate with your expectations, and the ample means which your care and liberality placed at my disposal.

I express my appreciation and thanks to Mr Evans, the deputy Surveyor, Mr Alan Cunningham, the King's botanist, Mr Fraser and Mr Parr."[184]

---

[184] Oxley Journals and Reports to Governor Macquarie

MOVEMENT TOWARDS EDUCATION

Economic events in the Colony were all instrumental in encouraging population growth, both by natural increase and by immigration. It had been Governor Macquarie's ambition to develop a kinder, gentler colonial atmosphere which would enable the free settlers to take great pride in the settlement, which in turn would lead to a feeling of permanency and security.

We consider the growth of the Education movement in the Colony in economic terms. Education achieved many goals: It created employment for builders, teachers, administrators, and increase the literacy rate to over 70% to under 20% in a relatively short period of time. This in itself assisted economic growth by a declining crime rate, by offering better educated workers to employers, and by bridging that generational gap and ensuring that illiterate parents did not restrict the opportunities for their children.

The earliest days

The First Fleet arrived in the Colony with 17 children belonging to the convicts and 19 children belonging to the Marines.

Nowhere in Governor Phillip's commission or instructions was any mention made of these children or their future, or of the child convicts whom the British Government saw fit to transport (there were 47 child convicts in Sydney and 36 at Norfolk Island—HRA I i,203), for it was alien to the official mind of the late 18th Century to feel any interest in the welfare of these children. By 1809 the War Office had been persuaded to appoint regimental schoolmasters, and by 1833 the Colonial Office was prepared to sanction an experiment in the reformation of child convicts in VDL, but in 1788 the education of these children formed no part of the business of any department of state.

A. G. Austin in his work 'Australian Education 1788-1900' outlines the approach to education of all the Colonists, both the children and the adults.

"The early governors of New South Wales, soon found it necessary to contradict their masters in Westminster, for 'Botany Bay ' was not to be a fragment of English society transformed to the Antipodes, but a military and penal garrison in which they (the Governors) were responsible for every aspect of daily life. In a settlement where the maintenance of discipline, the regulation of food production, the rationing of supplies, the employment of labour and the administration of justice were committed to one man's hands, there was no room for the laissez-faire indifference which characterised the conduct of public affairs in the Mother Country. Not only were they moved by the misery of the convict's children, but they realised that the future of the Colony had to be built upon these very children. In a colony where there were three times as many men as there were women, and where the distribution of female convicts were never properly supervised, there was, as might be expected, a high proportion of illegitimate and abandoned children. In 1807, on Bligh's testimony, there were 397 married women in the colony. 1,035 'concubines', 807 legitimate children and 1,024 illegitimate children; something as Governor King had already pointed out, had to be done to rescue these children' from the future misery to be expected from the horrible examples that they hourly witness from their parents' and those they live with. "

Phillip had been instructed by the King that ' a spot in or as near each town as possible be set apart for the building of a church, plus land there for a Minister and for a school-master.' (HRNSW 1 Pt 2)

In all this the Governors were not concerned to assert the supremacy of either Church or state. All their actions were matters of expediency. To finance schools they had made direct land grants, assigned convicts and issued rations; they had accepted Special Purpose Grant funds and subscriptions from the public; they had diverted money from fines and impositions and had made grants from public revenue. To staff the schools, they had used soldiers, convicts, dispossessed missionaries and any other literate person they could find; to accommodate the schools they had used churches, barracks, store-houses and private buildings, and to supervise them, they had used the colonial chaplains.

The first Governor to actually make real progress as opposed to the lazy ideas put forward by Richard Bourke (Governor 1831-1837), was Sir

George Gipps (Governor 1838-1846); from the outset Gipps clearly defined the educational problem and with great clarity wrote a report and recommendation to the Colonial Office Secretary—Lord Stanley.

"The great dispersion of the population of New South Wales, renders a system of education necessary, that shall be as comprehensive as possible. In large towns, or in a densely populated country, separate schools for each Christian denomination can be established, and in a qualified manner may answer the object of their Institution; though if in NSW each separate denomination shall have its separate school, then a large portion of the population shall remain uneducated and out of Sydney, or for the poorer classes of society the shall be scarcely any education at all. Schools are springing up in many of our country towns, but unless they combine they will be but ephemeral."

Establishing the Government System

This period of educating the populous was purely denominational and left to the churches, but as Gipps foresaw, the growth of educating the people should lay with the Government, not the Church, because the Colony was too diverse and sparse, and the cost of education would easily blow out their budget, as could happen to the Colonial budget unless certain limitations were imposed. There had been no provision made for the establishment of schools under State control.

In 1834, the first attempts were made to modify the system in force and by 1839 the first grant was made for the purpose of 'imparting instruction', free from sectarian influences to the children of those who objected to denominational education. It was not until the time of Gipps that any definite steps were made to the educational policy of the State. In that year a committee recommended the adoption of the Irish National School system, and in 1848 an Act created two school boards, and to each respectively was passed the denominational and non-denominational (or National) administration .

This progress commenced the second period of primary education in the Colony. The anomaly of two Boards was abolished in 1866 (the Public Schools Act), after 18 years of operation., and so all schools receiving aid from the State under the control of a Council of Education board. The public schools were totally administered by this board whilst the denominational schools were jointly administered in conjunction with the various religious bodies. Education commenced making considerable progress during this administration. This eventually proved impossible to maintain, because the majority of the people in the Colony were opposed to granting State aid to religious schools, and in 1880 State aid to denominational schools was abolished by Sir Henry Parkes, who had long advocated 'Free, secular and compulsory education'.

Under the Public Instruction Act of 1880, the entire educational system of the state was remodelled. The Council of Education was abolished and all educational matters placed into the hands of a Minister for Education. Provision was made for the establishment and maintenance of public schools, to afford primary instruction to all children without sectarian or class distinction; of superior public schools, in which additional lessons in the higher branches might be given; of evening public schools, with the object of instructing persons who had not received the advantages of primary education while of school age; and of high schools for boys and girls, in which the course of instruction should be of such a character as to complete the public school curriculum, or to prepare students for the university.

Although it was designed to be strictly unbiased it was decided that four hours of tuition each day would be sectarian whilst one hour could be devoted to religious instruction, to be given in a separate class room by a clergyman or religious teacher.

It was compulsory for parents to send their children to school for at least 70 days in each half-year, unless exemption was approved Penalties were provided for breaches. Although considered 'free', parents are required to pay a weekly fee of 3d per child but not to exceed 1s per family. These fees are paid into consolidated revenue. Children were allowed to travel free each way by train. Provision in the Act was also made for training schools, and for regular inspection of school by Local Boards. These boards were designed to review facilities, suspend teachers not performing, and take action on absentee children.

Illiteracy

At the census of 1881, out of the 751,468 people listed, 195,000 were illiterate or 26%. Included were 154,000 children under the age of 4, so there were 41,000 people over the age of 5 who were unable to read (or under 6%).

Of the 5,800 people married in 1857, 28% were illiterate while by 1900 only 1.5% were illiterate.

As of 1901, the number of school age children was 263,835 of which 172,352 were receiving instruction in State schools 12,755 were instructed at home and the rest by church schools. There were 583 students at the University of Sydney, which had been commenced in the 1850s.

The cost per child in attendance in NSW was 4.6.7, compared with Victoria at 4.12.2.

In a debate in the Victorian Parliament (Legislative Assembly) of 12th September, 1872, Attorney-General Stephens introduced a Bill into the House in which the NSW concept of 'free, compulsory and secular' education was adopted for Victorian schools. Stephens stated:

"The political desire to avoid sectarian conflict has always been paramount, but it is not the sole cause of the system; voluntarism, liberalism, and even agnosticism are all influential at a time when the fundamental beliefs of the Christian are being questioned. However, religion is not being driven out of schools. The new policy is to stop tax-payer's money being given to Church schools, to educate voters, and thereby build up prosperity, at a time when the population is increasing rapidly and also dispersing widely in the rural areas. Victoria is to lead the way."

The other Colonies were to follow over the next twenty years.

The Churches, in particular the Catholic Church reacted strongly to these bipartisan moves towards secular education and in a Pastoral Letter in New South Wales the Archbishop reminded his flock that "it is self-evident that education without Christianity is impossible; you may call it instruction, filling the mind with a certain quantity of secular knowledge, but you cannot dignify it with the name education; for religion is an essential part of Education, and to divorce religion or Christianity from Education is to return to paganism, and to reject the Gospels."

So the story of education in Australia is essentially one of neglect for the first One Hundred Years of settlement, during which time it appeared that the challenges of the wide open space of the rural colony and the internal conflicts between Church and State were just too much for the Administrators to handle. In Victoria where the conflict between Church and State ran deeper than any other Colony, the rival claims of denominationalism and secularism to dictate the nature of the education system dominated the debate. State aid to education had increased from 6,000 pound in 1851 to 30,000 in 1853 and despite bitter dispute to 50,000 in 1853, a considerable portion of the Colony's tiny 2 million pound budget of that year.

The debate would continue on in each Colony, even until Menzies in 1964 re-introduced Government contributions to private schools. At least Henry Parkes, in New South Wales, cooled the ardour of the senior churches in the debate and rationalised religious instruction in government schools sufficiently for the children in attendance to get some learning'

<u>THE PASTORAL SYSTEM AND LAND REFORM.</u>

Edward Pulsford, the doyenne of Free Trade in the colony wrote in a learned work on 'Trade & Commerce in NSW'(1892) that

"New South Wales is not great in agriculture, unless the term be used in the wide sense accepted in Great Britain and the United States, where it includes the pastoral industry. It is difficult to say why the distinction should be made in Australia, but at all events it is made. 'Agriculture' in Australia is divided into (1) the pastoral industry (2) agricultural farming and (3) the dairying industry

Agriculture in New South Wales has yet (as of 1892) to achieve great distinction, but steady progress is being made. In 1871 only 417,000 acres were under cultivation; by 1881, it had increased to 710,337, and by

1891 it had grown still further to 1,241,419 acres; about ¼ of the area is under artificially grown grasses. During the last harvest a little over 10 million bushels of grain was grown in the Colony . Maize was the largest grain at 5 million bushels , a little more than sufficient to meet local needs and so a small inter-colonial export trade has commenced; wheat stood at 4 million bushels; hay at 210,000 tons; potatoes at 62,000 tons, and the rest of the acreage is in sugar cane and a small acreage in tobacco.

There is potential for great diversity and the future should hold plenteous bounty for the inhabitants of the Colony and certainly self-sufficiency in food production."

'Wool remains and should continue to remain', wrote Pulsford, in 1892, 'the backbone of our commerce'. Since 1871 the number of sheep has risen to thirty-six million, from sixteen million in that earlier year. in 1871 one-third of the sheep were in NSW, in 1881 there was one-half , in spite of bad seasons. The losses from 1876 to 1885 were twenty-eight million, not including the lambs not realised. The year 1884 was a horror and the biggest drought year seen since the Colony began. In 1871 wool production stood at 65 million lb. Full details are to be found in the Appendix of Statistics.

Up until 1890 the whole of the wool clip had been shipped to London, and dispersed there by public wool sales. Since that time, a growing percentage of the clip is being sold in Sydney to representatives of English, German, French and Belgian wool-spinning firms. This trend is both to the advantage of the producer and the buyer. It is noteworthy that as of 1895 there were no American, Chinese or Japanese buyers in the Sydney markets. The former situation, that of the missing American buyers was of particular concern to the Government of New South Wales, as imports were increasing from that country but without any increase in exports. The Premier of the day, Cowper declared ' trade cannot attain its natural development unless it is conducted on a basis mutually satisfactory to the countries engaged in it; and it cannot be mutually satisfactory if one of the countries finds its products excluded from the markets of the other.'

Agriculture lost some of its gleam during the gold rush years. Being labour intensive and with labour more attracted to the riches under the ground, farmers waited to plant crops until labour was more readily available and a little less expensive. For example the acreage under crop in 1851 was 153,000 but for years 1852-55 the acreage fell to 134,000, but in 1869 it was 469,000 and 1871 fell further (because of the drought) to 417,000. On the other hand, in Victoria during the 1850s agriculture was almost 'extinct'. During this time wheat was being imported from America, Chile, Brazil and Britain, whilst even butter was being imported from Britain. Any farmer who had stayed with agriculture during this time, must have struck greater riches than on the gold field.

In the same way gold excitement delayed agriculture, it also delayed manufacturing, due to the large number of artisans seeking gold in the fields. Yet in the end many new arrivals chasing the gold fever in the Colony, and then returned to paid employment, used their lifelong skills to advance many industries with rapidity that would not otherwise have been possible.

Squatters had first grazed the coastal belt until following the explorers they ranged further and further with their flocks into the inland.

Although the pastoral industry is principally restricted ,in the Australia of pre-1901, to sheep and cattle grazing, our objective is to examine the growth of the sheep and wool industry.

However, we find in the 1874 edition of W. H. L. Ranken's The Dominion of Australia' a keen observation of the cattle industry.

"In the earlier days, before gold was thought of, as herds of cattle increased beyond the capability of their pasturages, they used to be sent out to the nearest unoccupied good country. Thus , the western streams of New South Wales became stocked, and the country occupied. This system arose when cattle were decreasing in value, and when it was therefore indispensable to breed them, at least cost, so that these herds were inferior, they often became wild and unmanageable, and only rose in value when the crowds of gold-diggers arrived and paid any price for meat. But these cattle proved how good all the interior was for stock, and convinced people that the land which seemed a desert, was the most fattening pasture. They discovered 'salt bush' and gave a character to the eastern portion of the great plain which, as the Riverina, it has ever held since. The Riverina became the fattening ground for Victorian meat, and the outlet for squatting enterprise.

History of Sheep Breeding in Australia

From humble beginnings a magnificent industry rose, to lead the way in opening new districts, to creating great wealth, but to stumbling when droughts and floods and plagues of pests transformed the landscape periodically and challenged the strength and commitment of the squatters and pastoralists.

Included in the humble beginnings were 29 sheep brought with the first fleet. Although the great flocks had not sprung from those humble few alone, it is important to set the scene as a witness to a triumph over adversity. Between 1788 and 1800 there were imports of some sheep from India, and in 1823-25 imports came in from Spain. By the end of 1792 there were 105 sheep and by 1796 the numbers had increased to 1,531 sheep; in 1800 there were 1,044 sheep; and 1803 there were 10,157; 1825 there were 237,622 sheep and in 1842, the number was 4,804,946.

year	sheep numbers
1788	29
1792	105
1796	1531
1800	6124
1825	237622
1842	4804946
1850	13059324*4
1861	5615054
1871	16278697
1881	36591946
1891	61,831,416
1900	40,020,506

The average rate of increase for the period was 4.8 %.

It was John Macarthur's breeding for wool types and yield rather than meat that led to a most profitable industry in fine merino wools, readily marketable to English and European manufacturers.

Heavier fleeces came about by an increase in density and length, both leading to a continued improvement in quality. By 1891 it was obvious that the pastures were overstocked and this led to a push for exploration. As well, many sheep were boiled down for tallow and killed for export, with the advent of refrigeration and freezing. Thus in 1894-95 of the decline of 9 million sheep, half was due to the drought and the balance to export and rendering.

The size of flocks took a strange turn towards the end of the century. In 1891 there were 73 holdings carrying more than 100,000 sheep, while in 1897 there were only 21 and in 1900 only 14.

CHAPTER 9

IMMIGRATION & INVESTMENT

The Economic Theory of 19th Century British Investment

Before we can complete the task of identifying capital formation by the British investor (both Public (Government) and Private Investment), let me review a piece by Sir T. H. Farrer (Bart) from his 1887 book ' Free Trade versus Fair Trade'. The notation on the front-piece of the book shows the Cobden Club emblem with the words 'free trade, peace, goodwill among nations'. We will discuss Cobden a little later when we review the work of the Australian Senator Edward Pulsford – another outspoken supporter and devotee of the Cobden philosophy, and free trade and open immigration.

"The amount of English capital constantly employed abroad in private trade and in permanent investments, including Stock Exchange securities, private advances, property owned abroad by Englishmen, British shipping, British-owned cargoes, and other British earnings abroad, has been estimated by competent statisticians as being between 1,500 and 2,000 million pounds, and is constantly increasing. Taking the lower figure, the interest or profit upon it, at 5 per cent, would be 75 million pounds, and at the higher figure it would be 100 million pound."[185]

Farrer then equates this income figure to the spread of imports over exports and finds that the two compare. But then he argues there is the question

[185] Farrer, T.H *Free Trade or Fair Trade*

of freights. "A very large proportion of the trade of the United Kingdom is carried in English ships, and these ships carry a large proportion of the trade of other countries not coming to England. This shipping is, in fact, an export of highly-skilled English labour and capital which does not appear in the export returns of the 19th century, and considering that it includes not only the interest on capital but also wages, provisions, coal, port expenses, repairs, depreciation and insurance; and that the value of English shipping employed in the foreign trade is estimated at more than 100 million pound per annum, the amount to be added to our exports on account of English shipping, must be very large". [186] But he goes further, "add to this the value of ships built for foreigners amounting to over 70,000 ton per annum, worth together several millions, and all these outgoings, with the profits, must either return to this country in the shape of imports, or be invested abroad—I believe 50 million pound is too low an estimate of the amount of unseen exports. In addition there are the commissions and other charges to agents in this country, connected with the carriage of goods from country to country, but each of these items do not appear in the statistics of exports. I can only assume that we are investing large amounts of our savings in the colonies, such as Australia".[187]

The Farrer argument in favour of 'free trade' then turns to the 'fair trade' objections to foreign investments.

Farrer writes "When we point to the indebtedness of foreign colonies to England as one reason for the excess of imports, they tell us that we have been paying for our imports by the return to us of foreign securities; and at the same time they complain bitterly that, instead of spending our money at home, our rich men are constantly investing their money abroad, and thus robbing English labour of its rights here"[188]

But we know that is not the whole story.

When England investors transferred capital to the colonies, it is not only in the form of cash (which would come from savings) but it is more

[186] Farrer *ibid*

[187] Farrer *ibid*

[188] Farrer *ibid*

often in the form of capital goods. England sends iron; the shipbuilders who make the ships that carry the goods, and the sailors who navigate them. When they reach the colonies, what happens then. They return with grain, or coal, or wool, or timber, and that makes those commodities cheaper in England. The investor receives the interest or profits on that capital invested which would generally be greater than what could have been earned if the capital had been invested in England. Now that return can be spent on luxury goods, invested locally or re-invested overseas to commence the whole cycle again. That return will be employed in setting to work English labour, earn a return and so on.

It remains true that on the whole, based on the Farrer argument, the transfer of English capital from an English industry that does not pay to a colonial industry which does pay, is no loss to England generally, and causes no diminution in the employment of English labour. There are at least two drawbacks to colonial investment by a maritime power; one, in the event of a war, the returns would be open to greater risk, and two; the investors can more easily evade taxation by the English Government.

Obviously since 1886, when Farrer constructed this argument, the world has changed, investment opportunities have changed, England has fallen from its pinnacle as a world power and international commercial leader and the improved collection of statistics now recognises movements of goods and investments on both current account and capital account. But the concept helped put the Australian colony on the map and attracted enormous amounts of private capital into the colony to make it grow and prosper.

Farrer concludes his argument with this observation.

"The desire to make profitable investments, however valuable economically, is not the only motive which governs rich men; it's the love of natural beauty; interest in farming and the outdoor life; personal and local attachments; all of which are quite sure to maintain a much larger expenditure on English land than would be dictated by a desire for gain. Let these other motives have their way, as these investors still contribute to the welfare of the toilers and spinners who produce the goods, and make a good return that in the end makes England wealthier"[189]

Factors Affecting British Investment in the Colony

A number of factors affected the level of capital investment into the colony – many were ill informed and relied on delayed newspaper reports on activity in the various settlements.

a. The offer of assisted migration
b. The failing economic conditions in Britain
c. Economic expansion for the pastoral industry due to successful exploration in the colony
d. The settlement at Port Phillip and the eventual separation of Victoria from New South Wales would promote great investment opportunities
e. The rise of the squattocracy
f. The crash of 1827-28 in the colony shakes British Investors
g. The Bigges' Report of 1823 breathed new life into capital formation especially with Macarthur sponsoring the float of the Australian Agricultural Company
h. Further along, the good credit rating of the colonies (and there being no defaults on loans) encouraged larger investments and loans into the colonies
i. Shortage of Labour in the colony and the offer of land grants to new settlers became a useful carrot to attract small settlers bringing their own capital by way of cash or goods or livestock with them.
j. Two other steps had important consequences, one in the colony and the other in Britain. In 1827 Governor Darling began to issue grazing licenses to pastoralists, and the terms were set at 2/6d per hundred acres, with liability to quit on one month's notice. From this movement grew, writes Madgwick in Immigration into Eastern Australia, the squatting movement and the great pastoral expansion, and the idea of the earlier Governors that the colony of New South Wales should be a colony of farmers was thus abandoned. The concurrent event was the floating of the

[189] Farrer *ibid*

Australian Agricultural Company in London. Development by the AAC and by the free settlers brought increasing prosperity. Exports tripled between 1826 and 1831.

k. There is a connection between availability of factors of production and the level of investment. In the early days of the colony, labour was present—bad labour, convict labour, but still labour. The governors had demanded settlers with capital to employ that labour and develop the land. They proposed to limit land grants in proportion to the means of the settler. Governor Darling declared (HRA ser 1, vol 8) that 'when I am satisfied of the character, respectability and means of the applicant settler in a rural area, he will receive the necessary authority to select a grant of land, proportionate in extent to the means he possesses.

Let us examine some of these important elements commencing with the Bigge Report into Agriculture and Trade of the Colony.[190]

1. The Australian Agricultural Company

J.F. Campbell wrote about the first decade of the Australian Agricultural Company 1824-1834 in the proceedings of the 1923 RAHS.

"Soon after Commissioner Bigge's report of 1823 became available for public information, several enterprising men concerted with a view to acquire sheep-runs in the interior of this colony, for the production of fine wool.

The success which attended the efforts of John Macarthur and a few other New South Wales pastoralists, in the breeding and rearing of fine woolled sheep and stock generally, as verified by Bigge, gave the incentive and led to the inauguration of proceedings which resulted in the formation of the Australian Agricultural Company.

The first formal meeting of the promoters took place at Lincoln's Inn, London, (at the offices of John Macarthur, junior).

---

190 Bigge, John Thomas *Commissioners' Report into Agriculture & Trade in NSW – Report No. 1 1823*

Earl Bathurst, advised Governor Brisbane in 1824 that.

His Majesty has been pleased to approve the formation of the Company, from the impression that it affords every reasonable prospect of securing to that part of His Majesty's dominions the essential advantage of the immediate introduction of large capital, and of agricultural skill, as well as the ultimate benefit of the increase of fine wool as a valuable commodity for export.

The chief proposals of the company are:

xiii. The company would be incorporated by Act of Parliament or Letters Patent.
xiv. The capital of the company was to be 1 million pound sterling divided into 10,000 shares of 100 pound each
xv. A grant of land of one million acres to be made to the company
xvi. That no rival joint stock company to be established in the colony for the next twenty years
xvii. That the agents of the company would select the situation or the land grants.
xviii. The shepherds and labourers would consist of 1,400 convicts, thereby lessening the maintenance of such convicts by an estimated 30,800 pound or 22 pound/per head/ per annum

The Royal Charter of 1824 forming the company provided for payment of quit-rents over a period of twenty years, or the redemption of the same by paying the capital sum of 20 times the amount of the rent so to be redeemed. These quit-rents were to be waived if the full number of convicts were maintained for a period of five years. No land was to be sold during the five-year period from the date of the grant".

Being important that the investment be seen to have the support of strong leaders in Britain, and democratic governance, the company operated with

- A Governor
- 25 directors
- 365 stockholders (proprietors)

Leading stockholders included

- Robert Campbell
- Chief Justice Forbes
- Son of Governor King
- Rev Samuel Marsden
- John Macarthur
- Each Macarthur son, John jr, Hannibal, James, Charles, Scott & William

John Oxley, the Colonial-Surveyor had recommended the area of Port Stephens as an eligible spot for the land grant. The local directors inspected and approved the site but John Macarthur was extremely critical of the selection, the management plan and the extravagance of the first buildings.

This venture was the first major investment into the colony and set the scene for later developments. In 1825 the Van Diemen's Land Company was chartered by the British Parliament and granted land on the northwest corner of the territory.

Both the A.A. Coy and the VDL Coy still operate today after nearly 180 years of continuous operation, a record beaten only by the operation of the Hudson Bay Company in Canada.

2. Macquarie's Bank

Nothing quite engenders confidence in an investor like the thought of a new bank opening for business.

Less than three months after his arrival in the colony, Macquarie foreshadowed his plan for a bank on the South African model, as a 'remedy' to 'be speedily applied to this growing evil' of private promissory notes. With some exaggeration he explained that there was 'no other circulating medium in this colony than the notes of hand of private individuals' which, as he said, had 'already been productive of infinite frauds, abuses and litigation'. He accordingly announced his intention to' strongly recommend the adoption here of the same system of banking and circulating medium as is now so successfully and beneficially pursued at the Cape of Good Hope'.

By June 1810 Macquarie had developed his plan for 'The New South Wales Loan Bank' as a government institution ' as nearly as possible on the same system and principles as the Government Loan Bank at the Cape of Good Hope'. There, he explained the government issued notes by way of loan on the security of mortgages at 6 per cent per annum. He also pointed out that in England the government borrowed on exchequer bills at 5 %, so that the Cape was 11% better off. 'It appears to me' was his conclusion, ' the most perfect model in all its parts that could be possibly adopted here' By October 1810, he was willing to accept any alternative form of bank which Liverpool (Secretary for the Colonies) might believe to be 'better calculated to effect the desired object'.

Obviously a Bank would form the foundation for a monetary policy in the colony, and stop the use of Commissary receipt (store receipts) as an exchange mechanism, promote a currency and an official exchange rate for traders and cease to rely on bills drawn on the British Treasury to pay for goods and services.

3. The British Scene

Circumstances in Britain contributed greatly to the climate of 'greener pastures' over the seas.

Conditions were never more favourable for emigration than they were during the 1830s. The decade had opened with rioting in the agricultural districts in the south of England. This was followed by the upheavals of the Reform Bill of 1832, the Factory Act of 1833 and the Corn Laws, which kept wages low and unemployment high. The Poor Law of 1834 withdrew assistance from the poor and re-introduced the workhouse. The Irish rebellion was creating both upheaval and poverty

These conditions were met by the enthusiastic reports coming from Australia of the progress being made in agriculture, commerce and the pastoral industry. The assistance granted to emigrants as a result of Edward Gibbon Wakefield's reforms made possible the emigration of people who had previously been prevented by the expense. It is almost certain that free passage would not have been a sufficient enticement if conditions in Britain had not been unfavourable. It is significant that years of small migration coincided with good conditions in England accompanied by unfavourable reports from the colony.

4. Creating Opportunities in the Colony

Availability of land and labour to yield profit on invested capital is the constant decisive condition and test of material prosperity in any community, and becomes the keystone of an economy as well as defining its national identity.

British Government policy for the Australian colonies was formulated and modified from time to time. Policies for the export of British capital and the supply of labour (both convict and free) were adjusted according to British industrial and demographic and other social situations, as well as the capability and capacity of the various colonial settlements top contribute to solving British problems.

By the 1820s there was official encouragement of British Investment in Australia by adopting policies for large land grants to persons of capital and for the sale of land and assignment of convict labour to those investors. Then followed the reversal of the policy of setting up ex-convicts on small 30 acre plots as small proprietors. The hardship demanded by this policy usually meant these convicts and families remained on the commissary list for support (food and clothing) at a continuing cost to the government. It was much cheaper to assign these convicts to men of property and capital who would support them fully – clothe, house and feed them.

6. What led directly to the crash of 1827?

g. Firstly, the float of the Australian Agricultural Company raised a large amount of capital, mostly from the City of London investment community, and this contributed to speculation and 'sheep and cattle mania instantly seized on all ranks and classes of the inhabitants' (written by Rev John Dunmore Lang) 'and brought many families to poverty and ruin'.

h. When capital imports cease, the wherewithal to speculate vanished; speculation perforce stopped; inflated prices fell to a more normal level, and wrote E.O. Shann in Economic History of Australia 'because those formerly too optimistic were now too despairing, and people had to sell goods at any price in order to get money; men who had bought at high prices were ruined, and perforce their creditors fell with them'.

i. In 1842, it was the same. The influx of capital from oversees, pastoral extension, and large-scale immigration, caused much speculation. The banks, competing for business, advanced too much credit. Loans were made on the security of land and livestock, which later became almost worthless; too much discounting was done for merchants (Gipps, HRA Vol 23) In the huge central district on the western slopes, along the Murrumbidgee and the Riverina, the squatters triumphed, as was inevitable. He had the financial resources to buy his run – especially after the long period of drought. Four million acres of crown land was sold for nearly 2.5 million pound. The confidence of British investors was waning. A crisis in the Argentine and the near failure of the large clearinghouse of Baring's made them cautious. Stories of rural and industrial strife in the colony were not inducements to invest: and wood and metal prices were still falling Loan applications being raised in London were under-subscribed, at the same time, the banks were increasingly reluctant to lend money for land development, which was so often unsound.

7. Assisted Migration

The dual policy of selling land to people with sufficient capital to cultivate it, and keeping a careful check on the number of free grants was adopted after 1825. 'Yet the Colonial Office', says Madgwick, 'failed to administer land policy with any certainty (R.B. Madgwick ' Immigration into Eastern Australia'). There was no uniform policy adopted to encourage economic development in a systematic and rational way. The Wakefield system found new supporters. The principle had been established that the sale of land was preferred to the old system of grants. The dual system of sales and grants had failed to encourage local (colonial) purchases. They were willing to accept grants or even 'squat' rather than purchase land. Sales to absentee landlords and investors stepped up, and as can be seen from the following table, provided extensive revenue to the British Government to promote free and sponsored migration.

Exploration

Successful exploration promotes new interest in the Colony

A period of rapid expansion followed the change in economic policy. Wool exports by 1831 were 15 times as great as they had been only 10 years earlier (in 1821). The increase in the number of sheep led to a rapid opening of new territories for grazing. It was the search for new land with economic value that underpinned most of the explorations. Settlers and sheep-men quickly followed exploration, and growth fanned out in all directions from Sydney town.

However, exploration was not the only catalyst for growth.

a. The growing determination to exclude other powers from the continent stimulated official interest in long-distance exploration by sea and by land and in the opening of new settlements. For instance, J.M. Ward in his work ' The Triumph of the Pastoral Economy 1821-1851' writes that Melville and Bathurst Islands, were annexed and settled between 1824 and 1827, whilst Westernport and Albany were settled in order to clinch British claims to the whole of Australia
b. When Governor Brisbane opened the settlement at Moreton Bay in 1824, it was to establish a place for punishment of unruly convicts and a step towards further economic development, and of extending the settlements for the sake of attracting new investment

8. Colonial Failures fuel loss of Confidence

The collapse of British Investment can be traced to one or two causes, or indeed both.

a. The British crisis of 1839 reflected the availability of capital for expansion by the Australian banks of that day – The Bank of Australasia and the Union Bank. These banks, three mortgage companies and the Royal Bank went into a slump due to shortage of available funds and deferred the raising of new funds until after the crisis. Stringency in the English Capital market had a serious impact on the capital raising opportunities in the colonies.
b. The second possibility is that the sharp decline was initiated by bad news of returns in the colonies, and that its role accentuated a slump with the dire consequences experienced in 1842-43. Recovery was delayed and made more difficult as there was 'no surplus labour in the colony'

It would be dangerous to imply or decide that every slump in Australia could be explained as being caused by economic evens. British investment was independent then, as it is now, and so the more valid explanation of the downturn in British investment in this period is that negative reports from the colonies disappointed and discouraged investors with capital to place.

Most facts about public finance in New South Wales lead to the conclusion that it was disappointed expectations that caused the turn down in the transfer of funds. At this same time Governor Gipps (Sir George Gipps) was being pushed by bankers and merchants to withdraw government deposits from the banks and thus this action caused a contraction in lending by the banks which in turn caused a slow down of colonial economic activity. The attached statistics of land sales, registered mortgages and liens on wool and livestock reflects the strong downturn in the agricultural economy, which naturally flowed on to the economy as a whole.

9. Some Leading Capitalists are drawn to the Colonies

Robert Brooks of whom Frank Broeze has written in 'Mr. Brookes and the Australian Trade' was a 'financier' whose activities were 'wide-ranging, diverse and flexible – he promoted a wide range of commercial business'

Benjamin Boyd used his association with the Royal Bank to influence that bank's policy to channel the capital of small investors into pastoral development in the colonies rather than the earlier policy of chartering the Australian Agricultural Company, whose shareholders were limited in number and based on patronage.

Donald Launach was an auditor in the Bank of New South Wales, which had managed to survive the crisis of the early 1840s. In the 1830s the banks had fuelled an unhealthy boom by offering discounts to customers and by accepting the bills of substantial landowners and merchants who themselves lent or gave credit to others. When in 1850 the British Government approved the separation of Victoria from New South Wales, the government gave the colonies the power to prepare their own constitutions. Larnbach led the way to establish a new bank in the Colony of Victoria, which area could not continue the services of the Bank of New South Wales whose charter restricted its business to that colony. This created an opportunity for new investment and new investors through the granting of fiscal independence to this settlement. As the London-based director of the Bank of New South Wales, Launach used the excellent credit performance of the colonies to raise further loan funds in London. Launach noted in his submissions to the City capital merchants that 'no Australian government has failed to pay interest on loans or repay on maturity in the nineteenth century'. It was a good record in an informed market with many knowledgeable Australians in London to give first hand views.

Henry Turner was another London banker who immigrated to the colony where he joined the Commercial Bank of Australia (CBA) as accountant. Turner would explain to his directors that 'the colonial practice of lending on security of land had grown out of colonial circumstances and was justified in terms of social and economic growth of the colony. Land selection acts before the mid-1850s had created a demand from squatters wishing to protect their possession of land by the judicious purchase of freehold. Rather than leave idle the deposits of the thrifty and prosperous, banks had met these demands, and later extended their organizations to help finance farmers, selectors, small graziers and storekeepers. Had they not done so, write Margot & Alan Beever in a biography of Henry Giles Turner, local enterprise would have been retarded. Instead there was the prospect of the growth of a class of industrious and enterprising agriculturalists, such as in England that might become one of the main sources of funds for investment.

Robert Nivison (the 1st Lord Glendyne) was active in the City of London. He would argue that 'Australians' live on our loans, they trade on our prestige, they presume on our protection; but they make sport of our interests, and do their best to exclude both our produce and our surplus labour'. These attacks elicited several articles defending Australia's credit, as well as further 'atrabilious and unwarranted onslaughts upon Australian manners, morals and money'. The specialist British financial press further weighed in with negative comments. They claimed that the debts of each colony had risen substantially, and found that such levels of indebtedness both ominous and deplorable. It noted that for expanding the railways network in Victoria, that colony borrowed at 4.21% but only earned 3.8% from its investment. For NSW the comparable figures were 3.91% and 3.5%. Only South Australia paid its way, returning 5.26% on money that had been borrowed at 4.08%.

Such attacks inevitably led to a decline of interest in investing in the colonies, and did much to slow the growth of the colonies, especially in the lead up to Federation.

10. Colonial Entrepreneurs

The chosen entrepreneurs are:

1. John Palmer
2. Robert Brookes
3. Thomas Sutcliffe Mort (1835 –1890)
4. Thomas Coghlan
5. Robert Campbell
6. Edward Pulsford
7. Lachlan Macquarie
8. Samuel Marsden
9. Simeon Lord
10. Francis Greenway
11. John Oxley

BRITISH COLONIAL INVESTMENT

In any study of British Colonial Investment one needs to define terms and establish parameters. Terms such as 'Investment' need a definition and a clarification.

For instance, does the term 'investment' include transportees, free immigrants, and supplies for the Colony? The answer is 'yes' to transportees, 'yes' to free immigrants, and 'no' to supplies. In this writer's opinion, human capital is as important as monetary capital.

The definitions will be expanded shortly after setting some parameters for the study. British investment into the new Colony of New South Wales from 1788 came in many guises. The British Treasury funded the ships, the supplies, the military payroll and its support; the civil list included the Governor, the clergy, the medical team, the surveyor, and the advocate-general. These people were salaried and supported. The convicts were clothed and fed. Tools were supplied, as were animals/livestock, building materials, and even a portable canvas 'house' for the Governor. This was the First Fleet.

The Second Fleet was little different. It carried badly needed supplies for a starving colony. The remote settlements of Parramatta, Hawkesbury and Norfolk Island, Windsor and Liverpool, all required investment. This was provided from the grant money allocated by the Treasury to support the Colony.

The first steps taken by Phillip at Sydney Cove – clearing the land, erecting tents, planting crops – are all a mechanism of investment. The second step was to make these facilities 'permanent', in a less temporary way. The crops had failed for want of local knowledge, and the earliest attempts to cut trees for structural timbers was again a failure, because of the inadequate tools and the lack of local knowledge of the moisture content of the trees. The results were that the wood, being undried and erected in a 'green' condition, bowed, twisted and cracked as the wood dried in place. These second steps included the assembly of a kiln for making bricks and tiles, and erection of a windmill, observatory, wharf, and a permanent Government House.

From 1802,only 14 years after establishing the colony, and with the colony still without a 'treasury', Governor King, (Hunter's successor) decided that the need for social services towards the growing orphan population in the colony should be met by local revenue. However, without any form of taxation and without a treasury, the Governor was breaking new ground, and decided to raise the first import duties imposed on the colony.

The first form of indirect taxation attempted in the colony was commenced in 1800 by applying a duty or tariff on all imported items of spirits, wine, and beer, for the purpose of providing funds for completing the erection of a Gaol in Sydney, a work which had previously been carried on by a voluntary assessment, levied in the first instance on the inhabitants of Sydney, but afterwards on the community at large. As the produce of these imposts was found inadequate to complete the work, duties on other articles (of luxury) were resorted to which, with some slight modifications, were continued to be collected under Proclamations of successive Governors till the year 1840. When Governor Macquarie assumed the government in 1810 the population was 11,500 and the duties about 8,000 pound a year. On his retirement from office, in 1821, the population had increased to 29,783 and the port duties to nearly 30,000 pound. This Gaol Fund, as it became known, was the first of the private funds, run on behalf of the Governor, but handled by private individuals – Mr. Darcy Wentworth was appointed to be treasurer of the 'Gaol' Fund sand then its successor, the Police Fund. He retired from this paid post in 1818 . . . During this time he also continued his work as Assistant Surgeon in the colony and as Police Magistrate. He also fathered William Charles Wentworth, one part of the threesome who crossed the Blue Mountains, trained in England as a lawyer, wrote two volumes of observations on the colony, which writings were slanted in favour of John Macarthur, whose son-in-law he had hoped to become.

The Orphan Fund had appointed the Rev Samuel Marsden as treasurer and board member of the Female Orphan Institute.

The parameters of studying British Investment must include an understanding of the source of revenues into the colony. There are three: direct funding by the British Treasury, local colonial revenue and bills drawn, in the colony, on the Treasury in London.

a. The British Treasury funded the

- Civil list (of salaried colonial officials),
- The military personnel
- The commissary (clothing, food, tool and material supplies)
- Convict shipping contracts, and
- Funds for operating the colony.

The attached table shows the funds furnished during this period, by the British Treasury direct and for the Commissary usage, local colonial operations, and the various 'funds'.

b. Local Colonial Revenue, as established for the Orphan, Gaol and Police Funds, were dispersed for items ranging from the purchase of Captain Kent's Home in Sydney for use as a temporary orphan residence, to the new building for female orphans in Parramatta, to improvements at the church of St. John in Parramatta to establishing schools in each of the settlements. The Gaol and Police Funds were used for another wide range of building and maintenance works, including:

- Work on new roads and streets
- Maintenance of roads and streets
- Fencing burial grounds
- Gates and fencing for gaols
- Materials for white-washing gaols
- Apprehending runaway convicts
- Purchasing police house in Newcastle
- Hospital supplies

Until 1835, import duties were over 50% of the colonial revenues and most often in the 70% range. By 1824, sales of crown land had commenced and were growing in importance as a source of revenue for the British Treasury, which maintained full control of the usage of those funds, until self-government in 1852, when they were relinquished as an offset to the colony accepting responsibility for the colonial funding and the civil list.

Reference to the Table 'Expenditure by British Treasury 1788-1835, shows classification of expenditures by

- Government Transport (of convicts to the colony)
- Victuals (stores and food)
- Other stores (tools and materials)
- Bills drawn by the colony on the Treasury
- The Civil Establishment (salaries and allowances)
- The Military and Marine personnel and their allowances

The annual expenditure by the Treasury rose from 18008 pound in 1788 to over 100,000 pound by 1792 before falling to 75,000 in 1795.

The Commissariat fund met obligations for local stores, materials and labour purchased by the Commissary for settlers, convicts and military personnel, with its source of revenue being bills drawn on the Treasury in London, and bartering of goods for goods and services with the farmers and settlers.

c. Bills drawn against the British Treasury were an important source of capital for the colony. It is difficult to imagine how the bills were accounted for in London with any degree of certainty. The first bill drawn on the Treasury was by Phillip who in 1787 was authorized to buy supplies and livestock in the Cape on his passage with the First Fleet to Botany Bay. Once the colony was under development, bills were drawn for a variety of reasons

    - Visiting ships were paid by a bill drawn on London for selling the badly needed provisions for a starving colony
    - Importers, such as Robert Campbell were paid by bills for bring goods and materials from India for use in the colony or for resale
    - The commissary purchased meat (Kangaroo) and vegetables from settlers and farmers, although the 'store receipts' were becoming a medium of exchange in order to eliminate the high discounting of bills trying to be cashed in the colony.
    - Private bills by military officers and traders were becoming of frequent use, except that there was no guarantee of payment

> upon presentment and some traders and settlers faced bankruptcy and many creditors.

So the parameters of our study are broad and must essentially cover the source and use of funds by the British Treasury, but this leaves two missing elements for our study, so we have top broaden it yet further.

- The private investment by the money market operators in London as well as holders of private investment capital needs to be examined and included in the study.
- There is then the important question of the 'opportunity' cost of the British Government 'investment'. Opportunity in this context is the alternative use that these investment funds could be put to; opportunity is also the alternative investment that may have had to be made if, for instance in this case, the colony had not been developable and become self-supporting to the extent that the approx.160, 000 convicts had not been able to be fed, clothed, and put to productive work in the colony. Our analysis of this opportunity cost will include statements as to what cost (thus the 'opportunity' cost) the British Treasury would have faced if a suitable colony had not been found to replace the Americas. Such costs would have included

The cost of building prisons to hold these prisoners, both convicted and held pending trial

The cost of guarding these men and women; and of feeding, clothing and keeping healthy them.

The costs of holding the prisoners in hulks and rotting barges on the English River System

An important cost is the continuing crime that would follow a release of prisoners from British gaols back into the community, as compared with ticket-of-leave or emancipated convicts being released only into the Australian landscape, usually never to see England again.

But what about the positive gains that are derived from opening the colony as a penal settlement with some free settlers. Again there are many and largely quantifiable.

The colony was built by convict labour, who were not paid (other than their 'keep') for their services

The extensive building program of public buildings, wharves, roads and infrastructure (water, drainage and sewerage).

The building program not only provided a useful employment for the convicts but created private industries wanting to supply materials and services for these important public programs.

Emancipated or ticket-of-leave convicts were returned to colonial society and many made significant contributions to the economic and social life of the colony.

The attached table shows the author's estimates of the 'opportunity' cost which estimate is approx 140 million pound.

The British expected their colonies to pay their way

We know that the British authorities had the choice of building new prisons in Britain and housing, feeding, guarding and clothing these prisoners, or relocate them to a 'penal colony'. The previous penal colony in America was no longer available because of the American Wars of Independence and the British were no longer welcome there. The recommendation of Sir Joseph Banks, after his voyage to the southern oceans with Captain James Cook, was to use the land and resources available in the newly charted East Coast of 'Australia'. The favourable opportunity cost of this arrangement was enormous. Britain was fighting wars in a number of areas and had numerous Colonies to administer, and one more Colony; supposedly rich in potential rewards and able to be converted to self-sufficiency was most attractive. So, the opportunity cost was became one form of savings.

By 1824 the convicts were also paying their way (in opportunity cost terms) by removing coal from the ground in the Maitland area and using it for heating purposes. No value was ever placed on this work, nor on the use of convicts as builders of roads, housing, barracks, storage sheds, port wharves, churches and government buildings. It would appear that the convicts earned their keep whilst the Colony paid its own way very quickly. The 'Blue Book' of 1828 states that there was revenue from the sale of convict produce such as 'coal, wheat, sugar, molasses and tobacco' but the value of convict labour was to remain unreported. Historians should recognise the value of the convict work as well as the opportunity cost of having transported the prisoners' offshore, when an assessment is made of the 'investment' made, and the benefits gained by Britain in the new Colony of New South Wales.

The original estimate of direct gains by the British authorities from the original and continuing investment in the Colony of New South Wales was based on 5 (five) identifiable and quantifiable events, even though the convicts were assigned jobs on the basis of 'full keep'.

1. The opportunity cost of housing, feeding and guarding the convicts in the Colony compared with the cost of doing the same thing in Britain.
   The original estimates, in this category, were based on an estimated differential of ten pound per head—an arbitrary assessment of the differential cost.
   However recent and more reliable information has come to hand which gives further validity to a number of 20 pound per head per annum, compared with the original 10 pound per head per annum.
   A letter to Under Secretary Nepean, dated 23rd August 1783, from James Maria Matra of Shropshire and London assists us in this regard.
   It was Matra, who first analysed the opportunity of using the new Colony as a Penal Colony; only his estimates were incorrect and ill founded. He had advised the Government that it would cost less than 3,000 pound to establish the Colony initially, plus transportation cost at 15 pound per head and annual maintenance of 20 pound per head.

In fact the transportation was contracted for the second fleet at 13 pound 5 shillings per head and Colonial revenues from 1802 offset annual maintenance.

However, Matra made a significant statement in his letter to Nepean, when he pointed out that the prisoners housed, fed and guarded on the rotting hulks on the Thames River were being contracted for in the annual amount of 26.15.10 per head per annum. He also writes that 'the charge to the public for these convicts has been increasing for the last 7 or 8 years' (Historical Records of NSW—Vol 1 Part 2 Page 7)

Adopting this alternative cost (of 26.75 pound) as a base for comparison purposes, it means that the benefit to Britain of the Colony over a twenty-year period increased from 140,000,000 pound to 180,000,000 pound. This calculation assesses the Ground 1 benefit at 84,000,000 pound.

2. Benefit to Britain on Ground Two is put at 70, 000,000 pound (again over a 20-year period) which places the value of a convict's labour at 35 pound per annum. Matra had assessed the value of labour of the Hulk prisoners at 35. 85 pound.
3. The valuation of convict labour in the new Colony should reflect the convicts not only used on building sites, but also on road, bridge and wharf construction. This would add (based on 35 pound per annum) a further 21,000,000-pound.
4. The Molesworth Committee (A House of Commons Committee investigating transportation) concluded that "the surplus food production by the convicts would feed the Military people and this, over a period of 10 years, would save 7,000,000 pound for the British Treasury.
5. The benefits of fringe benefit grants of land to the Military etc can be estimated (based on One pound per acre) at over 5,000,000 before 1810.
6. We learn from Governor King's Report to Earl Camden (which due to a change of office holder, should have been addressed to Viscount Castlereagh as Colonial Secretary) dated 15th March 1806 that the Convicts engaged in widely diverse work. The Report itself is entitled

"Public Labour of Convicts maintained by the Crown at Sydney, Parramatta, Hawkesbury, Toongabbie and Castle Hill, for the year 1805

Cultivation—Gathering, husking and shelling maize from 200 acres sowed last year—Breaking up ground and planting 1230 acres of wheat, 100 acre of Barley, 250 acres of Maize, 14 acres of Flax, and 3 acres of potatoes—Hoeing the above maize and threshing wheat.

Stock—Taking care of Government stock as herdsmen, watchmen etc

Buildings—

- At Sydney: Building and constructing of stone, a citadel, a stone house, a brick dwelling for the Judge Advocate, a commodious brick house for the main guard, a brick printing office
- At Parramatta: Alterations at the Brewery, a brick house as clergyman's residence
- At Hawkesbury: completing a public school
- A Gaol House with offices, at the expense of the Colony
- Boat and Ship Builders: refitting vessels and building row boats
- Wheel and Millwrights: making and repairing carts

Manufacturing: sawing, preparing and manufacturing hemp, flax and wool, bricks and tiles

Road Gangs: repairing roads, and building new roads

Other Gangs: loading and unloading boats"

(Historical Records of NSW—Vol 6 P43)

Thus the total benefits from these six (6) items of direct gain to the British comes to well over 174 million pound, and this is compared to Professor N. G. Butlin's proposal that the British 'invested' 5.6 million.

However, one item of direct cash cost born by the British was the transportation of the prisoners to the Colony, their initial food and general well being. Although the British chartered the whole boat, some of the expense was offset by authorising private passengers, 'free settlers' to travel in the same fleet. A second saving was the authorities had approved 'back-loading' by these vessels of tea from China.

Only limited stores and provisions, tools and implements were sent with Captain Arthur Phillip, the appointed first Governor, and his efforts to delay the fleet until additional tools were ready was met with an order to 'commence the trip forthwith'. This turned out to be a mistake as the new Colony could only rely on minimal farming practices to grow a supply of vegetables and without the tools to scratch the land, remove the trees and vegetation, little progress was made. This was a potentially big cost to the fledgling Colony.

i. The 'Blue Book' accounting records as maintained by Governor Macquarie from 1822 includes a reference to 'net revenue and expenses' which suggests an offset of all revenues against all expenses, and would include as revenue certain convict maintenance charges, to be reimbursed by the British Treasury. Such reimbursement was accounted for and reported only once—in 1825, when it is recorded as a 'receipt in aid of revenue' that an amount of 16,617 pound 'the amount of the parliamentary grant for the charge of defraying the civil establishment'. Prior to and since that date, there are only reports of payments and outgoings to the civil establishment, military and other personnel, without offset from reimbursement.
ii. Other notations in 1825 include revenues from rentals of government assets (Government outsourcing and privatisation obviously started back in 1825) such as;

£	
Ferries	1584
Toll gates	6554
Gardens	1835
Mill	1749
Canteen	910
Church pews	1296

The hire of convict 'mechanics' raised £6853.27 pound

Slaughtering dues contributed £975.54 whilst duty on colonial distillation reaped £4901.30 pound.

The biggest revenue earners were duty on imported spirits (£178,434 pound) and duty on imported Tobacco (£21,817 pound)

i. Even in 1822 the Colony was showing a small operating surplus. This surplus grew through 1828 until, other than for transportation of convicts to the Colony, the charges on account of the British Treasury were less than One Hundred Thousand pounds for protecting, feeding and housing nearly 5,000 fully maintained convicts. Against this cost, the charge for housing, feeding and guarding this same number of prisoners in Britain would have been substantially higher, since in addition to the 5,000 gully maintained convicts there were a further 20,000 being paid for by free settlers and used as supervised labour. Britain surely had found a cheap source of penal servitude for at least 25,000 of its former prisoners, and found a very worthwhile alternative to the American Colonies as a destination for its prisoners.
j. Revenue from Crown Land sales and rents was used to offset Civil (Crown) salaries and expenses.

The opportunity cost to the British Treasury includes not only the cost savings but also the lateral savings and benefits produced for England and the British Treasury.

Some of the other advantages to Britain include:

a. The build-up of trade by the East-India Company
b. The advantage of a secure, in-house, supply of raw wool, to keep the spinning mills occupied
c. The opportunity cost of housing, feeding and guarding prisoners
d. The use of convict labour in the new Colony, for such as

- Land clearing, farming, food production
- For road construction
  Building projects such as:
- Public wharves

- Barracks
- Public Buildings
- Productions of Materials supply eg brick & tile production.
- As unpaid day labour for the pastoral & agricultural industry.

e. We can assume that Land grants, in the Colony, to men on the military and civil list was a form of 'fringe benefits' and should be quantified as an alternative to paid remuneration for these people. Even land grants to emancipists were used as an incentive to increase food production.

f. We can quantify items C, D and E into a 'value of direct gain to the British economy of nearly 140,000,000 pound (refer details in 'Statistics'), compared with the publicly recorded expenditure on transportation, supplies, and military personnel of 5,600,000 pound, between 1788 and 1822.

The purposes of trying to quantify these benefits are to challenge to traditional concept that 'the British invested millions of pounds in the Colony of New South Wales'.

It is obviously only the case when the outlay is shown and not the on-going benefits for over fifty years, and indeed two hundred years. It is still arguable that the Continent of Australia is, in Captain Arthur Phillip's words ' the best investment Britain will ever make'.

Having established the parameters for studying British (private and public) investment in the Colony of New South Wales, the question must now be one of who else thinks this investment was of interest and relevance.

N.G. Butlin did not complete his manuscript of 'Forming a Colonial Economy' because his death in 1991.

However his notes to that time were edited and assembled into the book form and we can learn a great deal about the British motives for the colony and its economic development.

Butlin writes "Even though, there may have been other imperial motives behind the British settlement of Australia, there is no doubt that the transportation of convicts to the Antipodes was a convenient solution to social, judicial and budgetary problems in Britain in the 1780s"

Butlin further deduces that "Persons may move between countries (i.e. immigration) when the capitalized value of the differential in expected lifetime earnings abroad as compared with those at home exceeds the transfer and relocation costs." The good news of free immigration and the capital transfer into the colony was that between 1788 and 1800 is that 21,302 'free immigrants' arrived in the colony. There are 9 identified categories of 'immigrants' during this period.

- Military and civil officers and their families
- Former officials returning to the colony
- Convict families
- Indentured labourers
- Assisted immigrants
- Privately supported persons sponsored by colonials
- Free immigrants and their families

Given that Britain provided not only human capital but also fiscal resources to support the people concerned, the volume, nature and access to those resources became interesting. However, it remains the case that Britain, having put into place extensive levels of capital, certainly succeeded in withdrawing a great deal of its early fiscal support and bringing the Commissariat effectively under military control.

Obviously another form of 'investment' is public debt, and public borrowing, secured by the full faith and credit of the colonial government

The 'works outlay' is another element of 'public investment' and was not fully accounted for until 1810, upon the arrival of Governor Macquarie. From that date, works outlay (i.e. Capital expenditure from the revenue of the local colony) grew annually from 2194 pound (1810) to 14700 pound (1821). However this is a small component of total works outlay or capital expenditure, since a Mr. Henry Kitchen, in a submission to

Commissioner J.T. Bigge stated that his estimate of building construction under Macquarie was in excess of 900,000 pound.

A table included in Australians Historical Statistics refers to 'Gross Private Capital Formation at current prices do not commence until 1861 and later in this study we will try to accumulate both public and private capital formation from 1800 – based on a separate studies of colonial industrial development and colonial building and construction development. This table is derived from Butlin's 'Australian Domestic Product, Investment & Foreign Borrowing 1861-1938'. It appears that no previous studies have been undertaken of Private or Public Capital Formation between 1788 and 1861.

T.A. Coghlan is generally recognised as a significant contributor to Colonial Economic History and he writes in Volume 1 of 'Labour and Industry in Australia' of another phase of Public Investment, or its encouragement in the colony, by favourable official policies.

Coghlan writes "Under the Governorship of Macquarie the infant town of Sydney grew considerably. King had been the first Governor to grant leases there (Sydney), but as the leases were only for five years the buildings erected were naturally not of a substantial character. Macquarie granted a number of leases also, but gave permanent grants of land in cases where valuable buildings were to be erected, so that at the end of his term of office Sydney had grown considerably, having the appearance, according to W.C. Wentworth in his Historical and Statistical Account of the Colony, of a town of 20,000 inhabitants though its population, numbered only 7,000; and while the houses were for the most part small one-storied dwellings, it contained buildings, private and public, excellent both in construction and in design, and many stores where goods of all kinds could be bought. The Government Store continued in existence as a shop open to the public until January 1815, when Macquarie, considering that its purpose had been served as a means towards keeping down prices, closed it to all except the military and the convicts in government employment"[191]. So having fixed the short-term land lease, Macquarie actively encouraged public and private investment in building and construction.

[191] Coghlan, T.A. *Labour & Investment in Australia Vol 1*

Coghlan provides an insight into another Macquarie step to encourage investment. He writes "Until Macquarie arrived, the means of communicating between one part of the settlement and another was difficult, as all roads were poor. Macquarie had a passion for construction, and his roads were excellent. He made a turnpike road from Sydney to the Hawkesbury, completing it in 1811. Now goods and passengers did not have to be carried by boat, as previously was the case. A few years later he constructed the great road over the mountains to the western plains, and also extended his roads in other directions. With the construction of the roads, internal trade and all the industries dependent thereon developed. It took a further time before travelling by road was safe, as many convicts escaped and took to the bush, preying upon defenceless travellers; journeys to any part of the settlement was usually made in company and it was customary to make even the short journey from Sydney to Parramatta about 14 miles in parties."[192]

If we intend to extend our parameters to further analyse the types and amount of public and private British Investment in the colony of New South Wales, we will have to now review certain other matters:

- The development of private industries eg boat-building; timber harvesting and processing; agriculture sand pastoral pursuits, whaling and overseas trading – all of which were reasonably capital intensive operations, and which would have attracted both overseas investors and a local breed of entrepreneurs
- The development of building and construction in the colony, including reference to the public buildings completed in the period, how much they would have cost and how they were paid for.
- We will try to assemble a table of public and private overseas (British) investment, and establish the background to debt in the colony from overseas sources.
- We will attempt to recreate the level of Investment in the colony by category by first identifying the various sources of both public and private investment and relating value to each one

---

192 Coghlan *ibid*

- We will endeavour to track bank deposits and advances, which until the 1850s were generally in the negative (i.e. advances exceeded deposits and it fell to the local banks to accept British deposits for fixed terms of 1,2 or 3 years. Banks advanced money by way of pastoralists' overdrafts, on city land and on stocks and shares. Land banks offered mortgages. Banks liabilities before 1850 by way of term deposits from overseas depositors were almost 40 million pound.
- One gauge of how much money was flowing through the domestic economy is the volume of cheques, bills and drafts passing through the clearing-house. By the 1860s, this amount had risen to almost 6 million pound each week.
- Coghlan's 'Wealth and Progress of NSW' for 1900 reflects on the source and disposition of Public Capital and can be tabulated as follows:[193]

Source of Funds

Treasury bills & debentures	81688554
Transfer from Consolidated Rev.	1668640
Sum Available for Expenditure	82430777

Use of Funds

• Railways	40450473
• Tramways	2720338
• Telegraphs	1255600
• Water supply & Sewerage	9878833

[193] Coghlan, T.A. *Wealth & Progress in NSW 1900*

Catalysts for Immigration

Free Immigration into the Colony – A New Perspective

Introduction

The need for education in the colony is an interesting pre-emptive to the need for free immigrants. Immigration would help solve numerous gaps in the colony—capital and labour, societal demands and the imbalance of men and women, the demand for a free enterprise economy and 'foreign' investment. The direct association then as now, between education and investment, knowledge and growth is unmistakeable. It was largely left to Macquarie to juggle the need for balance in the penal colony, but this was not a high priority and it was passed to Brisbane and then Bourke. Before migration could be practiced, thought Macquarie, I need to rid the streets of the waifs, orphans and unwanted children of a largely immoral society. Bligh had first drawn official attention to the deteriorating social fabric with 3 times as many 'kept' as married women, the dazzling count of illegitimate children compared with those that numbered in the legitimate category. Education would help not only with this social dilemma but also with the illiteracy that was rampant in the colony. The three Rs were down to one R and 'riting was largely limited to an X on the spot.

Education, a construction program, local discretionary revenue raising and elimination of spirits as the currency of the day, were Macquarie's top priorities – only then could free immigrants be welcomed. Of course a bank would be helpful in cementing the colony as a land of opportunity. The English thought in terms of symbols even if they were thin.

So, in this paper on free immigration, understanding the needs for education as a precursor to establishing a migration policy will set the scene. The economy was at the top of the triangle pointing the way ahead. That 'the colony has no treasury' was a disincentive to migration, and Macquarie believed in balancing finely the needs of a despotic governor and the daily demands on government with the desire for free enterprise. Macquarie had decided that government had the need and responsibility to encourage and sponsor exploration, and it was the crossing of the mountain range west of Sydney town that inspired and commenced the first sustained economic expansion in the colony. The pastoral movement led the way for encouraging migration. The financing mechanism for the new policy was the sale of crown or 'waste' lands. The boom and bust syndrome was set in place by speculators in both land and livestock. The market economy would be in tatters within 20 years of Macquarie's exit.

This is the story of the need for education and a sound economy leading to migration as a catalyst for growth in the 'new' economy.

The early days of Education

A.G. Austin in Australian Education 1788-1900 offers an explanation as to the lack of interest in educating the lower classes.

"Nowhere in Phillip's Commissions or instructions was any mention made of the children accompanying the First Fleet, or of the child convicts whom the British Government saw fit to transport, for it was alien to the official mind of the late 18th century to feel any interest in the welfare of these children. By 1809 the War Office had been persuaded to appoint regimental schoolmasters, but in 1788 the education of these children formed no part of the business of any department of state.

The conservative opinion in Britain was convinced that education was exactly the wrong remedy and agreed with the Bishop of London's conviction that it was 'safest for both the Government and the religion of the country to let the lower classes remain in that state of ignorance in which nature has originally placed them'.

In this atmosphere anyone who undertook the education of the poor became an object of suspicion. Even the devout Hannah Moore had to defend her schools against charges of Methodism, Calvinism and subversion. Ms. Moore wrote: 'they learn such coarse work as may fit them as servants. I allow no writing for the poor. My object is to train up the lower classes in habits of industry and piety'. Nearly a century later John Stuart Mill still thought it necessary to warn his readers that 'a general state education . . . established a despotism over the mind'.

The Pitt Tory Government resisted those favouring State intervention in education. They saw no reason to meddle in the upbringing of other people's children, and no reason to suppose that the new Governor of NSW would presume to dispute their opinion.

The early governors of NSW soon found it necessary to change their adoption of British policies, especially regarding education in the colony, since Britain was not a fragment of English society transplanted, but a military and penal garrison in which the governors were responsible for every detail of daily life. In a settlement where the maintenance of discipline, the regulation of food production, the rationing of supplies, the employment of labour, and the administration of justice were necessarily committed into one man's hands, there was no room for that laissez-faire indifference which characterized the conduct of public affairs in Britain.

Not only were the governors moved by the misery of the convicts' children but also they realized that the future of the colony had to be built upon these children. In a colony where there was three times the number of men as there were women, a deplorably high proportion of illegitimate and abandoned children required some measure of protection and supervision. In 1807 on Bligh's testimony, there were 387 married women in the colony, 1,035 concubines, 807 legitimate children and 1,024 illegitimate children.

Phillip had set aside, near every town, an allotment for a church and 400 acres adjacent for the maintenance of a minister and 200 Acres for the schoolmaster. However the governors were not really concerned to assert the supremacy of either Church or State. All their actions were matters of expediency. To finance schools, they made direct grants of land, assigned convicts and issued rations. To staff schools they had used soldiers, convicts, missionaries and other literate person they could find. To accommodate the schools, they used churches, barracks, storehouses and private buildings. It was Macquarie who first set down the staging order of divinity. All clerics would be, for the first time, from 1810, responsible to the principal chaplain.

By the end of the Macquarie era, many changes had been made to the social order in the colony, including education, and most of these changes were in principal accepted by J.T. Bigge in his reports to the British Commissioners. Bigge's reported that ' the flow of immigrants and the increasing number of emancipated convicts has so increased the population of free settlers that the prosperity of the settlement as a colony has proportionately advanced, and hopes may reasonably be entertained of its becoming perhaps at no distant period a valuable possession of the crown. This makes me think that it is no longer fit for its original purpose'.

For public education to be considered as a government responsibility and controlled by a cleric meant that part of the cost could be defrayed by public revenue. The suggestions made by the new Archdeacon (Hassall – Marsden's future son-in-law) of the colony were that public education be controlled by a cleric who was also placed at the head of the Church Establishment. The costs could be defrayed, was the suggestion, by the parents contributing, annually, a ' bushel of good clean sound wheat, or equivalent value in meat, or 1/8th of the colonial import duty could be diverted to education; governments could subdivide its land at Grose Farm, Emu Plains, Rooty Hill and Cabramatta into small farms and apply their rents to the endowment of schools in general'. The last suggestion and the one that attracted Lord Bathurst's ear was that a 'new land reserve of some 25,000 acres should be established near Bathurst or Newcastle'.

The British Government ultimately decided in 1825 to direct Governor Brisbane to form a 'corporation and invest it with clergy and school estates, and from the proceeds it should support the Anglican Church and schools and school masters in connection with the established church' The territory of NSW was to be divided into counties, hundreds, and parishes as a result of a survey of the whole colony. The Corporation was not a success largely because it was never properly funded the way it was expected, nor did it enjoy the high enthusiasm or interest of the governor.

Macquarie 'reported' to Viscount Castlereagh on 30th April 1810 on the progress in carrying out British instructions

'In pursuance to your Lordship's instructions, I lost no time in directing my attention to the principal object pointed out in them, namely, to improve the morals of the colonists, to encourage marriage, to provide for education, to prohibit the use of spirituous liquors, and to increase the agriculture and livestock so as to ensure a certainty of supply to the inhabitants under all circumstances'. In his next dispatch Macquarie reported that 'with a view to the decent education and improvement of the rising generation, I have established several schools at head quarters and the subordinate settlements, which I trust will not fail of being attended with very desirable effects'. He also requested 'a few more chaplains and some additional schoolmasters which are very much required, and it would be very desirable if some should be sent out as soon as possible'.

Alan Barcan in his imaginative work 'History of Australian Education' notes that, in line with regular military policy the NSW Corps brought their own tutor with them for teaching the children of military personnel. No such luxury was available for the residents of Norfolk Island. In 1793, Lieutenant King (Governor of the island) established an import duty on liquor in order to raise funds for education. King built the first stone schoolhouse in 1794 and a second in 1795. Collins records ('An Account of the English Colony in NSW') that 'the first school was for young children, who were instructed by a woman of good character; the second was kept by a man, who taught reading, writing, and arithmetic, for which he was well qualified, and was very attentive'.

In Sydney Governor Hunter met with the school children each year, and as David Collins records, in 1797, Hunter inspected the children from three schools and 'was gratified with the sight of 102 clean and decently—dressed children, who came with their several masters and mistresses'.

In 1798, the Rev'd Richard Johnson (the first cleric in the colony, who had arrived with the First Fleet) amalgamated the three schools in Sydney and the three joint teachers held classes in the church. They had 150 to 200 children enrolled of 'all descriptions of persons, whether soldiers, settlers, or convicts' (/Johnson's Rules). After the Church was burnt down on 1st October 1798, it moved to the courthouse and then to a disused warehouse, but enrolments halved.

King, as a subordinate and assistant to Hunter, also opened an Orphan Institution in 1795 when by this time there were 75 destitute children. These children were taught, fed, clothed, and given vocational training.

When King arrived to take over as Governor in 1800, he continued his deep interest in education and 'education expanded significantly'. (Barcan). There were three main reasons for this expansion.

a. King himself took a deep interest in education and brought with him the experience gained from his Norfolk Island success
b. Increased colonial prosperity and better financial provision. King imposed an import duty on goods to establish a fund for education. When the Female Orphan Fund opened in August 1801, there were 54 girls aged from 7 to 14 in the school. In August 1804, King gave it an endowment of 13 000 acres to secure its economic stability. Samuel Marsden, its Treasurer and religious guardian commented that the Orphan School is 'the foundation of religion and morality in this colony'
c. The growth of population, which produced both the need for and the ability to sustain schools. By 1800 Sydney was a town of 2 000 and the colony had some 5 000 inhabitants. Significance could be seen in the

    - Growth of a small commercial middle class,
    - The publication of the Sydney Gazette, which offered an avenue for expression of opinion
    - A 'distinction' between state-aided 'public schools' and 'private' education

Vocational training was possibly the most important challenge and target of the education system. In 1798, Hunter reported that young male convicts had been assigned to an 'artificer's gang in order that they may be useful mechanics'. In 1805, King developed a system of apprenticeships for boys. In the same year advertisements appeared in the Sydney Gazette for apprentice seamen. The Female Orphan School developed some vocational training for the girls by offering 'needlework, reading, spinning and some few writing'. A few of the girls became servants with them being 'bound as apprentices to officer's wives'.

The overall shortage of labour in the colony caused vocational training to make only slow progress.

Immigrants and Free Settlers

Collins records that on the 15th January 1793, the Bellona transport ship, arrived in Sydney Harbour with a cargo of stores and provisions, 17 female convicts and five settlers one of whom was a master wheel-wright employed by the governor at a salary of 100 pound per annum. A second was a returning skilled tradesman who had been previously employed as a master blacksmith. All five settlers had brought their families.

Collins conjectures that these first five settlers had received free passage, a promise of a land grant and assistance with farming, as the incentive for becoming the free settlers,

Manning Clark (A History of Australia) records that in 1806, 'a dozen families from the Scottish border area arrived as free emigrants and each received 100 acres of land on the banks of the Hawkesbury River in a place they called Ebenezer. They were devout Presbyterians, and were allowed to worship in the colony according to their own lights'. However the authorities were not prepared to tolerate the practice of the catholic religion, because they saw it 'as an instrument of mental slavery, a threat to higher civilization, and a threat to liberty' (Clark Vol 1)

Free Immigrants 1788-1810

Insert Table (refer 'Australian History' Bessant)

Developing Immigration

Even by the census of 1828, NSW had fewer than 5,000 people who had come out voluntarily, in a population of 36 598. The colony had the attractions unavailable in the USA, free land and convict labour. Settlers were given land for agriculture and pasture usage. This meant freehold land, and it only applied to men who had immigrated as private citizens, to military officers who had decided to stay and to pardoned convicts who had been granted land.

In 1831, the British Government, against the opposition of many in the colony decided to stop giving away land grants to settlers and chose instead to 'sell' the land and use some of the proceeds to sponsor migrants to the colony. The initial sales price was 5 shillings an acre. It was a way of inducing poor families to leave the country, but as well of relieving the labour shortage. Between 1831 and 1840 about 50,000 prisoners were transported and about 65,000 free men and women chose to emigrate

The balance of the sexes was more equal amongst emigrants than among convicts: but even South Australia, which was wholly an emigrant's colony, had only 8 females for every 10 males by 1850, and in Australia as a whole there was fewer than 7 for every ten. The resulting challenge was only partially met by Caroline Chisholm who met every convict and emigrant ship to stress the dangers to young unmarried women. Her main accomplishment was to convince the Colonial Office, in 1846, to offer free passage to all families of convicts resident in the colony. Her detractors suggested that the result of her efforts towards convict families and emigrating poor families would be to create an imbalance of Catholics in the colony, who were already twice the proportion of the Australian population as they were in England.

'Populate or Perish'

The history of Australia is bound tightly into two aspects—the economics of colonization and the story of immigration.

The first free immigrants came out on the Bellona, and were given small landgrants on Liberty Plains (the Strathfield-Homebush area). The first family to arrive included a millwright who had been on the hulks in Britain for a minor crime and been released. It was Major Grose, acting as the Administrator after the departure of Phillip, who observed ' from some dirty tricks he has already attempted, I fear he has not forgotten all he learned as a former prisoner. He is evidently one of those that his country could well do without'.

Governor King wrote in his report – The State of the Colony in 1801 – on the subject of free immigrants:

"Settlers are of two classes i.e. those who come free from England and those who were convicts and whose terms of transportation are expired, or who are emancipated. Of the first class, I am sorry their industry and exertions by no means answer the professions they made in England, several of whom are so useless to themselves and everyone about them that they were not only a burden to the public but a very bad example to the industrious. As they brought no other property than their large families, many have been and will continue an expensive burden on the public, or starve. The settlers are maintained by the crown for eighteen months and have two convicts assigned to each, which is very sufficient to provide against the time of doing for themselves, but that period too often discovers their idleness and incapacity to raise the least article from a fertile and favourable climate, after having occasioned an expense of upwards of 250 pound for each family, exclusive of their passage out The desirable people to be sent here are sober, industrious farmers, carpenters, wheel and mill wrights, who having been used to draw their food from the earth, secure sand manufacture it, would here find how bountifully their labour would be rewarded".

It appears that King did not have a very high opinion of the potential for free migration to the colony.

Phillip's successor – Governor Hunter—was instructed by the Colonial Office to 'encourage free settlers without subjecting the public to expense'. They were to be given larger land grants than the emancipists and as much convict labour as they wanted. Hunter observed in one of his submissions to the Secretary of the colonies that 'free immigrants would not come to the country whilst the needs of the colony were supplied from Government farms'.

The economic factors hit the immigration concept in 1801 when Governor King, as Hunters successor wrote to the Duke of Portland, as Colonial Secretary and suggested family immigration. It was turned down on the basis that transporting a family would cost 150 pound and annual maintenance until they were self-supporting would cost 250 pound (HRNSW)

In 1802, the HRNSW records that free settlers (28 in one group) arrived by the Perseus and Coromandel. More came in the Navy ship Glatton, including a person supposedly bearing 'perfect knowledge of Agriculture, having held a very considerable farm in his hands, but which through youthful indiscretion, he found it necessary to relinquish'. The governor was asked to place him 'above the common class of settlers'. The government, Governor King wrote 'was much imposed on' by these free settlers. The Glatton settlers were sent to the Nepean, where they were wrote King ' going on with great spirit and well applied industry'

King reported to Lord Hobart in 1804 that 'there were 543 free settlers supporting 351 wives and 589 children and utilising 463 convicts'. Further free settlers are recorded as being in the William Pitt in 1805, mainly because land and subsistence was being replaced by the lure of wealth coming from the fine wool being promoted by John Macarthur. This endeavour and attraction of wealth brought a different and probably better class of free settler – the Blaxland brothers arrived on a charter vessel with their families, servants and capital of over 6,000 pound. Again the governor received instructions. 'They are to be allowed 8,000 acres of land and the services of up to 80 convicts for 18 months at the commissary store's expense. Governor Bligh was given similar instructions in reference to a 'lady of quality' – a Mrs Chapman, a widow, Governess and teacher. Bligh was directed to 'afford her due encouragement and assistance'. The next governor, Lachlan Macquarie took a different stance – he discouraged free immigration, probably because the flow of convicts was almost overwhelming his administration. His position is not readily understandable. As a quasi social reformer and developer of free enterprise in the colony, one would have expected Macquarie to welcome free settlers for what social and economic values they could contribute. When the Bigge report was published in London, it raised the interest of men of wealth in the colony and a Lieutenant Vickers, an officer of the East India Company, volunteered to emigrate with 10,000 pound of capital, an unblemished reputation and a purity of private life ' not previously known in any class of society', and in return demanded privileges by way of land grants, livestock and a regular seat at the governor's table. Brisbane, as governor, was directed by Lord Bathurst as Colonial secretary to give Vickers 2,000 acres of land and a house allotment near Newcastle. Brisbane investigated Vickers and found him to be little more than 'an adventurer, a bird of passage, and boycotted by his fellow officers'. Marjorie Barnard concluded, 'Only distance made his deception possible'. Opportunities followed good publicity, and the floating of the Australian Agricultural

Company in London in 1823 did much to promote the colony in Britain, and brought another spate of free settlers to the colony.

This then is the early trend in the free settler movement – it had not been seen yet as a government opportunity. But that was about to change. Lord Bathurst came along with an idea, urged by the Wakefield supporters and the rash of economists waging war on the increasing unemployment, poverty and lack of investment opportunities in Britain.

A privately sponsored scheme was funded by a loan to Dr. J.D. Lang by the governor in the amount of 1,500 pound, which brought out 100 selected 'mechanics' (semi-skilled labourers) and their families. Lang used a charter vessel to transport these immigrants, and the understanding was that the immigrants would repay their expenses from future wages. In 1831 this was an inspiring move to privatising a government policy.

Three factors were set to establish an on-going immigration policy. The three factors were bad times in England; shortages of skilled labour of both men and women in the colony; and the cessation of the assignment system.

A commission on Emigration was established in England to select and despatch suitable agricultural labourers. A plan to tax landowners of assigned convicts failed when the difficulty of collection was recognised. There were still 13,400 convicts on assignment in 1831.

The governor agreed that official funds would contribute 20 pound towards each immigrant family and try to recover it after the family settled. The collections were rarely made.

It was left to Governor Bourke to formulate a workable plan. The 'bounty system' relied on sponsored workers funded by government. The government paid 12 pound out of the 17 pound passage money. The Emigrants Friendly Society existed in Sydney to help and protect these sponsored migrants.

A more refined method was needed to select and sponsor these migrants. Glenelg reformed the financial side in 1837. He allocated the revenue from land sales in the colony as a means of affording immigration. The land as well as any revenue derived from its sale, lease or rental, had remained the property of the crown, not the colonial administration. Two-thirds of these funds were to be allocated to migrants by way of grants – 30 pound for a married couple, 15 for an unmarried daughter, 5 and10 pound for children depending on age.

The zenith of immigration success could be seen in the 1830s under Governor Gipps. Land revenue was high, the colony was prosperous and plenty of migrants were on offer and the colony could successfully absorb them. The severe drought at the end of decade (1838) cause land revenue to fall sharply. Gipps proposed a loan to the Land Fund in order to continue the immigration program. He requested of the British Treasury a loan of 1 million pound. The intention of floating the loan would ensure the repayment of the loan. English interest still dwelt on the export of her paupers and her unemployed. The response by Gipps to Lord John Russell's criticism of the Gipps approach to immigration was that the bounty system had caused the depression of the 1842-44 periods and not the reverse.

The Report of the 1837 'Committee on Immigration' opened up for opposition to the traditional White Australia policy.

"This committee was appointed to consider and report their opinion made to the government of New South Wales, for introducing into the colony certain of the Hill Labourers of India; and to consider the terms under which Mechanics and Labourers are now brought from Europe".

Summary

The British trait of pomposity came to the fore during the days of early migration to the colony. 'We are British, we are free, we are pure of spirit and more worthy than the prisoners already shipped' they thought' but we will take or families, our servants, our capital and relocate to the new colony, provided we are treated as privileged persons and given land, livestock and a seat at the governor's table'.

But establishing a class structure was not on the list of plans for Brisbane, Bourke Darling or Gipps. They hands their hands full keeping the economy moving forward and keeping the economy afloat. Although they were guided by an appointed Legislative Council, the governors role was an onerous one – balancing the ever-changing political scene in Britain with the ever-diminishing financial support coming from the British Treasury for colonial operations, and the growing relaxing of isolation of the colony in world events. Trading ships of many nations were daily arrivals into the splendid harbour. The other settlement under the governor's watchful eye was taking more and more time. It was fortunate that Port Phillip settlement was a net contributor to the New South Wales coffers, whilst Morton Bay, and VDL were still being supported out of Sydney. The huge influx of convicts made life difficult in the settlements. Finding places to put these people to gainful employment at little (if any) cost to the Treasury was growing more and more difficult. It was largely 'out of sight, out of mind'. Until they engaged in crime, or the landowners ran into hard times and suddenly the convicts were unwanted and thrown back onto the charity of the government. Free settlers were fine in theory but their growing influence in the political and financial arena of the colony, made both political and economic decisions difficult. The constant pressure to open up new land, build new roads, carry out surveys, create new settlements – was a continuing problem for the governor who kept demanding more and more money to run the colony. That placed pressure on raising more and more revenue, especially for public works, education, migration and government services.

Migrations soon became the life-blood of the colony. They brought their capital, their worldly goods, their ways of life, and over all made a valuable contribution to their new land. They were the basis of attracting new investment from the motherland. But migrants down through the years were always to be attractive in the Australian physic. This was to be a nation of immigrants, but society had to be built around the needs of this new world.

Special Events –Colonial Education & Immigration Policies

Synopsis

As the first of the special events to be examined, we can review the impact of both education and immigration, from the standpoint of the economy, the social framework, the political structure and look at the rocky road that was created by religious bigotry and factions within the colony. Naturally as a bi-product of the immigration policies, the transportation (of convicts) program was its first and most significant contributor. Education was a significant economic tool, as the rate of illiteracy within the colony fell from 75% before 1800 to 25% by 1830. The development of local industry was most dependent then, as it is still today, on a literate and educated workforce. Immigration of free settlers hastened the end of the transportation program and although the mass of people supported and approved of its cessation, the pastoralists, traders and merchants bemoaned the shortage of labour and the high price of skilled labourers arriving from Britain. Naturally the discovery of gold in the early 1850s drove those same prices and shortages even higher, since many in the population looked to find their fortune on the goldfields and gave up regular employment in order to move to the goldfields.

Free Immigration into the Colony – A Different Perspective

A.G. Austin in Australian Education 1788-1900 offers an explanation as to the lack of interest in educating the lower classes.

"Nowhere in Phillip's Commissions or instructions was any mention made of the children accompanying the First Fleet, or of the child convicts whom the British Government saw fit to transport, for it was alien to the official mind of the late 18th century to feel any interest in the welfare of these children. By 1809 the War Office had been persuaded to appoint regimental schoolmasters, but in 1788 the education of these children formed no part of the business of any department of state.

The conservative opinion in Britain was convinced that education was exactly the wrong remedy and agreed with the Bishop of London's conviction that it was 'safest for both the Government and the religion of the country to let the lower classes remain in that state of ignorance in which nature has originally placed them'.

In this atmosphere anyone who undertook the education of the poor became an object of suspicion. Even the devout Hannah Moore had to defend her schools against charges of Methodism, Calvinism and subversion. Ms. Moore wrote: 'they learn such coarse work as may fit them as servants. I allow no writing for the poor. My object is to train up the lower classes in habits of industry and piety'. Nearly a century later John Stuart Mill still thought it necessary to warn his readers that 'a general state education . . . established a despotism over the mind'.

The Pitt Tory Government resisted those favouring State intervention in education. They saw no reason to meddle in the upbringing of other people's children, and no reason to suppose that the new Governor of NSW would presume to dispute their opinion.

The early governors of NSW soon found it necessary to change their adoption of British policies, especially regarding education in the colony, since Britain was not a fragment of English society transplanted, but a military and penal garrison in which the governors were responsible for every detail of daily life. In a settlement where the maintenance of discipline, the regulation of food production, the rationing of supplies, the employment of labour, and the administration of justice were necessarily committed into one man's hands, there was no room for that laissez-faire indifference which characterized the conduct of public affairs in Britain.

Not only were the governors moved by the misery of the convicts' children but also they realized that the future of the colony had to built upon these children. In a colony where there was three times the number of men as there were women, a deplorably high proportion of illegitimate and abandoned children required some measure of protection and supervision. In 1807 on Bligh's testimony, there were 387 married women in the colony, 1,035 concubines, 807 legitimate children and 1,024 illegitimate children.

Phillip had set aside, near every town, an allotment for a church and 400 acres adjacent for the maintenance of a minister and 200 Acres for the schoolmaster. However the governors were not really concerned to assert the supremacy of either Church or State. All their actions were matters of expediency. To finance schools, they made direct grants of land, assigned convicts and issued rations. To staff schools they had used soldiers, convicts, missionaries and other literate person they could find. To accommodate the schools, they used churches, barracks, storehouses and private buildings. It was Macquarie who first set down the staging order of divinity. All clerics would be, for the first time, from 1810, responsible to the principal chaplain.

By the end of the Macquarie era, many changes had been made to the social order in the colony, including education, and most of these changes were in principal accepted by J.T. Bigge in his reports to the British Commissioners. Bigge's reported that ' the flow of immigrants and the increasing number of emancipated convicts has so increased the population of free settlers that the prosperity of the settlement as a colony has proportionately advanced, and hopes may reasonably be entertained of its becoming perhaps at no distant period a valuable possession of the crown. This makes me think that it is no longer fit for its original purpose'.

For public education to be considered as a government responsibility and controlled by a cleric meant that part of the cost could be defrayed by public revenue. The suggestions made by the new Archdeacon of the colony were that public education be controlled by a cleric who was also placed at the head of the Church Establishment. The costs could be defrayed, was the suggestion, by the parents contributing, annually, a ' bushel of good clean sound wheat, or equivalent value in meat, or 1/8th of the colonial import duty could be diverted to education; governments could subdivide its land at Grose Farm, Emu Plains, Rooty Hill and Cabramatta into small farms and apply their rents to the endowment of schools in general'. The last suggestion and the one that attracted Lord Bathurst's ear was that a 'new land reserve of some 25,000 acres should be established near Bathurst or Newcastle'.

The British Government ultimately decided in 1825 to direct Governor Brisbane to form a 'corporation and invest it with clergy and school estates, and from the proceeds it should support the Anglican Church and schools and school masters in connection with the established church' The territory of NSW was to be divided into counties, hundreds, and parishes as a result of a survey of the whole colony. The Corporation was not a success largely because it was never properly funded the way it was expected, nor did it enjoy the high enthusiasm or interest of the governor.

Macquarie 'reported' to Viscount Castlereagh on 30th April 1810 on the progress in carrying out British instructions

'In pursuance to your Lordship's instructions, I lost no time in directing my attention to the principal object pointed out in them, namely, to improve the morals of the colonists, to encourage marriage, to provide for education, to prohibit the use of spirituous liquors, and to increase the agriculture and livestock so as to ensure a certainty of supply to the inhabitants under all circumstances'. In his next dispatch Macquarie reported that 'with a view to the decent education and improvement of the rising generation, I have established several schools at head quarters and the subordinate settlements, which I trust will not fail of being attended with very desirable effects'. He also requested 'a few more chaplains and some additional schoolmasters which are very much required, and it would be very desirable if some should be sent out as soon as possible'.

Alan Barcan in his imaginative work 'History of Australian Education' notes that, in line with regular military policy the NSW Corps brought their own tutor with them for teaching the children of military personnel. No such luxury was available for the residents of Norfolk Island. In 1793, Lieutenant King (Governor of the island) established an import duty on liquor in order to raise funds for education. King built the first stone schoolhouse in 1794 and a second in 1795. Collins records ('An Account of the English Colony in NSW') that 'the first school was for young children, who were instructed by a woman of good character; the second was kept by a man, who taught reading, writing, and arithmetic, for which he was well qualified, and was very attentive'.

King also opened an Orphan Institution in 1795 when by this time there were 75 destitute children. These children were taught, fed, clothed, and given vocational training.

In Sydney Governor Hunter met with the school children each year, and as David Collins records, in 1797, Hunter inspected the children from three schools and 'was gratified with the sight of 102 clean and decently—dressed children, who came with their several masters and mistresses'.

In 1798, the Rev'd Richard Johnson (the first cleric in the colony, who had arrived with the First Fleet) amalgamated the three schools in Sydney and the three joint teachers held classes in the church. They had 150 to 200 children enrolled of 'all descriptions of persons, whether soldiers, settlers, or convicts' (/Johnson's Rules). After the Church was burnt down on 1st October 1798, it moved to the courthouse and then to a disused warehouse, but enrolments halved.

When King arrived to take over as Governor in 1800, he continued his deep interest in education and 'education expanded significantly'. (Barcan). There were three main reasons for this expansion.

d. King himself took a deep interest in education and brought with him the experience gained from his Norfolk Island success
e. Increased colonial prosperity and better financial provision. King imposed an import duty on goods to establish a fund for education. When the Female Orphan Fund opened in August 1801, there were 54 girls aged from 7 to 14 in the school. In August 1804, King gave it an endowment of 13 000 acres to secure its economic stability. Samuel Marsden, its Treasurer and religious guardian commented that the Orphan School is 'the foundation of religion and morality in this colony'
f. The growth of population, which produced both the need for and the ability to sustain schools. By 1800 Sydney was a town of 2 000 and the colony had some 5 000 inhabitants. Significance could be seen in the

    - Growth of a small commercial middle class,
    - The publication of the Sydney Gazette, which offered an avenue for expression of opinion
    - A 'distinction' between state-aided 'public schools' and 'private' education

Vocational training was possibly the most important challenge and target of the education system. In 1798, Hunter reported that young male convicts had been assigned to an 'artificer's gang in order that they may be useful mechanics'. In 1805, King developed a system of apprenticeships for boys. In the same year advertisements appeared in the Sydney Gazette for apprentice seamen. The Female Orphan School developed some vocational training for the girls by offering 'needlework, reading, spinning and some few writing'. A few of the girls became servants with them being 'bound as apprentices to officer's wives'.

The overall shortage of labour in the colony caused vocational training to make only slow progress.

Immigrants and Free Settlers

Collins records that on the 15th January 1793, the Bellona transport ship, arrived in Sydney Harbour with a cargo of stores and provisions, 17 female convicts and five settlers one of whom was a master wheel-wright employed by the governor at a salary of 100 pound per annum. A second was a returning skilled tradesman who had been previously employed as a master blacksmith. All five settlers had brought their families.

Collins conjectures that these first three settlers had received free passage, a promise of a land grant and assistance with farming, as the incentive for becoming the free settlers,

Manning Clark (A History of Australia) records that in 1806, 'a dozen families from the Scottish border area arrived as free emigrants and each received 100 acres of land on the banks of the Hawkesbury River in a place they called Ebenezer. They were devout Presbyterians, and were allowed to worship in the colony according to their own lights'. However the authorities were not prepared to tolerate the practice of the catholic religion, because they saw it 'as an instrument of mental slavery, a threat to higher civilization, and a threat to liberty' (Clark Vol 1)

Developing Immigration

Even by the census of 1828, NSW had fewer than 5,000 people who had come out voluntarily, in a population of 36 598. The colony had the attractions unavailable in the USA, free land and convict labour. Settlers were given land for agriculture and pasture usage. This meant freehold land, and it only applied to men who had immigrated as private citizens, to military officers who had decided to stay and to pardoned convicts who had been granted land.

In 1831, the British Government, against the opposition of many in the colony decided to stop giving away land grants to settlers and chose instead to 'sell' the land and use some of the proceeds to sponsor migrants to the colony. The initial sales price was 5 shillings an acre. It was a way of inducing poor families to leave the country, but as well of relieving the labour shortage. Between 1831 and 1840 about 50,000 prisoners were transported and about 65,000 free men and women chose to emigrate

The battle of the sexes was more equal amongst emigrants than among convicts: but even South Australia, which was wholly an emigrant's colony, had only 8 females for every 10 males by 1850, and in Australia as a whole there was fewer than 7 in every ten. The resulting challenge was only partially met by Caroline Chisholm who met every convict and emigrant ship to stress the dangers to young unmarried women. Her main accomplishment was to convince the Colonial Office, in 1846, to offer free passage to all families of convicts resident in the colony. Her detractors suggested that the result of her efforts towards convict families and emigrating poor families would be to create an imbalance of Catholics in the colony, who were already twice the proportion of the Australian population as they were in England.

'Populate or Perish'

The history of Australia is bound tightly into two aspects—the economics of colonization and the story of immigration.

The first free immigrants came out on the Bellona, and were given small landgrants on Liberty Plains (the Strathfield-Homebush area). The first family to arrive included a millwright who had been on the hulks in Britain for a minor crime and been released. It was Major Grose, acting as the Administrator after the departure of Phillip, who observed ' from some dirty tricks he has already attempted, I fear he has not forgotten all he learned as a former prisoner. He is evidently one of those that his country could well do without'.

Governor King wrote in his report – The State of the Colony in 1801 – on the subject of free immigrants:

"Settlers are of two classes i.e. those who come free from England and those who were convicts and whose terms of transportation are expired, or who are emancipated. Of the first class, I am sorry their industry and exertions by no means answer the professions they made in England, several of whom are so useless to themselves and everyone about them that they were not only a burden to the public but a very bad example to the industrious. As they brought no other property than their large families, many have been and will continue an expensive burden on the public, or starve. The settlers are maintained by the crown for eighteen months and have two convicts assigned to each, which is very sufficient to provide against the time of doing for themselves, but that period too often discovers their idleness and incapacity to raise the least article from a fertile and favourable climate, after having occasioned an expense of upwards of 250 pound for each family, exclusive of their passage out The desirable people to be sent here are sober, industrious farmers, carpenters, wheel and mill wrights, who having been used to draw their food from the earth, secure sand manufacture it, would here find how bountifully their labour would be rewarded".

It appears that King did not have a very high opinion of the potential for free migration to the colony.

Phillip's successor – Governor Hunter—was instructed by the Colonial Office to 'encourage free settlers without subjecting the public to expense'. They were to be given larger land grants than the emancipists and as much convict labour as they wanted. Hunter observed in one of his submissions to the Secretary of the colonies that 'free immigrants would not come to the country whilst the needs of the colony were supplied from Government farms'.

The economic factors hit the immigration concept in 1801 when Governor King, as Hunters successor wrote to the Duke of Portland, as

Colonial Secretary and suggested family immigration. It was turned down on the basis that transporting a family would cost 150 pound and annual maintenance until they were self-supporting would cost 250 pound (HRNSW)

In 1802, the HRNSW records that free settlers (28 in one group) arrived by the Perseus and Coromandel. More came in the Navy ship Glatton, including a person supposedly bearing 'perfect knowledge of Agriculture, having held a very considerable farm in his hands, but which through youthful indiscretion, he found it necessary to relinquish'. The governor was asked to place him 'above the common class of settlers'. The government, Governor King wrote 'was much imposed on' by these free settlers. The Glatton settlers were sent to the Nepean, where they were wrote King ' going on with great spirit and well applied industry'

King reported to Lord Hobart in 1804 that 'there were 543 free settlers supporting 351 wives and 589 children and utilising 463 convicts'. Further free settlers are recorded as being in the William Pitt in 1805, mainly because land and subsistence was being replaced by the lure of wealth coming from the fine wool being promoted by John Macarthur. This endeavour and attraction of wealth brought a different and probably better class of free settler – the Blaxland brothers arrived on a charter vessel with their families, servants and capital of over 6,000 pound. Again the governor received instructions. 'They are to be allowed 8,000 acres of land and the services of up to 80 convicts for 18 months at the commissary store's expense. Governor Bligh was given similar instructions in reference to a 'lady of quality' – a Mrs Chapman, a widow, Governess and teacher. Bligh was directed to 'afford her due encouragement and assistance'. The next governor, Lachlan Macquarie took a different stance – he discouraged free immigration, probably because the flow of convicts was almost overwhelming his administration. His position is not readily understandable. As a quasi social reformer and developer of free enterprise in the colony, one would have expected Macquarie to welcome free settlers for what social and economic values they could contribute. When the Bigge report was published in London, it raised the interest of men of wealth in the colony and a Lieutenant Vickers, an officer of the East India Company, volunteered to emigrate with 10,000 pound of capital, an unblemished reputation and a purity of private life ' hitherto known in any class of society', and in return demanded privileges by way of land grants, livestock and a regular seat at the governor's table. Brisbane, as governor, was directed by Lord Bathurst as Colonial secretary to give Vickers 2,000 acres of land and a house allotment near Newcastle. Brisbane investigated Vickers and found him to be little more than 'an adventurer, a bird of passage, and boycotted by his fellow officers'. Marjorie Barnard concluded, 'Only distance made his deception possible'. Opportunities followed good publicity, and the floating of the Australian Agricultural Company in London in 1823 did much to promote the colony in Britain, and brought another spate of free settlers to the colony.

This then is the early trend in the free settler movement – it had not been seen yet as a government opportunity. But that was about to change. Lord Bathurst came along with an idea, urged by the Wakefield supporters and the rash of economists waging war on the increasing unemployment, poverty and lack of investment opportunities in Britain.

A privately sponsored scheme was funded by a loan to Dr. J.D. Lang by the governor in the amount of 1,500 pound, which brought out 100 selected 'mechanics' (semi-skilled labourers) and their families. Land used a charter vessel to transport these immigrants, and the understanding was that the immigrants would repay their expenses from future wages. In 1831 this was an inspiring move to privatising a government policy.

Three factors were set to establish an on-going immigration policy. The three factors were bad times in England; shortages of skilled labour of both men and women in the colony; and the cessation of the assignment system.

A commission on Emigration was established in England to select and despatch suitable agricultural labourers. A plan to tax landowners of assigned convicts failed when the difficulty of collection was recognised. There were still 13,400 convicts on assignment in 1831.

The governor agreed that official funds would contribute 20 pound towards each immigrant family and try to recover it after the family settled. The collections were rarely made.

It was left to Governor Bourke to formulate a workable plan. The 'bounty system' relied on sponsored workers funded by government. The government paid 12 pound out of the 17 pound passage money. The Emigrants Friendly Society existed in Sydney to help and protect these sponsored migrants.

A more refined method was needed to select and sponsor these migrants. Glenelg reformed the financial side in 1837. He allocated the revenue from land sales in the colony as a means of affording immigration. The land as well as any revenue derived from its sale, lease or rental, had remained the property of the crown, not the colonial administration. Two-thirds of these funds were to be allocated to migrants by way of grants – 30 pound for a married couple, 15 for an unmarried daughter, 5 and10 pound for children depending on age.

The zenith of immigration success could be seen in the 1830s under Governor Gipps. Land revenue was high, the colony was prosperous and plenty of migrants were on offer and the colony could successfully absorb them. The severe drought at the end of decade (1838) cause land revenue to fall sharply. Gipps proposed a loan to the Land Fund in order to continue the immigration program. He requested of the British Treasury a loan of 1 million pound. The intention of floating the loan would ensure the repayment of the loan. English interest still dwelt on the export of her paupers and her unemployed. The response by Gipps to Lord John Russell's criticism of the Gipps approach to immigration was that the bounty system had caused the depression of the 1842-44 periods and not the reverse.

The Report of the 1837 'Committee on Immigration' opened up for opposition to the traditional White Australia policy.

"This committee was appointed to consider and report their opinion made to the government of New South Wales, for introducing into the colony certain of the Hill Labourers of India; and to consider the terms under which Mechanics and Labourers are now brought from Europe".

CHAPTER 10

ELEMENTS OF POPULATION INCREASE

Sex distribution

Australia has, since the first settlement of the continent in 1788, differed materially from the older countries of the world. Older countries, that are countries having an established civilised population, have, in general, grown by natural increase and their composition usually reflects that fact with the numbers of males and females being approximately equal, with a tendency for females to slightly exceed males. This slight excess arises from a number of causes

- Higher rate of mortality amongst males
- Greater propensity of males to travel
- The effects of war
- Employment of males in the armed forces
- Preponderance of males amongst emigrants

Masculinity of the Population

"The changing population structure necessarily implied a radical alteration in the size of the male workforce in the total population. The increasing numbers of young males and of all females compelled this change as shown below.

Year Workforce Males % of Total Popln

1790	1784	77.7
1795	3692	79.1
1800	4555	74.1
1805	5981	70.7
1810	7100	63.0
1815	9575	61.4
1820	22822	71.1
1825	34565	71.4
1830	47180	69.4

MASCULINITY OF THE NSW POPULATION 1800 to 1855

Year	%
1800	44.91
1805	40.00
1810	31.16
1815	30.76
1820	41.81
1825	53.00
1830	52.06
1835	45.71
1840	34.25
1845	21.05
1850	16.13
1855	11.14

This compares with other countries in various years, which would create a guide and average for base purposes

Canada	1911	6.07
India	1911	2.24
New Zealand	1919	1.15
Australia	1919	1.00
Poland	1914	0.41
Hungary	1912	-0.94
Ireland	1915	-1.36
England	1917	-16.43

Age Distribution

During the first 80 years of settlement, the age distribution of the colonial population has varied considerably. Prior to1856, the distribution averaged as follows:

Males >15	31.4
Males 15-65	67.4
Males <65	1.17
Total	100%
Females >15	43.0
Females 15-65	56.2
Females <65	0.77
Total	100%
Persons>15	36.28
Persons 15-65	62.72
Persons <65	1.0
Total	100%

Sources of Race & Nationality

The primary distribution is between the aboriginal natives and the immigrants, who since 1788 have made the colony their home. Under immigrants would come not only the direct immigrants but also their descendants. For the first 60 years after settlement, the Aboriginal population was in decline (refer also to Chapter 3 of this study – The Aboriginal Economy of 1788). It is of interest to note that in the first census of the aboriginal population in 1911, the Commonwealth statistician made the following reference.[194] "At the census of 1911 the number of full-blood aboriginals who were employed by whites or who lived on the fringe of white settlement was stated to be only 19,939. In Queensland, Western Australia and the Northern Territory, there are considerable numbers of natives still in the 'savage' state, numerical information concerning whom is of a most unreliable nature and can be regarded as little more than the result of guessing".

---

194 *Commonwealth Year Book 1901-1919* (1920) p.88

"The academic studies by Dr. Roth, formerly Chief Protector of Aborigines in Queensland puts the number of full-blood aborigines in the 6 colonies at 80,000 in 1919"[195] As a matter of Commonwealth census policy no count was attempted of 'half-castes' as 'no authoritative definition has yet been given.

The predominant race of immigrants and their descendants is British. Howevcr, by 1900, thc local born population had reached 83%. The figure in 1856 was calculated to be in the 52.5% vicinity. The other main birthplaces included Germany, China, Scandinavia, Polynesia, British India and Japan

Rate of Increase

The rate of increase in the early colony rose quickly but then steadied as migration took on a smaller 'net ' effect. After 1830 the average rate was only 4% but then declined steadily until by 1901, the rate was only 1.38. NSW always enjoyed the highest rate of increase and averaged over 5% before 1850 declining to 4.83 from 1860. The 1850s were a period of low natural increase and high net migration with the gold fields being the main catalyst.

Density of Population

From one aspect the total population may be less significant than in respect of the absolute amount than in respect of the density of its distribution. The total land area of the country is 2,974,581 square miles, and at the time of the Constitution of 1901, the country only had a population of 5,347,018 persons, with a density of 1.80. Even today that density is only a little less than 7. The comparative densities are, for the earliest period of statistics maintained (1919 – Statesman's Yearbook), Europe at 122.98, Asia 54.45. Americas 16.87 and Australasia 2.38

[195] CYB *ibid* p.89

Urban Population

One of the key features of the distribution of population in Australia is the tendency to accumulate in the capital cities. In every colony the capital city had a greater population than any other town in the colony. It was the hub and as such it carried certain features. The main population area was a port for international shipping. There were adequate fresh water sources servicing the population. In the early days of the colony of NSW the 'urban' population would have been close top 100%, but as Macquarie developed and serviced his regional towns, the urban percentage declined until by 1900, Sydney had only 41.38 % of the colonial population

Aboriginal population

The Commonwealth Year Book of 1901 reminds us that "The Commonwealth Constitution Act makes provision for aboriginal natives top"be excluded for all purposes for which statistics of population are made use but the opinion has been given by the Commonwealth Attorney-General that 'in reckoning the population of the Commonwealth, half-castes Are not aboriginal natives within the meaning of Section 127 of the Constitution', and should therefore be included in any census count."[196] Thids is one reason that the ABS (Australian Bureau of Statistics had so much doubt over the number of aborigines in the country – they had not been counted and would not be counted at any time until 1966. The ABS records guesses ranging from 150,000 to as low as 61,705 in 1925[197]

Enumeration

In colonial NSW, the system of 'musters' was the way chosen to count the free settlers. The governor would 'gazette' or announce the date and place of the next muster, and usually commissariat officers would officiate at the count. The basis of the count was often widened to include a record of the number and type of livestock, of acres cultivated and would be

---

196 Commonwealth Year Book #3– W. Ramsey-Smith ' *Special Characteristics of Commonwealth Population*' P.89

197 4The count in each state is estimated at 30th April 1915 by Ramsey Smith as NSW-6,580;Victoria 283; Qld 15,000; SA 4,842; WA 32,000; NT 3,000 for a total of 61,705

used to verify the rations receivable by that family 'off the store'. In 1828 the muster system was replaced by the first 'census' where a more detailed record was made of the population demographics including ages, sex and birthplace of each inhabitant and whether 'free' or 'convict'.

Natural Increase

The two factors, which contribute to the growth of a population, are the 'natural increase' by excess of births over deaths and the 'net migration', being the excess of arrivals over departures. In a new country such as the colony of NSW between 1788 and 1856, the 'net migration' occupies an important position as a source of increase of population especially as the early imbalance of sexes and the shortage of females in the colony, allowed for only a relatively small natural increase.

Net Immigration

The quinquennial period in which the greatest net migration to the Colonies occurred is outside our study period but was that of 1881-85 with a total of 224,040, whilst the period 1901-05 departures exceeded arrivals by 16,793

Total Increase

The total increase of the population is found by the combination of the natural increase with the net immigration

Musters

J.C. Caldwell writes in the introduction to the Chapter on 'Population'[198] "For the first 40 years of the Australian colonies, our knowledge of population numbers is derived from the musters. Their major deficiencies are that of the omission of the native peoples. Even in 1800 the musters perhaps account for only 1 or 2 percent of the actual population".

[198] Australians: Historical Statistics

Official musters were held in 1799,1805,1810,1817,1820 and1821. The first full-scale census was held in November 1828.

Most announcements of intentions to account for all persons were generally signed by the Governor of the day and the task assigned to the Commissary officials. Governor John Hunter issued the following General Order on the 23rd September 1795[199].

> *A general muster will be held on Saturday next, the 26th instant at Sydney; on Thursday, the 1st October, at Parramatta and Toongabbie; and on Saturday, the 3rd October, at the settlement at the Hawkesbury – at which places the Commissary will attend for the purpose of obtaining a correct amount of the numbers and distribution of all persons (the military excepted) in the different aforementioned settlements, whether victualled or not (victualled) from the public stores.*

Notice is hereby given to all persons concerned to attend, so that every man be accounted for; and such as neglect complying with this order will be sought after and be either confined in the cells, put to hard labour, or corporally punished.

> *The sick may be accounted for by the Principal Surgeon, and officers' servants by their masters*

199 HRNSW – Governors Despatches 1795

CHAPTER 11

REVISIONISM

Overview

There is a traditional viewpoint on Australian Colonial Economic History as espoused by Shann, Fitzpatrick & Fletcher and repeated by Butlin (N.G Butlin) to the effect that Australia was an area of very ancient settlement, within which the Aboriginal economy was a stably ordered system of decision-making that satisfied the needs of its people. British occupation (without any apparent deliberate intent) soon destroyed the Aboriginal economy and society with the accompanying decimation of its population[200]

We may not need to yet re-write our economic history but it does help to understand the economic setting that gave rise to the rapidly expanding British society in the new settlement of Botany Bay, with its rapidly declining native population and a developing economy that met the needs of Britain as being a valuable source of raw materials for its industry, as an outlet for its trading and the resulting transfer of resources (a takeover) by the new economic managers (the British autocratic governors). These new managers, in fact, faced much higher costs than expected, in achieving 'success'. Their 'success' was to be measured by being able to commandeer these natural resources and transfer them from an ancient society to the new society. This takeover was never the apparent original intent, but

200 Butlin uses some of these expressions in '*Economics and the Dreamtime*' p.184

rather the official intention was to seek a type of merger rather than a takeover. However, the gulf between the two societies was too large to be bridged and British settlement succeeded while the ancient society was destroyed.

Butlin finds a similarity between the 'economic' invasion of Britain by the Romans and the 'takeover' of economic interests in the Great South Land.[201] It is quite a stretch of the imagination but there are certain similarities that given the 1600-year time-span can be identified. Similar strategies learnt from history are probably what Butlin is offering.

"Rome had the essential springboard from Italy to develop a vast network of imperial control[202] extending over much of Europe and the Mediterranean. For 500 years these traditions were injected into England. On one hand Rome delivered a military market, a money economy, organised administration, a villa system of agriculture married to the Celtic farming of Britain, improved agricultural productivity, urban centres, transport systems and extended trade contacts with Europe. On the other hand, it was military control and reflected the hierarchical organisation and exploitation of unfree labour on which the ancient world depended. Butlin acknowledges that these thoughts are derived from Salway in *Roman Britain.*

One can see the similarities between the Roman takeover of early Britain, and the British takeover of New Holland. G. Arnold Wood in his prehistory of Australia makes a similar point but concludes, "It is scarcely conceivable that a transfer of influences corresponding to those of Rome on Britain could have been spread by Asians to Australia".[203]

For all the attribution that we can validly extend to the British for the takeover of Aboriginal economy, many questions remain unanswered. For instance,

- What were the economics of the 'takeover'?

---

201 Butlin *Economics and the Dreamtime* p.187

202 Butlin uses the word 'imperial' often and probably means 'British' rather than royal or monarchist

203 G.A. Wood *The Discovery of Australia*

- What were the legalities of the 'takeover'?
- Who were the major players?
- Was disease the main or only component of the Aboriginal depopulation?
- What were the real intentions of Britain in the 'takeover'?

One must ask if the success of establishing the colonial settlement by the use of the seven conditions referred to below were a result of a tightly planned economy or a mixture of planned or under-regulated, penal or free. It would seem that many of the elements of success had to have been part of an integrated planning process. For instance, the instruction for Bills to be drawn on the Treasury in London was a better alternative for a penal settlement not having an exchequer and any means of exchange, by way of coinage; the competition with and elimination of Aborigines may not have been British government policy but it was a consensual (by British Colonial Office policy) internal struggle for land and hunting rights; whilst the early privatisation of the settlement came about by the failure of government to produce sufficient food locally. The resulting issuance of land grants to the military officers and emancipists gave this new land-owning class the opportunity to either make money or feed themselves and their families adequately; the privatisation of the treasury by King and Macquarie was both a convenience and a display of not really wanting to get involved or know the details of local expenditures. It was both cheaper and less onerous to the governor not having to account for every penny of this discretionary and illegal revenue to the British Government; British financial support and legal and administrative oversight was necessary because it was a penal settlement rather than a 'slave' market, where convicts were sold to settlers and taken off the hands and the 'books' of the British government – this again was a deliberate policy decision by the British authorities; the supply of human capital with skills appropriate to a relatively advanced society may or may not have been deliberate—it is still a matter of conjecture as to whether convicts were selectively chosen in Britain (at the court or even the prison level) for transportation as Phillip and his successors had requested – but, at least we know from the records that Macquarie attended each arriving ship to select the skilled mechanics that he most needed for government service; the lack of economies of scale was a matter of transition from commissariat policy to import replace and make what could be made locally (and on a timely basis) and then turn it over to private enterprise for convenience. Butlin properly identifies 7 early achievements as if they were 'manor from heaven', but most appear to be deliberated policy ideas whose time had come.

A Revisionist Theory of the Colonial Origins

It is probably not surprising that an Economic Historian, more so than an Historian, would ask for a more rational explanation of the reasons for the formation of the Colony of New South Wales in 1788. Although not traditionally a matter of Australian economic history, this study has grown into one where the regular understanding is clarified and revised by an interpretation and understanding of events that cross over the boundary from history into historical economics. It would seem that the authorities in the British Treasury would have raised consideration, if not in the Home Office, as to what impact another British Colony would have on the Treasury funds. The economic argument would have been more than the mere 'opportunity' cost of not having a penal colony as a repository. The first question becomes, is it wise or proper to question the traditional understanding and theories of history? If schoolchildren have been taught for at least 50 years (I can verify from 1950) that Australia was selected as a penal colony and for the transportation of prisoners from British prisons, then why do we raise doubts in 2001?

A.G.L. Shaw introduces '*Great Britain and the Colonies 1815-1865*' with this rather exculpatory comment

"The fate of any historical interpretation about a problem or a period is to become itself re-interpreted. Not infrequently when a reigning hypothesis gets unseated, clarity and simplicity gives place to complexity, conflicting evidence, a melange of contributory causes. And, as the inexact science which history will undoubtedly remain, introducing 'multi-variables' is to lose at once that sense of certainty and intellectual satisfaction. Many major themes in the explanation of 19th century British history are currently in need of re-examination."

In this study we are revisiting the traditionalist theory that the only reason for the colony of New South Wales was as a penal settlement. It was carefully planned and discussed at all levels based on the simple submission by Sir Joseph Banks in evidence before the House of Commons Select Committee on Penitentiaries in 1774.

The <u>traditionalist argument</u> is, in its most simplistic structure:

Upon Cook's news that he had taken possession of a great country (New South Wales), England did not immediately decide to colonise it. She already had a huge empire, and wanted no more for the present, for colonies were expensive to govern, and they oftentimes caused wars. With the American Colonies in mind, it seemed that colonies brought no profit while they were struggling and expensive, and that when they became prosperous they rebelled.

Even though Cook and Bank's journals were doctored by Hawkesworth before publishing to make NSW sound better than it was, the choice of a new colony would have been (in the opinion of F. Hawke) New Zealand or the Friendly Islands before Botany Bay was selected.

However the need was different now with the revolt by the Americas and the accumulation of over 1,000 prisoners each year in Britain. They were being kept in prison and in hulks tethered together in mid-stream, and soon became over-full. It was Banks that suggested Botany Bay as a new penal colony, which is surprising when we remember what Banks said about NSW. He now seemed to think it was just the right place. It was far away and no danger of prisoners escaping. Thus the colony was simply to be used as a jail for prisoners and a repository for the poor of England! Russel Ward in *Australia* puts it simply "In 1788 the Australian nation was founded by and for Great Britain's surplus of convicted criminals, a fact which used to give many respectable Australians pain and which threatened a few with schizophrenia."

But this is over-simplistic, for Ward implies that Britain was blinded to all other considerations other than the placement of prisoners somewhere else than in Britain. As any economic Historian would know, if nothing else the economic considerations of adding another colony to the British Empire was just extra expense. But there was something else! Foreign policy issues, trade and industry issues, ridding the homeland of the poor and unemployed, following the Industrial revolution were all considered and the penal colony idea was the icing on the cake, and not the sole determinant.

Why does the traditional view need reviewing?

The record needs setting straight for future generations and at least for the next 50 years!

The answer to the question 'what are the reasons for the settlement' once seemed obvious. In the 1780s England was facing an urgent problem – jails were overflowing, crime was increasing; the solution was transportation – but to where? Botany Bay was selected!

This is the traditional copybook answer repeated for the past half-century!

In 1888, a British historian, Gonner, suggested a larger story – Botany Bay was settled for economic reasons, to compensate Britain for the loss of her American Colonies. This theory found no support in Australia until K.M. Dallas (a Tasmanian historian) discussed it in 1952. Dallas asked – Why would a nation of merchants go so far and pay so much money, if it were merely to dump convicts? It was Dallas that even set Geoffrey Blainey to rethinking the rational explanation.

Lord Sydney, as Secretary of State, had stated the problem and the government's position in 1780: The traditionalists bought this explanation without much question or even concern.

"The several gaols and places for the confinement of felons in this Kingdom, being in so crowded a state that the greatest danger is to be apprehended not only from their escape, but from infectious distempers which may hourly be expected to break out among them".

However these were the reasons for the policy of 'transportation' and not for settling the colony!

Some Background to Events leading to the Government 1786 decision

In the 18th Century, England was in the throes of domestic upheaval. She was going through the Industrial Revolution. The country was being transformed from a rural-based economy to an industrial one. Farms were closing. Factories were opening. People were relocating from the country to the city. The results were overcrowding, primitive sewerage, disease and an increase in crime, mostly due to higher levels of poverty. On top of that there was no police force, only a collection of corrupt wardens. The English penal code was to be made even more severe than it already was! Gaol was to be no more of a rehabilitation or preventative strike then, than it is now. The gaols were overflowing and short-term (7 years or less) convicted persons were placed on 'hulks' tied together in mid-stream of the Thames

Men were escaping from the hulks in growing numbers and there was a real fear that the situation would get out of hand. Crime, cost and prisoners were increasing – finance, accommodation and patience with the problem were not.

Building more prisons (made permissible by the Penitentiary Houses Act of 1779) was one solution, where convicts could be employed in hard labour. The scheme foundered because of wrangles over location and cost. By 1784, the authorities moved again to transportation and a 1784 Act to resume transportation was passed but without a specified location. Parliamentary Committees investigated Africa, but the unhealthiness of the climate, the infertile soil and a fear of hostile natives combined to rule out the region. A disastrous experiment at Cape Coast Castle resulted in a 45% death rate amongst convicts in a single year.

Even in 1785 and 1786, sites in Canada and the West Indies were under consideration, but by 1779 Joseph Banks had proposed Botany Bay just before Matra wrote his report to the Admiralty in 1883. Matra emphasised the great commercial advantages of Botany Bay, based on his having been a midshipman under Cook during his 7-day stay on the East Coast of new Holland. The colony could serve as a base for trade with China (tea), with

Nootka Sound (furs) and the Moluccas (spices) and for the cultivation of flax.

Sir John Young, another adviser to the Peel government, submitted a plan in 1785 for a settlement suitable for convicts and commercial gain. The Beauchamp Committee of the House of Commons rejected both schemes. The cost of transportation was the main objection. The evidence suggested a passage cost of about 30 pound, which was 6 times the cost of passage to America. Although Botany Bay was rejected in 1785 as too expensive, just one year later, on 18th August1786, it was chosen as the site. Botany Bay was selected as the last resort, almost in desperate circumstances. Circumstances pressuring the decision included the debts of the Prince of Wales, negotiations for a treaty with France, and growing agitation against the 'slave trade'. The convict problem appeared small, in comparison, but deserved and got a rapid solution. The government's aim was mercantilist – colonies or settlements were only useful if they benefited the mother country. England was a trading nation with imperial ambitions. Botany Bay was selected for the general advantages it offered as well as being a place suitable for transportation.

These general advantages included:

- Botany Bay was useful as a naval base and a refitting port in the South Seas.
- England's interest in the Pacific had increased, especially after the loss of the American colonies.
- Rivalry with the French in the East became a foundation for a base.
- The colony of NSW had important commercial attractions; flax and timber, essential for naval supplies could be grown there. Convicts were not dumped at Botany Bay; they were sent as the first settlers for a naval base and refitting port.
- That is why the early emphasis on rehabilitation. From that base, the vital trade routes could be tapped—tea from China, fur from North America, the whaling industry, and South American loot carried on Spanish ships.

After 1785, when the French, and Dutch alliance was renewed, the French revived their-own East India Company into the Pacific. In 1786 the British annexed Penang and Botany Bay was settled as a useful base for trade. The official documents do give us the profit motive, which the English needed to undertake the venture. These official documents included

- Cook's report of Norfolk Island having superior quality of the 'spruce pines and flax'; and the 'greatest consequence to us as a naval power'—Matra.
- Phillip was instructed to cultivate flax, which Phillip did within one month of arriving at Botany Bay. The flax and pine timber were as important in 1788 as steel and oil are today.

However, the traditionalists still argue that Botany Bay was settled *at a certain point in time* because the government needed to solve its convict problem. The revisionists argue – why that place and not another? The pressure groups won the day in 1786 –

- the politicians saw the disgraceful and frightening state of the hulks;
- the 'opposition' in parliament needled the government for its failure to find a solution;
- powerful economic groups (of merchants) were well represented in the discussions for protecting trade against competition from national rivals.

The government made a sudden, but not hasty, decision in the face of all this pressure.

Revising the Interpretation

A revisionist theory draws a very different analysis whereby there were numerous basic determinants (other than the penal colony) of the formation of the colony and that it became only a means to an end to send convicts from the overflowing British prisons to the early colony.

For a start, the fact was that no British government in the past had been directly responsible for initiating the permanent settlement of any territory.

The American colonial enterprises, dating back to the early seventeenth century, had been the work of individuals seeking a better life, or of companies acting with the general support of the government or under Royal charter, but none had been directly fostered by the government. With no private or commercial interests likely to set up a pioneering enterprise in the newly chartered territories, emigration from the British Isles to various American colonies went on free from any thought of the more distant places as alternatives. 'Not only remoteness but the very nature of the lands observed by members of Cook's expedition inhibited serious interest', writes Younger in *Australia and the Australians* 'whilst New Zealand's ferocious tribesmen inspired fear, and Sir Joseph Banks wrote of New South Wales that "a soil so barren and at the same time entirely void of the helps derived from cultivation could not be supposed to yield much towards the support of man" '.

The British government supported privatisation of colonisation, but the settlement of such remote and unproductive places did not appeal to any private group, and the British government saw no reason for action. A readiness to take possession (as Cook had done in the name of King George III) did not imply a readiness to follow such action with occupation; nor did the mere declaration of possession in itself confer any substantial right or obligation on the British government.

These basic determinants of whether or not to settle the area of *New Holland* included:

- Foreign Policy considerations
- Military (in particular, naval) considerations
- Scientific & technical considerations
- The tyranny of the distance
- Economic (in particular, trade) considerations

Only after quantifying the strategic criteria within these five categories did the rationale of the colony being developed at government expense but being made to pay its own way, as rapidly as possible, did the formation of a penal settlement come about as a means to underpin the economics of the future colony.

Foreign Policy Considerations

Commodore John Byron sailed from Plymouth in 1764 with orders, that in order to avoid arousing Spanish jealousies and retaliation were kept secret. After passing through the Straits of Magellan he sailed on the familiar north-westerly course over the Pacific, making few discoveries; he sighted only outlying islands of minor groups, and after visiting Tinian he went on to Batavia and returned home, completing the circumnavigation in the record time of twenty-two months. On his return to England in 1766 his ship, the frigate *Dolphin*, was placed under Captain Samuel Wallis who, with Captain Philip Carteret in the *Swallow*, set off on another circumnavigation. The two ships were separated soon after passing through the Straits of Magellan. Wallis reached Tahiti (Naming it King George Island), the Society Islands, and the Wallis Archipelago, sailing home by way of Batavia. Carteret discovered Pitcairn Island and sailed through St George's Channel, so proving that New Ireland and New Britain were separated.

For much of the eighteenth century there was a distinct possibility that naval warfare (between France and Britain) would be extended into the Pacific. Both the French and English were doing their share of voyaging in these waters, sometimes no more than a few months, or a few leagues, apart. England's victory in the Seven Years war, acknowledged at the Treaty of Paris in 1763, resulted in England's supremacy over the French in India, and the loss of France's North American colonies to England. (France, however, retained some possessions in India and the best of her sugar-islands.) In the long run the English victory also decided the future of the Pacific.

Scientific & technical consideration

During the years of struggle, increasing attention was given to scientific inquiry and geographical speculation, both in England and France. Now that practically all the remainder of the world was charted, the Great South Land – Terra Australis or Terra Incognita – had become a matter of immediate concern. Books about voyages in the Pacific and southern seas, proposing further exploration or the founding of settlements, and speculating about unknown parts, contributed to the growing interest.

It was also an era of scientific exploration, undertaken against a background of great expansion in scientific thought. Significant advance in the theoretical sciences of mathematics and astronomy had been made in the 17th century; now these new principles were being applied to navigation. The invention of the sextant in England in 1730 and the subsequent development of the chronometer, made it possible to take exact celestial measurements, and so to chart a ship's position with accuracy. These inventions, with modifications in ship-design resulting in greatly strengthened vessels, opened the way for new geographical discoveries.

Economic & trade considerations

With the founding in 1711 of the South Sea Company, one of London's joint-stock ventures to seize public imagination, the distant Pacific became a region for more than literary fantasy. The South Sea Company was to trade with Spanish America and concessions were gained for it for that purpose, but its great appeal to the speculator lay in its hoped-for trade with the rich lands thought to await discovery in the Pacific. Expectations of dazzling wealth were conjured up, although operations never became profitable. The fraudulent booming of the company's shares were followed by a collapse of the so-called South Sea Bubble in 1720, causing disillusionment as well as great scandal. The collapse brought to a sudden and calamitous end, all speculative interest in nebulous plans for trade in the Pacific. Nevertheless, the English period of discovery had begun.

Distance personified

Between 1744 and 1748, a handsome new edition was published in London of the *Complete Collection of Voyages and Travels* (which had originally appeared in 1705 edited by John Harris) urging further discoveries. As well as narratives of navigators, the book contained prefaces and notations by John Campbell, who sought to draw attention to opportunities for new enterprise believed to exist for enterprising Englishmen. Pointing to the value of commerce, Campbell explained the narratives of travel in the South Sea in terms of the new challenge that awaited those with foresight and courage to act:

'It is most evident from Tasman's voyages that New Guinea, Carpentaria (i.e. Cape York Peninsula), New Holland, Van Diemen's Land and the country discovered by Quiros make all one continent, from which New Zealand seems to be separated by a strait, and perhaps is part of another continent'.

Campbell went on to suggest that there were great prospects for Britain if settlements (or, as he termed them, plantations) were established there. Convinced of the immense value of the southern continent, which he termed Terra Australis, he was opposed to a monopoly being granted to the East India Company to trade there. He made a strong plea that the South Sea Company should have rights there 'as a point of high importance,' and wrote that if Britain wished to make the greatest gain 'it may, indeed be requisite to remove ill judged prohibitions, and to break down illegal exclusions'.

He urged that New Guinea should be settled at once, 'and with competent force, since without doubt the Spaniards would leave no means unattempted to dispossess them.' In the space of a very few years, he believed settlement of New Guinea (and a trade in slaves from there) would prove of great consequence to the South Sea Company. He also recommended the formation of a settlement on the southern coast of Terra Australis. This, he believed, would lead the way to the opening of a new trade route 'which must carry a great quantity of our goods and manufactures.' Such a settlement would also be attended by other advantages. 'There is in all probability,' Campbell wrote, 'another Southern continent which is still to be discovered.'

'Perhaps it was the aura of unreality associated with the southern lands as much as the British preoccupation with European wars, that held back further exploration for so long' writes Marjorie Barnard in *A History of Australia.* Dampier had returned to London in 1701, hinting at prospects in lands still untouched. Yet, apart from the wartime expedition of Captain George Anson in 1739, it was not until 1764 that the British government sent another ship into the Pacific area.

Investigating the New World

These voyages were all undertaken by Britain to advance 'the honour of this nation as a maritime power – and the trade and navigation thereof' (Lord

Sydney). The English ships each followed a course through the Straits of Magellan and then struck northwest, finally reaching the coast of New Guinea. Close behind them were the French, who had the same objectives and who directed their efforts to the same area. Captain Louis Antoine de Bougainville reached the Society Islands and Tahiti a year after Wallis, and continued westward, making some new discoveries in the Samoa group. His next landfall was an archipelago that he decided – correctly – was Quiros's long lost and long-sought Australia del Espiritu Santo. Here, he told himself, was the opportunity to solve the old riddle of the Southern Continent.

'So Bougainville sailed away from the Great Barrier Reef. He still believed he had been close to land, but consoled himself with the reflection that it could easily have been 'a cluster of islands' not the east coast of New Holland. His subsequent course took him through the hazardous waters of the Louisiade Archipelago, through the Solomons and New Britain, and north of New Ireland to the Moluccas and eventually to Europe' (Younger).

An English geographer, Alexander Dalrymple, had written a book, in 1769, in which he explained how easy it would be move into what he imagined to be the great, rich, populous continent of the south – a land 'sufficient to maintain the power, dominion, and sovereignty of Britain by employing all its manufacturers and ships.' Dalrymple, who had spent many years in the employ of the East India Company, had returned to London in 1765 and set about a study of material available on the South Seas. He secured a copy of a memorial printed in 1640 – discovered by the English expedition that captured Manila in 1762 – and from this long-hidden document he deduced the existence of a strait to the south of New Guinea. In a little book, *Discoveries in the South Pacific to 1764*, which was written in 1767 but not published until 1769, Dalrymple included a map in which the strait was marked, as well as the routes of Tasman and Torres. In this booklet he recapitulated all the discoveries that had been made in the South Pacific, including Juan Fernandez Islands off the coast of the Chile, the discoveries of Quiros and Tasman, and those of Le Naire to the north of New Guinea. He drew the conclusion that all these widely separated fragments were probably parts of the same great continent – a continent possibly extending over a hundred degrees of longitude in latitude 40°S, so that it was larger than the whole of Asia from Turkey to the extremity of China!

Cook had no idea of the importance of his discovery of and claim over the East coast of New South Wales. He and his superiors were much more interested in the Great South Land, whose whereabouts were such a puzzle. His second and third voyages were spent in searching between NZ and South America, and between Alaska and northeastern Asia, but did nothing more in 'our' part of the world. Haskell records that 'England then joined the loyalists in fighting 'our' cousins, the Americans; in the end 'we' were defeated but it set men thinking of the new land in the southern seas. James Matra, a midshipman on the *Endeavour*, drew up a scheme by which loyalists should be set down in NSW to found a colony there, with labourers brought from China and the South Sea Islands to do all the hard work for them. The great difficulty was that the French were also interested in exploring the South Seas, and if Matra's suggestion had been formed as Matra proposed, a strong French fleet would come down upon it and seize the country. Matra asked the Government for help on the grounds that if the scheme were carried out under the direct orders of the Government, there would be no fear of a French attack'. (*Australia and the Australians* – Haskell)

The recent war in the Americas served another argument in favour of Matra's suggestion:

- England had been fighting Spain as well as France; so, if England had to fight them again, NSW would be an admirable centre from which to attack the Dutch and Spanish Islands in the Malay Archipelago. But the argument that prevailed in the end was much more persuasive than that. It was that NSW would be a most suitable place to which to send prisoners.

The Goals of the Transportation Program

The aims of the British authorities in transporting criminals can be deduced from instructions to their representatives, the governors, from Westminster debates and from official regulations. The colonial office made one such statement, in 1789:

"Transportation seeks three ends – the prevention of crime in Britain, the moral reformation of the convicts themselves and the welfare of the colonies to which they are removed". To these should be added a fourth aim: that Britain would simply be rid of an unwanted element in the society. But would it be the deterrent in Britain and become an integral part of the penal system of the time. The assumption behind the penal system was that the individual broke the law of his own free will. He must then pay for his crime and be an example for others. Transportation as a major punishment was supposed to serve this end. As an aim, rehabilitation was observed to be a failure. In the colonial experience, the prisoners would not accept that they should contribute to the 'welfare of the colony'. This concept had been incorporated into the laws of Britain. If prisoners were to be punished then it should be undertaken in the most useful way possible. The colony should be sufficiently remote to prevent fleeing. No prisoner was to return to England, even as an emancipist. The penal colony was to become self-sufficient and self-supporting as soon as possible. This meant that the system was to operate with as little expense to the mother country as possible. England's welfare was not to be forgotten.

There were many contradictions in the transportation system. Punishment by transportation was different to each individual involved. For some, the release from the hulks was a blessing. For others, separation from family was a giant burden. The punishment was meant to be severe, consistent and considered by the public to be so. This was supposedly the deterrent. Communication meant that the details of colonial life had to be shared with the public over 12,000 miles away. With social policy being so paramount, at least in theory, it is enigmatic that between 1788 and 1850, all but four governors were drawn from the navy and the military ranks, to which control and discipline, not reformation, were the keynotes to the system

The element of chance determined the treatment, response and attitude of the prisoners. Convicts were subject to meeting officials, directly under the governor – the surgeon, the ship's captain, the military officers, overseers and the free settlers to whom the prisoner would be assigned. Many of these officials would be hard and tireless in their intentions to extract the last pound of flesh from the 'free labour'. A convict's actions alone did not determine his, or her, treatment by the system. Typical was the treatment of the women – they were 'damned whores, beyond redemption, worthy only of punishment'. They did however have another use. They were to ensure the normalcy of the penal settlement by being sexual partners for the men of the colony and mothers of their children.

There was a wide diversity of opinion in Britain and the colony on what benefits accrued to the colony as a result of transportation, which suggests that we cannot arrive at a definitive answer.

The simplistic answer that transportation provided the colony with a population really begs the question.

Would there have even been a colony had it not been needed for a transportation program?

That there was need for a transportation program therefore ensured that the capital requirements for creating a secure penal colony were provided. This funding assisted with infrastructure, buildings for housing, barracks, stores, offices, roads, wharves, and bridges all in the name of gainful employment of these transportees. So, from the colonial viewpoint, the supply of capital led to employment, local industries, free enterprise, farming opportunities, trade, local revenue, a growth population, a sinecure for the military officers. Self-sufficiency at the lowest possible cost was always the goal. Arthur Phillip questioned the value of convicts as workers. He claimed, as did his successors, that 'they were used to lives of indolence and thievery, and were poor workers'

Summary

As Marjorie Barnard points out:

"It is difficult to conceive of a plan that is based on a colony of social misfits on a coast that all reports had described as barren, waterless and dangerous. James Matra put a more credible plan forward in 1783. He had at least seen the east coast of the continent and Joseph Banks supported his scheme. Matra wrote

The climate and soil are so happily adapted to produce evert various and valuable production of Europe that with good management and a few settlers, in twenty or thirty years they might cause a revolution in the whole system of European commerce and secure to England a monopoly of some part of it, and a very large share in the whole."

These schemes, however credible the source would have fallen on stony ground but for an uncomfortable by-product of the American War of Independence. In the days of the Old Dominion, England had got rid of her felons very easily and inexpensively by shipping them off to the plantations of Virginia. At first the government paid contractors 5 pound a head to carry them across the Atlantic. Later it became a better bargain. The contractors made their profit at the American end. The services of a skilled man for the term of his punishment were sold for between 15 to 20 pound. Women brought from 8 to 10 pound each. This showed a good profit although deaths were usually heavy. The convicts were slaves in all but name. Once handed over the government took no more notice of them.

Our revisionist theory is much more complex than the simplistic traditional opinion. It would seem that

- foreign policy,
- trade and economic policy,
- scientific and technical opportunities, and
- supplying the military (mainly the naval stores)

were the fundamental considerations in determining to occupy the colony, following which the answer to the question – how are we going to pay for any settlement, especially since this excursion will be government sponsored – was answered with the suggestion that the prisons are overflowing in Britain; it is costing the government upwards of 32 pound per convict per year; why don't we transport the overflow of convicts and the poor and unemployed people to the new colony as fodder for its economic development and divert some, if not all of the funds used to support them in Britain to the support of these people in a new colony; it will only be the original shipment that will be degenerates; their successors will be free peoples able to look after themselves both financially and economically, and Britain will not only have rid itself of these drains on the economy of Britain but have created the basis for future trade with the mother country and its colonies.

Matra's Figures of the Cost of Establishing the Colony

From the HRNSW we find that "Mr. Matra's proposal was placed before the Coalition Government of Fox and Lord North but they left office before full consideration. The Pitt Ministry considered the Matra suggestions to send out the convict population from England to New South Wales. The proposal had the support of Admiral Sir George Young, and eventually appeared in a paper circulated in January 1785 entitled 'Heads of a Plan for effectually disposing of convicts by the establishing of a Colony in New South Wales'. This plan (set out in full in Appendix B) includes a proposal for a penal settlement, the use of ships and marines, the immediate and forward provisioning requirements, including livestock and seed, and sundry matters such as guards for the ships and transports, surgeons, trade in flax and timber and tropical products. The estimate of expenditure was given as being 1,497.10.0 per annum for staff, and a clothing allowance of 2/19/6 for each convict per annum. The cost of supplies, including tools, was estimated to be in excess of 1,300 pounds, to which Matra would have added the transportation and food cost per head of ' a sum not to exceed 3,000 pound'. Matra observed in his proposal that "most of the tools, saws, axes etc for the use of the party left may be drawn from the ordnance and other public stores, where at present they are useless; and the vessels also, being part of the peace establishment can, nor ought to be, fairly reckoned in the expenditure. The Matra Proposal is attached at Appendix A.

Summary and Conclusion

Does logical thinking apply in these circumstances? If we were planning on settling a newly discovered land, having just lost access to another, would there be only one consideration? I think not! The best report to the authorities would be one that set down the present circumstances in 'our' region, and in 'our' sphere of influence, and then list all the benefits that would accrue to 'our' country, upon making the move to settle or colonise on that new land. It would be a stepping-stone, and not an end in itself.

There would be expenditures associated with the establishment, and thus a cost-benefit analysis would be set down. Even if the costs were to be diverted from another government outlet for expenditure, there would be benefits and the support for that first step would be stronger if the 'opportunity' cost in favour of the new colony was stronger and more favourable than the cost under the former expenditure.

And so it was with Cook's discovery, except the British neglected for 'cost' reasons, the most fundamental of steps – that of reconnoitring the colony before despatching the First fleet. Matra, Phillip and others had strongly suggested a 'forward party' to select the best sight, to commence preparing the sight, commence a basic building program and ensure fresh water and appropriate crops were available when the main party arrived. The authorities refused to go along with this commonsense approach and the consequences were enormous for Phillip. Cook and Banks believed, in an untested theory, that pockets of soil near the coast could support small colonies of Europeans – so long as the colonists imported their seeds, plants and livestock. Blainey concludes that Cook and Banks arrived at a good time (both month and year – 1st May, 1770) for witnessing 'vast quantities of grass and vegetation'. But he suggests that they could 'not possibly assess the soil and climate during such a brief (7 day) visit. Here was a new land, lying on the opposite side of the equator and growing exotic plants; a land occupied by people whose way of life offered few clues about the land itself'.

It was on the misconception of 'rich and fertile soils' that Britain was to locate their first settlement on the new land. The choice would have been very different if the Endeavour had landed during a hot dry spell.

This analysis we mentioned being completed for the authorities listing the costs and the benefits as well As the strategic value of the land, would also have included a statement on the integral value of the land itself. However, the conclusion would and must have been that thew country, by the standards of the age, was valueless.

We know now that the stony plains and hillsides conceal minerals and oils of immense value, and that pipelines and railways can move huge resources quickly and efficiently from remote and isolated areas to the nearest port. But the 17th and 18th century decision-makers did not have that knowledge. They knew the limitations of the world and sensibly ignored the new land. There seemed to be no riches near the coastline, and it did not appear to offer (as did most other colonies) energetic, docile labourers. There were no apparent new timbers, spices, vegetables or fibres. What the British desperately hoped for was access to tall pines, to flax and hemp or at least soil which could grow such crops, but it was the prospect only that caused excitement. And that excitement turned out to be badly misplaced. The new land appeared to explorers before Cook, not to even provide a port of call for refitting, restocking and refreshment.

Was this land really worth claiming, let alone settling? Blainey acknowledges in his source notes to '*A Land Half Won*' a different perspective from the one he submitted ten years earlier in *The Tyranny of Distance*. By 1980 he was able to write "my view now is that Botany Bay was settled for four distinct reasons: the search for new naval supplies, the need for a half-way house on new trade routes, the convict problem, and not least the over optimistic assumptions held about the climate and soils of Botany Bay". Blainey goes on to admit that 'further re-reading of the Cook and Banks Journals has convinced me that their mistaken deductions about the climate and soil of Botany Bay were vital prerequisites for the English settlement in Australia.

So to our conclusions about foreign policy, defence, trade and law and order considerations we should add misstatement about and misunderstanding of the new land as a significant factor in determining the final outcome.

Although the House of Commons passed the first Transportation legislation in 1717 (4 Geo I, c.11), it remained high on the agenda in Britain as both a social policy as well as an economic policy through the rest of the 18th century. It surely was a neat policy to implement and administer. Convicted felons, who had done little to deserve a 7-year transportation sentence, were handed over to contractors, who without charge to the government would ship these offenders to North America and sell them to the plantation owners in the Carolinas, Maryland and Virginia. It was a winning answer for everyone involved except the prisoner, who was being sold into virtual, if not actual, slavery. The contractor made money, the government had a monetary obligation as well as a future commitment taken off its hands, and the plantation owner, for a small sum of between ten and twenty-five pound (the British government was adding a bounty of 5 pound until 1772) got a worker for life.

It was when the Americans of more independent mind saw the better opportunity came with the huge number of black slaves from Africa than the white trash and waste from England, that the Loyalists came under challenge and the War of Independence threw out the English from the colony. So Britain now needed a colony for the American Loyalists as well as the growing number of human waste being processed through the courts.

But how could the authorities locate a refuge that was under way and would offer the same benefits as the North American colony had offered. The obvious places were Canada and Africa. So the answer to the question of a transportation destination was simple. However the better answer was to locate a destination that cold assist in solving other challenges. A naval supply base, a transit base for traders, a base from which to launch interference against the Spanish, Dutch and French, who growing presence in the southern hemisphere was causing strategic concerns; these were questions awaiting an answer. When one combined with these the question of a transportation destination, the answer was a new colony in the Pacific with convicts being the icing on the cake. This is when the convict system became, in essence, a form of compulsory, assisted migration. The colony's main economic activities would be suckled by the convict system.

As a revisionist theory of the colonial origins, it is not new or even original it is commonsense and logical. It made sense to the merchant pressure group in London; it made sense to the Colonial, Home and Foreign Offices within the government, and the general population who were affronted by the hulks and overcrowded prisons, the growing poverty and social disorder. The only group not enamoured with the decision were the contractors who had carted so many prisoners to the North American colonies and had no wish to travel twice the distance and through unchartered waters to an unknown destination.

It took little enough time (12 years) for the naysayers in London to complain that the colony was leaning towards being a waste of money.

The 1798 Report of the House of Commons Committee on Finance included this reference to the colony of New South Wales." The labour of the whole number of persons sent to these colonies, whether as convicts or settlers, *is entirely lost to the Country*, nor can any return, to compensate such a loss, be expected till that very distant day, when the improved state of the colony may, by possibility, begin to repay a part of the advance, by the benefits of its trade". The attitude of the committee was simple; 'the more thriving the settlement the more frequented: The more frequented the less difficulty of return – The more thriving too the less terrible'.

Overall Summary of the Revision

The traditional reporting of Australian economic history is:

- Britain settled the continent for 'strategic' advantages and as a source of raw materials for its industry, and as an outlet for its trading and the transfer of resources (a takeover) by the new economic managers
- Economic development took place in the new land, beneficial only to British traditional interests (including the use of valuable raw materials, of the British trade, shipping, insurance and investment industries
- The official intention of settling the colony, was for peaceful & co-operative economic development of the new land, beneficial to British traditional interests and not undermine or war with the native population, and to share what food resources were naturally available. The gulf between the two societies was too large to be bridged and British settlement succeeded while the ancient society was destroyed. The destruction of traditional Aboriginal society was recognised by a depopulation from an accepted population of 1 million in 1788 to 250,000 by 1848 whilst an estimated 50% of Aboriginal resources were absorbed by whiter settlement between 1788 and 1809
- The traditional recounting of early Australian Economic History is that Britain decided to settle the continent for 'strategic'

advantages and as a source of raw materials for its industry, and as an outlet for its trading and the transfer of resources (a takeover) by the new economic managers.

- This new class of colonial economic manager, in fact, faced much higher costs than expected, in achieving their 'success'. Their target was to be a bloodless change of ownership followed by economic development of the new land, beneficial only to British traditional interests

The revisionist approach is that:

- Britain planned for a multi-purpose strategic settlement at Botany Bay
- Britain did not plan to diminish the native population by thinking that it was 'terra nullius' just because there was no signs of 'farming' or other physical improvements, but
- The settlement led directly to a presumption of British land ownership as well as ownership of all natural resources, and
- British development (as defined and outlined) led to a penal colony under autocratic governance before moving through a transition phase of free enterprise, semi-planned economy but still providing raw materials and markets for Britain. As Fitzpatrick points out "The phenomenon of British Industrialisation and not the enticements of colonisation filled the social foreground[204]

Why did the settlement achieve success after its early struggles? What steps did Britain take that led to a successful settlement and colonisation process?

Butlin thinks that the early achievements of the settlement are the result of seven major conditions:

(h) The early elimination of threats from Aborigines and their almost immediate depopulation.

---

[204] Fitzpatrick, Brian *The British Empire in Australia – An Economic History 1834-1939*

(i) The early privatisation of the settlement and the firm establishment of private property, private employed labour and market choice in the settlement
(j) The accession of substantial British support in kind, through the authority to issue bills payable by the British Government, and through the presence of substantial quasi-exports
(k) The desire for non-tradeables and for goods that could not be readily tradeable
(l) The supply of human capital with skills appropriate to a relatively advanced society
(m) The lack of economics of scale in large areas of non-food production, and
(n) The recovery of property rights in labour time by the majority of convicts

THE REASONS FOR THE COLONY

The purpose of this section is to examine the various theories by historians for the U.K. creating the colony under the British flag.

Some of these writers being examined include:

a. Haskell (The Australians)—1943
b. Mellor et al (Australian History – the Occupation of a continent) 1978
c. Blainey (The Tyranny of Distance) 1966
d. Barnard (A History of Australia) 1962
e. Coghlan (Labour & Industry in Australia) 1902
f. Younger (Australia & the Australians) 1970
g. Jose, A (History of Australasia) 1897
h. Wood, F.L.W. (A Concise History of Australia) 1935
i. Clark, C.M.H. (A History of Australia) 1962
j. Shaw The Economic Development of Australia 1944
k. Shann The Economic History of Australia 1930
l. Butlin, S Foundations of the Australian Monetary System 1953
m. Butlin, N Forming A Colonial Economy 1993
n. Beckett (An Economic History of Colonial Australia) 2000

F.L.W. Wood writes

Upon Cook's news that he had taken possession of a great country (new South Wales), England did not immediately decide to colonise it. She already had a huge empire, and wanted no more for the present, for colonies were expensive to govern, and they oftentimes caused wars. With the American Colonies in mind, it seemed that colonies brought no profit while they were struggling and expensive, and that when they became prosperous they rebelled.

Even though Cook and Bank's journals were doctored by Hawkesworth before publishing to make NSW sound better than it was, the choice of a new colony would have been New Zealand or the friendly Islands before Botany Bay was selected.

However the need was different now with the revolt by the Americas and the accumulation of over 1,000 prisoners each year in Britain. They were being kept in prison and in hulks tethered together in mid-stream, and soon became over-full. It was Banks that suggested Botany Bay As a new penal colony, which is surprising when we remember what Banks said about NSW. He seemed to think it was just the right place. It was far away and no danger of prisoners escaping.

Arthur Jose says

Cook had no idea of the importance of his discovery. He and his superiors were much more interested in the Great South Land, whose whereabouts were such a puzzle. His second and third voyages were spent in searching between NZ and South America, and between Alaska and northeastern Asia, but did nothing more in 'our' part of the world. England then joined the Loyalists in fighting our cousins, the Americans; in the end we were defeated but it set men thinking of the new land in the southern seas. James Matra, a midshipman on the *Endeavour,* drew up a scheme by which loyalists should be set down in NSW to found a colony there, with labourers brought from China and the South Sea Islands to do all the hard work for them. The great difficulty was that the French were also interested in exploring the South Seas, and if Matra's suggestion had been formed as Matra proposed, a strong French fleet would come down upon it and seize the country. Matra asked the Government for help on the grounds that if the scheme were carried out under the direct orders of the Government, there would be no fear of a French attack.

The recent war in the Americas served another argument in favour of Matra's suggestion. England had been fighting Spain as well as France; if England had to fight them again, NSW would be an admirable centre from which to attack the Dutch and Spanish Islands in the Malay Archipelago. But the argument that prevailed in the end was much more persuasive than that. It was that NSW would be a most suitable place to which to send prisoners.

Arnold Haskell says

In 1783, through a wilful ignorance of their way of life, we lost the American colonies. In 1788 the settlement of Australia began. There never was the slightest intention of compensating ourselves for the loss of the old colonies. There was scarcely a trace of idealism in the scheme. The very discovery of the east coast of New Holland left the greater thinker of the age (Samuel Johnson) completely indifferent. The only reason that a settlement was agreed upon was that, now that North America was no longer available, some answer had to be found to the question, What to do with our convicts? But there was a greater consideration; the convicts came from England as a result of English social conditions. Through this incredible muddle, misunderstanding and inhumanity, and working in a medium that had been condemned in the Old World as rotten, a band of exceptional men was to carve out a Dominion, men who risked more, gave more and created more than many of the more spectacular creators of our history – Phillip, Flinders, Macarthur, Macquarie, worthies whose deeds should be familiar in every British Schoolroom.

Suzanne Mellon, as editor, says

The answer to the question 'what are the reasons for the settlement' once seemed obvious. In the 1780s England was facing an urgent problem – jails were overflowing, crime was increasing; the solution was transportation – but to where? Botany Bay was selected!

This is the traditional copybook answer repeated for the past half-century!

In 1888, a British historian, Gonner, suggested a larger story – Botany Bay was settled for economic reasons, to compensate Britain for the loss of her American Colonies. This theory found no support in Australia until K.M. Dallas (a Tasmanian historian) in 1952. Dallas asked – Why would a nation of merchants go so far and pay so much money, if it were merely to dump convicts?

Lord Sydney, as Secretary of State, stated the problem in 1780:

The several gaols and places for the confinement of felons in this Kingdom being in so crowded a state that the greatest danger is to be apprehended not only from their escape, but from infectious distempers which may hourly be expected to break out among the.

However these were the reasons for 'transportation' not for settling the colony!

In the 18th Century, England was in the throes of domestic upheaval. She was going through the Industrial Revolution. The country was being transformed from a rural-based economy to an industrial one. Farms were closing. Factories were opening. People were relocating from the country to the city. The results were overcrowding, primitive sewerage, disease and an increase in crime. On top of that there was no police force, only a collection of corrupt wardens. The English penal code was made even more severe!

Men were escaping from the hulks in growing numbers and there was a real fear that the situation would get out of hand. Crime, cost and prisoners were increasing – finance, accommodation and patience were not.

Building more prisons (made permissible by the Penitentiary Houses Act of 1779) was one solution, where convicts could be employed on hard labour. The scheme foundered because of wrangles over location and cost. By 1784, the authorities moved again to transportation and a 1784 Act to resume transportation was passed but without a specified location.

Parliamentary Committees investigated Africa, but the unhealthiness of the climate, the infertile soil and a fear of hostile natives combined to rule out the region. A disastrous experiment at Cape Coast Castle resulted in a 45% death rate in a single year.

Even in 1785 and 1786, sites in Canada and the West Indies were under consideration, but in 1779 Joseph Banks had proposed Botany Bay, before Matra wrote his report in 1883. Matra emphasised the great commercial advantages of Botany Bay. It could serve as a base for trade with China (tea), with Nootka Sound (furs) and the Moluccas (spices) and for cultivation of flax.

Sir John Young submitted a plan in 1785 for a settlement suitable for convicts and commercial gain. The Beauchamp Committee of the House of Commons rejected both schemes. The cost of transportation was the main objection. The evidence suggested a passage cost of less than 30 pound, which was 6 times the cost of passage to America. Although Botany Bay was rejected in 1785 as too expensive, just one year later, on 18th August1786, it was chosen as the site. Botany Bay was selected as the last resort, almost in desperate circumstances. Circumstances pressuring the decision included the debts of the Prince of Wales, negotiations for a treaty with France, agitation against the 'slave trade'. The convict problem appeared small and deserved and got a rapid solution. The government's aim was mercantilist – colonies or settlements were only useful if they benefited the mother country. England was a trading nation with imperial ambitions. Botany Bay was selected for the advantages it offered as well as being a place suitable for transportation. Botany Bay was useful as a naval base and a refitting port in the South Seas. England's interest in the Pacific had increased, especially after the loss of the American colonies. Rivalry with the French in the East became a foundation for a base. The colony of NSW had important commercial attractions; flax and timber, essential for naval supplies could be grown there. Convicts were not dumped at Botany Bay; they were sent as the first settlers for a naval base and refitting port. That is why the early emphasis on rehabilitation. From that base, the vital trade routes could be tapped—tea from China, fur from North America, the whaling industry and South American loot carried on Spanish ships.

After 1785, when the French, Dutch alliance was renewed, the French revived their own East India Company into the Pacific. In 1786 the British annexed Penang and Botany Bay was settled as a useful base for trade. The official documents do give us the profit motive, which the English needed to undertake the venture. These documents included Cook's report of Norfolk Island having superior quality of the 'spruce pines and flax'; and the 'greatest consequence to us as a naval power'—Matra. Phillip was instructed to cultivate flax, which Phillip did within one month of arriving at Botany Bay. The flax and pine timber were as important in 1788 as steel and oil are today.

The traditionalists still argue that Botany Bay was settled *at a certain point in time* because the government needed to solve its convict problem. The revisionists argue – why that place and not another? The pressure groups won the day – the politicians saw the disgraceful and frightening state of the hulks; the 'opposition' in parliament needled the government for its failure to find a solution; powerful economic groups (of merchants) were well represented in the discussions for protecting trade against competition from national rivals. The government made a sudden decision in the face of all this pressure.

Marjorie Barnard says

It is difficult to conceive of a plan that is based on a colony of social misfits on a coast that all reports had described as barren, waterless and dangerous. James Matra put a more credible plan forward in 1783. He had at least seen the east coast of the continent and Joseph Banks supported his scheme. Matra wrote

The climate and soil are so happily adapted to produce evert various and valuable production of Europe that with good management and a few settlers, in twenty or thirty years they might cause a revolution in the whole system of European commerce and secure to England a monopoly of some part of it, and a very large share in the whole.

These schemes, however credible the source would have fallen on stony ground but for an uncomfortable by-product of the American War of Independence. In the days of the Old Dominion, England had got rid of her felons very easily and inexpensively by shipping them off to the plantations of Virginia. At first the government paid contractors 5 pnd a head to carry them across the Atlantic. Later it became a better bargain. The contractors made their profit at the American end. The services of a skilled man for the term of his punishment were sold for between 15 to 20 pound. Women brought from 8 to 10 pound each. This showed a good profit although deaths were usually heavy. The convicts were slaves in all but name. Once handed over the government took no more notice of them.

William Eden, Lord Auckland, in his scholarly *Discourse on Banishment (1787)* enunciated the legal principles behind transportation and revealed the general societal attitude towards the criminal. The convict was an outlaw, and, having offended society, could expect no mercy. Punishment was a mixture of vengeance with a forlorn hope of deterring other potential criminals. Any idea of reform was only a pious gesture. He (Lord Auckland) was not in favour of transportation. He thought felons could be more useful at home, in the salt works and in the mines, on dangerous enterprises when it would be wasteful to expend a valuable citizen, for experiments involving risk or to exchange them in Tunis and Algiers for the redemption of Christian slaves. He wrote also of banishment but gave no clues as to where, other than the Riviera. It could not have been NSW – he had not been there.

There was actually nowhere left, unpossessed, distant, and reasonably healthy except in the Pacific.

All the schemes for colonization of NSW have a neat, often unreasonably reasonable, profit motif, supported by deductions that smack of medieval dialectic. Joseph Banks offered the thought as to whether England could derive any advantage from settlement in Australia, answered, If the people formed themselves a civil government, they would necessarily increase, and New Holland, being larger than Europe, would furnish an advantageous return.

There were originally three reasons for considering a new colony in the Pacific

i. For the use of resettling the American Loyalists
ii. The persistent suspicion of the French and the Dutch
iii. The superabundance of convicts

Banks gave reasons for supporting Botany Bay before the 1779 Parliamentary Committee into locating a new penal colony.

a. He had spent 8 days there in 1770
b. There was water and timber, the climate was good
c. It was not the ideal home for Englishmen but for convicts, men and women who had forfeited all privileges, it was ideal.
d. He suggested an advance party be sent to plant crops and erect buildings (as had Matra and Phillip)

Timothy Coghlan says:

Joseph Banks and others holding influential positions advocated the establishment of a colony in NSW, the beautiful and, it was thought, fertile territory discovered in 1770 by James Cook, and some point was given to these representations by urgent demand made on the King to provide new homes for those American loyalists who preferred quitting the land of their birth to living under the rule of the successful republicans. It is fruitless now to enquire how much or how little the English Ministry were moved by sentimental considerations in founding a colony in Australia; the fact remains that the scheme of settlement actually carried out was purely penal and military. In truth the authorities saw clearly that the idea of a penal settlement and a free colony at the same place and under the same government was an impossible one. When the First Fleet set out, it carried no one that was not connected with the penal colony—the authorities were much opposed to free settlers entering the colony, and did not desire them in any way. They (the authorities) did not consider they were founding a mere gaol, but an industrial colony; from which would arise in due season a new home for British people. This foresight is evident from several contemporary writers but how the colony was to be evolved out of the penal settlement is not entirely clear. Indeed it is probable that it was a pious hope rather than a real expectation. Botany Bay had been selected by the English Government as a suitable place at which to establish a colony, and when Phillip set sail from England in May1787 it was thither he directed his course.

R.M. Younger says

With the founding in 1711 of the South Sea Company, one of London's joint-stock ventures to seize public imagination, the distant Pacific became a region for more than literary fantasy. The South Sea Company was to trade with Spanish America and concessions were gained for it for that purpose, but its great appeal to the speculator lay in its hoped-for trade with the rich lands thought to await discovery in the Pacific. Expectations of dazzling wealth were conjured up, although operations never became profitable. The fraudulent booming of the company's shares ere followed by a collapse of the so-called South Sea Bubble in 1720,m causing disillusionment as well as great scandal. The collapse brought to a sudden and calamitous end all speculative interest in nebulous plans for trade in the Pacific. Nevertheless, the English period of discovery had begun. It was an era of scientific exploration, undertaken against a background of great expansion in scientific thought. Significant advance in the theoretical sciences of mathematics and astronomy had been made in the 17th century; now these new principles were being applied to navigation. The invention of the sextant in England in 1730 and the subsequent development of the chronometer, made it possible to take exact celestial measurements, and so to chart a ship's position with accuracy. These inventions, with modifications in ship-design resulting in greatly strengthened vessels, opened the way for new geographical discoveries.

Perhaps it was the aura of unreality associated with the southern lands as much as the British preoccupation with European wars, that held back further exploration for so long. Dampier had returned to London, hinting at prospects in lands still untouched, in 1701. Yet, apart from the wartime expedition of Captain George Anson in 1739, it was not until 1764 that the British government sent another ship into the area.

For much of the eighteenth century there was a distinct possibility that this naval warfare would be extended into the Pacific. Both French and English were doing their share of voyaging in these waters, sometimes no more than a few months, or a few leagues, apart. England's victory in the

Seven Years war, acknowledged at the Treaty of Paris in 1763, resulted in England's supremacy over the French in India, and the loss of France's North American colonies to England. (France, however, retained some possessions in India and the best of her sugar-islands.) In the long run the English victory also decided the future of the Pacific.

During the years of struggle, increasing attention was given to scientific inquiry and geographical speculation, both in England and France. Now that practically all the remainder of the world was charted, the Great South Land – Terra Australis or Terra Incognita – had become a matter of immediate concern. Books about voyages in the Pacific and southern seas, proposing further exploration or the founding of settlements, and speculating about unknown parts, contributed to the growing interest.

Between 1977 and 1748, a handsome new edition was published in London of the *Complete Collection of Voyages and Travels* (which has originally appeared in 1705, edited by John Harris) urging further discoveries. As well as narratives of navigators, the book contained prefaces and notations by John Campbell, who sought to draw attention to opportunities for new enterprise believed to exist for enterprising Englishmen. Pointing to the value of commerce, Campbell explained the narratives of travel in the South Sea in terms of the new challenge that awaited those with foresight and courage to act:

It is most evident from Tasman's voyages that New Guinea, Carpentaria (i.e. Cape York Peninsula), New Holland, Van Diemen's Land and the country discovered by Quiros make all one continent, from which New Zealand seems to be separated by a strait, and perhaps is part of another continent.

Campbell went on to suggest that there were great prospects for Britain if settlements (or, as he termed them, plantations) were established there. Convinced of the immense value of the southern continent, which he termed Terra Australis, he was opposed to a monopoly being granted to the East India Company to trade there. He made a strong plea that the South Sea Company should have rights there 'as a point of high importance,' and wrote that if Britain wished to make the greatest gain 'it may, indeed be requisite to remove ill judged prohibitions, and to break down illegal exclusions'.

He urged that New Guinea should be settled at once, 'and with competent force, since without doubt the Spaniards would leave no means unattempted to dispossess them.' In the space of a very few years, he believed settlement of New Guinea (and a trade in slaves from there) would prove of great consequence to the South Sea Company. He also recommended the formation of a settlement on the southern coast of Terra Australis. This, he believed, would lead the way to the opening of a new trade route 'which must carry a great quantity of our goods and manufactures.' Such a settlement would also be attended by other advantages. 'There is in all probability,' he wrote, 'another Southern continent which is still to be discovered.'

The Seven Years War began in the year that de Brosses's book was published. The future of the Pacific was decided in the water of Quiberon Bay in 1759. This naval victory began a long period of English naval supremacy, not to be reversed except during the War of American Independence. England's maritime supremacy made it certain that in the long run the visions of John Campbell should prevail over those of Charles de Brosses. In ironical commentary on this, three years after the end of the Seven Years War there appeared in London the first three volumes of John Callender's *Terra Australis Cognita.* In this book the whole of the arguments put forward by de Brosses, including the details of his idea for settlement, were appropriated by Callender. The only difference was that these arguments were now advanced to urge Britain's discovery and settlement of the Great South Land!

Callender's book was timely. The British Admiralty had no intention of allowing the French to forestall them in the race to new lands, and after 1763 a number of expeditions to the far South Pacific were organized.

Commodore John Byron sailed from Plymouth in 1764 with orders that in order to avoid arousing Spanish jealousies and retaliation, were kept secret. After passing through the Straits of Magellan he sailed on the familiar north-westerly course over the Pacific, making few discoveries; he sighted only outlying islands of minor groups, and after visiting Tinian he went on to Batavia and returned home, completing the circumnavigation in the record time of twenty-two months. On his return to England in 1766 his ship, the frigate *Dolphin*, was placed under Captain Samuel Wallis who, with Captain Philip Carteret in the *Swallow*, set off on another circumnavigation. The two ships were separated soon after passing through the Straits of Magellan. Wallis reached Tahiti (Naming it King George Island), the Society Islands, and the Wallis Archipelago, sailing home by way of Batavia. Carteret discovered Pitcairn Island and sailed through St George's Channel, so proving that New Ireland and New Britain were separated.

These voyages were all undertaken by Britain to advance 'the honour of this nation as a maritime power – and the trade and navigation thereof.' The English ships each followed a course through the Straits of Magellan and then struck northwest, finally coasting New Guinea. Close behind them were the French, who had the same objectives and who directed their efforts to the same area. Captain Louis Antoine de Bougainville reached the Society Islands and Tahiti a year after Wallis, and continued westward, making some new discoveries in the Samoa group. His next landfall was an archipelago that he decided – correctly – was Quiros's long lost long-sought Australia del Espiritu Santo. Here, he told himself, was the opportunity to solve the old riddle of the Southern Continent.

And so Bougainville sailed away from the Great Barrier Reef. He still believed he had been close to land, but consoled himself with the reflection that it could easily have been 'a cluster of islands' not the east coast of New Holland. His subsequent course took him through the hazardous waters of the Louisiade Archipelago, through the Solomons and New Britain, and north of New Ireland to the Moluccas and eventually to Europe.

Meanwhile, an English geographer, Alexander Dalrymple, had written a book in which he explained how easy it would be move into what he imagined to be the great, rich, populous continent of the south – a land 'sufficient to maintain the power, dominion, and sovereignty of Britain by employing all its manufacturers and ships.' Dalrymple, who had spent many years in the employ of the East India Company, returned to London in 1765 and set about a study of material available on the South Seas. He secured a copy of a memorial printed in 1640 – discovered by the English expedition that captured Manila in 1762 – and from this long-hidden document he deduced the existence of a strait to the south of New Guinea. In a little book, *Discoveries in the South Pacific to 1764*, which was written in 1767 but not published until 1769, Dalrymple included a map in which the strait was marked, as well as the routes of Tasman and Torres. In this booklet he recapitulated all the discoveries that had been made in the South Pacific, including Juan Fernandez Islands off the coast of the Chile, the discoveries of Quiros and Tasman, and those of Le Naire to the north of New Guinea. He drew the conclusion that all these widely separated fragments were probably parts of the same great continent – a continent possibly extending over a hundred degrees of longitude in latitude 40°S, so that it was larger than the whole of Asia from Turkey to the extremity of China!

CHAPTER 12

PASTORAL EXPANSION, EXPLORATION & DECENTRALISATION OF POPULATION

Imagine the opportunity of starting a new colony. The possibilities are endless. The opportunity to plan a new town; lay out the streets, design the new buildings; put the people to work; protect the people from foreign adversaries; design the roads; plan what the farmers will grow.

Life should be that simple!

Phillip had these opportunities and spent two years planning before the event. But natural events and other unplanned circumstances thwarted his plans. The weather was not conducive to growing neither the vegetable seeds nor plants he had brought with him, and so the crops in the first year failed. The construction and building program he had so carefully planned out, was delayed from taking place, mainly due to the failure of Phillip to acknowledge that the convicts would not be willing pawns in his grand plan. It was a prison and penal colony, and even the Marines (the military) rejected Phillip's policy that the military should guard and supervise the convicts. This task, they declared, was for independent contractors, and since there weren't any available, convicts supervised convicts, and the building plan suffered accordingly.

The military waited for a surprise invasion that never came, and spent their time learning to take advantage of the convicts by becoming traders and commercial schemers. Who needed a town plan when there were no houses, no means of transport and thus no need for roads other than to guide the convict hauliers to their destination along basic 'goat' tracks. The only people that needed to work were the convicts—the penal settlement had no free citizens other than Government officials. For the first three months, the settlement was a 'tent city'.

Slowly the tents were replaced with crude wooden buildings. But, there was little knowledge of how to work with this new timber. The trees were axe cut, but then the saws could not easily cut the hard, moist logs. The stumps were extremely difficult to remove from this shale and shall soil ground. There was much rock around Sydney Cove and although Phillip had spent quite some days scouting for a good location, he couldn't have foreseen the disadvantages of settling around the Cove. The benefits of magnificent sheltered harboured and fresh running water couldn't offset the disadvantages of the site. Phillip had set a building schedule, which was to be finished in a fraction of the time actually taken. The convicts would be housed; the military would be housed, and then the officials; and finally the precious stores sufficient only for 2 years, if properly rationed, and supplemental food was located.

The pressure of finishing any form of cover for both the residents and the stores resulted in 'green' timber was used in construction, and as the planks and poles dried, they cracked and split and fell over. There was no roofing material so 'rushes' from Rushcutters Bay were used as a thatching. The stores were filled with the food supply, but two challenges had been ignored. The threat of fire was nearly as big a threat as the rat plague that enjoyed the stored food.

Lieutenant Collins recorded daily, in his diary, the growth of the small colony. He writes in his 'Account of the English Colony in New South Wales', and sets out a list of the earliest buildings as they were completed.

The Collins diary is an important record of those early days, as the dispatches from the Governor back to England were spasmodic due to the irregular shipping. Collins kept a commentary of the atmosphere and the physical environment; frequently noting the lack of incentive to the convicts to carry out assigned duties and the effect the continuos shortage of food was having on all the residents. He commented that although Phillip's official line was to be friendly to the natives, neither the military nor the convicts abided by Phillip's directions.

In spite of the times being very tough, and far different to those originally envisaged by Phillip when he would sit in front of his cosy fireplace in his cottage in England, great progress was made, and Collins maintained his list of changes and especially buildings under construction. After a few false starts caused by the misuse of tools and timber, the colony took shape. The first house used by Governor Phillip was prefabricated in England and brought out in sections in the First Fleet. The first permanent house commenced in November 1788 was built using bricks made at Darling Harbour. The brickworks were shortly afterwards moved to Brickfield Hill, but the product was inferior because of a change of clay and the inefficient kiln. Later, new brickworks were started at St.Peters, Granville and Gore Hill, before a distant opening of a new kiln at Rose Hill, near Parramatta, where a fresh, quality seam of clay had been found.

The Earliest Progress toward Town Planning

Governor Phillip's Plan for a Sydney Town

It is fortunate that Lt. David Collins, an officer with the first fleet, kept a diary of both the journey and the early days in the colony

The Collins list of building and development work undertaken includes such items as

- Barracks—prisoners
- Barracks – military
- Storehouses
- Observatory
- Hospital & dispensary
- Government House

- Senior officers & official houses—Ross, Collins, Johnson, Alt, Arndell and Irving
- A hut for Bennelong
- A Magazine at Dawes Point
- A Gun Placement on today's Bennelong Point
- Church
- Mills
- Cells
- Court-house
- Basic Roads

Phillip planned for all these items but lack of rapid or expected progress made him reach only to the Gun Placement at Bennelong Point, which Macquarie found to be so run down that he replaced this item with the Fort Macquarie on the same spot.

In a work commissioned for the sesqui-centenary of the City of Sydney, Paul Ashton writes in 'Planning Sydney-The Accidental City', "within months of the initial European colonisation, New South Wales' first governor, Arthur Phillip, had marked out the 'principal street of the intended town', defined 'the limits of future building' and ordered the preparation of a plan for the town of Sydney. Most likely executed by Lt William Dawes and Augustus Alt, Phillip's plan envisaged the 'principal streets . . . . placed so as to admit a free circulation of air'; they were also to be 200 feet wide. Other provisions were made to 'preserve uniformity in the buildings, prevent narrow streets, and the many inconveniences, which the increase of inhabitants would otherwise occasion hereafter'.

Phillip had made an early administrative decision to segregate convict, military and a number of civil establishments from bureaucratic and legal functions. This decision was to influence Sydney's development. Building was to concentrate in the western part of the fledgling town, while the eastern area, naturally separated by the Tank Stream, was to be characterised by open spaces and later provide the location of the Sydney's first 'genteel' suburbs. But the Governors somewhat ambitious plan did not materialise. His last order, that the crown within the town of Sydney retains land was likewise ineffective. After Phillip's departure from the colony in 1792, some of his successors leased into private hands and, from

1808, granted title to land within Sydney town. The alienation of town sites compounded Sydney's disorderly growth, so much so that by 1807 its most irascible governor, William Bligh, was to complain to his superiors in England 'how much government (was) . . . . confined in any arrangement it may think proper to make for its own use or ornament of the town'.

Before we take a look at the details of the constructions listed above, let us review the origins of town planning, keeping in mind that Phillip had a vision for the new colony, which had far from reflected the actual circumstances found on arrival in 1788.

It is the story of building and development progress in the colony that we shall review from the history and from the Records. The 'history' comes from the Collins, Tench, Hunter, King, Phillip diaries, and from the Macquarie and Greenway collected papers.

Governor Macquarie's Vision for a Sydney Town

When Macquarie arrived in Sydney in late 1809, the conditions were not conducive to planned growth or to his goal of 'having all Edifices within the town built on a regular plan, so as to combine convenience with ornament, and preserve the regularity of the streets and houses. Macquarie had clocks installed in the major buildings (those commissioned by Macquarie himself) in order to 'instil discipline into the colonial workforce, and he had also had a host of regulations decreed to bring order to the town. Thoroughfares were regularised and named; narrow streets were widened; building rules were promulgated. But he further alienated land from the crown and helped create property relations. All those 'able and willing to erect substantial and handsome buildings within the town' were also encouraged to do so by promises of land grants instead of leases.

William Charles Wentworth wrote in his 'Historical and Statistical Account of the Colony of New South Wales':

"Until the administration of Governor Macquarie, little or no attention had been paid to the paving of streets, and each proprietor was left to build on his lease, where and how his caprice inclined him . . . The town upon the whole may be pronounced to be tolerably regular; and, as in all future additions that may be made to it, the proprietors of leases will not be allowed to deviate from the lines marked out by the surveyor-general, the new part will of course be free from the faults and inconveniences of the old".

Timothy Coghlan in "Labour & Industry in Australia records that

"Phillip was expressly enjoined to pay attention to the laying out of townships, reserving land in each for military purposes, and for naval purposes also where such seemed desirable. The interests of religion as represented by the Establish Church were not forgotten, and he was instructed to set apart a site for a church in each township, close to which 400 acres were to be reserved for the support of a clergyman; a site for a school was also to be reserved, together with 200 acres for the schoolmaster."

In 1832 Surveyor General Mitchell recorded in his report ' Reports on the limits of Sydney' that "most of the peripheral town land has been alienated and that roads and boundary lines were oblique and irregular" Mitchell's decision to straighten roads and property boundaries resulted in many claims for compensation from land-holders and led to the appointment of a select commission on compensation. The commission decided not to pay compensation but did decide that "owners would not be compelled to follow the street alignments" and this in effect gave them carte blanche to build where ever they chose, and houses were even built across the very roads that formed the basis of Mitchell's grand plan for the extension of the town".

In 'Significant Sites' edited by Lenore Coltheart, we can find the confirmation that in the Police Act of 1833 a signal of the changeover to civil society from penal society was demonstrated. The Act allowed for the regulation of shop awnings and house gutters; directed that carriage and footways 'be marked by posts at the corners and intersections of streets; and ordered that the Surveyor General 'set out and name with sufficient marks the limits of the town' and its immediate port. The Act also made provision for the erection of boarding and scaffolding. A Street Alignment Act was then passed in 1834, which aimed to straighten and widen thoroughfares. The Sydney Building Act of 1837 was in effect only concerned with structural considerations and the 'security of property'

Financing the Development

The Police and Orphan Funds

Between 1802 and 1822, the Treasury reporting function was, in fact, privatised and outsourced—the only time in Australia's history and indeed a rare occurrence any where in the civilised world. Treasury recording and reporting has always been a task for official Government.

However it was Governor King, who having been driven into action by the hasty recall and dismissal of Hunter from the position, decided that a number of matters could be handled less expensively by combining duties. The Reverend Samuel Marsden was already the Deputy Chaplain in the Colony and was 'interfering' in Colonial Politics (such as they were), so an answer to two problems came to King's mind and in reality he solved all three problems with one sweep of the pen.

A senior officer and good citizen of the early settlement – a Lieutenant Kent, was leaving the service and returning to England. Kent had built a large (some said a 'magnificent' house (which Kent couldn't sell when he was about to leave the colony. He lobbied King for the Government to buy it for official purposes, at its valuation, but King did not have authority for those types of extravagances. But he did see its use in connection with the second problem.

The penal colony had grown such as a penal colony would – a low morale, little respect for social niceties, especially marriage or responsibility towards each other; spirits were consumed to excess, whilst spirits were the 'currency' of the streets. Men and women drank to cope and debauchery reigned. This lifestyle, although officially frowned upon, led to a state of children, of all ages, running the streets, most from one-parent homes and unmarried mothers. There was estimated to be 500 children of both sexes living on the streets as the nineteenth century came into being. King came to the idea that female orphans could be housed, educated and 'kept', as wards of the state – largely the influence of Wilberforce back in England, whom Marsden had been corresponding with and informing of the conditions and religious inaction in the colony. Marsden had forcibly lobbied both Hunter and King. Since Hunter was no longer around, Marsden directed the full force of his ideas at King, not expecting the repercussions that came swiftly.

Marsden was becoming a thorn in King's side. His plea for more churches – Parramatta, Windsor and Liverpool, could not be justified in terms of buildings or more preachers to service them.

So Kings three-pronged action solved all three problems at one time.

King bought Kent's house for use as the Female Orphanage and set up a committee (including Marsden) to organise it. 80-100 female orphans were planned o be housed, fed, clothed and educated. Marsden's task was to, not only chair the committee but be its Treasurer. Shortly, King having arranged a source of regular revenue for the Orphan treasury, extended the role of the treasurer's function and kept Marsden extremely well occupied and away from the Government residence.

That was how the Orphan Fund commenced and was still going strong in 1821, when Macquarie was told by the British Treasury to abandon his simplistic accounting systems and adopt the 'Blue Book' methods.

The second prong of the 'privatised' treasury recording system was the Gaol Fund, with the Police Fund being simply the successor (by name change) to the Gaol Fund.

When the original Sydney Gaol burnt down by suspected arson, King decided to rally the citizens of Sydney and build a larger, stronger and more attractive replacement. He was encouraged in his plan by the directions of the Treasury in London to keep costs down, so King decided to make it a building by subscription. He rallied the free settlers and 'encouraged' them to donate money to a building fund. Subscriptions were slow but initially sufficient to get the building started. But progress was then slow and after two years of construction, the building was still not complete and donated funds had run out. So King decided to finish the Gaol with

Government money. Thus the Gaol Building Fund was converted into the 'Police Fund', given an expanded role and placed into the hands of a second treasurer – Darcy Wentworth. Wentworth who was also the assistant surgeon in the colony was to be the father of William Charles Wentworth after marrying an ex-convict. Both Marsden and Wentworth filled their roles from 1802 through 1821.

It was Macquarie who decided to make the accounts and the reporting more transparent. In 1810 Macquarie subjected the payments from the two funds to scrutiny and set up a committee led by the Lieutenant Governor to review each months payments, after which Macquarie put his name on them and had the published in the Sydney Gazette for all the citizens to read and enjoy.

The reading was probably not the exciting news from 'home' that the residents wanted to hear but since the Sydney Gazette had become the official government organ for disseminating information to the populace, it was as good as the next story.

The source of revenues for both funds was the mainly import duties, imposed first by King in 1802, without official authorisation but readily welcomed by the British Treasury. Import duties were applied to all imported goods at an initial flat rate of 5%, but naturally this rate grew until by Macquarie's time it had grown well into double figures (see accompanying table). Other revenues raised were fees from tavern licenses, auction licenses, tolls (from June 1811) and Market duties, for stalls in the open-air market, near Sydney Cove.

Revenue varied significantly from quarter to quarter, such was the small size and irregular visit of traders to the Harbour.

The usage of funds was broad and never ending. It ranged from paying for repair work on the existing roads and bridges of Sydney to building new roads and bridges and even government buildings. In the early days, revenue was small and expenditures limited by the need to remain in credit and build to some type of surplus. Between July 1810 and November 1818 total revenue raised for the police fund was 125,598 pound, and this was all spent other than the final balance on hand (16,859) on

- Salaries 52927
- Repair work 9409
- New Wharf 2000
- New roads 6280
- Other contracts 15779
- Govt buildings 9920
- Sundry payments4000
- Hospital supplies2624

Macquarie's Loan Bank

Timothy Coghlan writing in his 'Labour & Industry in Australia – Volume 1' states that

"At an early period in his governorship, Macquarie prepared a plan for the establishment of a loan bank, on the model of that founded by the Dutch at the Cape. His idea was that the Bank should issue loans to landowners at the rate of 6%, taking a mortgage of their property as security; thereby he hoped to stimulate agriculture and establish credit for those who deserved it while doing away with the need for promissory notes. The Committee for Trade and Plantations in England was unwilling to sanction the experiment, and nothing more was heard of the matter. But then in November 1816 an official notice was issued to the effect that certain subscribers had obtained permission to establish a bank. This was the Bank of New South Wales which was to have a capital of 20,000 pound divided into 200 shares of 100 pound each, and was authorised to do all the usual business of banking, including the issue of notes. Very soon the evils of an unstable paper currency disappeared as the notes of the bank were everywhere received and the promissory notes of private persons were speedily withdrawn from circulation".

For an explanation of early revenues we can turn to James Thomson's ' The financial Statements of New South Wales' where we find in the Appendix an explanation and *"An account of the Rise, Progress and present condition of the Revenue of the Colony."*

Thomson records that "early in the year 1800, import duties on other articles of luxury were resorted to, which, with slight modifications, were continued to be collected under Proclamations of successive governors till the year 1840.

When Major-General Macquarie assumed the Government in 1810 the population was 11,590 and the port duties were about £8,000 per annum. On his retirement from office, in 1821, the population had increased to 29,783 and the annual port duties to nearly £30,000.

Some explanation is necessary to show where local revenues were used to supplement the civil list, since all military, government officials, including legal and medical, surveying and superintendence of convicts were meant to be allayed from the civil salaries provided by the British Treasury. Upon Macquarie's establishment of the permanency of the Police & Orphan Funds, salary payments began to appear with frequency. The first quarter of 1810 showed only £49 but this grew quarterly until second quarter 1812 it was £325 and by the fourth quarter of 1815 it had reached £4,012. By the third quarter of 1818 it was consistently 2,500 pound, giving in total for Macquarie's period over £50,000 pound of payments in the form of salaries not met by the civil; list from the British Treasury.

The expenditure on roads and bridges is likewise interesting to analyse. Darcy Wentworth was, as well as an assistant surgeon, appointed as a Police Magistrate. As treasurer of the Police Fund, he had an interesting conflict of interest and he used his position in an unusual way. Most of the road repairs were carried out under the direction of a police representative or military officer. In the early 1800s the military was in its prime as controllers of the trading scene in Sydney and especially the flow of spirits. But not all military officers were proficient or successful as traders, and this is where Wentworth was able to supplement those incomes by offering them supervisory work over road repair gangs. Over the period, 1810 – 1818, supplementary payments amounted to nearly 10,000 pound. Another source of supplementary income for the military officers not otherwise engaged in trade was to 'bring back' absconding convicts. This work generally carried a 25 pound per head fee, and was not difficult work for military men with some experience of tracking.

The most important question now that we have considered the rise of local revenues and the use of those funds is how to explain the 'gap' between the use of local building funds about 25,000 pounds between 1810 and 1818, but the known expenditure on new buildings by Macquarie of over $900,000.

The Henry Kitchen submission to Commissioner Bigge of 922,000 pound is obviously an attempt to blacken the reputations of both Macquarie and Greenway. We also know that it includes an 'allowance' of 3 shillings per day for convict labour which we have to ignore because the convict maintenance fund was separated kept by the British Treasury. Thus the generally agreed upon cost of materials for the period (accepting the Bigge papers identification of 63 buildings completed during this time) is approx 412,000 pound. The payment of 25,000 pound from local revenues (assuming it all contributed towards public buildings) leaves this gap of about 375,000 pound and we need to identify its source.

N.G.Butlin wrote 'Forming a Colonial Economy' but is silent on public funds prior to the commencement of official statistics in 1822, sourced from The Blue Books. He fails to discuss these early Funds, which became the 'unofficial' treasury of the colony between 1802 and 1821.

Macquarie commenced his rule in 1810 with a meagre surplus in the funds of less than 4,000 pounds – his predecessor. King, having spent rather lavishly on boat building and raising little revenue. Macquarie operated in surplus for most years in his era except for 1812 when he had a deficit of 523 pound; 1814, a deficit of 4,000 pound; and 1815 a further deficit of 4,000 pound. Prior year surplus covered these shortages, as did the accruals of government revenue for debts uncollected by the government on duties and other taxes imposed.

The answer to our question lies in the remarkable increase in the annual value of bills drawn and paid from the commencement of the Macquarie era, in 1810. Governors had the authority to arrange for bills to be drawn on the British Treasury in payment for goods and services purchased on behalf of the colony. From the last days of King when the total of bills drawn was less than 12,000 pound, Macquarie's first year was 78,000 and it rose from there.

The advantage from the Waterways

Captain Arthur Phillip, as a naval man, was overjoyed when he entered Port Jackson, describing it as 'one of the finest harbours in the world', in which a thousand ships of the line might ride in perfect security', and as one where 'ships can anchor so close to the shore that at very small expense quays may be constructed at which the largest vessels may unload.'

The author of the book – 'The Sydney Waterfront, 1788-1850', Graeme John Aplin, makes some interesting observations about the connectivity between growth in the colony and development of the waterfront.

"From the very beginning, the waterfront was seen as a desirable place for more than just wharves. Bond stores and warehouses naturally established themselves nearby. Industry gained advantages from proximity to both wharves and stores, was well as gaining water supply (if salt water could be used) and a virtually uncontrolled means of waste disposal. Waterfront areas away from industry and wharves became choice residential locations, because of their views and the refreshing sea breezes. Throughout Sydney's history, the harbour and other waterways have been a favourite site for recreation, either on or in the water and along the shoreline of headland viewpoints and secluded coves. Finally, there has always been a strong naval presence on the Port Jackson waterfront."

Phillip chose Sydney Cove as the site of the first settlement mainly because of the small freshwater stream (the Tank Stream) that would, at least, temporarily, provide an adequate water supply. Activity for the period to about 1890 thus centred entirely on this inlet and its neighbours, Cockle Bay (later Darling Harbour) and Woolloomooloo Bay. Sydney Cove itself was bounded to the east and west by rocky ridges of higher land, ending to the east in Bennelong Point and to the west in Dawes Point. The western ridge was soon developed and densely inhabited, becoming appropriately known as The Rocks.

These two ridges later had the effect of impeding movement on land and making waterfront development difficult.

Much of the history of Sydney's wharves, in fact, involves efforts to provide just such wharfage for increasingly large ships a process that proved much more difficult and expensive than Phillip could foresee. The security from nature was provided by the many small coves sheltered by the rocky, wooded headlands Phillip remarked upon; security from man came, it was hoped, from the many fortifications built over subsequent decades, but virtually never needed.

In the earliest years of the penal settlement only two small and soon inadequate jetties were built: the Government Wharf near the present Loftus-Alfred Street corner, and the Hospital Wharf (later Kings and then Queens Wharf) on the western side of Sydney Cove. In 1812 the Commissariat Stores were built next to Hospital Wharf as the main Government store and warehouse. Robert Campbell had built the first substantial stores as part of his wharf complex developed towards the northern end of the western side of the cove from 1800. By the time the Campbell's sold this facility to Australasian Steam Navigation Company in 1876, it included a continuous 300m wharf and an eleven bay, two-story brick store. In 1811 the first wharf had been built at the bottom of Market Street on the Cockle Bay or Darling Harbour. It was named the Macarthur Wharf and was used to unload produce by boat for sale at the new Market at George Street, at the site of the present Queen Victoria Building.

Two events then assisted the town to extend and grow. The building of the new Government House in the Domain allowed the 'third' government house and its extensive grounds to be removed to make way for new construction. The silting of the Tank Stream required extensive reclamation work on the landward side, which would provide much needed wharves and additional land for urban building. A sea wall was built around the cove, and further land between Macquarie place and the sea wall was also reclaimed. The sea wall linked and integrated the Queens Wharf and the Campbell's Wharf, giving the sweep known more accurately as 'semi-circular quay' but the named was changed to Circular Quay.

The wharves were given regula5r use as landing areas for river and harbour traffic. Regular services to Parramatta had begun in 1789; the north shore was serviced by rowboat in 1830. The Manly service began in 1831. Pyrmont Bridge was opened to traffic in 1858.

Industry grew up around the Harbour immediately upon settlement. The windmills were located on Dawes Point and Darlinghurst Ridge; by 1837 three steam mills were located on the eastern side of Darling Harbour.

The Bigge Report

The arrival of Commissioner Bigge with his wide-ranging terms of enquiry spelled the end of the Macquarie era.

Bills Drawn on British Treasury 1810-1819

Year	Amount of bills	Cumulative
1810	78805	78805
1811	92128	170933
1812	91019	261952
1813	57948	319900
1814	74174	394074
1815	86021	480095
1816	109118	589213
1817	101163	690376
1818	145520	835896
1819	163465	999361

(These figures sourced from the Bigge Report to the House of Commons and Australian Historical Statistics)

Although the British Government reacted to this high level of 'bill' expenditure and appointed John Thomas Bigge as Commissioner to investigate the operations of the colony, Macquarie's successor, Major General, Sir Thomas Brisbane was not able or unwilling to reduce the amount of annual expenditure in any category. One area of explanation for Macquarie's high expenditure over say, King's was that the costs for convict transportation also rose dramatically, a confirmation that a huge increase in convict numbers had occurred. To Macquarie's credit the cost of stores fluctuated downwards which indicated the movement towards self-sufficiency within the colony, and an explanation for the high cost of salary payments from local revenue is that Macquarie kept the civil list, for his whole ten years at less that the last year of King and in fact reduced it from 13,309 pound in 1811 to 12,423in 1816.The cost of victualling the colony continued to rise which indicates that in despite of the system of 'assignment' the demand for daily rations did not decrease but rather increased over the 10 year period.. Macquarie had kept the majority of the arriving convicts out of the assignment program in order to use them in his construction program. The total of bills paid under Macquarie at close to One million pound was obviously not all allocated to the construction work but would have covered most of operating costs for the colony by way of injection of funds for public finance, and community works in particular. Macquarie provided new sources of public water, and commenced a basic sewerage works program – both services were to become a considerable expenditure of colonial funds.

a. Our intent in relating this story is to allow us to trace and follow the building construction sequence and the town planning policy for the colony between 1788 and 1820, estimate the cost, location, dimensions and construction type of each asset and locate an early sketch of each building. We will follow a guided path through official records and mostly convict sketches of the day.

DEVELOPING A COLONY

A. The origins of the Building Program

1. The need for a prison colony

The British Government had gone to war in the American colonies and the outcome was to abandon their sale of prisoners to American colonists as encumbered workers. A new source of moving prisoners from overflowing jails and hulks was needed. A House of Commons Committee reviewed Africa and a few other possibilities, but Sir Joseph Banks recommended Botany Bay.

2. The influx of convicts

The first fleet of prisoners left England in 1787 and arrived at Botany Bay in early January 1788. A week of surveying alternatives sites found that Sydney Cove, with safe mooring conditions, level land and fresh water was much better than Botany Bay and the fleet moved and arrived for settlement on 26th January 1788. Phillip had not considered the disadvantages of the site, being shallow soli, rock and shale and unfriendly natives on whose land Phillip had encroached.

3. Bringing a portable building to the colony

Captain Arthur Phillip R.N. had been appointed to lead the military officers, head up the Government and form a settlement, which was to be self-supporting within 2 years – for 2 years of provisions was all that had been carried to the new settlement, along with a few head of livestock, some plants, a portable house for the 'Governor' and lots of hope for a successful transformation.

4. Creating a new British outpost

The reality of the challenge was far greater than Phillip had realised. The land was not the deep rich soil, they had expected, so the plants would not grow; the natives became a problem; there were no free settlers so no free enterprise; the convicts were not in the mind to work hard, so productivity and morale was low. Food was in short supply and Phillip regularly trimmed rations until the prisoners claimed they couldn't work at all on such low rations

5. Establishing a new social order

With the new colony came a new order – the old English laws had to be amended to deal with the new circumstances. The colony commenced as a pure 'penal' colony without a treasury, without coins or any means of exchange; everything needed in the colony had to be 'imported', and the early shipping delay was seven months of sailing

B. Servicing the needs of the inhabitants

1. The Legal Authority for the Colony.

The establishment of a colony in New Holland at Botany Bay was authorised by letters from the British Home Secretary, Lord Sydney, in the last weeks of August 1786. These letters were addressed to the Treasury and to the Admiralty and ordered that "you do forthwith take such measures as may be necessary for providing a proper number of vessels for the conveyance of seven hundred and fifty convicts to Botany Bay, together with such provisions, necessaries and implements for agriculture as may be necessary for their use after their arrival." The commission to Captain Arthur Phillip was dated 12th October 1786 and signed by the King. The fleet, at the appointed time of its departure consisted of two naval vessels, six transports and three store ships.

2. The role of the commissary

The commissary was the 'storehouse' of the colony. It provided rations for every person on the military and civil list. It provided rations, clothing and tools for every convict worker. It held a store of food, grain, tools and material supplies. Every request for a product in the colony passed through the commissary. It was responsible for projecting ahead the rations required and ordering supplies from local farmers or, as was the general case in those early years, from overseas suppliers. It paid for its purchases by a bill drawn on the Treasury in England. Payment to the commissary could be by way of barter items, for instance, grain or other rural commodities, sometimes in the barter of labour to perform certain approved tasks, but because there was no currency in the colony, there was no payment, other than 'in kind'. In the early 1800s the currency became rum or spirits. The commissary traded heavily in this commodity. The commissary kept 'accounts' of what was owed by residents, other than convicts, and would carry these accounts for an extended period in the trust that the account would one day be settled by produce or in another for. However, many ' bad debts' were incurred and had to be either pursued vigorously by the Governor's staff or written off.

3. Working for the 'Civil List'

Until free settlers were encouraged into the colony – the first free settlers arrived in the Second Fleet – all 'free' residents were employed on the civil list. This list was of people employed by and paid by the British Government and included the chaplain, medical specialists, the Governor, lieutenant-governor, judges and the commissary-general. From year to year the list grew as the demand for government services expanded and soon the list included surveyors, engineers, architects and building supervisors.

4. Town Planning for the early stages

Phillip arrived in the colony with a 'plan' for controlled development and growth for the colony, in his mind. But circumstances rendered it in tatters. The shortage of food, the lack of understanding of the soils and the climate generally, the unusual terrain encountered, the inability to use and understand the timber available, the unrest among the natives and the attitude of both the convicts and military, all made Phillip struggle with his administration of the Colony. He had planned a town centre with wide streets, a residential area, a military and convict area, and a 'farming' area. His town plan had to be shelved for the reasons set out above, and even after Phillip returned to England and the colony became self-supporting and self sufficient, it was not until Macquarie wrote a Plan for Development, that town planning and construction control became part of the government operations. Captain Arthur Phillip captured the essential character of Sydney Harbour in his account from the very earliest days of the new colony.

"It runs chiefly in a western direction, about thirteen miles (21 kilometres) into the country, and contains not less than an hundred small coves, formed by narrow necks of land . . . . covered with timber, yet so rocky that it is not easy to comprehend how the trees could have found sufficient nourishment."

5. The need for exploration

The town of Sydney grew quickly with the arrival of more and more convicts. Phillip had encouraged the satellite towns of Rose Hill, Parramatta and the Hawkesbury. The grazing area known as the 'cow pastures' became too small, and the need for more and fertile farming and grazing land became number 1 priority for the Governors. The Governor encouraged 'exploration ' and decentralisation. Windsor, Liverpool and Castlereagh became new settlements, but in 1813 the great success of Blaxland. Lawson and Wentworth of crossing the Blue Mountains opened up the western pastoral plains to livestock grazing. Macquarie built a road traversing the mountain range and set up the first inland town of Bathurst.

6. Growth, decentralisation and creating small towns

If the need for new grazing lands became the catalyst for decentralisation, then the mechanics of growth were led by the surge of inland exploration – the story of the inland New South Wales rivers was unfolding, whilst many moves were being made to discover the inland routes to Port Phillip and northern areas, north of the established Newcastle. Small towns sprung up, as trading posts, stops for the Cobb & Co coaches and along livestock routes. It would not be until the discovery of Gold in 1851 that a population surge would follow new industry in regional type centres.

7. Roads and infrastructure

Macquarie quickly followed the crossing of the Blue Mountains and the opening up of huge pastoral runs with roads and bridges leading inland and along which, coaches and livestock could travel. His plan to make most of the main roads into toll roads, from which revenue for maintenance could be derived. This scheme was promoted and supported by the British Treasury and Macquarie tried to implement the proposal. but with limited success. Toll bridges at Windsor and across the Hawkesbury had not raised the level of revenue expected. The toll road between Sydney Town and Parramatta was the exception, and Greenway designed flamboyant style tollgates for the corner of George and Pitt Streets, and at the other end, just east of the Parramatta River crossing. The Governor had arranged for tenders to collect these tolls but this arrangement became the source of great irritation to stock movers and residents living adjacent to the tollgates, with their need to regularly cross through the gate or bridge system.

8. The continuing needs of the new settlement

Law and order, government building and buildings, importing goods, wealth creation (traders, spirit merchants)

C. The Economics of the Colony (what did it all cost?)

1. How the public funding system work

There is some disagreement over the actual funding of the new colony. The colony raised funds on its own account from duties, harbour and port charges, lighthouse charges, and wharfage as well as for the freshwater taken on by visiting sailing ships. In addition to locally raised revenues the British Treasury remitted funds for the civil list salaries and made payment for all supplies and provisions sent to the colony. As well as paying bills of Exchange drawn by the Commissary and Governor in the colony, the Treasury paid for the contracts to transport the convicts, provision the ships, clothe the prisoners and meet the freight charges for provisions being moved to the colony. These revenues and expenses are contained in a number of documents. The Treasury kept the accounts from 1788 to 1802 when the 'Gaol' Fund was established by Governor Hunter to try and replace the burnt out Sydney Jail through public subscription. There was a short fall in th4e fund and so the Governor advanced the required funds to finish the building and simultaneously appointed the Reverend Samuel Marsden to be Treasurer of the Orphan Fund, the purpose of which was to support the growing number of abandoned orphans roaming the streets of the town. The Female Orphan Fund was given a share of the revenue raised in the colony and charged with expending those funds on equipping the orphan school, housing feeding and clothing the orphans selected for support and then of educating them. The second fund set up was the 'Police' Fund – a successor by name change to the Gaol Fund. The appointed Treasurer of the Police fund was Darcy Wentworth. The gross revenue coming into the colony was shared between these two funds, which became the de facto treasury of the colony and the treasurers became the official recorders of the finances of the colony. This situation was confirmed again by Macquarie who left the arrangement in place until 1822 when the British Treasury designated an official office and a new recording and reporting system to operate the finances of the colony. Thus the 'Blue book ' era came into being, and continued in practice until self-government in 1855.

2. The Growth of Public Finance

Public Finance grew from these first two 'funds' in a penal colony without a treasury into a self-supporting colony without Treasury support by 1817, at which time Macquarie sponsored, firstly, coinage as a medium of exchange instead of 'bills' and a barter system including the 'rum' system as an exchange medium, and secondly he sponsored the Bank of New South Wales. By the end of the Macquarie era and the commencement of the 'Blue book' period, Britain no longer put its hand in its pocket all the time and in fact made the colonial treasury pay for free immigration to the colony. The first sale of crown land was the means of raising extra finance to operate the colony and pay for shipping convicts to the colony. As part of self-government Britain even made the colonial treasurer pay for the Civil List, if it was to keep all local revenues under its control.

3. The early Treasury functions (coins)

The first coins came in the pockets of seamen, the military officers and merchant traders, thus the coinage in the colony prior to 1810 was a mixed bag, with the Governor trying to apply an official exchange rate. Hunter tried to extend the usage of coins by punching the centrepiece out of the dollar thus making it the 'holy' dollar and when the Treasury finally sent a large quantity of coins to the colony, the residents found the means of hording the coins and really defeating the purpose of the exercise. The result was a return to using spirits as a medium of exchange.

4. Sources of revenue funds

The sources and use of funds are derived from a number of sources between 1788 and 1828. Between 1788 and 1802, the British Treasury paid for all payments in and on behalf of the colony. These direct payments included:

From 1802 the colony commenced to raise its own revenues by way of 'import' duties, harbour duties, lighthouse and wharfage fees, purchase of services from local residents, trading in government livestock and purchase of free labour for construction. These items of revenue are identified through the 'Orphan & Police Funds) between 1802 and 1822. During these years, the British Treasury 'topped' up the general revenue by meeting the on-going obligations for the convicts, the military and the civil list. From 1822 the 'Blue Books' recorded the revenue and expenditure for the colony and took the Treasury functions out of the hands of the two private individuals previously operating the Orphan and Police Funds accounts. The Governor in Council (the Governor had appointed a select panel of advisers in the form of a Legislative Council) was always seeking new ways of raising revenue, the demand for which just grew and grew. A significant Part of the British Treasury contribution was being raised from the sale and lease of Crown Lands, which the British had reserved exclusively for their own use, until 1856 when they released this revenue to the NSW Legislature in exchange for the Legislature accepting responsibility for paying the 'Civil ' list.

5. Use of Treasury Funds

The use of funds ranged from supporting exploration trips, to employing surveyors, architects, and public works supervisors for local purposes, outside the approved scope of British Treasury work. The commissary drew bills for supplies and provisions, purchased locally or from visiting ships, on the British Treasury, and sold provisions to local residents on a barter system until 1813. The locally raised revenue was used to pay for road and infrastructure maintenance including bridges, ferry services between Sydney and Parramatta, and the tolls raised were treated as general revenues rather than being reserved in a specific fund. From 1825, and the successful operation of the Bank of New South Wales, the Colonial Treasurer opened numerous 'funds' as a means of partitioning and isolating funds. For instance there was the Colonial Fund; the Aboriginal Welfare Fund; the Church & School Fund; The Civil Service Superannuation Fund; The 'scab in sheep' fund; The Orphan, Police and Gaol Funds

6. The opportunity cost to Britain

It is still a matter for great academic debate as to what the real cost of establishing the colony was to Britain. On one hand, the argument runs that it cost the British Treasury over $127 million pound sterling to set up and operate the colony (Professor N.G.Butlin). On the other hand, it is argued that there was an opportunity cost attached to the settlement that saved England much, much more than it cost. The traditionalists versus the rationalists. The opportunity costs are easily accounted for:

The savings in operating traditional prisons

The savings from paying contractors to feed and house the prisoners on the hulks and in the prisons

The savings from using convict labour to build up the colony (assuming Britain wanted another overseas colony)

The benefits from traders using British manufacturers to source materials and supplies for the colony.

The benefit to British textile manufacturers to have a reliable and cheap source of quality raw material (wool) for value adding and re-exporting throughout Europe and Asia.

The benefits of having the colony be the source of food and naval supplies (the navy wanted Norfolk Island as a source of flax –for sail-making, and pine trunks for masts

D. The Portfolio of Improvements

1. The early years of building

As would be expected Philips first priority was to get shelter for the convicts, the military, him and the stores. By good planning, Phillip had brought with him a prefabricated house for himself, costing the Treasury 125 pound. The other buildings were slow to erect. Step one was to clear the ground, and the convicts were set to this task but were ill equipped with poor and inadequate tools against the harsh terrain. Phillip had not anticipated the shallow soil over rock and shale; nor had he anticipated the very different types of timber to that commonly found in Britain or Europe. The Australian 'Gum' or Eucalyptus is very high in moisture content and very slow to dry. In normal open air rack drying, it takes almost two years to dry sufficiently so that with nailing it does not crack, split, warp or bow. With Phillip in a great hurry to show progress with establishing the settlement, he decided not to wait two years whilst the timber was drying before use. He ordered the trees to be cut, split and used immediately. Within months the buildings constructed from 'green' timber had twisted and split, and the buildings collapsed. Phillip set up a Lumber Yard as part of the Commissary Store, and directed that they be responsible for forestry operations, especially storing and stacking on drying racks all timber designated for construction work. The commissary decided to sub-contract this work and was within four years able to negotiate supply contracts with reputable timber cutters, for dried, quality-sawn timber. When the Sydney area could no longer supply the quantity required, especially during the Macquarie era, regular supply was found from the Newcastle area.

The early buildings were constructed to British standard design. Barracks, both military and convict were generally 100 feet long and 24 feet wide. This conformed to the configuration specified by the British military throughout the Empire. In addition to barracks, the governor ordered, storehouses, wharfs, a hospital, houses for senior civil list personnel and finally administration offices, and a new house for the Governor.

2. Inventory of the First Fleet

An inventory of goods shipped with the first fleet was assembled by John Cobley in his work ' Sydney Cove 1788'. Contents included:

3. Resources of the colony eg timber, bricks, tiles, tools

Phillip obviously planned for a reliable supply of natural and local resources to build his colony with and on. But many expected resources were not available. His food supply dwindled without ability to be replenished; his worker resource fell far short of expectations and the productivity per head was a fraction of what was expected; the military refused to supervise the convicts at work and so convicts were to be supervised by convicts; the available timber supply was unsuitable for immediate use; the tools he had brought with him were largely inappropriate, unreliable, scarce and easily stolen by the convicts and the natives. Phillip had a brick making operation set up in the Domain area within months of arrival and he located a small supply of second quality clay nearby. By mid-1789 this operation had been transferred to a new place at Brickfield Hill and a second better supply of clay had been located at Rose Hill, thus making this second small settlement area a staging toward Parramatta. The failure of the timber supply to fill the needs of the construction plans meant there was a growing reliance on and importance to the regular and reliable supply of bricks and tiles. Within months the new facility at Rose Hill was turning out 25,000 bricks each week.

4. Shortage of skills

Tools and materials were not the only items missing and missed in the colony. There were few, if any, skills amongst the convicts that could be used or relied upon to assist in forming the colony along the lines Phillip had envisioned. He needed brick makers (and had only one man experienced in this trade; he needed carpenters and mechanics; he needed engineers, surveyor, clerical assistance, but none of these trades was readily available. His appeals to the British Colonial Office for supervisors were ignored, as were his calls for more and better tools and general building materials.

5. Designing by default

Each governor had his own ideas on town development. Phillip had to set the basis for future development by clearing land, laying out streets, giving some intention of future sites for key government buildings such as government house, courts, military bases, convict barracks etc. Governors King and Hunter, both associates of Phillip during his term of office were happy to just keep Phillip's work moving ahead without appearing to strike out into new territory. Bligh, on his arrival had few supporters and did little to improve the settlement other than make a few land grants and some controversial appointments, most of which Macquarie reversed upon his term commencing in 1810. It was left to Macquarie to re-assess the whole future direction and development of the town and its various satellites and try to meet more of the objectives of the colonial office in London. The colonial office wanted expansion for more convicts to be transported and put to gainful work – all such activity to be with minimal cost to the Treasury.

6. Paying in Kind – a Barter economy—'The Colony has no Treasury (1788-1802)'

Being a penal colony, the first Governors – Phillip, King and Hunter, did not worry about coinage or the development of a monetary system as a means of exchange. The commissary coped by drawing 'bills of exchange' in favour of visiting traders, shippers and local purchasers, on the British Treasury in London. The barter system became established as the means by which freemen could sell their labour, settlers could sell produce to the commissary and settlers could trade between each other. It was Professor S. J. Butlin who coined the phrase 'the country has no treasury in his work "Foundations of the Australian Monetary System". He writes that the commissary store receipts were, for many the means of exchange on the streets of Sydney town. The medium of exchange for the military officers was the Paymaster's Bills, again drawn on the Treasury in London. There were a few 'scanty' coins, says Butlin, and a few private bills. Those who had credit balances or credit in London that is mainly the military and civil officers could only draw private bills. In 1799 a 'few tons' of copper coins was shipped to the colony and Hunter decided to assign varying exchange rates to the various coins rather than their face value of farthings ¼ penny, halfpenny 1/2 penny and the penny

7. Traders set the pace

Each new colony attracts those traders seeking new outlets for their goods or new markets to supply their wares or new sources of supply to ship back to the primary locations. Robert Campbell was no exception. An English trader, who had moved to India to further his career and success, arrived in Sydney in 1793 with the intention of building a trading relationship between India and the new colony. From the time of its establishment in 1788, writes Margaret Steven in "Merchant Campbell1769-1846 – A study in colonial trade", the colony's immediate and spontaneous links were with India. Bengal was British and prosperous, and the colony of Botany Bay figured spasmodically in the affairs of Calcutta, which for the first twenty years, played the part of general store to the penal establishment." Campbell's business flourished and this led to convicts and early release convicts being used as 'front' men for firstly the military officers who engaged in trade, and then becoming traders in their own right. For instance Simeon Lord, not long after finishing his sentence became a very wealthy and respectable trader, magistrate and government confidante. Being so isolated, and with a surge of growth from both convicts and free settlers, there was no shortage of those willing to take risks as a trader. Even John Palmer the commissary-general engaged in questionable trade practices whilst still the operator of the commissary, and the ignoble Robert Brookes of London, became one of the largest traders and encouraged the shipping of wool to the English auction houses before the trend was to sell the wool in Sydney sales houses.

E. Specialised development

1. Wharves, harbours & navigation

The need for wharves is obvious in any port town. The fleets (both first and second) could not get close to the shore, and so required unloading facilities, row boats etc to transport convicts, military personnel and stores to dry land. However, even in1811, there existed only three landing places around Sydney Cove. The Governor's Wharf on the east side of the cove, the Hospital Wharf adjacent to the market house and store house, and Robert Campbell's wharf further north on the west side of the cove. Phillip had built the Dawes Point observatory and the magazine on Bennelong Point, and when a sailing vessel was expected, lit fires on South Head. It took until Macquarie's era to have a lighthouse built on the South Head (Macquarie lighthouse) and Fort Macquarie replaced the old magazine on Bennelong Point.

2. Military accommodation

The first military accommodation was on the shore of Sydney Cove in tents, whilst they awaited the building of barracks. Most of the officers remained in tents until mid-1789 (records the diary of Lt David Collins). The priority set by Phillip was for him and the senior civilians to be houses, the convicts to be placed in Barracks, a hospital to be built and storehouses. The military was then to have their barracks built. The whole process was delayed by the use of green wood, which soon twisted and split in the drying process, causing the huts and houses to fall over.

3. City beautification

It took until the arrival of Macquarie for any Governor to show or take any interest in aesthetics. Macquarie built Macquarie Square and incorporated an obelisk and fountain into the landscape. He instructed Greenway, as his official architect to design attractive (if not ornate) toll-gates in both Sydney and Parramatta, and ordered the Government Stables in the Domain area next to Government House to become a magnificent edifice to inspire the colonists and demonstrate how attractive buildings would improve the landscape and the quality of life in the town. He broadened the streets and planted trees along those streets.

4. Road and Bridge Development

'Roads' were little more than cart tracks before Macquarie brick-paved the first road – George Street—in 1814. The first bridge was built over the Tank Stream in July 1788, with a bridge built over the Parramatta River in 1794. Macquarie introduced the 'turnpike' or toll road in 1810. The Windsor Bridge of 65 m in three spans was completed in 1813 and by March 1814 the Sydney to Liverpool road was completed. The crossing of the Blue Mountains in 1813 gave Macquarie reason to build an inexpensive road from Parramatta to Bathurst using convict labour with the incentive of freedom upon completion.

5. Expansion of the settlements – Liverpool, Windsor, Castlereagh & Parramatta

It was Phillip and his earliest successors who, in their search for food production decided to make grants of land to freed convicts, military people and free settlers. In the effort to find better grazing and farming country, they set up in Rose Hill, Parramatta, Toongabbie, Windsor and Hawkesbury (Castlereagh). The results were immediate. Food production and grazing too place and by 1792 the colony was moving steadily to self-sufficiency. Phillip distributed breeding livestock to selected farmers in an effort to grow the animal numbers to a point where the salt pork could be replaced by fresh meat, and fresh vegetables were available to all.

F. Development Plans for the Future

1. The rise of the Banks

It was the Macquarie observation to Lord Bathurst that " . . . the colony had no provision for public credit . . ." that becomes the first indication that Macquarie was mindful of the need for a bank in the colony (Banks, or credit and discount houses had been operating in England for many years). However it took until 1817 for Macquarie to sponsor and indeed 'charter' a bank – the first bank being 'The Bank of New South Wales'.

Crowley in Colonial Australia –Volume 1 writes "Private banks played a leading role in the development of the New South Wales economy in the 1820s and 1830s. The first was the Bank of New South Wales, which opened for business in Macquarie Place, Sydney on 8th April 1817. Governor Macquarie had granted to the President and Directors of the new bank a special charter for their incorporation as a limited liability company, and had therefore legalised thew institution pending final approval from London. In fact, Macquarie had no legal authority to issue such a charter, and this was later made clear to him and to his successors; it was not until seven years after the bank had opened that it received official approval. It was established to meet the need for a stable local currency and to establish credit facilities for trade, commerce, manufacturing and land settlement. Crowley quotes from the rules and regulations which were adopted for the bank's conduct."

2. Gold Discoveries

The last few days of May 1851 saw Sydney town in a flurry of excitement, after the reports of 'The Gold Fever' reached the town on 20th May, 1851 and were published in the Sydney Morning Herald, and followed with hundreds of men walking the road over the Blue Mountains; the shops were crowed with buyers of suitable clothes and tools, appropriate to a 'digger'. The immediate effects of the gold discovery were a sudden increase in the size of the population in eastern Australia and the export to Britain of large quantities of gold bullion. Crowley points out that "at first, wool growing and cattle raising suffered from the loss of workmen, but the squatters quickly adapted to the new situation, mainly because of the new increased demand for meat and grain, and the higher prices brought for these items. Freight costs were also reduced to Britain by the new keen competition between ship owners, at a time when wool prices were also rising."

Rising wages for the manufacturing industry was held partly in check by the constant arrivals of new immigrants in ships with their holds full of pots, pans, tools, clothing, lanterns and cheap furniture. The commercial boom in Sydney and Melbourne led to a land boom and the inevitable speculation in building in the two capital cities as well as the central gold towns, such as Ballarat, Bathurst, Orange and Goulburn.

3. Traders in Control

During the 1820s the colony changed from a 'paternally administered jail into a free—market capitalist economy' (Crowley) in which the everyday use of money increased in importance, private banks increased in number, privately arranged foreign exchange became important, share deals and bill-broking became common, and pastoral expansion was financed by bank overdraft and imported capital. 'Pastoral settlement in the Hunter, Bathurst and Goulburn districts was rapid, and the colony's population increased from 24,000 in 18250 to 36,100 in 1825 and 41,000 in 1829. Wool exports to Britain increased from 175,000 lb in 1821 to 1,106,000 in 1826, and then doubled in the next four years. New settlers brought in capital and in July 1826, the new Bank of Australia opened in competition to the Bank of New South Wales. The dominance, once again, of the traders and great pastoral houses was entrenched.

The Commencement of Town Planning.

Phillip approved the earliest 'Public Buildings' with little benefit of forethought or planning. The earliest known layout of the colony is dated July 1788, showing Phillip's thoughts as to the layout of streets and the location of these public buildings. The references include"

- "A small house building for the Governor
- A farm of 9 acres in corn
- The lieutenant-Governor's house

- The principal street marked out
- Ground intended for the Governor's new House, Main Guard House and Criminal Court
- Ground intended for building hereafter
- Ground intended for Church
- Grounds intended for Storehouses
- The Hospital
- The Observatory
- Temporary Buildings and huts—military and convict use."

Phillip's plan showed that at the junction of the cove with today's bridge street, a road was marked. This road Phillip planned to be the town's principal street, 200 feet wide. The road was never made.

This map was forwarded with Governor Phillip's despatch of 9th July 1788 to the Colonial Secretary, Lord Grenville, and is attached for reference purposes.

Subsequent maps are dated 1800 (Grimes); 1807—drawn by ex-convict and official Surveyor James Meehan; 1808—Governor Bligh's plan of the Town of Sydney; undated Macquarie era plan (probably 1817-18) showing all town streets named and blocks marked and identifying main buildings and improvements; an 1822 map by Greenway, showing the prominent buildings and locations; and an 1827 'View of the Town of Sydney' showing the development in an elevation perspective, including items such as

- New goal
- Prisoners Barracks
- Government Domain
- General Hospital
- The various chapels and churches
- Botany Bay
- Road to Parramatta
- School of Industry
- Natives
- Orphan school
- Various official houses

- Fort Phillip
- Blue Mountains
- Law Courts

By 1800 the population of the town was 3,000. A further 3,000 residents were located in Parramatta, Toongabbie and Hawkesbury. Governor Hunter had opened up the fertile Hawkesbury River area for settlement in 1794, with Windsor being the first town centre of the region and replacing Parramatta as the principal rural district.

Earlier (in 1789), Phillip had given an acre of land at Rose Hill to James Rouse, an industrious ex-convict. Rouse became the colony's first independent farmer, and was followed by numerous other 'settlers, under Phillip's land grant scheme. Time-expired or pardoned convicts were 'granted' 30 acres with an additional 20 acres for a wife and 10 acres for every child. The obvious explanation is that Phillip wanted to encourage marriage in an otherwise immoral society and control the growing wave of orphan children roaming the streets. Phillip's hunt was for food production via an expanded agricultural base for the colony.

Phillips town planning was complicated by the need to separate and expand the colony into rural and town. Only the class responsible for town planning decisions understand the rationale behind their plan. The rationale was based on 'commonsense' for the colonial administration of the day, which policy was implicit in government for almost 100 years and is inherent in the building heritage of that period. Phillip built the town centre around the port, and the source of fresh water. The convict barracks were initially on the outskirts of the town boundaries, alongside the military barracks and main guard. The storehouses were centrally located to the wharf area and adjacent to the residential area whose inhabitants were the main customers of the public stores. The residential blocks were all sized 60 feet x 150 feet. There was commonsense symmetry in the street pattern—the main thoroughfares ran north/south from the wharves of today's circular quay towards Ultimo and Brickfield Hill and led the main thoroughfare all the way to Parramatta. The east/west streets traversed the main thoroughfares and linked the Domain to the smaller docks of Cockle Bay and today's Pyrmont. Macquarie completed and supplemented the first plan of Phillips, and although Bligh put his name to the 1808 map, his was a small contribution to the town plan.

By examining the public buildings and planned open public space we can understand a little better these 'commonsense' rules. The initial stage of military government was gradually transformed into the phase of civil type construction. Phillip and his two working associates, Hunter and King, had completed the basic structure and organisation of the town and it went to Macquarie to imprint the town with the embellishments that differentiate a town from a city. King & Hunter barely touched, let alone refined the Phillip plan mainly because they had had a hand in its formulation. Macquarie changed the pattern immediately because he found the town 'run down and decrepit looking, and wanted to make it a 'good place' to live, even though the majority of the residents were still convicts.

Buildings of new grandeur, buildings designed mostly by Greenway, an ex-convict, but also by Lafleur, made quite a contribution. The Macquarie era was the high point of the change, which affected the development of the primary and secondary towns as well as the styles of building. Macquarie developed Sydney's town centre on a plan 'for the ornament and regularity of the streets of Sydney, to secure the peace and tranquillity of the town'. The early timber structures had decayed rapidly, so Macquarie established the civic institutions in local sandstone: the schools, churches, public buildings of various kinds including even the asylums (for orphans and the aged), and the barracks. Through the architectural skills of Greenway, Macquarie placed the town centre further away from the shoreline. Macquarie also attempted to impose a town plan on an irregular topography and tidy up the rather haphazard streets and buildings clustered around the Tank Stream and Sydney Cove. This is in stark contrast to the geometric layout of Adelaide Streets on a level site beside the river Torrens set out by Colonel Light a generation later.

Macquarie encouraged the shift of the central civil authority away from the Rocks area, and allowed that part of the town (built literally on 'rock') to be the first area of urban decay. By re-locating the military barracks from Sydney Cove to Wynyard in George Street, Macquarie brought protection to the new middle class area around Hyde Park, Elizabeth Street and

Macquarie Street. The gaol and police station remained in 'The Rocks' area and reminded the population that this was the original settlement of early convicts, as well as of trade and a source of great thievery and low-life haunts.

Macquarie was the colony's fifth official Governor and when he arrived in 1810 with his wife, Elizabeth, and his own regiment, he found the colony only just self-sufficient, with poor roads, crumbling building and a great deal of general maintenance work unfinished.

Macquarie had announced on 11th August 1811 a new town plan for Sydney, with road widths of 50 feet including footpaths and he set minimum building standards and construction regulations.

As well, the local agriculture and enterprise was at a low state. Public morale, after the removal of Bligh, was also at low ebb and the convicts after a tortuous period at the hands of the Rum Corps had lost all interest in other than just staying alive.

During the next eleven years of the Macquarie era, the colony would grow from 11,590 to 38,798 people and the amount of land under agriculture from 7,645 acres to 32,267 acres. Animal numbers grew in numbers enormously, particularly sheep; from a flock of 26,000 in 1810 to 290,000 in 1820; Cattle numbers increased 10 fold from 12,442 to 109,939. During these same years, the Bank of New South Wales was founded; a police force and police districts were created; currency was introduced, as was cart registration, horse racing and the first public markets. Sunday liquor sales were stopped and convicts were forced to attend church.

However, it was the public works program that brought Macquarie under special Colonial Office attention, and it was this program, along with his town planning skills, which have left the greatest legacy.

Macquarie had developed a proper plan for the town of Sydney as well as the settlement at Parramatta and the smaller towns in the Hawkesbury. Rather than allowing the city to develop in its own way, Macquarie named all the streets and, by regulation, required that all building plans be submitted for approval prior to construction.

He told Greenway that Government buildings should be of quality construction, and thus lead to a higher standard for all building work. In all he built 67 public buildings in Sydney itself (refer "Appendix A"), 20 in Parramatta, 15 at Windsor, 12 at Liverpool, as well as in Tasmania (Van Diemens Land) and Bathurst. Probably his greatest engineering achievement was the building of the Western Road over the Blue Mountains; 60 convict workers and their overseers completed the 126 miles in just six months. The road had cost zero in labour. Macquarie had agreed that any convicts, who worked on the road at no pay other than food and shelter and completed the task quickly, would be given their freedom.

Macquarie chose to meet every convict transport ship arriving and 'select' qualified or suitable convicts for special government service. He justified new buildings, constructed in a belt-tightening era, in an unusual way. For example, he used a 'defence' need as justification for constructing the Government House Stables (now the Conservatorium of Music). The 'Rum' Hospital was a 'free' building—he exchanged the finished hospital for the free importation (free of duty) of 45,000 gallons of rum. However, Commissioner John Bigge brought the era to an end with the charge of extravagance against Macquarie, which led to his recall back to England.

If Macquarie were being examined today, in front of an enquiry panel into his actions, he would be applauded as choosing the most logical way of improving the economy. Increasing wealth within the colony and keeping costs (compared to benefits) to a manageable and justifiable level. However Bigge did not put it in this light. He reported excess expenditure (in his opinion) and reported scurrilous, damaging criticism to his superiors in London without ever placing Macquarie's explanations or justifications before the same authorities. Macquarie was damaged beyond redemption by the Bigge report, unjustly and unjustifiably, and as a result he personally and his health, suffered. He retired a shattered and broken man, without ever living to see the enormous contribution he had made to the fortunes of the colony.

CHAPTER 13

BUILDING PROGRESS FROM THE RECORDS

Building Progress

From the Historical Records of New South Wales, we find an attachment to an official Report to London, by Governor Hunter, a list of buildings completed between October 1796 and June 1797. This list includes:

1. Log prison in Parramatta 100 feet long x 24 feet wide
2. Log Prison in Sydney—80 feet long x 24 feet wide
3. Windmill in Sydney with a stone base
4. Granary in Sydney with a capacity of 10-12,000 bushels of wheat
5. Whitewashed & repaired all military barracks, storehouses, hospital, officers houses, and all other brick buildings in Sydney
6. Widened and repaired the public roads
7. Built an additional storehouse in Sydney
8. Employed 24 men making bricks & tiles at Brickfield Hill and Rose Hill – producing over 25,000 bricks each week, but still not sufficient to meet the demand.
9. Built a windmill with stone base for Parramatta
10. 2 stockyards for Government livestock—Parramatta & Toongabbie
11. Rebuilt several Government boats
12. Prepared ground and sowed 300 acres of wheat

13. Divided the Town of Sydney into 4 sections, and placed a watchman in each
14. Built houses for the two assistant surgeons
15. New gaol—created from the 'Gaol Fund'—in Sydney.

In a Report by Phillip to Lord Sydney (Secretary for the Colonies) 9th July 1788, found in HRNSW—Vol 1 Part 2.

" . . . . 70-100 convicts are constantly employed on building the Military barracks."

Phillip enclosed the 'intended plan for the colony'. A house was being built for the Lt. Governor. The second Gov. House was to be built opposite the Lt Gov on a corner of Bridge Street adjacent to the Parade ground. Convict huts are located on both sides of the parade. An observatory was built at Dawes Point. The streets are 200 feet wide, and public buildings will be placed in situations that will allow for expansion. Only one house per allotment dimensioned 60 feet frontage and 150 feet depth.

I propose building barracks between the town area and the hospital. I shall next build a 'secure' storehouse and in future, all buildings shall be covered in shingles."

Further extracts from Phillip's reports demonstrate the progress as well as the difficulties of trying to create the new settlement:

Gov Phillip wrote to Lord Sydney on the 28th September 1788

"The officers now have separate houses. The former barracks are used as convict quarters. The barracks, officer's houses, hospital, storehouses for the military and for the public stores are going to last for many years. They are to be walled up with brick or stone, if limestone can be found in the country (it was found near Newcastle)" and again on 12th February 1790,

"All buildings are now of brick or stone. My house was only designed as three rooms but having as solid foundation, it was enlarged to 6 rooms and being well built should stand for many years."

Phillip wrote to Lord Grenville on the 4th March 1791

"The new stores in Sydney and Parramatta are of brick and tiled so there are no apprehensions of an accident from fire. A barracks is finished in Parramatta for 100 men; all the convicts are now in good huts."

We find that in 1800, King had determined to buy the house of retiring military officer Lt. Kent, and use the house for an Orphan lodging. He wrote to the Treasury in London looking for support on his having given Kent a Bill of Exchange in payment for the house. King justified the cost by 'valuing the replacement cost of the property.

The value of Lt Kent's house appeared to Gov. King as too expensive to acquire for an Orphan Home.

King wrote, "It is valued at 1,539 pound, made up of:

Bricklayers, plasterers, mason	568.02.3
Carpenters, Windows, shingles, nails, glue	818.00.0
Glaziers, glass putty	63.15.0
Locks, bolts, hinges, sashes, pulleys, etc	90.00.0
Total	1539.17.3 pounds

Governor King

In 1800, King proposed to the Treasury Commissioners to build a new Orphan 'asylum' from revenue raised 'from the entry and clearance of ships, and a duty from landing articles for sale, together with revenue from fines, charitable donations. In the meantime, the Kent home would be bought for that purpose until sufficient revenue was accumulated to build a new building. This is the first recorded plan to raise local revenue other than Hunter's endeavours to replace the burnt down gaol with a new one funded by settler's subscriptions.

Public Buildings—Value at 13th August 1806

- Granary at Hawkesbury 600
- Church and school house at Hawkesbury 400

- Brewery at Parramatta 1,000
- Port Phillip works to-date 1,909
- Salt Works—Sydney 500
- Church—Sydney—Wk to-date 500
- Guard-house at Sydney 600
- Other works 1,000

(Gov. King assembled these figures from Commissary Accounts and other Public Documents

Governor Hunter

Governor Hunter (King's successor), writing in September 1800, stated that a great deal of repair work had been undertaken recently. He noted:

- that the large brick barracks in Parramatta (100 feet long) much decayed was now repaired, with an additional 60 feet to be added to serve as storage for wheat—there being no granary in the town.
- A strong windmill tower has been erected above Sydney town; the mill was finished and put to work
- A set of barracks, built of brick, built in Sydney between the hospitals and the surgeon's house
- A strong gaol of 80 feet in length, with separate cells for prisoners, built in Sydney
- Two log granaries—both 100 feet long for wheat and maize on Green Hills at Hawkesbury.
- Whitewashed two government houses, military barracks, store-houses, granaries, officers dwellings and all the public brick buildings—all for the purpose of preservation
- "Made good the public roads and repaired them at various times through the different parts of the settlement and threw bridges over the gullies"
- Converted the old Grose mill-house in Sydney into a good granary—72 feet by 21 feet wide, with two floors
- Built another stone windmill in Sydney 36 feet high
- Built a weatherboard store-house in Sydney with two wings, one wing being converted into a temporary church

- Built a blacksmith's workshop in Sydney with 6 forges
- Built a brick granary in Sydney of 100 feet by 22 feet wide with three floors. An addition was built of a further 70 feet for a kiln for drying grain
- Built an elegant church in Parramatta 100 feet by 44 feet with an extra room of 20 feet long for a council room
- Built a steeple tower in Sydney of brick for a town clock
- Built an apartment of brick in the yard of the old gaol for debtors containing three cells
- Built a stone house near the naval yard for the master boat-builder. On the same naval yard built a joiners and blacksmiths shop + sheds for repairing vessels, a storehouse, a steamer, a warders lodge and clerk's house.
- Built a stone gaol in Sydney
- Built a large and elegant Government House at Parramatta
- Built a new dispensary and hospital (with store attached)
- Prepared foundations for a new powder magazine in Sydney
- Fenced and paled in the military barracks and exercise ground in Sydney
- Paled in a cooperage beside the provision store at Sydney
- Paled in the public tanks and around the spring head at Sydney and cleaned them of filth.
- Built a Military Hospital and dispensary at Sydney
- Built an officers room at the Main Guard at Sydney
- Built sheds for Government boats
- Repaired a house for use as a School
- Erected nurses home in the hospital yard
- Built stockyards for the Government cattle

Buildings Required in the Colony

Gov. Hunter then submitted a list of Public Buildings he proposed to build, by utilising the convict labour readily available, but not overly willing:

a. **Water mill at Parramatta**
b. Church at Parramatta
c. Court-house at Parramatta

d. Church (made of stone) in Sydney
e. Gunpowder magazine—Windmill Hill, Sydney
f. 2 new stores + 1 guardhouse for Hawkesbury colony
g. Modify stone mill in Sydney to make it higher
h. Log Prison for Hawkesbury
i. Stockyard at Portland Place for Gov. cattle. Cut down 100 acres at Portland Place ready for buildings (near Parramatta)
j. Stockyard for Pendant Hills
k. Boat for coastal pursuit of deserters
l. Boat for carrying supply to and from Norfolk Island

Public Works in hand during 2nd Quarter 1803

a. Brick granary at Hawkesbury—101 feet x 25 feet wide; 23 feet high (3 floors)
b. Public School for boys
c. Public Brewery
d. 2 story Stone Barracks for convicts at Castle Hill—100 feet x 24 feet-
e. Stone Church at Sydney
f. Stone Gaol at Parramatta
g. Stone Bridge at Sydney Cove
h. Water-Mill at Sydney + associated dam
i. Enlarging the Wharfs, building vessels

Estimated values of completed work as of 1st July 1804 (Pound Sterling)

a. Colonial vessels and boats		2,250.00.0
b. Public Buildings		54,100.00.0
• Hospital	4,000	
• Gov house	5,000	
• Gaols	6,000	
• Churches	7,000	
• Granaries & Store-houses	12,000	
• Barracks	8,000	
• Mills	4,000	
• Orphan houses	3,100	

- Magazines 500
- Batteries 500
- Other 4,000

Public Labour of Convicts as at 31st December 1805

- Fort Phillip—Stonework—
- Building stone house over the salt pans + dwelling house + wharf
- House for Judge-Advocate
- Brick house for main guard + officers quarters
- Brick printing office
- Repairing store-houses, offices, soldiers barracks

Governor Lachlan Macquarie 1810—1821

At the time of Macquarie's arrival in the colony, at the head of his Regiment – the 73rd Dragoon Guards—Lt-Col Foveaux (as Acting Governor) wrote to Viscount Castlereagh on 9th November 1808 that a number of urgent repairs as well as new works were required in the colony.

"A substantial brick barracks (the Wynyard barracks) in Wynyard Square 180 feet in length and two stories high to accommodate the increased strength of the NSW Corps have been commenced, however, there is a present shortage of mechanics and labourers which does not allow me to carry on with new work or even the necessary repairs of existing buildings"

Foveaux wrote to Gov Macquarie, (shortly after Macquarie's arrival in the colony) on 27th February 1810 claiming to have completed the military barracks at Wynyard Square, together with officer's quarters and gaol, as well as the store granary at Parramatta and new brick convict barracks at Sydney; a new commissary store had been built and completed close to the waterside at Sydney Cove. Bridges were constructed which would afford land carriage and travelling in safety from Sydney town to other settlements."

In a communication from Macquarie to Castlereagh 8th March 1810, Macquarie wrote:

"I found the public stores almost empty of dry provisions—being occasioned by the flooding of the Hawkesbury River and the total ruination of all crops. There will be absolute necessity for building a new general hospital, the present one being in a ruinous state. Granaries and other public stores, as well as barracks for new male and female convicts are also very much wanted"

On the instruction of the British Treasury, in an attempt to make users of roads pay for their upkeep, Macquarie approved the installation of 'toll-bars' on roads between the Sydney markets and residential areas of Hawkesbury and Parramatta, for a period of seven years—the proceeds were to be used to improve and expand the public road system.

Macquarie appointed Samuel Marsden, Simeon Lord and Andrew Thompson to be trustees for a 'turnpike' between Sydney and Hawkesbury on the 31st March 1810. Marsden (because of an inability to work with the former convict—Lord-) declined to act and W.C. Wentworth was appointed in his place.

Macquarie declared, on that date—31st March 1810, "the cost of making the Sydney-Hawkesbury road would initially come from the Colonial Fund, which he had recently formed. Tolls would be used to repay the amount and to repair the road". (HRNSW) However Butlin writes in 'Forming a Colonial Economy' that the Colonial Fund was not formed until 1822.

Macquarie had announced on 11th August 1810 a new town plan for Sydney, with road widths of 50 feet including footpaths and set minimum building standards and construction regulations.

In the "Epitome of the Official History of NSW" (1883), it is recorded that "One of the most remarkable features of Governor Macquarie's time was the number of public buildings erected, the total reaching 250. Commissioner Bigge however, sets the accurate number at 73 (based on a submission from the Colonial Treasurer's office.

Macquarie returned to England in the middle of 1822. In defence of his policies, which had come under such severe, personalised attack from

Bigge in his final report to the House of Commons, Macquarie wrote to Earl Bathurst, upon his arrival in London, as follows:

"I found the colony barely emerging from infantile imbecility, and suffering from various privations and disabilities; the country impenetrable beyond 40 miles from Sydney; agriculture in a yet languishing state; commerce in its early dawn; revenue unknown; threatened with famine; distracted by faction; the public buildings in a state of dilapidation and mouldering to decay; the population in general depressed poverty; no public credit nor private confidence; the morals of the great mass of the population in the lowest state of debasement and the religious worship almost totally neglected. Such was the state of New South Wales when I took charge of its administration in 1810. I left in February 1822, reaping incalculable advantages from my extensive and important discoveries in all directions, including my supposed insurmountable barrier called the Blue Mountains, to the westward of which are situated the fertile plains of Bathurst; and in all respects enjoying the state of private comfort and public prosperity.

John Thomas Bigge & the Bigge Report

From the Bigge Report Vol 3 P 101 (printed on 3rd July1823) we find that Bigge reported, "Such is the extent of demand for timber in the town of Sydney that timber is being used in an unseasoned state. The gangs of timber fellers working in Sydney and Pennant Hills were insufficient to meet the demand and 90,946 super feet of timber of all sorts was imported from Newcastle to Sydney valued at 1,136.16.6 pounds, in 1820. In addition New castle exported to Sydney 3,915 tons of coal and 42,800 bushels of lime. These were wholly expended upon the public works of Sydney . . .

I procured a list of buildings and works undertaken, in progress or completed since 1st February 1810. It appears (from this document) that 73 buildings of various kinds, including two vessels and several boats, have been commenced, and the greatest portion of them has been completed.

The most useful buildings on the list are:

- The Commissariat (King's) Store at Sydney

- St. Phillips Church at Sydney
- St. Matthews Church at Windsor
- Church at Liverpool
- Chapel at Castlereagh
- Improvement of Government Houses at Sydney and Parramatta
- Clearing of grounds contiguous to the Government Houses
- A Parsonage House at Sydney, Parramatta, Liverpool
- Military Barracks at Sydney
- Hospital at Parramatta
- Hospital at Windsor (formerly a brewery owned by Andrew Thompson)
- Hospital at Liverpool
- Military Hospital in Sydney
- Improvements to Lumber-Yard and Dockyard at Sydney
- Convict Barracks at Sydney and Parramatta
- Carters Barracks and gaol at Windsor
- Female Factory at Parramatta
- Light-house at Sydney South Head
- Houses for Judge-Advocate, Judge of Supreme Court
- Court-house, school-house and market house at Sydney,
- An asylum for the aged and infirm near Sydney
- Government stables at Sydney
- Fountain in Macquarie Place
- The Turnpike Gate
- Fort (Macquarie) at Bennelong Point
- Battery at Dawes Point
- 2 Windmills (built at Public Expense)—one at Garrison barracks, a second at the Domain.

At Newcastle the buildings erected were:

- Church
- Hospital
- Gaol
- Commandant House
- Surgeons Quarter
- Workhouse
- Blacksmiths Forge

- Pier
- Windmill
- Parsonage House "(Bigge Report)

Francis Greenway

M.H. Ellis in his biography of Francis Greenway records that a vitriolic and noisy opponent of Greenway was a Mr Henry Kitchen, who had become a 'voluntary and enthusiastic adviser to Bigge'. Kitchen, a 'sour rival of Greenway, was burning to revenge the ruin which Greenway had brought upon him' (Ellis)

Kitchen considered that the appropriateness of Greenway to be civil architect (Colonial Architect) could be judged from 'my opinion upon many of the principal works of his design and erection' (Ellis)

Kitchen pledged to examine the cost of the Government building program for Bigge, but decided that 'the obtaining of information as to what value any building or work has been to the Government is absolutely impossible'. (Ellis)

However "the assessment of the expense (apart from the Sydney hospital) is 922,857.13.11 pound." (Kitchen's estimate)

Kitchen's complaints were numerous and commenced with:

- The Government's energy was being devoted to the wrong sort of building eg only 2 months supply of grain can be stored instead of at least twelve months requirements.
- The sole attention of the Government is to employing the labours of a vast proportion of convicts (Here Kitchen was being mischievous, as this was the sole purpose of the colony and what the British Government was providing financial support to achieve.
- 'Enormous expense' and 'monopoly of useful labour' were the two main complaints of Kitchen, together with observations that the convicts were continually drunk, worked under a lax system and were lazy and unproductive

- Exorbitant and high expense can be demonstrated by the fact that one set of barracks for the convicts cost 36,000 pound. Thus, says Kitchen, the 'mere house rent of 700 convicts at the current rate of interest (being 10%—the discount rate) is 3,600 pound per annum.'
- The workmanship was shoddy—the' barracks referred to above, had been completed for only two years but already needed re-shingling. The materials of the Macquarie lighthouse and Tower were extremely bad.
- The tollgate, says Kitchen, was an extravagantly expensive trifle. The commissariat stores in Parramatta were trembling to their fall. The female factory in Parramatta was defective in plan and building. The magazine at Fort Phillip was a 'trifling toy'. The church of St. James was too near adjacent buildings, and an obstruction to the thoroughfare.

Kitchen was not only criticising Greenway, but also the actions of Macquarie, who had chosen not to use Kitchen's drafting skills – probably for goods reason!

The following notes in relation to Greenway's architectural and Project Superintendence on behalf of Macquarie, in Sydney, are taken from the Greenway Papers A1451, as recorded in the M. H. Ellis biography of 'Francis Greenway' (Angus & Robertson—1949)

From an official copy of documents in the handwriting of Robert Crawford, Clerk to the Colonial Secretary between 1816 and 1820, it can be seen that Greenway credited himself with entitlement to a fee from the Colonial Treasury of 8% of the assessed value of all works done under his supervision by convict labour, including St. James' Church and other buildings which were only in the initial stages of erection when his estimate of what was owing to him was prepared.

Ellis records "It will be noted that his charges for travelling expenses for five buildings alone—Mr Marsden's parsonage, the Windsor Church. Liverpool Church. Parramatta Women's Factory and Parramatta Gaol—total 327 pound.

At the proper scale of 17 shillings each day, this works out at 387 days—a good indication of Greenway's unbusinesslike nature and the utter undependability of his mind when applied to practical matters. 387 days out of Sydney would have meant that two workdays each week between 1816 and 1820 were spent 'on the road' and away from his drawing table. 'Just not believable,' concludes Ellis.

Ellis further points out 'his figure does not square with his statement at the end of the document that 'it has cost me twenty pounds per annum travelling expenses more than I received from the Government'. Again, his estimate is in conflict with the fact that he was prepared, under Macquarie to accept 7 shillings per day travelling expenses before 1819, and that before the court in 1822 he affirmed under oath that he had spent more than 80 pounds more than the 32 pound he received before 1819.

However, the report by Greenway is of interest to us for reasons other than his poor business skills, and these relate to the listing he made for Commissioner Bigge of 'The measure and work done by Government men according to the plan and direction of F. H. Greenway, Acting Civil Architect, Assistant Engineer'

Construction Job	Greenway's estimate of cost
Magazine Fort Phillip	1,240.
Macquarie Lighthouse	7,050
Hyde Park Barracks	30,600
Officer Quarters-Hyde Park	10,600
Fort Macquarie	21,000
Judge Field's House	4,800
Alts to Judge Advocate's Hse	600
Alts to Lumber Yd bldg	2,000
Alts to Dawes Battery	1,200
Windsor Church	5,600
Gov House Stables	9,000
Alts to Liverpool parsonage	520
Portico, Gov House, Parra	1,120
Alts to Orphan School, Syd	640
St. James Church, Hyde Pk	6,240
Court House	6,450
St.Andrews Church found'n	2,500
Market House Foundation	300

Alts to Gov House, Sydney	600
Dockyard & Offices	3,500
School Hse in Hyde Park	4,600

This list is most interesting not only because it outlines the range of new construction work undertaken by Macquarie, but also it gives us a basis of identifying direct costs, at that time, of materials and the skills available in the infant colony.

Greenway adds a personal observation to his list by stating "In carrying into effect these public buildings by government hands it has not cost Government one-half the sum it would have cost by the lower contract that would have been obtained, and the same buildings, five years ago, would have cost nearly double what is now calculated by contract."

In trying to explain his concept of changing building values, Greenway adds "The contracts carried into effect by me fore Government, but for the line of conduct pursued by me, would have cost Government double the money. The buildings carried into effect by my perseverance in getting better workmanship and materials, is of double value to Government, than they would otherwise would have been."

He then lists minor work completed by him such as:

- Plans for Mr Marsden's House at Parramatta
- Survey for the new General (Rum) Hospital
- Plans for the Windsor Church
- Plans for the Liverpool Church
- Plans for Judge Field's house
- Plans for Parramatta Female Factory
- Survey of Parramatta Bridge
- Survey of Sydney Gaol
- Measuring work by contractors at Sydney Gaol
- Plans for Windsor Court-house
- Plans for new toll-gate
- Plans for Obelisk in Macquarie Place
- Plans for fountain in Macquarie Place.

This latter list is the one Greenway presented to Commissioner Bigge in 1819 as part of a claim in which Greenway states he saved the Government (by not being paid for this work) over 11,000 pound.

However, Greenway helps us in another way—he sets down some cost figures for contract work at that time, and from these figures we can verify the Greenway estimate of how the Government stables should have cost only 2,500 pound, instead of the 9,000 pound Greenway quoted as the cost of contract labour and materials.

In the Appendix to the Bigge Report, we find an 'estimate ' by Greenway of the cost of replastering the interior of Chief Surgeon Sir John Jamison's house.

463 yards ceiling @2s 6d	= 57.17.6
1960 yards walls	=196.01.9
16 enriched blocks	16.0
1 centrepiece	10.0
Cornice 211.5 @2s 6d	26.08.9
30 @ 1s0d	4.10.0
TOTAL	286.03.3

The Greenway estimates for the Government Stables

No. of days worked by various 'mechanics'	834.06.6
Bricks used—650,000 @10s/'000 (inc ctge)	325.00.0
Lime & loam required for brick laying	260.00.0
Scantling, nails, battens for 104 sq roofing	210.00.0
304 hundred lin.ft of joists & flrg brd	121.12.0
3 tons lead @46 pnd/ton	138.00.0
Cost to Finish Out (est.)	600.00.0
TOTAL	2,488.18.6

The Plan for a Settlement

The development of the colony followed a relatively orderly and logical sequence, thwarted only temporarily by the continuing famine and understandable poor attitude of the convicts towards work. By the time

Phillip returned to England, the basics had all been completed and everyone was housed, or at least had a roof over their head. Regular major storms over Sydney destroyed much of the early development, including the first gaol, giving residents and officials a good sign of just how flimsy the earliest method of construction was. The bowing and splitting of undried wood continued until a good stock of timber was available to the store and a 'Lumber Yard' was established at the top end of High Street (later George Street). The main role of the Lumber Yard was to organise the 'cutting crews' in the forests around the Town and haul the logs by hand to the Yard before sawing into useable lengths and placing on racks for proper drying. Until a stock of dried wood was built up, the Yard would release semi-green sawn timber, which after a time would split around the large nails as well as bow and bend. Eventually when the immediate need for lumber slowed the Yard built up its stocks and even made sawn timber available to private buyers.

It was only much later than the Lumber Yard found that Yellow, Blue and White Gum dried at the rate of about ½ inch per year, so the drying process is extremely slow. In addition, the whitewashing process acted as a sealer and kept as much moisture in the timber as it was meant to keep out. Being used to the cedar and birches found in England, the tools that came with the first fleet were both inadequate and inappropriate to meet the demands of local hardwoods and gum found around Sydney town.

Observations from Historians

F.L.W.Wood, a New Zealand Academic makes two statements of some extended interest, in his work "A Concise History of Australia"

It was the Greeks (2,350 years ago in 384-322BC) who first proved that the earth was round and who identified a 'terra Australis' – they were certain that it was vastly bigger than the lands and oceans that they knew. Their scientists knew that there was a temperate zone in the South, corresponding to that which they knew in the north. It followed, they thought, that there might well be a great southern continent where white men could live.

Wood surmised that when Cook and Banks returned to England their opinions were that—'if a colony was to be founded then it should be at New Zealand, Friendly Islands or the Sandwich Islands, but not at Botany Bay'. However, their journals were 'edited' and published by a Dr. Hawkesworth, who 'made considerable changes in what the two explorers had written, and in particular made Botany Bay seem a much better place for a colony than they had said it was.

In 1779, Banks recommended Botany Bay as a place to send convicts which is surprising when it is recalled that he wrote in his original journal that Botany Bay 'was the most barren place he had ever seen'. Possibly that is why he thought it may be a good place for convicts. He also thought that 'if the convicts worked hard, they could make the settlement self-supporting in a year'.

"If Phillip had great powers (he had been given despotic powers by the British Parliament) he also had great difficulties to overcome. Some of these were from the same Government that provided his powers – not enough tools had been sent out and many of these were bad. Then a party of marines had been sent to keep order. They refused to overseer the convicts and make them work. The greatest difficulty was that the great bulk of the people to be governed were convicts. It would be wrong to say that all of the convicts were lazy and wicked; however the bulk of the convicts were not suitable colonists and were unwilling to do more work than they could help. The barrenness of the land around Sydney Cove caused a problem of food production – there was no good grass for animals brought from South Africa. Crops were carefully sown but came to nothing. He scouted the harbour and inland areas and eventually discovered the fertile area of Rouse Hill where he started a second settlement. Then in June the next year (1789) he explored broken Bay and the Hawkesbury area – an untold value of fertile land.

The convicts were more use than the soldiers – freed convicts were given small parcels of land to cultivate for producing food, and it seemed that Australia was to become a country of small farmers.

Phillip opened up the Parramatta region in 1789 and determined to make it a rural urban location. It was clear that they could not make the colony self-sufficient in the two years foreseen, although the original food supply, brought with the first fleet was only intended to last two years.

The convicts came from a variety of backgrounds most having limited skills other than a nose for getting out of work. Poachers and Petty offenders headed the list but many future leaders were born of this initial misery. William Redfern became a leading doctor. Simon Lord a trader and magistrate; James Ruse an agriculturalist; Francis Greenway became the Colonial Architect. Wood believes that the convicts fared much better under the humane Macquarie than they did under a William Bligh or the stern Governor Arthur.

The happiness of a convict depended largely on the Governor's character with the policy of the Government towards rehabilitation being the task of the sentence and the conduct of the convict. Sometimes convicts flourished e.g. Greenway, Ruse, Lord, Redfern,

Phillip had carefully drawn up plans for the town of Sydney. All streets were to be 200 feet wide, straight and well laid out; public and private buildings were to be so placed and so built that Sydney would be a model town. But these plans were swept aside and the town grew up with narrow and criss-cross streets and badly planned buildings. By yielding to the interests of the military, Grose (the acting Governor after Phillip's departure,) made the officers wealthy, the colony self-supporting in food terms, an exporter of wool, furs etc and made the colony wealthy as well – a nation of traders and small farmers, at least until the rise of the pastoralists and their mighty sheep flocks, grazing the open western ranges.

The British Government could not allow the self-serving interests of the military officers to dominate the operations of the colony, but unfortunately put in place a weak, but honest and well-meaning Governor (John Hunter) who was not strong enough to deal with the selfish military. Wood states that practically <u>every</u> officer in the colony traded in rum. In September 1800 even the two chief medical officers had for sale about 4,500 gallons of spirits between them. Hunter failed and was recalled in disgrace. Both Hunter and his successor King were compatriots of Phillip and wanted to follow Phillip's initial plans for the colony.

The third Governor was Phillip King, who tried to strong-arm the military but who also failed to destroy the rum trade. The Irish revolt in 1804 was easily suppressed but the health of King failed him.

His successor was Captain Bligh, a career officer with a fierce reputation and a person much stronger than King. Again the military revolted when they determined that Bligh was going to have his way in policy matters and closing down the rum trade. He gave his enemies many chances to attack him until in 1807, Bligh quarrelled with McArthur, one of the richest and most enterprising residents in the colony. The officers chose rebellion and arrested Bligh in Government House, and the colony awaited his successor for almost two years – during which time the military resumed governing the colony.

Phillips ideas for town planning had been forgotten and the town moved into very bad condition. Phillips plans had been forgotten and the Sydney streets had grown up narrow and without plan. Macquarie set to work to make the streets straight and wide. By then most of the buildings were miserable – many being just wooden huts. Macquarie taught the colonists to build houses of brick and stone and set the good example by putting up fine public buildings. Many, including the British Government, thought he spent too much money on these buildings and this may have been so, however, when he arrived in the colony, many of the public buildings were falling to pieces for they had been built of green timber in the days of Phillip and the wood had warped. Macquarie's buildings were excellently planned, and gave accolades to Greenway as one of the best ever Australian architects. Under his guidance Sydney became more and more like a good-class English town, with well laid out streets and fine buildings. It was an orderly town for Macquarie successfully reorganized the police and made Sydney safer THAN London. Macquarie decided that the farmers would not flourish unless they could get their crops top market so he built roads from Sydney to all main settlements – Parramatta, Liverpool, Windsor and Bathurst. Altogether he built 276 miles of public roads.

In A History of the Colony from the Records, it is recorded that in 1794, acting-Governor Grose informed Chaplain Dundee that he had erected 'a church containing three hundred people, which contradicts what Revd Richard Johnson wrote to the Archbishop of Canterbury . . . 'there is no place for public worship except in a building put up at my own expense' . . . . and after six years of the colony this was the only sign of matters ecclesiastical' The Johnson chapel according to a Johnson letter to Dundee could accommodate 500 people and cost Johnson personally (subject to reimbursement) 67.12.11 ½ pound

Phillip reported to Lord Grenville on 4th March 1791, "Three stores, sufficient to contain two years provisions in Sydney and Rose Hill are built. They are brick and tile, so we no longer fear accidents from fire. A barrack is finished at Rose Hill for convicts and we are starting on barracks for officers and men in Sydney. Storehouses in Rose Hill –100 feet long x 24 feet wide, were begun and finished in November, a rainless month. In December the foundations for a storehouse in Sydney were laid. Although Phillip's dispatches show that a large proportion of the convict population was employed in erecting public buildings (there were only 450 men available for agriculture, including those given to officers and settlers, on 4th October, 1792) there is little reference in the dispatches to the building work undertaken. Collins diary records that a good deal was accomplished including two large storehouses at Parramatta together with a town hall and a hospital. The town hall included a market place, and the usual barracks for convicts and military men. Collins refers to brick huts for convicts and the construction at Sydney of a tank holding nearly 8,000 gallons of water. Collins records that the traditional barracks design was 100 feet by 24 feet, at each end were two apartments for officers, 75 feet x 18 feet, each apartment containing four rooms for their accommodation with a passage of 16 feet

In April 1794 shortly after Phillip departed the colony, Grose claimed that ' I have the satisfaction to say that military officers are all in good barracks. We have three large mills at work sand 2,962 acres of ground have been cleared.'

Contrary to thinking that development under Grose was haphazard, we learn that Grose's grand plan was 'to form a chain of farms between Sydney and Parramatta, the object being to bring the two centres of population into communication with each other. Most of the land grants issued in early 1793 after authority had been received to give land to all military officers were made in accordance with Grose' plan. HRA records that "the permission given to officers to hold lands had operated powerfully in favour of the colony. They were liberal in their employment of people to cultivate these lands; and such had been their exertions that it appeared many valuable acres had been cleared and cultivated and much food production had been completed" David Collins recorded in his diary of the same period that "the colony never wore so favourable an appearance as at this period; our public stores are filled with wholesome provisions; five ships are on the seas with additional supplies; and there is wheat enough in the ground to promise the realizing of many a golden dream; a rapidly increasing herd of livestock, new country gradually opening, and improving everywhere opening to us as it opens; with a spirit universally prevalent of cultivating it".

In 1788 the prefabricated canvas and timber house Phillip had brought on the first fleet and which he erected on the east side of Sydney cove had cost 125 pound and was the colony's first Government House.

During the 1790s stone footings and thresholds, whitewashed hessian ceilings and walls of grass reinforced mud and cow dung on timber frames were characteristics of early cottages. Measuring at least 7.3m x 3.6m, they were contained one room for sleeping and one room for eating.

In 1790 brick maker James Bloodworth completed the first dry store on the east side of Sydney Cove.

In 1793 Richard Johnson built the first chapel in the colony near the present day intersection of Hunter and Bligh Streets. It was 22.2m x 19.8m (built of wattle and daub) but burnt down in 1798 (arson)

In 1797, Governor Hunter began a building program of a new Government House, surgeon's quarters, a second St. Phillip's Church on Church Hill and a 45 m clock tower, which collapsed a few years later.

In 1798 the 2 storied Union Hotel was built of weatherboard exterior and plank lining on the inside

By 1800 tongue and grooved flooring, smooth lime-plastered internal walls and ceilings used cedar joinery and glazed windows were used on the typical house of free settlers.

In 1807 the Ebenezer Church was commenced, situated on the Hawkesbury River north of Windsor, it survives as the nation's oldest church.

On Dec 15, 1810 Macquarie set down the first building regulations. 'Dwellings were to be of brick or weatherboard with brick chimneys and shingle roofs

On 9th July 1788 Phillip submitted a town plan calling for 200 feet (60 m) streets, but the plan was not followed

In October 1788 the first bridge over the tank stream was construction (near the present corner of Pitt and Bridge Streets). David Collins recorded in his diary that a 'group of convicts were employed, rolling timber together to form a bridge'.

In 1794 Grose, acting Governor completed a bridge over the Parramatta River at Parramatta. It was washed away in the 1795 flood. He completed a road from Parramatta to Windsor.

In 1810 Macquarie introduced the turnpike or toll-road system for maintenance by contractors.

The 1881 stone arch bridge over the Tank Stream was crossed upon payment in spirits

In 1813, under Macquarie, the longest bridge in the colony was constructed being 200 feet long in 5 spans across South Creek at Windsor

In 1814 the Sydney—Liverpool road was opened and a cattle track was made down the Bulli Mountain north of Wollongong.

Before 1811 only three landing places existed around Sydney Cove: the Governor's Wharf on the east side of the cover; the Hospital Wharf adjacent to the market place and store house, and Robert Campbell's wharf further north on the western side. Neither the Hospital or Governor's wharves had any depth of water or any effective device for unloading equipment. In 1803 Campbell's wharf was described as being in good condition. Until Macquarie's arrival, all goods were unloaded at the rather dilapidated Hospital Wharf within easy reach of the market place, situated where the Cahill Expressway now passes over George Street. Its shallow water was only sufficient to accommodate the small craft coming down from Rose Hill with agricultural produce but Macquarie announced in 1811 a new wharf at Cockle Bay (now Darling Harbour). This new Market Street wharf was a factor in determining the geographic centre of the town and underpinned the new growth corridors of the settlement. In essence, the building of this important wharf created a new hub for the settlement and enabled Macquarie to establish a new system of streets extending back from Sydney Cove, with the new marketplace at the centre. The author of 'Seaport Sydney' observes that 'had this port facility been located elsewher5e on the peninsula, or even at Farm Cove, the future central city structure would have been established on very different lines.

a. The new wharf was to generate for Macquarie commercial development in the western sector of the town and became a determinant of urban development as well as heralding a period of significant and intensive growth in the Woolloomooloo area
b. Patrick White in Voss writes that 'the romance of the clipper sailing ship and the beautiful green-blue waters of the Sydney Cove at the heart of a delightful Georgian town ended with the impact of the great gold rushes on the economy.

M. H. Ellis wrote two detailed works by way of historical biographies of lives that for some significant period intertwined – the lives of Greenway & Macquarie ran together between 1814(when Greenway was transported to the Colony of New South Wales as a prisoner on a 14-year sentence. Macquarie had arrived in 1810 with the commission as Governor of the Colony replacing the disgraced Bligh. It was shortly after Greenway settled into his routine as convict that he showed signs of design experience and made observations on the ruinous condition of many Public Buildings. Macquarie, who was in the mindset of reform – keeping a growing number of convicts fully occupied in the colony, and himself wanting to leave a Macquarie 'stamp' on the development progress of the town – heard of

Greenway's proposals, sent for him and requested some small designs to demonstrate his knowledge and art.

Coghlan (T.A. Coghlan –"Labour & industry in Australia") argues that the current wage rates in July 1800 were:

Felling, burning & breaking up 1 acre = 5.03.0
Reaping wheat per acre = 0.13.11
Sawing 100 feet of plank =1.01.3
Day labour – no board = 5.0

Macquarie, Governor from December 1809, continued the rates existing at that time, but there is no doubt that certain employers paid premiums for good labour. The premium payers were usually small settlers who had no assigned convicts. This practice was given in evidence before the Select Committee of the House of Commons in 1812. John Palmer who was Commissary-General for the colony until the arrival of Macquarie gave evidence that the lowest weekly wage was 24s, but skills brought a premium as well as scarcity of good labour – a shipwright could earn 10-s per day in 1808. Another witness stated that blacksmiths, carpenters, tailors and shoemakers could early 5 pound per day

Coghlan opines that Macquarie was a great builder. His roads, bridges, churches, public buildings required for their construction large numbers of labourers and he allowed assignment of convicts only on a small scale. Under Macquarie, an assigned servant/convicts whole time again became his masters as Phillip had contemplated, so the wage rates changed once more. The summary of official wages payments is:

Assigned servants not working after 3 pm:—no wages
Assigned servants working all day fully found—7 pnd p.a.
Farm servants fully found—10 pnd p.a.
Day labourers—4s per day
Mechanics—5s per day
Caulkers—6s per day
Shoemakers—5 s per day

From "An Economic History of Australia" by E.O Shann, we learn that:

"Macquarie's general order after a first tour of the settlements upbraided his subjects for their unsuitable houses, the absence of barns and their miserable clothing—a lack of standards bespeaking the despair of exiles. In spite of directions that 'no public buildings whatsoever, will be commenced unless indispensable to the public service'. The bills drawn by Macquarie for building materials soon mounted up:

25,000 pound	1818
16,738	1809
59,738	1810
71,085	1811
30869 (4 months)	1813
75,000	1815

Macquarie's defence was simple ' no-one else, in any of H.M colonies had been more rigidly vigilant and watchful of public expenditure of money, provisions and stores belonging to the crown'. Greenway won support by offering to 'erect more and better buildings in four years'. Greenway's best buildings included; Hyde Park Barracks; St. James Church, Sydney; St. Matthews, Windsor; Burdekin House in Macquarie Street, and Subiaco in Rydalmere. He worked in a style 'simple and stately, although of humble execution'.

a. During the post-war period after 1813, a big surge of convicts arrived in the colony. The post Napoleonic era in Britain brought widespread industrial unrest and increased crime, thus the increase in the transportation program of prisoners to Botany Bay. From the high expenditure on public buildings, which had offended the cash-strapped Treasury, another form of public works commenced, enabling these convicts to be put to gainful work. Exploration over the Blue Mountains opened up large quantities of grazing land, which required access roads, clearing, sheep and cattle shepherding, and much assigned convict labour. Macquarie sanctioned a 'road ', a cart track according to Evans, over the Mountains to be made by convicts who, upon completion, would receive no remuneration

> but would receive their freedom. Macquarie decided that making bridges and permanent roads was ' one of the first steps in improving a country'. Any cost to an empty British treasury was a burden and Liverpool wrote to Macquarie that 'if the spirit duties were spent on roads, they could not be used to lessen the burden of sending and maintaining the convicts'. He (Liverpool) argued that 'if the free settlers could not pay for the roads, this proved the colony was not advanced enough to need them'. A new Secretary of State had sanctioned other turnpike (toll) roads on the ground that tolls would recoup the expense, but bridled at offering free roads whilst the Treasury is paying 100,000 pounds per annum for the support of the colony.

The Treasury thought Macquarie was out of control. With his excessive spending. However the circumstances required Macquarie's touch. The colony was growing; the colony had accepted 16,493 convicts between 1810 and 1820. 11,250 of who arrived between 1816 and 1820. Colonial revenues from import and port duties had increased from 10,000 in 1810 to 125,884 in 1820. But Macquarie spent them without much caution – 3,005 in 1811, 6,920 in 1815 and 16,486 in 1819 (all values are in pounds sterling). Floods along the Hawkesbury River had cost the colony much in lost production and thrown many assigned convicts back on Government rations. The colony's bills drawn on Treasury for rations and stores had amounted to 227,000 in 1814 and 240,0000 in 1817

SOME ECONOMIC HIGHLIGHTS OF THE BRITISH COLONIAL RULE

Any volume of economic history for Australia must acknowledge the master works by Butlin, Clark, Buxton and others who have covered each topic in such great detail, and with such authority, knowledge and skill. It is presumptuous for any non-academic to question or 'profane' the methodology or conclusions of these giants, especially when one's criticism is somewhat pre-empted and answered in advance by an author's statement and then counter-claim such as 'Buxton (P285—The Riverina 1961-1891)

"It could be argued that the influx of population during the gold-rush years would, as a result of natural increase, have generated pressure on existing resources, including land, and that this may have inevitably led to a struggle for redistribution of wealth."

But then he goes on to say "Recently N. G. Butlin has suggested in *'Investment in Australian Economic Development"* that the selector-squatter struggle has been over-emphasised by historians, but an adequate knowledge of this struggle is necessary for any real understanding of the coarse of pastoral investment in New South Wales and the development of Australian rural society and its politics."

In preparing a work such as this one must set the goals and select the events to be analysed. One goal must be to explain to the reader that one man's opinion of 'key' events would be but one of hundreds of selections by learned men. However in this case, the rise of the Colony from nothing to a self-contained, self-sufficient member of the world economic community must be considered a starting point.

That the British overlorded the Colony for the first 112 years and imposed their own ways, standards and conditions, might well be considered another significant step in our economic history, and then the growth of the rural economy and the definite boost thereto from the coming of the railway system should be another . The great contribution of the wool industry and the coal industry , added to the growth and strengths of the wool and pastoral industries are all significant, and an admirable lead into the economic considerations for the federationists.

There is little controversial about all these subjects, or is there?

Our starting point is the 'economic prologue' of the Colony in New South Wales from the first fleet to Federation; the Federation story accounts for the outline of the Financial aspect of the Federation debates and introduces a prime mover in the Federation movement, Edward Pulsford, the leader of the Free Trade Association. The last section covers that most basic of a state's right, that of regional development, the successor by name change to decentralisation.

Each article issues a challenge to the reader—the conclusion in the Development of Public Accounts is that the 'traditional' view of historians that 'Britain invested millions of pounds in the Colony' is disproved; the Pulsford story is one of supporting 'White Australia' for election purposes—he became a Senator in 1901—and is disproved by his frenzied support of ,firstly, free trade within the Empire and then unrestricted Asian migration; the financial aspects of Federation reveal that insufficient attention was given in the Constitution to long term protection of the states and successive High Court challenges and Commonwealth manipulation have left the State's as mere pawns in a 'Federal' system. A new concept in Regional development should be used to turn the state governments against old policies and platforms.

CHAPTER 14

SUMMARY & CONCLUSION

APPENDIX A

Australian Statisticians and the development of official statistics

(Year Book Australia, 1988)

Article reproduced from Year Book Australia, 1988 (ABS Catalogue No. 1301.0) Written by Colin Forster and Cameron Hazlehurst.

Contents

PART I: IMPERIAL STATISTICS 1788-1855

THE EARLY YEARS 1788-1822

Arthur Phillip was the first Australian statistician. In 1787 he was appointed Captain-General and Governor-in-Chief of New South Wales and its dependencies with the widest powers: powers necessary to transport a fleet of convicts and establish and maintain a settlement far beyond immediate supervision from London. With this freedom of action however went accountability. The settlement was seen as an economic means of disposing of felons, but only time and comprehensive accounting records would show whether the experiment was a success. More than economics was involved, with the British authorities requiring reports on social and legal matters. Accountability is implicit throughout the Instructions given to Phillip in April 1787, and this involved the collecting and collating of information in numerical form. Some tasks were specified. He was required to issue tools and utensils and use every proper degree of economy, and be careful that the Commissary so transmit an account of the issues from time to time to the Commissioners of our Treasury, to enable them to judge of the propriety or expediency of granting further supplies. The clothing of the convicts and the provisions issued to them, and the civil and military establishments, must be accounted for in the same manner. 1.

To the appropriate Secretary of State had to go 'an account of the numbers inhabiting the neighbourhood of the intended settlement'.2 Land grants could be made to emancipated convicts, in which case 'you will cause copies of such grants as may to passed to be preserved, and make a regular return of the said grants'3, not only to Treasury but also to the Committee for Trade and Plantations.

The type of statistical material produced by Phillip can be seen in his early reports on 9 July 1788 in his fourth dispatch to Lord Sydney at the Home Office, Phillip included, along with an account of population numbers, tables relating to livestock in the settlement, to a general return on the four companies of marines and to a return on the sick and the dead since the landing.4 The following day, reporting to the Admiralty, he referred to the inclusion with his dispatch of 'the weekly accounts'.5 On

28 September a Commissariat return was sent to the Home Office on the state of stores and the number of persons being victualled at Sydney and Norfolk Island.6 A detailed return of the whole population was included in Phillip's dispatch dated

25 July 1790; it was signed by the Commissary and numbered the population in categories of men, women and children classified as military, civil or convict.7 Phillip's first return with details of land grants was dated

5 November 1791; it listed the names of 87 settlers who had been granted land in New South Wales and Norfolk Island with details of their status, marital situation, date of settling, size and location of grant and area in actual cultivation.8 The following year on 16 October the return was able to indicate what crops were being grown on the cleared ground.9

On Phillip's departure in December 1792, Lieutenant-Governor Grose administered the settlement, and he was informed on

15 November 1793 that his duties included 'a yearly return . . . signed by the Governor of the settlement . . . of all births and deaths within the settlement'.10 Grose was also reminded of the detail reacquired in the Commissariat returns:

A like return should be transmitted of all provisions, clothing, and stores, annually received for the use of the settlement . . . [and] returns of their distribution, under separate heads, of clothing, stores, and provisions. The distribution of the provisions should appear in a victualling-book, which should be kept by the Commissary, in like manner as is usual with pursers in the Navy, bearing the persons on separate lists, where their rations differ, the title of each list expressing the ration; and the ready-made clothing should be distributed in the manner above mentioned; and a regular account, both as to the time and the numbers, mentioning their names to whom it is distributed, should appear in a yearly return of clothing.11

In the years that followed, a flow of statistics was sent from New South Wales to Britain, while for their part the British colonial authorities, with varying success, ordered more types of information, more accurate information and more regular information. The Governors not only had the duty of reporting on the state of the colony, they had actually to administer the colony: a colony established as a large gaol in a wilderness, which grew rapidly and in which free settlement soon became important. For their own use the Governors required detailed information, and the very nature of the colony, the fact that it was under firm government control, meant that from its beginning the statistics created were basically official statistics. Four areas of statistics are now considered.

Population

A gaol requires the careful counting and identification of prisoners. This requirement was reinforced in New South Wales because prisoners were not only the workforce of the settlement but had to be supplied from the public stores, which themselves were wholly imported and were at critically low levels in the first years of settlement. Phillip's first report on population was in his dispatch of 9 July 1788:

Of the convicts, 36 men and 4 women died on the passage, 20 men and 8 women since landing—eleven men and one woman absconded; four have been executed, and three killed by the natives. The number of convicts now employed in erecting the necessary buildings and cultivating the lands only amounts to 320—and the whole number of people victualled amounts to 966—consequently we have only the labour of a part to provide for the whole.12

Convicts then were constantly being counted and often as part of the total population. These counts took the form of 'musters', actual assemblies of the population, which were commonly supervised by the Governor or his deputy. Records of population musters exist for almost every year between 1790 and 1825. The method of mustering took many forms and was clearly much easier to organise when the population was small, wholly dependent on government stores and the area of settlement was limited. An early form of general muster is suggested by an order of 23 September 1795:

"A General Muster will be held on Saturday next, the 26th instant, at Sydney; on Thursday, the 1st of October, at Parramatta and Toongabbie; and on Saturday, the 3rd of October, at the settlement at the Hawkesbury,—at which places the Commissary will attend for the purpose of obtaining a correct account of the numbers and distribution of all persons (the military excepted) in the different aforementioned settlements, whether victualled or not victualled from the public stores.13

With the order went the threat that those who failed to attend would 'be either confined to the cells, put to hard labour, or corporally punished'.14

For administrative convenience this muster took place over several days, but Governor Hunter ordered a simultaneous muster because the previous method

"... gave good time for imposters and other villains to practise their tricks and ingenuity by answering the first call at Sydney, where they have received provisions and slops as one resident in that district; on the day of call at Parramatta they have appeared there, have been entered in the muster list of that place, and have been again victualled and sometimes clothed; the attempt has sometimes been made (and not always unsuccessfully) at the third muster.15

And in December 1796 in order to protect property when the population assembled at a muster, Hunter found it necessary to order that servants and labourers assemble one day and settlers the next.16 In 1801 Governor King summed up what he thought an unsatisfactory situation:

I have used every means to ascertain the numbers of every description of persons in the colony, which has not been done without much difficulty, owing to the scattered state they were in, the numbers who had obtained false certificates of their times being expired, and their being no general list whatever of the inhabitants . . . 17

By 1809 the muster extended over a fortnight with different classes of people assigned different muster days.18 By 1812 the period of muster had extended to almost one month19, and in 1819 it took from 27 September to 12 November 20. In 1820 expansion of settlement necessitated new methods: three new muster centres were added to the existing four and supervision was conducted by magistrates rather than the Governor and the Deputy Commissary-General.21 In 1823 there were sixteen muster-stations22 and 1825, twenty.23 The accuracy of the picture of the population presented by the musters must vary between individual years, but in general they appear to be in significant error. The change to the counting by magistrates in 1820 was a failure. Governor Macquarie found the returns so inaccurate that he felt unable to send them to England24, and even a second attempt by the magistrates was no more satisfactory.25 As a result, in 1821, Macquarie reverted to his method of personal supervision of the muster. Not that his method would guarantee satisfactory results: In 1823 and 1825 the official Population figures of 29,692 and 38,217 were made up partly from those who actually attended the musters, but also from an estimated 4,853 in 1823 and 5,203 in 1825 who were 'unaccounted for'.26

The Commissariat

The key economic institution in the settlement was the Commissariat. It was established to provide the supply of stores for the penal colony. From the beginning the task was a demanding one. In 1796 Commissary Palmer complained that he had been required to keep accounts in the same manner as the 'purser of a man-of-war',

. . . but when the numbers to be accounted for are from three to four thousand persons, the books then required to be kept become very extensive, particularly those of the slop and victualling accounts.27

Moreover, he went on, his duties were more than those of a purser since he was obliged to keep a particular account of all kinds of stores received and expended in the colony, and to transmit accounts of all ordnance, naval, victualling, and hospital stores, that may be received and issued to the different Boards . . . 28

And he foresaw great difficulties as both the numbers in the colony and the area of settlement expanded.

Already, by 1796, the Commissariat had expanded beyond its original purpose of a store of issue. It developed as the main market for local produce and the main retail outlet for supplies. Goods were sometimes bartered, but were more often sold on cash or credit. It was the most important source of foreign currency for the colony. It has been called 'Australia's first bank'. 29 The activities of the Commissariat were under the control of the Governors until 1813. Concern over misconduct in its administration then led to it being made directly responsible to the office of the Commissary General in London, itself a sub-department of the Treasury.

The activities of this institution were central to the functioning of the colony's economy for at least the first thirty or forty years. Its accounts and reports are the main source of economic statistics. These records would arise naturally in the circumstances of the operation of the business, but their extent, form and regularity of appearance were strongly influenced by a stream of complaints and instructions from London. The early Governors' dispatches regularly included such information as the stock of stores, rate of consumption, numbers and quantity of rations of those victualled at the store. The quarterly returns by the Commissariat of its accounts to the Treasury for auditing have been preserved.

Vital Statistics

Governors were required to report annually on the numbers of births and deaths. these reports, however, although headed births and deaths, record only some baptisms and burials. The position was summed up by the surgeon responsible for the returns in 1801:

The state of births and deaths in this report is accurate as far as comes within our knowledge, but people die and children are born without our being made acquainted herewith. 30

The various authorities debuted to record vital statistics—clergy, surgeons and magistrates—don't appear to have taken their duties very seriously, and difficulties became more pronounced as settlement spread. Moreover, the absence of Roman Catholic clergy until 1820 (except for 1803-08) seems to have meant the virtual exclusion of members of this sect from the returns. Indeed official figures for Roman Catholics do not appear until 1831.

Agricultural Statistics

Providing statistics of stock owned by the government in the early years of settlement was relatively straightforward. As agriculture expanded and increasingly was conducted in private hands, the collection of accurate statistics became much more difficult. One early method required military officers to put in a return on their own agricultural activities and constables to collect the information from settlers.31 Later, and more systematically, the collection of agricultural information was combined with the population musters. For example, a return in 1800 based on musters of 18 July and 15 August gave numbers for sheep, cattle, horses, goats, hogs, acres in wheat and acres of maize to be planted, according to ownership by government or individuals.32

This discussion of types of statistics transmitted to Britain is not meant to be exhaustive. Returns on other areas such as customs revenue and land grants were also made. It is obvious that the reliability of the statistics varied greatly, as did the punctuality and regularity of their appearance; for instance, in 1821 the Colonial Office drew Macquarie's attention to the fact that there had been no land grant returns since 1812.33 All these statistical reports may be regarded as official, but the relationship between the colonial and the British authorities meant that they were of the nature of documents reporting and accounting within government departments. Although the contents of some would find occasional publication in a British parliamentary paper, they were never published on any regular basis.

There has been no discussion so far of the colony in Van Diemen's Land. Obviously it has its own story, but in terms of the nature, problems and significance of official statistics, it is broadly similar to that of New South Wales. After 1822 and to 1855 this type of statistical reporting by New South Wales and Van Diemen's Land continued, and they were joined by other Australian colonies, Western Australia, South Australia and Victoria, as they were established. Although these returns continued, their importance in representing Australian official statistics was greatly diminished when they were largely incorporated in a single, annual volume.

THE BLUE BOOKS 1822-1855

The mainstream of official statistics in Australia begins with the Blue Books, the annual statistical returns of the Australian colonies to the Colonial Office. When self-government was obtained in 1855, the Blue Books were transformed into the Statistical Registers of the second half of the nineteenth century. Blue Books were not limited to Australia: all British colonies had to make the same type of statistical returns. Their emergence reflected the new imperial situation following the loss of the American colonies and the end of the Napoleonic wars.

In 1788 colonial affairs centred in the hands of the Home Office, but were administered simply as part of the general business of that department. Moreover, other departments such as Treasury, Admiralty, Ordnance and Customs had their own officials in the colonies who were responsible directly to them. A significant change took place in 1801 when colonial administration was turned over to the recently-created office of Secretary of State for War. War precluded much attention being given to the colonies, until the appointment of Lord Bathurst in 1812 heralded a sustained period of reorganisation. Continuity in the office was maintained, since Bathurst retained his post until 1827 and his Under-Secretary, Goulburn, stayed with him until 1822. Their achievements have been highly rated:

[They] unquestionably created a Colonial Office where none existed before, and in so doing they performed a task which was essential if the British Empire was to survive. To build a central machinery which could furnish information for the ministry and parliament on colonial affairs was the first step toward the reorganisation of the empire in the nineteenth century. 34

The continuing war probably delayed Bathurst from giving his full attention to the colonies until 1815, when the long-run overhaul of colonial administration began. Legal, economic, financial, social, military matters, all needed revision. Central to change and to efficient administration was the systematic gathering of information. Initially, the Blue Books were seen by Bathurst as supplying the financial data.

He first introduced the preparation of what were called the 'Blue Books', which name is now even adopted in Parliamentary documents; and when in my evidence before the Canada Committee in 1828 I stated my opinion 'that it was expedient that the most unqualified publicity should be given both in the Colonies and the mother country to all pecuniary accounts, appropriations and matters of finance,' I only stated the opinion which had led to the adoption of this Blue Book system, which system as far as I have been able to ascertain, has been approved by the most rigid economists.35

The origin of the term 'Blue Book' appears to lie simply in the colour of the report cover. It was sufficiently institutionalised by 1829, that when, in a dispatch Governor Darling referred to the 'Crown Book'36 Under-Secretary Hay replied that this had been noticed by the Secretary of State, and that 'I am directed to acquaint you that the original name given to this compilation, that of the "Blue Book", is preferred'.37 An early reference to the term was in 1817 when returns were made to a House of Commons Select Committee on Finances. The Committee had requested information from the responsible government departments concerning office holders in the colonies: office, possession or reversion, salary, name and date of appointment. Some departments were unable to provide this information in full. In its reply the Colonial Office named only fourteen officers in New South Wales (headed by the Governor) and four in Van Diemen's Land.38 It was probably this request from the Finance Committee which brought home to the Colonial Office its lack of information. In the same month it dispatched to the colonies forms which were to be filled in by all office-holders and collected by the Governor.39

The annual system of reporting by Blue Book was initiated with its dispatch from London in March 1822 to the Governors of the colonies. It was accompanied by a circular from Bathurst which began with a formal explanation:

I have had occasion to remark that a want of a regular form of transmission of detailed information respecting the financial resources of His Majesty's Colonies, and the several branches of their expenditure, is a deficiency which creates much inconvenience to the public Service.40

Bathurst went on to list the five main divisions of the book and to discuss the sort of information required. The topics reflected British preoccupation with the cost of the colonies: 'Abstract of the Nett Revenue and Expenditure'; 'Schedule of Taxes, Duties, etc.'; 'Military Expenditure'; 'Establishment'; and 'Schedule of the Fees, etc.' The Governors were informed that in future the books should be returned 'as soon as possible to this department after the close of every year'. Further, more general, information was required in a circular of April 1823, relating to 'Population'; 'Exports and Imports'; and 'Currency'.41 In the event, the first Blue Book for New South Wales was completed for the year 1822.

The table of contents of the first Blue Book consisted of the eight subjects listed above and at the bottom of this page was printed 'This Book and the Duplicate of it must be returned to the Colonial Office'. The inside pages had printed headings indicating in more detail what contents were required; the entries made in New South Wales were entirely hand-written. In length it was made up of 77 folios, not all of them with entries, with almost a half being given over to 'Establishment'; details were there required relating to each office holder, beginning with the Governor. The importance of the West Indian Colonies at this time is suggested by the population section which has headings referring to 'Free Blacks' and 'Slaves'. In New South Wales these pages were ignored and there are later entries for the civil and military populations.

The birth of the Blue Book in New South Wales was difficult. Governor Brisbane was unable to complete a return for 1821, and in May 1823 was sent a reproof from the Colonial Office urging him to 'lose no time' sending a return for 182242, for which fresh forms were enclosed. The timing was already late for 1822, because, as the Colonial Office later admitted, 'unfortunately, in consequence of accident, [they] were not sent to you as soon as to the other Colonies'.43 In January 1824 Brisbane could reply only with a summary statement of finance, pleading that this 'altogether new' form of presentation of information was 'attended with so much labor'.44

He was not able to dispatch the 1822 Blue Book until March 1825. He believed it 'to be as accurate as the time and the nature of so complicated an undertaking will admit of, for a first attempt'.45 For its part, the Colonial Office had continued to be laggardly: it did not send the 1823 Book to New South Wales until April 1824.46

There was no Book from New South Wales for 1824. After 1824 this annual report was always presented, but delays, recriminations and explanations continued. In June 1828 the Secretary of State wrote firmly to Governor Darling:

It is impossible for me to imagine why so little care seems hitherto to have been taken to send home the Blue Book regularly and in due time . . . I anxiously hope that you will not render it necessary for me to remind you again of His Majesty's Pleasure upon this subject. 47

He went on to order that the New South Wales Colonial Secretary should take responsibility for the Blue Book. The Colonial Secretary's problem, apart from overwork, was that of obtaining satisfactory accounts on time from the various officers responsible. For the past three years, although the Blue Book was compiled in his office, 'I did not consider that I was answerable for the financial Statements which it contained, any further than as to the correctness of the transcription'.48 Now that he was to be held personally responsible for their 'correctness', an immense amount of work was involved to 'put them into an intelligible form'. As a result, and because the 1828 Blue Book had to be printed, he could send only one incomplete copy in July 1829.49

The complete book was dispatched ultimately in October, and on the last page the Colonial Secretary cautiously wrote:

I certify that this Book has been compiled under my immediate inspection; and that the several Statements and returns contained in it are as accurate as the means in my power have enabled me to make them.50

Delays continued, the 1829 Blue Book was not sent from New South Wales until February 1831. Again the Colonial Office had been late in sending the blank Book; again there was pressure of work on the Colonial Secretary; but on this occasion he also pointed out: that the printed Books, which are sent to us to be filled up, are, in most of the Forms, not applicable to this Colony, and that our Returns must therefore be less perfect than they otherwise would have been.51

1833 brought copies of two circulars dispatched on the same date from the Colonial Office. One was a reminder of an increasing need for punctuality because of parliamentary interest; the other more positively made a contribution to punctuality since it was accompanied by six blank copies of Blue Books as a contingency reserve.52 However, in March 1840 the Colonial Office had still not received the 1838 Blue Book and the Secretary of State firmly reminded Governor Gipps of 'Chapter 5 of the Printed Book of Regulations, Page 51' which forbade him to pay 'the first Quarter of the year's Salary to the Colonial Secretary unless he shall have delivered the Blue Book for the previous year to the Governor for transmission to this Office'.53 The Governor responded promptly but shifted the blame from the Colonial Secretary:

. . . finding every exertion which I have hitherto used ineffectual to expedite returns from the different Heads of Departments, which are required for the compilation of this Book, I have this day given an order that no salary shall be issued to any person whom so ever, from whom returns for the Blue Book may be due on the 1st of March in every year.54

In January 1841, Lord Russell heartily commended Gipps' action,55 but several months later came the order that the Colonial Secretary should not escape the penalty if he was laggardly; it other public officers had not punctually submitted their returns then the Colonial Secretary, as a stopgap, should submit an incomplete Blue Book on time.56 Punctuality was now even more pressing because henceforth the Blue Book and the Governor's Annual Report accompanying it were to be submitted together to Parliament. To assist in meeting this timetable the accounting period was changed from the calendar year to the year ending 30 September, and a tight schedule was imposed on Governors to transmit the Blue Book by 30 November.57

The Annual Report now put the Governor in the firing line. He was strongly reprimanded for not sending a report for 1839.58 His 1840 report was 'not' of the character required:

The Report now before me describes merely the political and Judicial constitution of the Colony; whereas it was the object of the instruction to produce a review, retrospective and prospective, of the state and condition of the Colony, under each of the heads into which the Blue Book is divided.59

Gipps may have drawn some solace from a significant rider to this criticism: 'At the same time, I have pleasure in acknowledging the very satisfactory manner in which the Blue Book itself is prepared'.60 What the Colonial Office required in the Annual Report involved the presentation of a variety of statistical information, and a later Secretary of State (Earl Grey) was to refer to it as 'the Statistical report on the State of the Colony'.61

The change to the year ending 30 September was short-lived. Governors complained of difficulties and strict comparability with earlier returns was lost. From 1844 the calendar year was again used and three months grace was allowed for preparation and dispatch.62 This appears to have begun a period when the New South Wales returns were regarded as satisfactory. The fact that they were not dispatched until May rather than by 31 March was accepted apparently without comment by the Colonial Office.

New South Wales Blue Book: Size, Scope, Distribution and Accuracy

The changing size and composition of the New South Wales Blue Book between 1822 and 1855 reflects the increasing size and complexity of the New South Wales Government and economy, the changing British interest in New South Wales, and the production of statistics in response to local developments as well as British needs.

The 1822 Book consisted of 154 pages; it was 218 pages in 1830, 410 in 1840 and 803 in 1850. The inclusion of the census in the 1856 volume raised it to its peak of 1,020 pages.

The instruction for the contents of the 1821 Blue Book referred only to the establishment and to government financial matters. A broader coverage was indicated for 1822 with the addition of the topics of population, trade and currency. The 1825 Book had an appendix written in with results of the 1825 muster and some miscellaneous statistics.

In 1828 a wider range of subject matter was introduced into the Blue Book. Additional topics added to the printed table of contents, on which reports were required, included: Education; Agriculture; Manufactures; Mines and Fisheries; Grants of Land; and Gaols and Prisoners. These changes appear to stem from a new emphasis being given to the purpose of the compilation. In late 1828, the Secretary for State sent a circular to all Governors in which he made a very good case for the annual production of a wide range of official statistics. After referring to the importance of the Blue Book, he stated that an 'additional measure' would be for Governors to use their annual address to the legislature as a fit occasion for exhibiting in detail a view of the existing state of the Colony, and of exhibiting in a clear and methodical form such statistical information as is most important to a correct understanding of its past progress and future prospects.63

To this end he suggested a number of topics on which information should be gathered. The statement would then 'lead the mind of the governor himself to an exact scrutiny into all those circumstances which most affect the welfare'64 of his settlement. For the Colonial Office, knowledge of this material would permit 'good government', because 'an exact summary of facts with a careful though brief enquiry into their causes and probable results will supply a deficiency which is daily felt'.65 In 1836 a printed abstract of the 1836 census was included. What might be regarded as the first move towards the format of the Statistical Register was the inclusion in the 1841 Blue Book of a section headed 'Printed returns' (pp. 384-395) which presented economic and demographic statistics over a period, often from the 1820s, to 1840. In 1843 this became a section of 13 pages headed 'New South Wales: Statistical Returns: From 1822 to 1842', and it was in fact a paper printed for the Legislative Council. These returns, normally covering ten years were included in each subsequent Blue Book, and by 1855 had reached 44 pages. They normally arose from annual figures entered in earlier Blue Books. Other printed matter entered the Blue Book: returns of New South Wales banks, exports and imports; in 1855 the large section relating to Taxes, Fees, avenue and Expenditure was mainly printed. It should be emphasised that overwhelmingly the largest section of the Blue Book remained the civil establishment, which in 1851, for example, made up 274 pages, almost one-third of the total.

The Blue Book began, and essentially remained, a hand-written document. Initially the Colonial office appears to have envisaged a production run of two. On the cover of the New South Wales hook for 1822 was printed: 'This Book and the Duplicate of it must be returned to the colonial Office'. But another copy was made and retained by the Governor. Following representation from colonial legislatures the Secretary for the Colonies agreed they should retain a copy. In the case of New South Wales he instructed Governor Bourke in January 1837 to lay [a copy] annually before the Legislative Council . . . It is highly proper that the Council should have access to these Returns, and the knowledge that they will be subjected to the scrutiny of that Body will serve as an additional motive to correctness, to those officers in the various Departments, to whom you must look for the details of which the Blue Book is composed.66

At the bottom of the contents page of the 1836 Book was the additional statement: 'Triplicate to be retained for the Governor's information'. And added to this distribution in 1839 was: 'One for the Council, and the other for the Assembly'. An exception to the usual hand-written Book was the 1828 production. The Colonial Office wanted 30 printed copies to be prepared in New South Wales for a Parliamentary Committee. Printing posed problems and these were advanced by the Colonial Secretary as one reason for the lateness of the return:

I shall only observe on this subject that those, who have experienced the expedition with which such things are done in London, can form no idea of the difficulty of getting any printing containing what is called Ruled-work, or any thing out of the common way done in this Colony.67

New South Wales had considerable difficulty in arranging its financial accounts in the manner required for the Blue Book. This reflects both the casual accounting which existed and the lack of trained and experienced officials to introduce and operate the new system. Specific areas like the Commissariat and customs required overhaul. But pressure from Britain, auditing requirements and the growth of experience meant that by the beginning of the 1830s the accounts appear to have been in reasonable shape. Giving evidence to a Select Committee on Colonial Accounts in 1837, G. R. Porter, head of the newly-formed Statistical Department of the Board of Trade, said of the Blue Books in general: 'at first they were found to be exceedingly inaccurate68, but later he emphasised 'great and progressive improvement'69 especially over the last two or three years. Among the returns which were 'very good' he included those of New South Wales and Van Diemen's Land.70

In two areas the New South Wales returns were admitted to be in significant error. One was vital statistics where no attempt for complete coverage was made until the middle 1850s. The other was agriculture. There are numerous warnings as to the usefulness of the agricultural statistics; a very strong assessment was made as late as 1859:

It is much to be regretted that information of so much importance . . . should be left to the casual and unchecked collection of the constabulary . . . It would be a mere waste of time to enter upon an analysis of figures in which no one believes . . . 71

Blue Book: Other Colonies

Van Diemen's Land produced its first Book for 1822, the same year as New South Wales, and maintained annual delivery without a break. Two other colonies began completing their Books once they had overcome early settlement problems. Western Australia began in 1834 and South Australia in 1840. Victoria began in 1851, immediately after separation from New South Wales. As with New South Wales, these Blue Books reflected growing local concern with statistics, and small volumes of official statistical returns began to appear semi-independently of the Blue Book themselves. Possibly the earliest such volume was in Van Diemen's Land. In response to a request from Governor Arthur for a statistical coverage of his period of office, the Colonial Secretary produced the Statistical Return of Van Diemen's Land for the Years 1824 to 1835. It contained forty-six tables.

CENSUSES

New South Wales

The first formal census of the modern type in Australia was held in New South Wales in 1828. It had been recognised that the previous proclamations by the Governor calling free citizens to muster had no legal force, and this census was authorised by Act of the New South Wales Legislative Council (9 Geo. IV., No. 4) dated 30 June 1828. It was described as 'An Act for ascertaining the number, names, and conditions of the Inhabitants of the Colony of New South Wales; and the number of Cattle; and the quantities of located, cleared, and cultivated Land within the said Colony'.72 In framing their first census New South Wales administrators were of course aware of the English model of 1821, but in fact they appear to have been more influenced by Australian conditions and to have followed in the tradition of the musters. Information was obtained for New South Wales relating to age, sex, occupation and religion and for housing in Sydney. Details of 'class' were also required.

The Column for the 'Class' is to be filled up with one of the following Abbreviations, according to the Circumstances, viz., B.C., for Born in the Colony; C.F., for Came Free; F.S., for Free by Servitude; A.P., for Holding an Absolute Pardon; C.P. for holding a Conditional Pardon; T.L., for Holding a Ticket of Leave; C., for Convict; C.S., for Colonial Sentence; and G.S., for Government (or Assigned) Servant.73

This concern with civil status reflected the continuing penal aspect of the colony: of a civil population of 30,827 over 12 years of age registered at the census, roughly three quarters had been or were convicts. Other information obtained in the census related to numbers of stock and the area of cultivated land.

What was distinctively new in this census was the distribution of printed forms by responsible persons 'by whom, as well as by the respective Householders, who can write, each Form is to be signed when duly filled up'.74

How accurate was this first census? One observation in 1836 noted that all population enumerations in New South Wales 'are considered very inaccurate by those who know the colony well, especially that of 1828, when the settlers were apprehensive of the establishment of a poll tax'.75 This assessment of the 1828 census was repeated, perhaps not independently, in a paper read to the Statistical Society of London in 1849.76 An official recognition of inaccuracy in the total count is in a note appended to the 1828 return in the Blue Book. It declared that account should be taken of Runaway Convicts in the Bush', 'Persons who have no fixed Place of Residence' and 'Omissions that may have occurred', but that in total these 'do not exceed 2,000 persons.77

Censuses in New South Wales were carried out in 1833 and then after only three years in 1836, presumably to adapt planned five-year periods to the British decennial census dates which began in 1801. The five-year interval was maintained in New South Wales from 1836 to 1861. After 1828 the agricultural section of the census was dropped, and in 1833 and 1836, possibly because the Governor was sympathetic to public sensitivity, civil condition was simply distinguished as free or convict. Between 1841 and 1851, when the question was put for the last time, ex-convicts were identified. The census of 1841 was said by a contemporary to have been 'taken from the principle laid down in the former Census Acts of England, with such alterations as the nature of our society and our circumstances rendered expedient'.78 Supervised by the Colonial Secretary, E. Deas-Thomson, this census showed 'a marked advance over all preceding enumerations'.79'As well as a more detailed population census there was an enumeration of housing in New South Wales. In the 1846 census two new lines of inquiry, education and birthplace, were added to the seven of 1841; results were now presented in fifty-six tables instead of five.80 The 1851 and 1856 censuses were very similar to that of 1846; the 1856 census, the first after self-government, was introduced by a report analysing the returns.

Other Colonies

Beginning in 1841 the Port Phillip district was distinguished in the New South Wales censuses; by then the population was 11,738 compared with the 224 of 1836. Legal separation from New South Wales was accomplished in 1851, and the only census conducted by the Victorian authorities before self-government was in 1854—in the middle of a population explosion brought on by the gold discoveries. Formally it was in the hands of the Registrar General, and the British example was drawn upon heavily. British schedules were adapted by W. H. Archer, the Assistant Registrar General, 'to the circumstances and requirements of the Colonial Census'81, and the information was published in the British form 'to comply with the expressed desire of scientific men at home, that the statistics of every part of the Empire should be drawn up on one uniform plan'.82 There was little time for preparation for this census, and the Registrar General emphasised the difficulties he faced.83 In the event, the census showed a growth of population from 77,345 in 1851 to 236,798 in 1854. There is further discussion of this census in a later section.

There were censuses in 1841, 1844, 1846 and 1851 in South Australia. The 1841 census appears to have classified the population by age and district only. The later censuses added conjugal condition, religion, occupation and housing.

In this period the population of Western Australia was very small. The Registrar General in 1848 claimed that the count of that year was the first 'systematic census', although earlier, almost annual enumerations existed.84 In 1848 the total non-Aboriginal population was 4,622 and was classified in districts by age, conjugal condition, religion and occupation. Agricultural information was also obtained. By the next census in 1854, convicts had been introduced and the population was 11,976. At both censuses some information was collected on Aboriginal numbers.

Censuses began in Van Diemen's Land at a date considerably later than in New South Wales. They were held in 1842, 1843, 1848 and 1851. In 1842 the population of 57,420 was classified for each district by age, conjugal condition, civil condition, religion, occupation and housing. There was little change in the schedule over the four censuses. Like New South Wales, Tasmania was a convict colony and 'civil condition' specified whether 'free' or 'bond', and within the free group ex-convict's were distinguished. An assessment of these censuses describes them as being 'of doubtful accuracy'.85

CONCLUSION

Three main vehicles of official statistics have been identified for the period from the foundation of Australia to 1855. Up to 1822 attention was directed to a wide range of reports for the British authorities, a large proportion of which came directly from the Governor's office. From 1822 annual Blue Books of statistical information, designed by the Colonial Office, were the most important means of reporting. Local influences increasingly affected the character of these books, and the practice developed of retaining copies in the colonies for local use. The Governor remained formally responsible for their production, but the actual statistical collating devolved on to a public servant, usually the Colonial Secretary. The third type of official statistic was the census, the first being held in 1828 in New South Wales. The form and the timing of the censuses were decided in the colonies.

What was achieved in the Australian colonies must be seen in the context of developments in British official statistics. Although decennial population censuses began in 1801, it was not until the 1830s that attention was directed towards making some general use of the statistical material generated by individual government departments. Forth is purpose the Statistical Department of the Board of Trade was formed in 1832. Its head was G. R. Porter, a distinguished statistician, and it is claimed that under him 'the incoherent mass of periodical tables then prepared was for the first time reduced to orderly and comprehensive returns, accompanied by lucid explanations of the meaning and limitations of the figures . . . and giving to it a comparative character by including the figures for a series of years'.86 Further evidence of the growing interest in the social usefulness of statistics was the formation of the Statistical Society of London (later Royal Statistical Society) in 1834, the function of which, according to its prospectus, was to 'procure, arrange and publish facts calculated to illustrate the condition and prospects of society'.87

It was easier to impose the collection of such statistics on the colonies, than to negotiate their introduction into Britain. The annual production of statistical material in some thirty colonies throughout the world, required by the Blue Book, was a significant statistical achievement. Colonial practice was ahead of Britain's. Not until 1854 was the first Statistical Abstract produced for the United Kingdom: it covered the years 1840 to 1853 and was a mere 27 pages in length.88 The Statistical Returns prepared for the Legislative Council in New South Wales in the 1840s stand comparison with it.

At the beginning of the 1850s the five small Australian colonies, with a total population of some 400,000, were producing statistics relating to their societies which were impressive in quality and range. Their small bureaucracies had become accustomed to the discipline of the annual production of statistical material to meet the standards of an outside authority. The impact of self-government remained to be seen.

PART II: COLONIAL STATISTICS 1855-1900

INTRODUCTION

When the Australian Colonies of New South Wales, Victoria, Tasmania, and South Australia obtained self-government in 1855-56, they no longer had the obligation and discipline of producing statistics to meet the requirements of the Colonial Office. These statistics had been required to assist in the administration of an empire, but it has been shown that the colonies had already taken some steps to produce statistics to meet local needs. Now it was entirely for the colonies themselves to decide on the range and quality of their statistical records. Inevitably, there was a transition period and equally the responses of the colonies, although there were marked similarities, were different. What stands out in this period is the statistical work done in the two main colonies of Victoria and New South Wales. This work was associated in different periods with three distinguished statisticians: W. H. Archer and H. H. Hayter in Victoria and T. A. Coghlan in New South Wales.

In what follows, the discussion relates to three main themes: first, there is the production of an array of general statistics usually published in annual form; here, emphasis is placed on the volume which brought together these statistics, commonly called the 'statistical register', and on the 'year book' which commented on them.89 The second theme is the carrying out of the regular population censuses, and the third bears on the relations between the colonial statisticians and the attempts to coordinate their work. These themes are combined within three historical stages associated with the three leading statisticians: Archer in Victoria between 1853 and 1874, Hayter in Victoria from 1874 to 1886 and Coghlan in New South Wales from 1886 to the end of the century. In these periods the focus is placed on these particular colonies, but work in other colonies is also considered. 90

W. H. ARCHER AND OFFICIAL STATISTICS 1853-1874

W. H. Archer was born in 1825 in London. In 1841 he took employment with the Medical, Invalid and General Life Assurance Co. as a clerk under the actuary, F.G.P. Neison. Converted to Roman Catholicism in 1848 he took a professional interest in Catholic friendly societies, and in 1850 became the managing actuary to the Catholic, Law and General Life Assurance Co. This position could not be sustained by the company, and Archer, following his brother, migrated to Melbourne in 1852. 91

Archer's statistical apprenticeship and development were obtained when, for the first time, the systematic collection and analysis of social and economic statistics were being attempted in England. This 'statistical movement' has been identified by historians as one of the significant features of the period.92 Its main institutional aspects were the foundation of the Statistical Society of London (later Royal Statistical Society) in 1834, and the establishment of two government institutions: the Statistical Department of the Board of trade in 1832 and, in 1837, the General Register Office to collect and collate figures on births, deaths and marriages.

In the 1840s a strong emphasis was placed on the need for accurate social statistics, especially those bearing on health and education, so as to obtain the knowledge with which to reform and improve society.93 Two statisticians of the period had particular influence on Archer. One was the great William Farr who had a special interest in medical statistics; he corresponded with Archer throughout his life. The other was Neison, Archer's original employer. He was a professional statistician of standing, and his criticisms made him 'something of the enfant terrible of social statistics in the 1840s'.94 Archer was later to say that 'all my Studies and previous habits of life have been moulded under the ablest Actuary in England . . . '. 95

Archer's arrival in Melbourne in November 1852 was propitious. Victoria had been established as a colony separate from New South Wales in 1851, and until self-government was obtained in 1855, effective power lay with the Lieutenant-Governor and his nominated Council. The new colony needed able administrators, and the gold bonanza helped to provide the means to pay for them.96 More immediately, in January 1853 an Act was passed for the civil registration of births, deaths and marriages97 and, in February 1853, as Archer put it: 'the Colonial Secretary . . . placed in my hand the Act . . . requesting me to draw up a general plan for the guidance of the Registrar General, and rules in detail for the Deputy Registrars of Births and Deaths'.98

Archer's instructions on 25 February were 'at a moment's warning both unexpectedly and unprepared'.99 Nevertheless, he was able through two communications on 10 March and 22 March to respond quickly and fully to his commission, and the Colonial Secretary expressed his satisfaction: 'Let every arrangement be made as far as possible to carry the system proposed into effect—emendations and alterations may be made according to circumstances'.100

Archer was assisted, no doubt, by the fact that he brought with him from England 'the labour of many years under Mr. Neison'.101 Indeed, his proposals drew heavily on English experience and practice. In his 'Preliminary Remarks' he strongly recommended that the districts defined for registration and for the population censuses should be identical. Unless this was done 'a thousand social problems of vital interest to a state must remain wholly unsolved'.102 The absence of this identity in England had drawn Neison's strong criticism in 1845.103 In another and marked improvement on English practice, Archer recommended more details in the birth, death and marriage schedules 'in accordance with a report made by a Registration Committee appointed by the Council of the Statistical Society of London. 104

It is clear that in his proposals Archer saw himself as the agent for the establishment of the profession of statistics in the Australian colonies. He noted that the Act called on the 'Chief Registrar' to provide annually a general abstract of the number of births, deaths and marriages. He continued:

The proper compilation of such a document can be done by a Statist only. In England this duty has been performed by William Farr in a way to raise that nation in a Statistical point of view, to a high position in the eyes of the scientific and legislative world. And it has brought him into communication with the ablest statists on the continent, where the System of Numerical Observation has been carried to a degree of refinement, and a scientific excellence worthy of emulation by every state; particularly by the Colony of Victoria, in which is opened up a new and rich field for the cultivation of that most important branch of modern Philosophy Vital Statistics. The Government Statist of Victoria would doubtless find ready and willing operators in every direction; as all scientific minds must at once see the value of the peculiar developments likely to be manifested under the very singular social condition of the Inhabitants of this Colony.105

The whole emphasis of Archer's recommendations was on the collection of social statistics, especially as in the English tradition, those that bore on health and education:

After the great mass of material has been stored, then will come the necessity of analysing it, classifying it and deducing from it the general laws that govern our existence in relation to health, disease and morals. 106

Some particular areas in which Archer thought work could be done included 'the Sanatory Condition of the Registrars' Districts, and the state of Crime, Lunacy and Education with the extent of disease and intemperance among the general population. 107

Along with making recommendations for registration of births, deaths and marriages, Archer had been asked to prepare the Blue Book and a consequent collection of general statistics. Such tasks had been performed in the colonies in the office of the Colonial Secretary. In his report, Archer recommended in a few lines that the Registrar General, as one of his minor duties, should prepare the Blue Book. It may be that Archer thought it natural that the task should accompany his person. In fact, this was a development of significance. For the first time, the collation of general statistics was to be performed by the officer responsible for collecting and analysing an array of vital and social statistics. What had begun was the establishment of the Registrar General as the statistical officer for the Victorian Government.

Archer began the preparation of his first Blue Book on 11 March, the day after his first report. A major problem was to obtain the statistical returns from the heads of various government organisations: Archer found that not all returns had been made, and of those that had, only five were satisfactory; the ultimate threat of stoppage of salary had to be invoked.

The Blue Book was completed by 21 July to the Governor's satisfaction, and Archer was then given the task of writing the accompanying dispatch. Concurrently with the preparation of the Blue Book, he threw himself into setting up the administrative system for the registrations of births, deaths and marriages.

Archer's ability and vigour were recognised to the extent that he was made. Acting Registrar-General from 1 July to the end of the year, but his hope of being confirmed in that position was not fulfilled. He was informed in August that the office was to go to the Governor's private secretary, Major E.S.N. Campbell. Archer, who had previously been promised by the Governor that, whatever the decision, he would retain a degree of independence, was made Assistant Registrar-General.108 It is reported that the two men 'worked well together and held each other in high esteem'.109 After Campbell's death in January 1859, Archer was made Registrar-General, a position he held until 1874.

It took several years for the system of registration to come into full operation. Clergymen had to be instructed on the use of marriage forms; medical men educated in the use of William Farr's nosological table. A colony-wide network of deputy and assistant registrars to record births and deaths had to be established. For this latter task Archer rode the countryside during 1853 and 1854 recruiting suitable men who could cope with distance and scattered habitation.110 He selected all sorts: 'settlers, medical men, clerks of the peace and petty sessions, schoolmasters, postmasters, chemists and druggists, and sometimes storekeepers'.111 But he preferred medical men: 'they are about a good deal among their patients; they know personally or by repute most other people in their district, and are found to be intelligent and erlicient agents.'112 In April 1855, 127 registration officers were employed and 133 ministers of religion registered marriages.113 It was thought best, as far as possible, to avoid connection with the legal system. Popular distrust would have reduced registrations. Indeed, Archer was warned that some Irish, especially recent arrivals, avoided the Registration Officer: 'They suspected something disadvantageous would eventually result from it—on the part of the Government.'114

When the whole system was in place, Archer believed he had created something unique.

England has nothing so complete, nor has any other country that I am aware of. Victoria has therefore the honour of being the first to work out so uniform and elaborate a system; and hence the Mother country may learn something in the practice of the youngest of its Colonies. 115

Victorian Annual Statistics

In 1852 a statistical collection was printed by order of the Victorian Legislative Council entitled Statistics of the Port Phillip District, (Now the Colony of Victoria) for the Year 1850. Only thirty-five pages in length, it had its origins in the Blue Book and in form was simply a continuation of the series begun for New South Wales in the 1840s.

Archer was responsible for the next collection for 1852 entitled Statistics of the Colony of Victoria. This began a series which appeared annually under this name up to 1873, becoming the Statistical Register in 1874. This volume of forty-one foolscap pages was produced by Archer in the first hectic months of his appointment, and he felt it necessary to introduce them with an apology:

The 'Annual Statistics', being a formal document, the precedents of previous years have been strictly followed, and no important modification of the Tabular Matter has been made. The information had been applied for according to the old forms, before my appointment, and nothing was left for me but to make use of the particulars obtained in the old way.116

However, he went on to promise better things:

In future, more precise and methodised results will be obtainable with regard to the Statistics of the Colony, His Excellency having honoured me with commands to prepare an 'Annual Register,' which, I trust, will prove a truthful reflex of the Social and Physical Condition of Victoria throughout every coming year.117

It was probably the Governor's 'commands', referred to by Archer, which were responsible for his production in 1854 of a curious volume entitled The Statistical Register of Victoria, From the Foundation of the Colony with an Astronomical Calendar for 1855.118 The work of 447 pages gave principal space to the astronomical calendar; a rural calendar; a list of legislation, proclamations and proceedings of Council; an examination of the Registrar General's Department; and miscellaneous statistics between 1841 and 1853.

Archer saw the book as 'a humble attempt to commence a series of Registers, or Books of Reference, that may from time to time faithfully reflect the progress of this extraordinary Colony'. He acknowledged that 'mechanical difficulties' and 'pressure of multifarious duties' had given it 'somewhat of a fragmentary character'. And this was in spite of the 'warm interest' of Governor La Trobe, who 'read over with me several of the proofs . . . 119

As well as this single volume of Archer's, produced in 1854, the mainstream of Statistics of the Colony of Victoria continued. The 1853 introduction apologised, as it had in 1852, for the quality of the statistics. It maintained that what was 'urgently needed' was 'a more reliable and efficient system of collecting statistics, than that which has hitherto prevailed . . . 120 The agricultural statistics, which were collected by the police, were acknowledged to be most inaccurate. As a result, the Registrar General said that he proposed to try this year the experiment of collecting, through the medium of the Registrars, instead of that of the police constables, the materials for the various returns required for the Blue Book . . . 121

The use of his own department in the collection of agricultural statistics further strengthened the role of the registrar General as the statistical officer for the government.

At first, the Deputy Registrars had only moderate success in their attempts to gather the agricultural statistics:

It is more difficult in many cases to obtain information from the parties who alone are able to supply it, owing to prejudice or misconception of the objects of an enquiry which they deem to be inquisitorial, and it has happened in some instances that not only have gates been barred and dogs unloosed on the approach of the Collectors, but abusive language has been showered upon them, as the supposed precursors of increased taxation. 122

The 1855 Statistics were largely given over to the agricultural returns, but the Registrar General had to admit that 'that accuracy of the information . . . must . . . remain a matter of opinion . . . 123 However, rapid improvement was claimed. For the 1858 returns, the registrar General noted that 'the collectors are unanimous in bearing testimony to the general willingness of the people to afford them every information and assistance'.124 And by the early 1860s Archer could boast of the achievement:

Upon the whole, the machinery employed to procure these statistics may be considered to answer its purpose admirably well, and I believe that the returns, both in point of accuracy, and also in regard to the interesting nature of the details they exhibit, are fully equal, if not superior, to the agricultural statistics of any other country.125

1861 marks something of a landmark in the development of the annual statistics. Previously, the contents had not been organised in any systematic manner; in 1861 the format below was developed, and was maintained for the rest of the century.126

STATISTICS OF THE COLONY OF VICTORIA FOR THE YEAR 1861

CONTENTS

Not only was the formal shape of the volume determined in 1861, but the general thrust of the statistics had been made clear—especially by developments over the previous three years. During this period, the space devoted to statistics (not including the Civil Establishment) grew by some 275 pages. New material included: vital statistics; population material from the census; much more detailed information on foreign trade relating to value, quantity and country of origin or destination; a section on wages and prices; employment and power in manufacturing; and sundry statistics on migration, railways, interstate estates and banking.127

Between 1861 and 1872, the last year for which Archer was responsible, developments were not so marked. The statistics grew by some 75 pages, including friendly societies and more material relating to crime and punishment. The most significant change took place in the collection of agricultural and manufacturing statistics, where, Archer's claims not with standing, all was not well. At least by 1863, tenders were being called for the jobs of the collectors.128 In 1868 and 1869 Crown-lands bailiffs were used. Then in 1870 because, it was claimed, of the expense and the dissatisfaction with the quality of the figures, the job was given to the local authorities.129 Advantage was taken of amendments to the local government Act in that year to force local authorities, by means of their rate assessors, to collect the statistics. The result was much more detail in agricultural and manufacturing statistics, which were claimed to be 'most accurate'.130

Annual Statistics in Other Colonies: Production and Uniformity

Developments in other colonies followed a similar pattern to that in Victoria. But in the transition from the limited statistics of the Blue Book to the more wide-ranging statistics collected and presented primarily for local needs, Victoria was the pace-setter and example. In New South Wales annual volumes of statistics were published by the Colonial Secretary until 1857. From 1858, following the Victorian precedent, this responsibility was given to the Registrar General, C. Rolleston, who in that year produced the first Statistical Register for New South Wales. He saw his task as combining a condensed Blue Book with the annual statistical volume 'under a new title . . . 131. He wrote immediately to

Archer that he would 'like to be favored with a copy of all your general Tables, viz—Agricultural, Commercial, Mining, Manufacturing etc'.132 He later acknowledged Archer's leadership: 'I don't pretend to compete with you in the field of statistics. I am rather a humble disciple . . . '.133

Within a year of taking on his new statistical task, Rolleston saw himself as the 'Government Statist',134 and rather grudgingly accepted one of the duties.

For the information of the general public, who are not very well disposed to wade through the mass of Tabular Statements of which the Statistical Register is composed, it seems to be considered desirable that the compiler should enter upon a sort of analysis of the returns, point out the more striking features, and shew, with the aid of as few figures as possible, the comparative progress of the year past with others that have gone before it, in fact, that the Government Statist should do that which is more properly the business of individual inquirers, and of the people themselves.135

He thought there had been an improvement in New South Wales statistics, but 'we can never hope to attain such perfection as has been arrived at in the sister Colony of Victoria with regard both to punctuality and reliability'.136

In 1862 the statistics in the Register were classified under seven headings, similar to, but not identical with, those in Victoria. In the same year, Rolleston repeated earlier comments on the unreliability of the agricultural statistics, and recommended strongly that New South Wales should adopt the Victorian method of using the officers of the Registrar General to collect them rather than the police.137

The first Statistical Register appeared in South Australia for the year 1859. The first Queensland Register for 1860, the year after separation from New South Wales, was modelled closely on the example of that State.138 The lack of uniformity in the coverage and presentation of the statistics in these annual volumes was felt keenly in some colonies. The superintendent of the South Australia census reported that Rolleston and the New South Wales Government urged action, and that:

The Government of Victoria expressed a hope that the views of Mr Archer, to the effect that the three colonies should not only unite in regard to the enumeration of the people, but to recast and assimilate, in concert, all 'blue book' and other statistics, on a scientific and practical basis,' would meet with the concurrence of the Government of New South Wales and South Australia . . . 139

The South Australian Government responded to these views and the 1859 Statistical Register was the result. Nevertheless, in South Australia this was regarded as only a 'preliminary step' towards unity.140 Pressure for a meeting of statisticians built up, and it is claimed that the decisive initiative came from the Governor of South Australia, who obtained the backing of the British Government.141 He wanted a meeting in order to:

. . . not merely arrange there the forms of the most important and general statistical tables common to all these Colonies, but more especially investigate the process of obtaining, in the first instance, the details summed up afterwards in the annual statistical returns of each Colony.142

Melbourne was recommended as the meeting place 'as the most central capital',143 and the conference took place during October-November 1861.

There were local reasons for the conference, but what was happening was representative of a wider scene. The rapidly growing acceptance in advanced countries of the need for official social and economic statistics had led to international moves for statistical co-ordination and standardisation. The first international conference was held at Brussells in 1853. The year before the Australian meeting, the European International Statistical Congress was held in London in 1860. Archer had written to Farr that he was 'unable to get to England144 but all the self-governing Australian colonies sent representatives.

The Melbourne Conference was attended by the Registrars General of Victoria, New South Wales and Queensland and the South Australian Superintendent of the Census. Discussion centred on obtaining agreement on practical steps to achieve a degree of uniformity in content and classification of the annual statistical publications. Archer 'presided' and was the dominant figure.145 At the final meeting:

Documents illustrative of the system pursued in Victoria relating to the collection and tabulation of Blue Book and Census data were handed in . . . Mr Archer undertook to construct a model of a Statistical Year Book based on the resolutions of the conference just held such as would be suitable for Victoria and to submit it for consideration and final approval to the representatives of the other colonies as soon as it would be possible to do so.146

Population Censuses

Since the taking of the census had always been in local hands, the obtaining of self-government could not be expected to bring significant changes. The Victorian experience at this time was somewhat different from the other colonies. The 1851 census had been carried out as part of New South Wales, but separation meant the establishment of its own census administration while at the same time society was transformed by the inrush of population. Such change was being experienced that it was felt necessary to follow the 1851 census with two more within a short period—in April 1854 and March 1857. Responsibility for the 1854 census was given with very short notice to the newly-created office of the Registrar General. Previous censuses in the Australian colonies had been conducted by the Colonial Secretary. In his Report, the Registrar General described the circumstances of the difficult environment he found:

. . . a new country . . . about the size of England, Wales and Ireland united, devoid for the most part of public roads . . . and in some parts absolutely impracticable for travellers . . . These natural difficulties were in no small degree enhanced by the prejudice which unfortunately existed in the minds of many of the uneducated portion of the community against what was conceived to be an inquisitorial proceeding, and by the unsettled habits of a large body of the people perpetually on the move from one gold field to another by various routes, and whom it was exceedingly difficult to overtake. The absence of recent and complete maps was also much felt.147

The speed of preparation gave little time to prepare the population or to train the enumerators: 'Many of the 45,880 schedules were almost as difficult to decipher as an Egyptian inscription; not to mention the Chinese returns . . . '148 The schedules themselves were of the form employed in the United Kingdom, adapted by Archer to the conditions of the Colony. Questions were directed towards age and sex, religion, conjugal condition, education, occupation and birth place. As compared with the 1851 census, there were no questions on 'civil condition' (convict, freed or free) and housing. The form of presentation of the results of the census followed the example of the British Census of 1851, especially since it was 'considered advisable . . . to comply with the expressed desire of scientific men at home, that the statistics of every part of the Empire should be drawn up on one uniform plan'.149 There was nothing novel in the questions on the census schedule, apart from the classification of occupations. In 1851 the British had adopted a classification made by William Farr, and in 1854 Archer followed suit. The problem of occupational classification was to develop as an important cause of disagreement between the colonial statisticians. It is discussed later.

There were reservations concerning the accuracy of the 1854 census. More confidence was placed in the results of the 1857 census, because of the more careful preparation and the more settled nature of the population. Housing was added to the questions.150

Along with the attempts to produce uniform annual statistics in the second half of the 1850s, discussions and negotiations began to hold a census in 1861 in all the Australian colonies on the same date as that in Great Britain and Ireland. Victoria, New South Wales and South Australia were the main proponents. Archer wrote to Farr in 1859:

The Governor of South Australia is desirous to aid in securing a uniform Census throughout these Colonies in the Year 1861, when the South Australians are to have their Census. The registrar General of New South Wales and myself, wish to have it on the day of the English Census in 1861 & I am anxious at all events that Victoria and England should be enumerated in the same 24 hours. If you could kindly moot this at your Congress, and stamp the notion with your approbation, it will fillip the Australian Governments and support my efforts amazingly. 151

The South Australian Superintendent of the Census indicated some of the benefits that resulted from this attempt at co-ordination:

Considerable correspondence ensued with the Imperial and Local Governments in the arrangement of the facts to be inquired into, and the mode of procedure to be adopted in tabulating the results obtained, the effect being a valuable addition to our knowledge as respects existing methods, and the formation of the basis of one uniform system . . . 152

In the event, four colonies, Victoria, New South Wales, South Australia and Tasmania held their censuses within 24 hours of 7 April 1861. For the first time other colonies adopted the occupational classification used by Britain in 1851; the South Australian Superintendent had a slightly different emphasis:

The general grouping is precisely similar to that of Victoria, which was recommended as most serviceable by Mr Archer, the Registrar-General . . . It is also piratically the same as that of Great Britain . . . 153

Only three colonies, Victoria, New South Wales, and South Australia held their censuses on the same day in 1871.

Assessment

'We are all delighted to have hit upon you Mr Archer. You have the head that we wanted.' 154 La Trobe's early assessment was to the point. Victoria was extremely fortunate to obtain as its first statistician a man who had just completed his statistical training in England when, for the first time, considerable attention was being paid to the recording, collection and analysis for a large range of statistics.

There were two outstandingly weak areas of statistics in the old Blue Books. One was vital statistics which depended mainly on the clergy; the other was agricultural statistics which were collected by the police. Within a few years both had been tackled by Archer. Vital statistics were comprehensively recorded by agents responsible to the Registrar General, and with a wealth of detail far ahead of English practice. Much the same was done for agricultural statistics; a yearly series, and then only with very limited information, did not begin in England until 1868. Improvements were not limited to these two areas, but extended to the general range of annual statistics and the census.

Archer was the dominant colonial statistician. No other statistician had his connections with the wider world in England. His annual statistics were the model for the other colonies. He helped provide the leadership for obtaining uniformity in the schedules and timing of the census. Through his stature, and by combining a number of statistical roles in the one office, he paved the way for the later emergence of the specialised position of government statistician in Victoria and other colonies.

Archer's second decade was not as productive in statistical terms as his first. There is the appearance of administering an office rather than acting creatively. He was involved in political and administrative manoeuvres, studied law, added "register of titles" to his duties in 1868 and then in 1874 was promoted from Registrar General to Secretary of Lands and Survey. During this period in 1861, 1867 and 1873 he produced 'statistical essays' on the 'progress of Victoria'. These essays, which briefly discussed tables of Victorian statistics, were occasioned by 'exhibitions' held in Melbourne. No significant analysis of statistics emerged. In 1869, in a letter to Farr, he sought advice on administrative matters, complained that administering did not leave him time to work on a mortality problem, and hoped that Farr would make use of 'our Victorian data'.155

How much of the credit for developments in Victoria statistics from about 1860 should be shared with H.H Hayter (see later) is not clear. Hayter was a clerk in the statistical branch, and was later to agree that he had been 'in charge of the office since 1861', and that 'since I have been there' Victoria had tried to be 'foremost in the compilation of statistics'.156 He also claimed full credit for the taking of the 1871 census.

Whatever the balance of responsibility on the second half of Archer's term, in 1873 he recorded his satisfaction with his own role and with the results:

The statistical records of Australia are not excelled either in fullness or in accuracy by those of any other country; and as the statistical system initiated in Melbourne in 1853 is gradually being followed by statisticians in surrounding states, there is every reason to hope that, at no distant date, thorough unity will exist both of purpose and of action in relation to all the leading lines of statistical work throughout Australasia.157

H.H. HAYTER—GOVERNMENT STATISTICIAN OF VICTORIA

Hayter was born in England in 1821, migrated to Australia in 1852 and in 1857 began his long association with colonial statistics.158 In May of that year he began a period of temporary work for the Registrar General, which included the task of collecting agricultural statistics from an area in western Victoria.159 In 1859 he was appointed clerk in the Statistical Branch of the Central Office of the Registrar General; he was soon chief clerk and carried considerable responsibility for the production of Victorian statistics. In 1874, when Archer left, the Statistical Branch was separated from the Registrar General's Office and established as a separate organisation in the Department of the Chief Secretary, 'to deal exclusively with statistics'.160 Hayter was placed at its head as Government Statist, a position he held until his death in 1895.

The establishment of this separate organisation with Hayter in charge points to the status that both the office and Hayter had attained. It may also represent the fact that the Registrar General's Office had acquired considerable legal duties161, and that Archer was the only man who could span both the legal and statistical aspects. Once established in the new post, Hayter was soon acknowledged as the foremost statistician in Australia.

The Statistical Register

Hayter promptly used the name 'Statistical Register' to describe the volume of Victorian annual statistics. But, essentially, the volume had been created by the time he took office. No radical changes in structure took place, although the collection was improved in various ways. In trade statistics, for example, coverage was extended to include transhipments; more information was provided in such areas as government loans, crime and court activity, and individual manufacturing industries. Manufacturing was reclassified in the same manner as 'occupations' in the Victorian census.

An insight into the methods of collection and compilation of the Victorian statistics was given by Hayter in 1879 in his evidence to the British Official Statistics Committee. The material used in the Statistical Register was acquired in a variety of ways, and required different degrees of processing. First, there were government departments which provided statistics in their annual reports and sometimes published them independently; they nevertheless provided statistics for the Government Statist on forms provided by him. Foremost in this group were Customs (trade statistics) and Railways. Other government authorities provided unprocessed or semi-processed material: one hundred and seventy local authorities returned figures on agriculture, manufacturing, private schools and population numbers on the Statist's forms—there was, for example, a schedule agricultural holding; statistics of crime were obtained from the police who filled in a form for each individual—27,000 a year; prisons, friendly societies, banks and savings banks all made returns; tables on births, deaths and marriages were complied by the Statist's officers from the raw returns at the office of the Register General. Some statistics were obtained more directly by the Statist: the decennial census was carried out by him; the statistics generally supplied by local authorities, were collected by the Statist's temporary employees in areas not covered by the legislation—these included Melbourne, Geelong and outlying districts; data wages and price's were collected by the Statist's staff from newspapers and journals, with the assistance of police in country areas; information on religion was obtained by correspondence with the heads of the different denominations.162

This array of material was obtained partly through legal powers given to the Statist, and partly by his use of personal persuasion and pressure. One way or another, he claimed he got all the statistical material he sought.163 At the time, the permanent staff of his office who carried out this collection and compilation numbered eight and their annual salaries amounted to £2,700.

The Statistical Register was a significant achievement in international terms. The British Committee concluded: 'The system of statistics in this

Colony has evidently been elaborated with much care, and appears to have been brought, under Mr. Hayter, into an unusually perfect condition.164 Hayter thought such a volume would be possible in Great Britain, and the Secretary of the British Committee was sufficiently impressed to recommend a new statistical department which would

. . . produce annually a complete set of Blue Books, each forming a part or volume of one work, somewhat in the same manner as the several parts of the Statistical Register in the colony of Victoria.165

An immediate innovation of Hayter's in the 1873 Statistical Register was the inclusion of a small section of "Australian Statistics" for that year.166 Hayter mentioned that the Governor of New South Wales, Sir Hercules Robinson, had attempted much the same thing for the last two years. In order to obtain the material's, Hayter drew up a form which he sent off to the other colonies to be filled in , he noticed that some had considerable difficulty obtaining the information.167 Data on Fiji were added from 1878. In his introduction to the first issue Hayter said his aim was "to make the tables as comprehensive and clear as possible and they will, I believe, speak for themselves'.168 In succeeding years this practice was followed, but from 1875 they drew extensive comment in the Victorian Year Book.

Inter-Colonial Co-operation: Annual Statistics and the 1881 Census

In January 1875 statistical representatives of Victoria, New South Wales, South Australia and Tasmania met in Hobart to discuss presenting their statistics on a uniform basis. There was a problem in the absence of three colonies—Queensland and Western Australia had declined to attend and New Zealand had been given insufficient notice. One reason for the meeting was the request from Britain, reflecting the nineteenth century pre-occupation with the subject, for the supply of uniform crime statistics. More importantly, one of the resolutions of the Intercolonial Conference of 1873 had called for action 'to facilitate comparison between the official statistics of the various Australasian colonies . . . 169

The statisticians, in their report, made a large number of recommendations which were, in the event, very imperfectly acted upon.170 Hayter was able to congratulate the Victorian Government that most of the recommendations were intended to bring the other colonies to the Victorian standard. One important recommendation referred to the arrangement of trade statistics. In all colonies commodities were arranged in alphabetical order, and it was resolved that in future they should be classified in the same manner as occupations in the Victorian census—the Farr classification. Even Hayter was partly defeated here. The Customs Department complained 'they would have to alter all their books 171 and Hayter used the Farr classification only in his summary tables in the Year Book.

The statisticians also recommended that the population census should be taken on the same day, and with the same schedules and compilation procedures as in the United Kingdom. In fact, the census was carried out on the same day, 3 April 1881, in almost every country in the British empire. But Hayter was bitter that New South Wales was the exception to the uniform compilation of census tables. The Hobart decision, being in general terms, had required further and more specific discussion. According to Hayter, New South Wales proved unco-operative while other colonies consulted and then followed the Victorian example. As a result the New South Wales tables 'especially those relating to the occupations of the people, differ widely from those of Victoria and the other colonies.'172

In his Report, Hayter included an account of the methods used in his office to process the returns and compile the tables. One aspect of the account which is particularly interesting is Hayter's claim that the use of a card to record the details of each individual was a world first.173 He was proud also of his 'mechanical appliances', which he used to save clerical labour.

I would particularly mention Edison's electric pen, which, as an instrument for multiplying copies of written documents, is perhaps unequalled; numbering machines of simple and correct action, specially made to the order of Messrs Semple and Ramsay of Melbourne; also a French calculating machine, designated L' Arithmometre, by Thomas de Colmar of Paris.174

The Victorian Year Book

The great reputation that Hayter established depended in part on the presentation of the Victorian statistics in the Statistical Register. More important was the production of an annual 'year book', consisting of summary tables of statistics with considerable comment. It was a venture which probably had not been attempted elsewhere in the world on an official basis. In Victoria, as we have seen, somewhat similar publications had appeared occasionally, but they were more of the nature of statistical histories of the colony. Moreover, from quite modest beginnings, the Year Book expanded in scope and original plan. It was so identified with the man, that locally it 'Hayter's Year Book' or simply 'Hayter'. The Year Book had its origin in September 1874 'as a report upon the Statistical Register' made 'without instruction', to the Minister of Hayter's department.175 What was he attempting?

. . . my first object will be to draw up such an analysis of the contents of the tables embraced in the several parts of the Statistics as may be of material assistance to persons whose business or inclination may lead them to consult that work.176

But, he continued, since some people may not have the Statistical Register or may find it heavy going:

. . . it will also be my endeavour to make the Report as complete as possible in itself, and to that end I shall be obliged to quote somewhat largely from the figures embodied in the tables.177

The report, with only slight modifications, was very quickly published as the Victorian Year Book.178 In his preface, dated October 1874, Hayter gave the reason:

It was however, considered desirable by the Government that the information contained in the report should be disseminated somewhat largely, both in this colony and in Europe; and it wasn't that if the work were issued in a pamphlet or book form it would be more convenient for reference than if circulated on the large-sized and somewhat formidable looking pages upon which the Parliamentary Papers of this colony are printed.179

With this encouragement, Hayter said he would produce a similar volume each year, and he proceeded to set out the philosophy that would guide him:

It will be my endeavour in this succession of volumes to record facts with correctness and impartiality to comment upon them only so far as may be necessary to elucidate them properly, to set up no theories except such as may be fairly deducible from the materials before me, and in drawing inferences, to exercise perfect fairness to all sections of the community. By keeping these points steadily in view I shall, I trust, be able to give to the world a series of publications which will be of service to persons of many aims and ends not only Australia but in the mother country and elsewhere.180

The first issue of the Year Book contained 102 octavo pages of text which were further divided into 347 numbered paragraphs. It was firmly based on the statistics in the Statistical Register and subjects were classified in the same manner. Comment was simply the main drawing attention to the totals in the tables and comparing them with the Victorian figures for the previous year. In vital statistics, however, Victoria was compared with England and Wales, often over a ten year period. Apart from this exception it could be said that the Year Book was confined to two year periods with almost no international or inter-colonial comparisons. In succeeding years the scope future of the Year Book changed markedly. In 1874, to meet the needs for publicity at an international exhibition at Philadelphia, sections were added on discovery and history, geography, meteorology and climate.181 In 1875 a much more substantial change was made: figures for the other Australasian colonies were used 'for the purpose of affording means of judging of the progress, condition, resources and importance of each colony'.182 In 1877-78 the standard for comparison was widened.

. . . Statistical data, not only relating to Victoria and the other Australasian colonies, but also to other British dominions and foreign countries throughout the world. Such particulars, apart from the fact that they enhance the value of the work as one of general reference, are or great importance in showing the true position attained by this colony as compared with other portions of the civilised globe. 183

In the 1885-86 edition, Hayter indicated the wide range of official and non-official sources upon which he drew. It is worth giving in full.

In compiling the work, free use has been made, as usual, of the tables published by the Imperial Board of Trade under the direction of Mr Robert Giffen; the Reports of the Agricultural Department of the Privy Council Office; the Reports of the Registrar-General of England, Scotland and Ireland; the Reports of the Deputy Master of the London Mint; and other Imperial official documents. Occasional extracts have also been made from The Statesman's Year-Book (now ably conducted by Mr J. Scott Keltie); L'Almanach de Gotha; McCarty's Annual Statistician (San Francisco); Mulhall's Dictionary of Statistics; Kolb's Condition of Nations; The Statist and British Australasian (London Journals); The Transactions of the Statistical Societies of London and Paris; that excellent Melbourne publication The Australasian Insurance and Banking Record; and other works.184

As well as the expansion in coverage in the general body of the Year Book, substantial appendixes on various topics were added from time to time. All this meant a great increase in size: by the end of the 1880s it was published in two volumes and the 347 paragraphs of 1873 had become 1,749.185

The Year Book brought Hayter international acclaim and international honours.186 In the 1873 edition he had viewed his task as the straightforward, impartial presentation and description of statistics. In 1879 he expressed the task of a statistical department in similar terms.

I think the primary object of a Government Statistical department is to collect material for others to deal with. The function of a Statistical department is to write reports drawing attention to various matters, and instituting comparisons, but not to go deeply into the science of statistics.187

Hayter largely succeeded in his purpose. But he showed little explicit recognition that no array of statistics is impartial, that every fact is a theory. Inevitably, since one object of the Year Book was to publicise Victoria overseas, especially to encourage migration and Investment, comment in it emphasised the virtues of Victoria as against those of other colonies. Moreover, Hayter admitted that in the Year Book he had gone further than simple description—'I draw inferences'.188 In choosing areas for this, he was influenced both by his own competence and by prudence. He thought he had gone 'very fully' into vital statistics and crime189 but as a 'Government officer' he should not argue the case of protection versus free trade.190 He admitted that even the 'facts' could cause trouble.

Religious feeling runs high in Victoria, and I have shown that in some sects crime is much more prevalent than in others; that is, going a little beyond recording the facts.191

It was not only religious feeling that was sensitive in Australia. In the 1877-78 Year Book, the first to include statistics of other colonies, his facts showed that 'crime is much more prevalent in New South Wales than in Victoria 192 and he then moved on from description to explanation.

. . . the three colonies to which criminals were formerly transported, viz., New South Wales, Tasmania and Western Australia are, as will readily be supposed, those in which crime is more rife than in the remainder which have always been free from the convict taint.193

To some extent Hayter's Year Book was a product of inter-colonial rivalry and competition.194 Its success and prestige as a stimulating record of facts, not to mention the scope it gave for pressing Victoria's case, led to some resentment, especially in New South Wales. It was a major factor in encouraging that State to appoint its own statistician.

T. A COGHLAN

Born in Sydney in 1855, Timothy Coghlan was young to be appointed in 1886 as the first holder of the post of 'Government Statist of New South Wales'. The origin of the position lay in profound dissatisfaction with the quality and presentation of the New South Wales statistics, especially as compared with those of Victoria. In 1886 Henry Parkes summarised the background.

Some four or five years ago provision was made in the Appropriation Act for the salary of a government statist. Year after year we have had prepared a large volume of statistical tables—a very inconvenient volume, arranged in a very unscientific, not to say clumsy manner and the object of the provision in the Appropriation Act to which I refer was that we might get some officer who would give parliament and the country something like a lucid exposition growth of the colony. Every one must see what a great advantage it would be if we had that work properly done—that must be seen very clearly when we compare our so-called Statistical Register with the book which is issued in Victoria.195

Finding a suitable person was difficult, and consideration was given to seeking out an Englishman. What the office required said George Dibbs, the Colonial Secretary, was 'a man of peculiar talents . . . '.196 And certainly this is how Coghlan's qualifications were later to strike opponents of his appointment. Dibbs described him thus:

Mr Coghlan was assistant engineer in the Harbours and Rivers Department. He is a member of the Institute of Civil Engineers, and I am informed a good mathematician, and has some literary attainments.197

Although his career as engineer had been most distinguished, there is little indication in the formal outline of his background of the qualities required of government statist. To explain his change of direction, Coghlan simply says he felt his calling was statistics and not engineering . . . 198 Dibbs maintained that Coghlan was the best applicant, but certainly Coghlan had been able to establish personal contact with Dibbs who, Coghlan said, 'adopted him as his protege.199 Perhaps to appease critic's he was appointed on probation for two years.

The selection of Coghlan (at almost twice his previous salary), the establishment of Statist's Office separate from the Registrar General and demands for economy, combined to make his appointment a short run cause celebre. It forced Dibbs' temporary resignation, and Coghlan says his first six months were "chaos" and that for most of the period five of his seven clerks remained unpaid.200 Immediately on his appointment Coghlan was sent to Melbourne to study 'the working of the Statistical Department . . . '.201

In this background there is little to indicate that within a few years Coghlan would be acknowledged as a master statistician. He not only produced official statistics, he commented and analysed. Yet statistics were only part of his interests, and by the start of the 1890s he had emerged as an outstanding public servant and adviser to government on economic and financial matters.

In the statistical field, the rapidity with which he wrought changes in the official statistics is remarkable. Within eighteen months of his appointment, publications began to testify to his statistical ability and to his vision of New South Wales society and economy. The developments in New South Wales official statistics will be examined through their production in four channels: the Statistical Register; the census report; The Wealth and Progress of New South Wales; and The Seven Colonies of Australasia.

New South Wales Statistical Register

Coghlan inherited a Statistical Register which, in its basic structure had not changed since Rolleston had arranged the 1862 edition into six subject areas: Religion, Education and Crime; Trade and Commerce; Mills and Manufactures; Monetary and Financial; Production; Miscellaneous. The 214 foolscap pages of the 1862 issue had become 370 in 1885. Precedent seems to have ruled, while the Statistical Register grew in size; old categories remained and new statistics were pressed into the old framework. In effect, it had become a jumble of information.

The 1886 Register, the first to be issued from the office of the Government Statist, was transformed. Although it was only slightly larger in size than the 1885 volume and presented much the same statistics, what stands out was the systematic and orderly presentation of information. It is possible here only to highlight a few of the more obvious changes. The category Religion, Education and Crime (a remarkable group!) was divided into two—Education, Religion and Charities, and Crime and Civil Justice.

In the latter, crime statistics were arranged logically and Civil Justice had been moved from Miscellaneous. In the section Population, Immigration and Vital Statistics there were much more detailed vital statistics, and the price and wage statistics were removed. In Trade and Commerce the listing of imports and exports remained alphabetical, but there was more commodity detail and grouping was under more obvious names. There was a complete reclassification of manufacturing industries. Monetary and Financial for the first time included tables of government revenue and expenditure.

1886 was the year of greatest change: later years built on this framework. The 1889 edition was produced as an octavo volume of 594 pages with the advice that since it contained statistics only, it 'should therefore be read in conjunction with the "Wealth and Progress of New South Wales" '.202 Coghlan maintained the awkward octavo format and his last volume for 1904 reached 1,251 pages. By then, the eight section classification of 1886 had become fourteen with a number of sub-divisions. The great expansion reflected new material: there was, for instance, a section of 88 pages on industrial wages; but the growth also resulted from the desire for better and more detailed figures.

The new Statistical Register was well received. From the beginning of 1896 it appears not to have been completely under his direction; then, because of the pressure of other public service work, he reduced his statistical activities by giving up 'the immediate control of the compilation of the Statistical Register . . . '.203 Assessing the publication, Coghlan was well satisfied. He thought it had been 'recognised as, if not the best, amongst the best purely statistical registers published in any country'.204

The 1891 Census

For the 1891 census the colonies agreed on a common day, on a common core to the schedules and on the compilation of the returns on a uniform principle. This was an important achievement, and it meant that the major stumbling block for uniformity at the 1881 census, a common occupational classification, had been overcome. Agreement to use a common occupational classification in 1891 was significant, and not just because uniformity was desirable and the classification itself was an improvement on the old method. The new classification had been formulated by Coghlan and R.M. Johnston, The Tasmanian Statistician205, and had been opposed by Hayter. Its introduction symbolised the end of about forty years of statistical leadership from Victoria.

The occupational question was probably the most difficult one for the census-takers. Broadly speaking, the two main and related problems were to define occupations in an identifiable way and to classify them to permit useful conclusions. In 1851 in England, William Farr's occupational classification was adopted. It was based in the main on the materials used, because Farr, with his interest in medical statistics, thought a workers materials were an important determinant of his health. In other words he saw the census as yielding significant information on occupational morbidity and mortality. As we have seen William Archer, straight from England and with his own actuarial background, adopted (with some modification) the Farr system for Victoria the 1854 census. Victoria maintained this system up to 1881, when all the except New South Wales, agreed to follow the Victorian system.

At the pre-census conference of colonial statists at Hobart in March 1890, with Hayter as president, Johnston and Coghlan were deputed to draw up an entirely new occupational classification. Their position had been strengthened by strong criticism in England of the Farr system, and the use by Scotland of its own method in 1871. In particular that undermined Hayter's position was the fact of England's partial departure from the Farr system at its 1881 census. The main change which was then made distinction between the 'occupied' and the 'unoccupied' population. 206 In Hobart, Johnston developed his criticism of the Farr system along these lines:

. . . so far as minor groups or combinations are concerned this method was fairly successful, but as regards the principal classes of workers it could not form a guiding principle; for it is obvious all classes of workers must often be related to the self-same materials, and separation could not possibly be based successfully upon this method. It is therefore, that Dr Farr's classification should present many defects and anomalies. For example, Class II.—Domestic, and Class VI.—Indefinite and Non-productive, hopelessly mixed up Breadwinners and Dependants. Similarly, Primary

Producers, Distributors, and Manufacturers were indifferently mixed together under three very distinct Classes—viz., Commercial, Class III; Agricultural and Pastoral, Class IV.; and Industrial, Class V. It is apparent that the lack of any clearly recognised principle for determining the limits great Classes themselves led the original Classifier into great perplexities; for we find Fishermen, Veterinary Surgeon, and Farrier grouped under Class Agricultural and Pastoral; Chimney-sweep grouped under workers in Coal; and the Miner, Quarryman, and other Primary Producers are found classed together with a moiety of the Dealers, along with Night Soil Men, Artizans, and Manufacturers.207

Coghlan much more aggressively, defended past practice in New South Wales, and attacked the Farr system and Hayter's use of it.

[In NSW in 1881] a very different system was adopted, which, though marked by many imperfections was a distinct improvement on all preceding attempts, and in many important particulars was superior to the pretentious classification adopted in the other colonies, which was merely a servile adaptation of the system employed at the previous English census.208

Moreover, he continued, Hayter's proposal to use the Farr system in 1891, would 'commit these colonies to the principle of remaining ten years behind the English compilers.' 209

In drawing up their classification of occupations, Coghlan and Johnston were guided by some very general classificatory principles devised by Johnston 210 but more specific information is not available. They did not intend their classification to be used for medical purposes, but, in Johnston's words, to 'more fully meet the wants of the social economist and statesman . . . '. 211 The result was, according to Coghlan, 'not based on any previous system, and if there was any such it was unknown to the Conference'.212 It consisted of seven classes divided into twenty-four orders and one hundred and nine sub-orders; sub-orders were divided into groups of occupations which were named at the conference, but whose adoption was left to individual statisticians.213 To capture the essence of the change, Johnston's description of the main classes is set out below.

The amended Classification is divided into seven principal classes. The first six embrace all independent Breadwinners; the seventh, or last class embracing all Dependants. The three important classes related to Materials are kept separate by regard to the relationship which their differing services bear to the materials which pass through their hands, Thus, Primary Producers of Raw Materials directly acquired by labour from natural sources, bring naturally into one class (Class V.) those engaged in Agriculture, Grazing, Fishing, Hunting, and Mining. Transporters, Dealers or Distributors, who effect no material change in Producers' materials, come naturally together in Class Commercial (Class III.); while all skilled, and unskilled modifiers or constructors of materials, in a similar way, come naturally together in Class Industrial (Class V.).

The Domestic Class (Class II.) no longer includes wives and others engaged at home in domestic duties for which no remuneration is paid, nor dependent relatives or children.

The Professional Class (Class I.) only includes those ministering to Religion, Charity, Education, Art, Science, and Amusement, and those connected with the General and Local Government, and in Defence, Law, and Protection.214

Johnston did not mention the rather awkward but inevitable 'Class VI.—Indefinite', which consisted of 'persons whose occupations are undefined or unknown . . . '.215

Of the Australian colonies, Queensland and Western Australia did not attend the Hobart conference, but all followed its recommendations concerning collection and compilation. The new classification of occupations was substantially followed at the first Commonwealth Census in 1911.

Coghlan made a General Report ('Illustrated with Maps and Diagrams') on the 1891 census of New South Wales.216 It was the most comprehensive and longest (334 pages) statistical report on a census in the Australian colonies. It included an account of the taking of the census, but this was almost incidental to his analysis of the findings. The analysis was characterised by a strong historical emphasis, and in particular there was a masterly account of the growth of population in New South Wales since 1788. Thrown in was a chapter on the history of life tables and the construction of one for New South Wales. For good measure, the last chapter consisted of humorous anecdotes from the census.

A New South Wales Year Book

Coghlan's first Year Book, published in 1887, was entitled The Wealth and Progress of New South Wales 1886-87. It began a series with this title and produced by him of thirteen issues, the last being for the year 1900-01. The first paragraph of the first volume suggests both the historical approach adopted and an important impulse behind the work.

The following pages, which are designed to trace the progress of the Colony during the first century of its history, show that New South Wales maintains its position as the leading the Australasian Group.217

Early progress, Coghlan continued, would be dealt with 'in the form of an historical sketch, But since the separation of Queensland in 1859, the period 'has been treated statistically. 218

In the succeeding volume for 1887-88, Coghlan remarked on the 'uneventful' nature of Australasian history, so that 'the history of this continent is comprised almost entirely in that of its industrial progress'219 By implication, a Year Book such as his own, dealt with the essence of Australasian history. And, he continued, in explanation of the title of his series: 'To illustrate the wealth and trace the progress of the Colony is the aim of this volume . . . '.220 The list of contents in this issue, consisting of twenty three individual chapters, shows that Coghlan was able to deal with topics in a much more natural manner than Hayter. The Victorian Year Book was constructed in the same manner as the Statistical Register, so that topics were constrained into eights groups Coghlan was able to devote eight chapters to the relatively unchanging of the broadly historical and geographical type, whereas Hayter combined this in a few sketchy pages.

In the fourth year of issue, 1889-90, Coghlan was able to make a significant change to method of presentation because of the production of a new companion volume.

The necessity of comparing the progress of New South Wales with that of the other Colonies, except on the most important points, is obviated by the publication of 'The Seven Colonies of Australasia which deals with the Colonies as a whole, as well as with their individual resources.221

Comparative material remained in the local volume, but emphasis could be placed very firmly on developments in New South Wales itself. Lacking the encyclopaedic comprehensiveness of Hayter's volume, the work seems more purposeful. In Coghlan's discussion of the statistics, there is of course a good deal of formal comment—a noting of the figures and a brief description of institutions. But the overall impression is of the authoritative handling of the material, as Coghlan shows himself to be historian, economist and a man of affairs in administration and politics. Take the example of one of Coghlan's central concerns. In 1888-89 begins a historical discussion of real wages through a focus on money wages and prices. In 1890-91 this becomes a seventeen page section of a new chapter headed 'Industrial Progress', which historically 'is naturally divided into eight periods, each with some distinguishing characteristic . . . '.222 In 1894 'Industrial Progress' becomes 'Industrial History' and warrants a full chapter of sixty-three pages; it has now broadened, but its final thrust is still 'the condition of the workers'.223 What can be seen developing within the framework of the official Year Book is the genesis of Coghlan's great historical work, not published until 1918, Labour and Industry in Australia.224

Throughout the thirteen editions there was a massive accumulation of statistical information, with comment, about New South Wales. Information was broadened in scope and extended in time. Primary statistical material was moulded into such constructs as real wages, export price indexes and even estimates of the national income of New South Wales. It meant, of course, a great growth in size of Wealth and Progress. The 577 pages of 1886-87 had become 968 by 1892; in 1893 about one third more print was fitted to the page, and the 828 pages of that year grew to 1,043 by 1900-01 Coghlan gave New South Wales the Year Book it sought. The fourth issue was greeted by the Sydney Morning Herald:

The great statistical handbook of the Colony, which has now become invaluable as a book of reference . . . nearly 900 pages full of information upon every point relating to the material, physical, and moral welfare of the people of this colony . . . pages of interesting explanatory letterpress, by which the points brought out in the various tables quoted are emphasised in an instructive way.225

In Victoria, on the other hand, all was not well with the Year Book Hayter died in office in 1895 after some years of ill-health and financial problems, and economies meant it was a number of years before a new government statist was appointed; indeed, there was no issue of the Year Book between No. 21 of 1894 and No. 22 of 1895-98. In 1886 it was Parkes in the New South Wales parliament who had deplored his State's backwardness: in 1895 it was the turn of a Victorian parliamentarian.

He . . . believed the Government Statist of New South Wales was paid £800 a year, and, judged by the way in which he had managed his business, Mr. Coghlan had been worth £80,000 a year to New South Wales, because he had published works which had been most magnificent advertisements for that colony, just as in the olden times Mr. Hayter's publications did magnificent work for this colony. He . . . esteemed Mr. Hayter very much, but towards the end of that gentleman's career he did not retain his initial vigour, and there were defects in the Year Book which ought to be remedied forthwith.226

An Australasian Year Book

Coghlan's decision to begin a new series of Year Books covering all the colonies has been noted. The first issue for 1890 was entitled A Statistical Account of the Seven Colonies of Australasia. The series, consisting of eleven editions, ended in 1902-03, the last two, in deference to the fact of Federation, being called A Statistical Account of Australia and New Zealand.

In the first issue Coghlan set out the purpose of the series.

To afford information by which the progress of these Colonies may be gauged is the object of the present work, which aims to exhibit at a glance the position held by each Colony individually, and by the country as a whole, with regard to all matters connected with its moral and material welfare. Such an account cannot fail to be of interest—so much has been attempted in directions in which old-world experience was of little avail, and so much has been accomplished in the development of the material resources of a new land, and the social well-being of its people.227

It was a smallish volume of 186 octavo pages in which the contents were divided, and the commentary made, in much the same way as in Wealth and Progress. There were also 'Concluding Remarks' which express the emotion and confidence of 1890.

Enough has been said, however, to show how these great Colonies, from the humblest beginnings, have grown and expanded into important provinces, peopled with a race of hardy, enterprising, and industrious colonists, with free institutions such as are enjoyed by few nations in the old world, and without those social and caste impediments which are in older countries so great a hindrance to the march of civilisation. 228

Succeeding issues of this series reflect Coghlan's increasing knowledge and maturity in much the same way as did developments in Wealth and Progress. New topics were added and significant interpretative essays were built around the tables of figures in such areas as capital imports and land settlement. Inevitably, the size of the volume grew, reaching 543 pages by the seventh issue for 1897-98. The next issue for 1899-1900 with 836 pages was much larger: the imminence of Federation induced Coghlan to insert historical chapters on all the colonies. In the 1901-02 issue Coghlan began a chapter on the 'industrial progress' of Australasia. The final issue, dated 1 December 1904, was a voluminous 1,042 pages and included material on Federation Constitution. This was Coghlan's last Year Book: he left for England two months later. It could be seen as a monument to his work: a mass of statistical, coherently ordered and arranged, and always accompanied by authoritative discussion and interpretation, the end of the series left a gap which was only by the first Commonwealth Year Book in 1908.

CONCLUSION

It is not simply local pride and hyperbole that have judged the official statistics of the Australian colonies in the second half of the nineteenth century to be of the highest international quality, both in content and presentation.229 What may be thought surprising is to find such an achievement in colonies remote from the main stream of statistical development, recently settled and having just obtained self-government.

To a considerable extent the achievement was, for a number of reasons, a legacy of British colonial rule. First, the colonies had been required to produce official statistics on an annual basis; collection was not based on periodic censuses as in the United States. Second, the statistics had to be of a range and quality to satisfy the British authorities, who required them for efficient administration. Third, the statistics brought together by a single officer, the local Colonial Secretary, who took some final responsibility for their accuracy and their presentation; there was therefore a central statistical authority and this contrasted markedly with the British position. Finally the authority was required to present all the relevant statistics of the colony in a single volume—the Blue Book. As an offshoot of these developments, it was natural for the colonies to begin the production of a consolidated volume of annual statistics for their own use.

Self Government meant the inheritance of a most favourable institutional arrangement. But adaptation and progress were not automatic: freedom and changed circumstances gave the opportunity for stagnation. That there was such a successful outcome on a number of factors, of which the most important was the discovery in this small community of three remarkable statisticians.

W. H. Archer, well-trained and fresh from the invigorating statistical climate of England arrived in Victoria in 1852 just as the public service was being shaped. Previously, the Colonial Secretary, as part of his numerous duties, had taken responsibility for the census, the Blue Book and the compilation of the statistics for local use. In the English tradition, it was probably inevitable that responsibility for the census would be given to the registrar General's Department, but Archer's presence led to that office taking over all the statistical work done by the Colonial Secretary. At the same time, the Registrar General set up a prestigious system of recording vital statistics began collecting more general statistics in his own right. In Victoria, then, central statistical control was continued, and Archer's status and authority gave the Registrar General the informal mantle of government statistician. His methods set the pace for the other colonies.

In 1874, in the newly-created post of Government Statist of Victoria, Henry Hayter had a more specialised role. He was no longer responsible for what was now the routine collection of vital statistics, but took charge of the census, the collection of a variety of statistics and the production of the Statistical Register. He maintained Victorian leadership in statistical standards, and added a new dimension to official statistical activities through the innovation of his famous Year Book, which publicised Victoria through informed comment on the statistics.

Colonial governments needed good statistics. There was also early recognition that the Statistical Registers could be used overseas in a manner which could encourage the flow of capital and migrants. Hayter's Year Book went a step further in that direction. In this situation inter-colonial rivalry and competition were important in ensuring some flow-on of best statistical practice. British pressure and the natural desire to harmonise census-taking also raised census standards. Inter-colonial rivalry was greatest between Victoria and New South Wales, and was a major factor in the establishment of the post of government statist in New South Wales. Timothy Coghlan was the first appointment in 1886, and as Hayter's innovations and drive were beginning to decline, Coghlan was able to build on Hayter's work. He improved dramatically the conventional array of statistics in the New South Wales Statistical Register, and he made important improvements in the census schedule. His most significant achievement in official statistics was through his Year Books. With imagination and vision he translated the tables of figures into an interpretative picture of his society, and this involved the formulation of statistical constructs out of the raw data. Not only was this done for New South Wales, it was also extended to meet the more complex challenge of Australasia. In their genre the works are classics.

Federation on 1 January 1901 had many implications for official statistics in Australia. In the short run, a new Commonwealth Statistician could draw on the output from the centralised statistical offices in the States. It would be a challenge, however, to maintain the progress that had been achieved by his distinguished colonial predecessors.

PART III: STATISTICS FOR THE NEW NATION

STEPS TOWARDS UNIFORMITY

At the beginning of the Commonwealth period, the six States were spending a total of about £18,000 a year on statistical work, of which £2,000 was for the tabulation of vital statistics. The costs associated with decennial censuses were additional as were those of printing, stationery, postage, and telegrams. In a report prepared at the request of the federal government in April 1903, Timothy Coghlan estimated that the States spent between 0.76 pence and 2.82 pence per inhabitant on statistics. The cost comparison alone was of minimal value, as Coghlan pointed out, since the range of statistics covered varied significantly. In some States, 'even statistics relating to the greater primary industries and to Manufactures are neglected or imperfectly collected and presented.1

While colonial statisticians, particularly Coghlan and R. M. Johnston, had played notable parts in the federation debates as financial experts, national responsibility for censuses and official statistical compilation was not a subject of controversy.2 Federation could be seen as a step towards the elusive goal of statistical uniformity. Some statisticians saw advantages in the prospect of a national statistical authority that might lend its weight to the decisions of the professional conferences which had become the recognised forum for co-ordination. No one disputed that the new nation should have both a responsibility and a capacity to undertake statistical inquiry.

Sir Samuel Griffiths' drafting committee at the National Australasian Convention in March 1891 produced a draft constitution Bill in which Chapter 1 Part V sub-section 12 was to give the Commonwealth the power to make laws in respect of census and statistics. The words 'census and statistics' appear to have come directly from the British North America Act Section 91 sub-section 6.3 There was no debate on this issue and the Australasian Federal Convention in 1897-98 accepted the sub-clause from the Commonwealth Bill of 1891 again without debate. Under Section 51 (xi) of the Constitution, the Commonwealth Parliament was given a concurrent power to make laws with respect to census and statistics. It was not immediately apparent how this power might be exercised. Later events were to suggest that little thought had been given to how the statistical interests of the States and Commonwealth could best be served in the new era.

The first major statistical business of the twentieth century was the 1901 Census. In March 1900 a conference of statisticians, including a representative from New Zealand, was held in Sydney to arrange for the uniform collection of the 1901 Census. Coghlan, as president of the conference, reported to Lyne, Premier and Treasurer of New South Wales, that the conference broke up into three sub-committees: the first to deal with drawing up a uniform householders' schedule; the second to revise the classifications of occupations; and the third to draw up the reasons which led the conference to recommend 28 April as the day for taking the Census.

It was decided that there would be only one question additional to those asked in 1891. It related to the length of residence for those not born in the particular colony. The reasons for not expanding the Census further were explained by Coghlan:

There were several suggestions for increasing the number of questions to be asked of the people, but the majority of the members of the Conference were of the opinion that it would be unwise to extend the inquiries beyond the class of subjects usually presented in countries where the census is taken upon schedules. If, as in some countries, the plan were adopted of appointing enumerators whose business it would be to make personal inquiry from house to house, and fill up their books from the particulars thus obtained much more elaborate inquiries might be ventured upon.

The conference decided not to change any of the classifications and to accept those drawn up by Johnston and Coghlan in 1890:

The experience of ten years has suggested a few changes, but these are all of a minor character, such as may be looked for in the, development of the population and industries of a young community.

A number of the colonies had proposed incorporating with the householders schedule a return relating to land and crops. But this proposal was not adopted. Most of the figures were in any case available in the colonies on an annual basis; and it was contended that the census was not the most opportune time for pursuing investigations relating to land and industries. Coghlan put certain resolutions to the conference regarding uniformity which

. . . if strictly adhered to, will ensure the possibility of exact comparison being drawn between the conditions of the various colonies . . . They consider that uniformity is especially desirable at the present time, when five of the colonies are about to enter upon a federation, as there is every probability that the figures obtained in the coming Census will form the first population statistics of the Commonwealth, and be the basis of many important arrangements in regard to finance and electoral representation.4

The actual date of the census also had to be settled. The night of the first Sunday in April had been the usual time of census taking, but in 1901 the first Sunday in April was Easter Sunday.

The effect of taking a Census at a time of general migration like Easter would be to enumerate the population in places in which they do not usually reside, and to increase unduly the population of some localities at the expense of others. The result would be utterly misleading so far as localising the population, and would also affect the number of males resident in given areas.5

The choice of April 28, though a departure from the imperial census, would give people time to settle down after holidays and after harvesting.

From the outset it was clear that generally accepted population figures would be essential as a basis for apportioning payments to or for the States. In September 1901 the Prime Minister wrote to all State Premiers asking if they were willing to use figures supplied by the Victorian Government Statistician for the purpose of calculating the future distribution of 'other' new expenditure. Alone of the respondents, New South Wales proposed a different approach. They would prefer to include half-castes in the figure for their State, bringing the total to 1,356,090.6

Another conference of statisticians was held in Hobart in January 1902; it was called specifically to look at uniformity in preparation of statistical returns. All the States except Western Australia were present and a representative from New Zealand also attended. This conference had been proposed by Coghlan in a letter to Johnston on 25 June 1901:

I have long considered it would be extremely desirable that the statistics of the States should be placed upon a uniform basis . . . Such uniformity is all the more desirable, since the Statistics of Australia (now that the States have accomplished Federation) will be quoted as for the Commonwealth, and not for the individual States . A year or two ago I arrived at an understanding with Mr Fenton of Victoria as to the compilation of statistics relating to Manufacturers and Works, and I see no insuperable difficulties in placing the statistics relating to Education, Law and Crime, Public Finance, Land Settlement, Agriculture, Vital Statistics, and so forth, upon a uniform basis throughout the six Colonies.7

In his letter inviting the various State Premiers to send a statistician to the proposed conference, N. E. Lewis, Premier of Tasmania, said that besides the question of uniformity there was a need for a conference:

To advise upon all matters where dual functions of Commonwealth and States respectively may be carried out by the same machinery in the various branches of State Bureaux. For example the whole question of the dual relationship, organization etc., between State and Commonwealth must be carefully gone into so that no confusion may arise, as would be the case if a double set of machinery were employed in collecting statistical and other matters in the same region.8

The report of the conference dealt with the need for a 'harmonious relationship' to be established between the various State bureaus and the soon to be formed Commonwealth Bureau:

Having devoted some considerable thought to this important matter of the harmonious relationship . . . it is the general opinion among the members of the Conference that the whole work of collection of the materials of statistics, whether for State or Commonwealth, had better be deputed to the officers of the several State Bureaux of Statistics. This would avoid confusion and extra expense such as would surely arise if double machinery were employed upon the same statistics within the same region; that is the local State officers would be charged with dual functions. As officers of the State, they would be under the direction and discharge the functions which they now carry out for the State. In addition they, co-operating with the Central Bureau of the Commonwealth, could prepare all statistics required in a more concentrated form for the publications of the Commonwealth, of course, under a definite agreement between the respective Governments of State and Commonwealth.9

Prior to Federation, the statistics of commerce and shipping were a major part of the work done in each colonial statistical office. Federation had taken from the States their largest source of revenue—the right to levy customs and excise duties. But, after protracted negotiation on principles and procedures, it had been agreed that, for ten years after the determination of a uniform tariff, at least three quarters of the revenue collected by the Commonwealth would be returned to the States. A 'book-keeping system' was devised which kept an account of the destination of all dubitable goods entering the country and each State was to be credited with the revenue deemed to have accrued from goods destined for consumption within its boundaries. Principles of classification were agreed at the Hobart meeting to facilitate the compilation of statistics on a comparable basis. But the classification scheme was not in fact followed by the State bureaus.10 Although the Commonwealth was to turn to Coghlan for advice, the categorisation of items in trade and customs statistics was to be a recurring problem for which the Commonwealth authorities had no great enthusiasm.

The other important financial loss for the States resulted from the transfer of postal administration to the Commonwealth. Except in South Australia, all statistical returns were carried free of postage charges. The conference strongly recommended: the retention of the free franking system for the transmission of public business communication in connection with the State Statistical and Registry Department.

There were a number of other recommendations:

(1) That the conference recognises the necessity for recording all persons engaged in industrial pursuits or attending school in Census enumeration, including aborigines.
(2) That, as the 5,137 aborigines included in the Queensland Census are engaged in industrial pursuits, or attending schools subsidised by the Government, they should be included in the general population for all purposes except those relating to the Commonwealth.
(3) That, owing to the difficulty of estimating the numbers of the people at long intervals, it is desirable to take an intermediate Census five years after each general Census—showing at least the Names, Sexes and Ages of the people, and distinguishing Chinese and other coloured Races, so that it may be possible to separate them from the general population, if thought desirable.
(4) That, in the opinion of this Conference, it is desirable that legislative authority be provided in any State of the Commonwealth not yet possessing permanent Census and Statistics Acts, so as to enable needful information to be efficiently collected. 11

The treatment of Aboriginal people was to be a recurring issue and the concept of a quinquennial census was to be urged without success for another half century.

Concerned at the absence of uniformity in estimating the population of the States, Coghlan decided the New South Wales Premier, Sir John See, to suggest another conference in 1903. Coghlan and the other five State statisticians agreed on a uniform basis for estimating the population, with Coghlan apparently the chief architect the reforms. The Census of 1901 was taken as the starting point. Various percentages were to be added to the individual States, allowing for unrecorded departures by land, sea or rail. Population figures were henceforth to be published quarterly on a uniform basis and the mean of the four quarters was to be taken as the mean population for the year. The population statistics had a special significance in the context of federal state financial relationships. Up to 30 June 1910 all 'new' Commonwealth expenditure was debited to the States according to their population. Thereafter payments to the States were also based on population. Moreover, the number of members of the House of Representatives was dependent on population calculated so as to exclude Aboriginals and aliens disqualified from voting by State electoral laws. In determining the population of the various States as at 30 June 1902 full blooded Aboriginals were excluded of was dependent on population calculated so as to exclude but the numbers were to be shown on a separate line in the various estimates.

CREATING A NATIONAL ORGANISATION

While the Constitution gave the Commonwealth a concurrent power over census and statistics, the qualified enthusiasm of the States made it by no means certain what this would mean in practice. Federal Cabinet decided in March 1903 that the Minister for Home Affairs, Sir William Lyne, should ask Coghlan to advise on the 'probable extent and costs' of establishing a federal bureau of statistics. Coghlan incorporated in his report the view's of his colleagues, J.J. Fenton (Victoria), J.Hughes (Queensland), L.H. Sholl (South Australia), M.A.C. Fraser (Western Australia) and R.M. Johnston (Tasmania). All had been asked:

Do you consider it will be necessary or desirable to maintain a State Statistical office after the establishment of a Federal Bureau, supposing the latter to be on an entirely efficient basis?

So blatantly contrived a question unsurprisingly elicited a unanimous declaration in the affirmative. Coghlan's conclusion was that however matters were arranged there would remain with the States important work connected with vital statistics, land, labour, and licensing laws, public and private charities, 'and other subjects connected with the social and industrial well-being of the community, and in regard to which State Parliament have the rights of legislation'.12 The Commonwealth intention to set up a body that would in some respects at least supersede or pre-empt the States receive little encouragement from Coghlan's peers. In a report written on 4 April 1903, R.M. Johnston made plain his belief that a federal bureau 'could not possibly be established on an entirely efficient basis without the aid of auxiliary subordinate local Statistical Bureaus in each independent State'. Nevertheless the plan urged by both the Federal Government and the Governments of New South Wales and Victoria at the 1905 Premiers' Conference in Hobart was to create a federal department and abolish State offices.13

In the meantime Coghlan had been engaged to shape the statistical branch of the Customs Department with the intention of developing a model organisation that would be adopted for other federal departments. It seems to have been envisaged that these departmental offices would be linked under a central bureau. Coghlan also supervised the preparation of the Commonwealth Trade and Commerce Returns for 1903 and 1904.

In March 1904 Coghlan was offered the position of federal statistician. He declined the post. According to his own autobiographical account, 'on pointing out the difficulties surrounding the establishment of a Statistical Office to Sir William Lyne, provisional arrangement was made, under which he agreed to prepare yearly an edition of the "Seven Colonies".14 The offer was renewed by George Reid later in the year. But Coghlan had decided to go to London in response to the urging of the New South Wales Premier, J. H. Carruthers, who was anxious to re-organise the work of the Agent General's Office. Coghlan had shown no enthusiasm for an earlier proposal Carruthers that he fill the specially created post of Financial Adviser to the New South Wales Treasury. Believing that the London appointment was only temporary, Reid agreed to defer the establishment of the new bureau until Coghlan's return.

In fact, Coghlan was already turning to fresh fields. He told friends that he was concerned about his pension rights if he 'threw over my own Government'. But he also aspired to be Australia's first High Commissioner, seeing in that post the chance to "make Australia hum"15 It was not until the Commonwealth census and statistics enacted that Coghlan finally advised Deakin not to consider him further for the post of Commonwealth Statistician. Carruthers was unwilling to release him pending completion of 'financial transactions' on behalf of New South Wales and had suggested that he accept the position on condition that he be allowed to take it up after the appointment of a High Commissioner had been made.16

Coghlan deliberately did not discuss his London ambition with Deakin, having already disclosed it to Sir John Forrest only to discover that Forrest also coveted the post. But Coghlan's temporising and ambivalence were ultimately self-defeating. He was never a serious contender for a job that was to be ornamented by a succession of ex-Prime Ministers. And his self-serving lament about the absence of qualified rivals for the Statistician's post did not deter the government from proceeding to make an appointment from the available candidates. Littleton Groom, the Minister for Home Affair's had been willing to pay Coghlan £1,200 a year, but the position was eventually advertised an annual salary of £800 to £1,000.17

In February 1905 a conference of Commonwealth and State Ministers was held in Hobart and Sir George Turner, the federal Treasurer, pointed out that the States were spending about £20,000 a year on statistics, and £120,000 every ten years on the census. Prime Minister Reid, in referring to various powers, including that of legislating on census and statistics, said:

We want to explain that the Commonwealth proposes to take over these departments. But, in as they are State departments and departments transacting business with the public, we want to take them over with due consideration, in order to avoid dislocation, and little inconvenience as possible to the public . . . We will therefore invite the State Governments to co-operate and help us exercise these powers in the most convenient way.

J.G. Jenkin, the Premier of South Australia, stated that:

Under the heading of census and statistics we know that means the employment of a good many State officials to get the information. I hope it is not the intention to establish a complete new department of Federal officers to carry out the work. If it means that it will be an expensive luxury.

Allan McLean, the Minister for Trade and Customs, replied:

It is not intended to do that in connection with any service taken over. We desire to take over such services as are included in our constitutional powers, and which can be better managed by one central department.18

The Census and Statistics Bill was introduced into the House of Representatives by the Minister of Home Affairs, Littleton Groom, on 23 August 1905. His second reading speech noted that the Commonwealth power in relation to census and statistics was a concurrent power. He went on to say:

The object of the Bill is to enable the Commonwealth to establish a central bureau of statistics in order that it may furnish to the world statistical returns with respect to the matters under its special jurisdiction, and also publish certain statistics having reference to the affairs of Australia as a whole.

Even though a central office with a Commonwealth Statistician was to be established the States were still to retain their own offices and officers.

We start on the assumption that the States will require to have their own local statistics for their own purposes . . . I think it would be advantageous for them to have one Commonwealth department; but judging from the tone of replies received from them I am inclined to think that some negotiations will be required before they will be prepared to hand over their own departments.

Groom explained that there were two possible courses:

We might have a central statistical bureau with branches in each of the six States; which could be used for State purposes as required. As an alternative we could establish a central Commonwealth bureau and enter into negotiations with the various States with a view to utilising their departments to the fullest possible extent. During the early stages of the organisation of the Commonwealth departments the latter will be found to be the most practical course to pursue.

The reason for a centralised Bureau was given as a need to: bring into line the statistics of the States for the purpose of comparison, to lay down a uniform method for the collection of statistics.

In addition:

The central department will collect all information in regard to subjects specially controlled by the Commonwealth, such as imports and exports, trade, and commerce generally including inter-State transactions, navigation and shipping, postal, defence and other matters.19

It would remain a power of the States to collect their own census data. But the proposed Commonwealth census would be decennial and would rely on a parliamentary appropriation.

When the debate resumed on 3 October 1905 the Bill was closely scrutinised. In the Senate the clause dealing with free postage, which had attracted much attention at the 1903 Conference of Statisticians in Hobart, was deleted. It was also argued unsuccessfully that the census schedule should be approved by Parliament before it could be distributed. The Census and Statistics Act was assented to on 8 December 1905. Part II of the Act dealt with the appointment and powers of the Statistician, arrangements with the States for collection of data, and secrecy provisions. Part III related to the taking of the census. The first census under the new Act was to be taken in 1911. Part IV of the Act covered statistics and laid down the areas where the Statistician was to have authority:

16. The Statistician shall subject to the regulations and the directions of the Minister, collect, annually, statistics in relation to all or any of the following matters:

(a) Population;
(b) Vital, social, and industrial matters;
(c) Employment and non-employment;
(d) Imports and exports;
(e) Interstate trade;
(f) Postal and telegraphic matters;
(g) Factories, mines and productive industries generally;

(h) Agricultural, horticultural, viticultural, dairying, and pastoral industries;
(i) Banking, insurance, and finance;
(j) Railways, tramways, shipping, and transport;
(k) Land tenure and occupancy;
(l) Any other prescribed matters.

The Statistician was given wide powers. He was able at any time during working hours to enter any factory, mine, workshop, or place where persons were employed to make inquiries or inspect all plant and machinery. The penalty for hindering an officer under this section of the Act was ten pounds. Penalties for supplying false information or failure to supply information were also prescribed. A severe penalty of fifty pounds applied to any officer of the Bureau who divulged the contents of any forms or any information furnished to the Bureau. 20

At a conference of State and Commonwealth Ministers in Sydney in April 1906 it was resolved 'that the general statistical departments should be handed over to the Commonwealth'. Meanwhile, the position of Commonwealth Statistician had been advertised in the Commonwealth of Australia Gazette on 24 February 1906. 'I wish I could see someone fitted for the post in the service of the Commonwealth or of the States', Coghlan intimated to Deakin. 'The only man of ready talent fit for the work is a young man named H. A. Smith in my office in Sydney.21

Smith was chief compiler in the vital statistics branch of the New South Wales Statistician's Office but manifestly too junior, notwithstanding Coghlan's lukewarm patronage, for the federal appointment. In 1919 he became New South Wales Statistician. R. M. Johnston, at 62, declined to be a candidate for a position that would take him away from Tasmania. But George Handley Knibbs was deemed suitable. His appointment, at a salary of £1,000 a year was announced in the Gazette on 26 May 1906. Knibbs, born in Sydney in 1858, and formerly a surveyor and lecturer in the engineering school at Sydney University, had been president of the Institution of Surveyors 1892-93 and 1900-01, honorary secretary of the Royal Society of New South Wales for nine years and president in 1898-99. He was co-author of a report on education prepared for the New South Wales Government after an overseas study done in 1902-03 and was appointed Director of Technical Education in New South Wales early in 1906, following a brief period as Acting Professor of Physics at Sydney. Although he had been in 1887 a foundation member (with Coghlan and Hayter) of the Australian Economic Association, whose second but unfulfilled object had been the compilation of a statistical history of the various Australian colonies, Knibbs had hitherto had little direct involvement in the kind of official statistical work for which he was to be responsible.22

Sir William Lyne, whom Groom consulted about Knibbs, reported that 'he used to be a very bitter opponent and writer to the press, always against our party'. But Knibbs had 'been for some time past rather reasonable' Lyne admitted. 'I know nothing against him,' the Minister for Trade and Customs concluded, 'and probably he would make a very good man. 23

In an early private assessment of the Commonwealth Statistician Coghlan had commented:

Knibbs will have a very uphill job. As at present situated he can do his work only thru' the State Offices, and he will speedily find himself in difficulties for lack of information. He has great abilities and attainments, but his lack of acquaintance with the technique and presentation of statistics are great obstacles to success, but of all the applicants he was certainly the best.24

Writing to Alfred Deakin, Coghlan conceded that the 'appointment of Mr Knibbs should carry with it a good share of support in the States'. But the praise that followed was obtrusively faint. 'Mr Knibbs has high mathematical attainments, he is earnest, hardworking and scrupulously honest but he must be given experienced assistants, a knowledge of the technique of statistics is absolutely essential to even moderately good work.' 25 A few months later another friend was invited to tell Coghlan 'how Knibbs is shaping—badly, I should say, every man whom I discarded as worthless seems to have got into Knibbs' good graces'.26

Those who had most conspicuously got into Knibbs' good graces were the five principal professional officers appointed, as Knibbs' first Year Book put it, 'to the command of the various greater divisions of statistic [sic] in this Bureau'. They were John Stonham, 'M.A., Sydney University (Chief

Compiler)', Henry Spondly 'Zurich University', Charles Henry Wickens 'Associate of the Institute of Actuaries', Frederick Dalglish Rossiter 'M.A. Melbourne University', and Edward Tannoch McPhee 'Tasmanian Statistical Bureau'.

Spondly's province was vital statistics. Rossiter was recruited from the Victorian Bureau and was responsible for defence and the library. Wickens, who had recently composed Western Australia's first life tables after conducting the 1901 Census there, came to be supervisor of census. Stonham had been with the New South Wales Bureau and was given responsibility for 'general administration'. Though remaining nominally the senior officer, Stonham was passed over for both Wickens and McPhee (who had been in charge of trade, customs, and commerce) as well as by L. F. Giblin when the post of Commonwealth Statistician was vacant in later years. In May 1933, in the course of an unsuccessful appeal against a recommendation by McPhee that Roland Wilson should normally act as Statistician in McPhee's absence, Stonham claimed

. . . I was mainly instrumental in laying down the main lines of procedure at the inception of the Bureau. I was secretary to the first Conference of Commonwealth and State Statisticians . . . Mr Knibbs (as he then was) freely admitted that it was largely due to my official work that the Bureau proceeded on successful lines . . . In addition to being the original author of three chapters of the Official Year Book, I contributed portions to others, and some of my original writing in them remains to this day. 27

The conference at which Stonham served as secretary was held from 30 November to 8 December 1906. In the preceding months Knibbs had travelled to each of the State capitals to examine their methods and 'legal and administrative powers' as well as to seek out potential recruits. He also made an 'exhaustive but rapid examination of the whole range of Australian Statistic [sic]'. Knibbs' plan for the subjects to be covered by the new Bureau were foreshadowed by Senator J. H. Keating, Minister without Portfolio, on 11 October 1906 during discussion of the Appropriation Bill. Keating noted that the transfer to 'the Statistical Department' of the statistical officers of the Customs Department was under consideration.28

Knibbs went to the 1906 conference armed with 'a comprehensive memorandum and a complete series of forms, indicating what might be attempted through an adequate organisation of the State Statistical Bureaus, and illustrative of the range of requirements of the Commonwealth Statistician'.29 His lengthy opening speech was a blend of credo and tactical compromise. The Commonwealth and the States were not 'different and mutually exclusive entities, as in the case, let us suppose, of different nations, but a single entity-the people of Australia'. There had been ministerial agreement earlier in the year, Knibbs pointed out, 'to the effect that general statistics should be relegated to federal control'. This was not a very enlightening formula. In reply to a request by the Prime Minister for elucidation, the States had offered a variety of self-serving interpretations which negated the agreement. The South Australian Premier had the singular honesty to confess on 19 July 1906: I have the honour to state that I am not aware of the meaning which these words were intended to convey'. Undaunted, Knibbs declared that the 'scope of the statistical requirements of the Commonwealth . . . cannot be less exhaustive than those of the States'. The Commonwealth was 'materially interested' in all of the available statistical data for State. Without a 'complete statistical record' it would be 'practically impossible to for the Commonwealth Government to be adequately and accurately advised in connexion with its administrative and legislative functions.30

No one was disposed to challenge these propositions. Nor was there significant The disagreement with the details of the 145 'common statistical forms' which Knibbs submitted for adoption. The conference unanimously adopted a series of resolutions that stated and elaborated on the desirability of uniformity in method, order, and date of 'co-extensive' statistical collection, compilation, and publication of statistical information by the State bureaus. Co-operation and consultation was pledged. Exchange of information, initially within the scope of the approved forms and thereafter by agreement, was to be free of charge 'and with the greatest punctuality of which the circumstances admit'.31

Some old problems were tackled and new ones identified. It was agreed that the services of the police rather than ordinary enumerators or direct enquiry should be used for the collection of information 'as far as practicable'.32 A quinquennial enumeration restricted to sex and age was seen as essential for ensuring accuracy in determining the fluctuation of population in the States.33 (The Victorian Statist, having discovered what he believed to be a flaw that greatly exaggerated the loss of his State's population by sea, dissented from the recommendation that the method of estimating inter-censal population changes should not be altered until the next census.)34

In his speech, Knibbs had argued that a 'principle of localisation' was needed in order to rationalise the 'determination of statistical aggregates within localities fixed by definite boundaries'. His declared preference for using police patrol areas, at least to as an interim procedure, did not win assent. But it was resolved that steps ought to be taken 'for the determination of definite statistical units of area, due consideration being given therein to local enactments, and existing State divisions'.35 (In 1919 Knibbs was to publish a monograph on local government as a prelude to the proposed use of 'the municipal subdivision of the States as a basis for the presentation of data in connexion with next the census'.)36

One of the benefits of localisation of statistical aggregates would be the availability of data linking specific forms of primary industry to 'means of communication'. Knibbs emphasised that such information was vital to determination of 'a true solution' for the management principles to be adopted for government railways. Should railways be run as commercial concerns intended to yield a profit or 'as means of developing a territory' without regard to 'immediate or direct profit'? Whatever the 'true solution' to this or other questions, improvements were also necessary, Knibbs noted, in factory, forestry, water and irrigation, fisheries, banking, private finance, and insurance statistics. Estimates of the value of agricultural produce needed to be put on a more consistent basis so that 'questions of economic loss arising from lack of co-operative effort or from difficulty in placing on a suitable market would be possible of fuller and more satisfactory discussion'.37

Knibbs could be well pleased with the cordiality and consensus achieved at this meeting. Translating it into concerted action was to prove another matter. During 1903, 1904, and 1905 New South Wales, Queensland and Tasmania had adopted a system of classifying causes of death introduced by the British Registrar-General in 1901. In spite of agreement at the 1902

Statisticians' Conference, Victoria, South Australia and Western Australia had persisted with the Farr-Ogle system. At the Melbourne conference Knibbs successfully recommended the use of the International Institute of Statistics' Bertillon Index. But it was not until 1917 that he was able to report that all of the States were employing the Bertillon System in their monthly and quarterly bulletins of vital statistics.38

Among Knibbs' earliest tribulations was confusion over the activities of Coghlan. In July 1906 Knibbs had concurred with a proposal that Coghlan should publish a volume of statistics on Australia and New Zealand for 1904-05. Coghlan had offered to undertake the task, contending that it was very much a personal work; and the Premier of New South Wales had sought the agreement of the Commonwealth Government to this once-only sequel to the now discontinued New South Wales publication, A Statistical Account of Australia and New Zealand. A grant of £500 was made to Coghlan in return for the supply of copies of the work but nearly a year later Coghlan advised that he was abandoning the project.39

In the meantime the Bureau staff had been examining existing statistics prior to establishing their own procedures. 'So many discrepancies were found', Knibbs advised the Secretary of the Department of Home Affairs, 'that it became necessary to compile authoritative statistics for whole Commonwealth period, 1901 to 1907'40 In a draft response to a parliamentary question on whether the government intended to authorise the annual issue of a statistical publication 'on similar lines to that compiled by T. A. Coghlan, and entitled "A Statistical Account of Australia and New Zealand"' Knibbs wrote that he had been authorised to publish 'an Official Year Book for the Commonwealth'. However, the volume 'will not be based upon "Australia and New Zealand" as a model, but its form has been decided upon after a comparative study of the annual statistical publications of the civilised world'.41

Eight thousand copies of this innovative book were to be printed, half of which were to be taken by the Department of External Affairs. Knibbs had recommended a 'liberal supply' to British, American and other foreign libraries, as well as to schools, public libraries, steamers, trains, schools of arts, mechanics institutes, agricultural societies, mining institutes, farmers' associations and 'debating societies with proper libraries'. In order to 'meet the difficulty of excessive demand for gratuitous copies', 1,000 copies were also to be placed on sale at 3/6d plus postage. 42

Arrangements for the printing of the Year Book were themselves the source of prolonged controversy. Knibbs had to overcome Treasury opposition and gain ministerial approval in order to call for tenders rather than rely on the slow and allegedly inferior work of the Victorian Government Printer. He insisted that the entire body of type should be set by hand rather than by linotype or monotype machines. Although one prospective tenderer had indicated that hand setting would double the cost, Parliament was assured on 9 October 1907 in answer to a question on notice to the Prime Minister: the work is of a special nature, involving a large amount of tabulation, and is subject to continual alteration, as fresh data comes to hand, and in the opinion of experienced statistical officers and printers, it cannot with advantage and economy be dealt with by machine setting.

Only a handful of large firms—John Sands, Sands & McDougall, and McCarron, Bird—could readily meet the requirements of the tender, especially restrictions on sub-letting portions of the contract. McCarron, Bird of Melbourne were the successful tenderers.

It was possible to expedite printing—'a private firm has to please, or the custom is lost' Knibbs noted in a memorandum of 21 February 1907, to the Acting Secretary of the Home Affairs Department. But there was little that could be done to overcome the dilatoriness of the States in submitting information. 'Under existing arrangements this Bureau has to wait until the States of the Commonwealth have compiled the information before we can even start to compile, and owing to the unequal efficiency in the staffs of the several State Offices some of them are much later than others. Further the compilation of individual subjects is not contemporaneously carried out in several States.' 43

Nearly a year later Knibbs advised his Minister that the Commonwealth Bureau 'is at the mercy of the slowest and least efficient State Bureau for the completion of practically the whole of its statistics'. This crippling dependence was obviously irksome. 'Unless more strenuous efforts are made by the States to supply the Commonwealth with statistical information it will become necessary for the central authority to obtain statistical information directly instead of through the State Statisticians.' 44

The long awaited first edition of the Year Book was widely welcomed. Six months after publication Knibbs forwarded ten pages of extracts from press and personal comments to his Minister, Hugh Mahon. From the range and tone of newspaper reviews it was clear that the volume had achieved its objective of promoting overseas appreciation of Australia. Walter Murdoch, lecturer in English Literature at Melbourne University, commended the work as 'a miracle of clearness'. The German Acting Consul-General in Sydney and the Commander-in-Chief of the United States Atlantic Fleet found the book 'of great service' and 'invaluable' respectively.

As for the Minister, he minuted that it was 'a triumph of industry, discrimination and judicious arrangement'. Diffidently, he suggested that 'a more copious index to the multitude of facts' might be desirable.45

The only sour note to find its way into the files was an anonymous review in the Bulletin on 7 May 1908 which, the Minister was assured, 'Misrepresents the facts and figures in a very remarkable way'. But the Bulletin's most wounding shaft was aimed not at the Statistician's 'columns of figures and his mathematics' but at his efforts as a 'descriptive writer'. 46 The unstated contrast with Coghlan leaped from between the lines. Coghlan's own judgment was unflattering:

Knibbs, I take it, must have the ear of the press, as I do not hear of any complaints. His yearbook is full of errors, being so inexperienced, I wonder that he did not lay himself out to make a success of one thing at a time. 47

'To be a successful Statistician, one needs to be an economist', he explained to Deakin, 'statistics and mathematics are often directly opposed'. To another old friend Coghlan wrote 'I feel vexed with Knibbs who deprecates everybody's work and does very little himself'. Candidly he confided that he was not enamoured of his post as Agent-General. 'I would rather be Statistician any day. 48

Coghlan's regret at taking a wrong turning in his own life blinded him to the substance of Knibbs' achievement. The Year Book was an outstanding production. In 29 chapters spread over 931 pages, the Commonwealth had a remarkable compendium of data, historical summaries, and occasional commentary. While there was consider-able thematic continuity between Coghlan's Statistical Account and the Year Book, Knibbs' volume had a more austere tone. There were no chapters corresponding with Coghlan's 'Food Supply and Cost of Living', 'Social Condition', and 'Religion'. Where Coghlan had written of 'Industrial Progress', Knibbs dealt with 'Industrial Unionism and Industrial Legislation'. Nevertheless, the new reference book provided glimpses of the Statistician's personal judgment. In discussing 'Causes of Decrease in Crime' Knibbs noted that 'collaterally with the introduction of ordinary intellectual education certain people have departed from their pristine virtues'. He remarked on the 'mistaken zeal' of police in informing employers about the prison records of prospective employees, and condemned the 'danger and absurdity of sending drunkards to gaol'. On the contentious question of 'Trade of the United Kingdom with Australia. Has it been Diverted?' he relied heavily on quotations from a report of the Advisory Committee on Commercial Intelligence of the United Kingdom Board of Trade.49 The following year, however, there was a much expanded chapter on commerce, including articles on the customs tariff of 1908, and the development of trade with the East. In succeeding years specially contributed essays became a feature of the Year Book covering such topics as the kindergarten movement (1909), Aborigines (1910), the Commonwealth seat of government (1911), preferential voting (1912), and anthropometrical measurements of military cadets (1918).

GEORGE KNIBBS: INITIATIVE AND ACHIEVEMENT

Knibbs' philosophy and vision were further expounded in a series of publications, in addition to the annual Year Books. 'Uniformity in Statistic [sic] an Imperative Necessity', Knibbs' first Year Book had proclaimed in a bold heading.50 Statistical uniformity, Knibbs said, was an urgent requirement of Commonwealth administration. But, while the Commonwealth 'is directly concerned with the good of the whole as well as that of the individual States' the thrust of his argument remained the same as that of his address to the State statisticians in November 1906, that the well-being of the Commonwealth implies the 'well-being of its integral parts, viz. the several States therein'.

In a lecture on 'The Problems of Statistics' delivered to the Australasian Association for the Advancement of Science in 1910, Knibbs disclosed his conception of the purpose and agenda of modern official statistics:

Official statistics . . . arise from a clearer perception of what is essential for productive administration, and for what has been called, in the wider sense of the term, police regulation.

The raison d'etre of official statistical organisations was the need for 'an adequate statistic [sic]' that would make it impossible 'to distinguish between results which may be properly credited to wise or bad government and what may more properly be credited to the lavishness or niggardliness of Nature'.

Knibbs saw it as a fundamental task of economics to investigate 'the economic efficiency of the human unit'. As he conceived it, this entailed calculating the energy spent in nurture, education, and 'general maintenance' and setting it against 'productive activity'. It would be desirable, he contended, to know the extent to which the activity of productive units was affected by disease, and variations in efficiency according to age and natural and acquired endowments. The cost of general and preventative medicine, and of education and occupational training, would also need to be considered in 'any equitable adjustment of the social system'. A 'complete analysis of the total economic effect' of public hygiene measures remained to be made. And, without explicitly endorsing the arguments of eugenicists, he noted that 'eugenic considerations were increasingly influencing public opinion, and commended the 'systematic examination of school children from an anthropometric and hygienic point of view'.

Returning to one of the subjects he had put before his fellow official statisticians in 1906, he articulated his argument that 'too strict an adoption of the commercial principle may be detrimental to the general interest of the community' when applied to the nation's railway system. Knibbs left no doubt that he had a vision of the role of statistician guided by a 'high aim' of understanding 'the inter-relations and inter-dependencies of man with his fellow-man, and, from his position of professional expert in statecraft, assisting the administrative statesman with his counsel and advice'.51

High minded utterances combined with what W. M. Hughes, the Attorney-General, characterised as 'wholesale condemnation of his predecessors' exposed Knibbs to criticism for 'the extraordinary amount of corrigenda in his own work'. Hughes told Knibbs' Minister, Hugh Mahon, in April 1909, that the Commonwealth Statistician is 'purely a theorist'. 'If you were to make enquiries into the work of his office you would find', Hughes forecast, 'that what he does himself is very little indeed'.52

The source of many of the adverse assessments of Knibbs was the acerbic pen of Coghlan. Thus when Knibbs travelled overseas to study census methods he was derided for taking 'a jaunt'. And, in a letter to a friend at the Bulletin, Coghlan confided that 'I think his work is of poor quality, and he suffers terribly from swelled-head'.53

Critical perceptions of Knibbs' activities were associated with State resistance to Commonwealth ambitions. When the Western Australian Government introduced a statistics Bill in July 1907, Knibbs pressed for federal intervention to prevent it, but the Attorney-General, Groom, advised that a State Parliament had the right 'to legislate to obtain certain statistics for itself independently'. It was a question of policy whether representations should be made 'in respect to the unnecessary duplication of machinery'.54 Persistent efforts by Knibbs from 1907 onwards to persuade his Ministers that 'federalising of statistical services' was essential were to no avail. While the principal State statistical officers of Queensland and South Australia had been appointed as Commonwealth officers as envisaged in the 1905 Act, they operated under an uneasy formula—which encountered prolonged resistance from other States—that entailed their acceptance of 'professional directions' from the Commonwealth Statistician without being under his 'immediate administrative authority'. 'The present system of dual control is conducive to delay, incompleteness and want of uniformity in presentation', Knibbs complained to his departmental head on 26 November 1909 after vexing correspondence with Queensland and frustrating delays in obtaining returns from the under-staffed Tasmanian statistician. Nevertheless, because of the need for co-operation on the

Census, he suggested the following April that 'the matter of assuming the whole range of statistical functions' should be deferred until after the main part of the Census work had been completed.55

The 1911 Census was the first major opportunity for Knibbs' counsel (and the talents of Wickens as a vital statistician) to be implemented. Knibbs adopted the innovative New South Wales and Victorian question of 1901 about the number of children born to the marriage and extended it to previous marriages. (Ex-nuptial births were not recorded and data on women who were separated, divorced, or widowed were collected but not tabulated.) He introduced questions about race, the occupation of a person's employer, and the length of time unemployed persons had been out of work; and made it possible to distinguish between house-owners and tenants. The weekly rent of tenants was asked but the Senate refused to sanction questions about alcohol consumption, wage rates, and the amount of currency in circulation. Information was to be supplied on cards by each individual rather than on a household schedule. The British were planning to transfer data from householders' schedules to Hollerith punched cards for storage and processing. Knibbs decided, however, that electric adding machines and calculators, but not tabulating or sorting machines, were to be used for computation. In a widely circulated pamphlet, Knibbs explained the historical background, purposes, and operations of the Census. As a 'national stocktaking' for 'sociological, economic and hygienic purposes' the data would enable the government to deal more effectively with 'the most urgent problem of the day', the declining birth-rate. In explaining some of the administrative, financial, and social policy objectives of Census taking, Knibbs made an effective case for the prospective temporary employment of 350 enumerators, 6,000 collectors, and 150 clerks.56

Among the 1911 findings, published in seventeen bulletins and a three volume report, were some with significant policy implications, notably the estimates of the male population aged between 18 and 60 who were eligible to serve in the Citizen Forces in time of war (57 per cent), and the revelation that 4.5 per cent of the population was eligible for old age pensions. Because of mis-statements by respondents, calculations of age based on previous censuses were believed to be very inaccurate. Knibbs and Wickens introduced a process of 'age smoothing', but the problem persisted, posing a puzzle for successive Statisticians. As the 1933 Census Report put it, 'unassailable generalisation' about the reasons for mis-stating age was not possible. Ignorance and carelessness were factors, as were a more or less conscious preference for certain attractive digits, such as 0,5, and even numbers, and possibly unconscious aversion to certain odd numbers such as 7; and some wilful misrepresentations arising from motives of an economic, social or purely individual character.

By 1961, the problem had largely evaporated, probably as a result of improved educational standards and 'a more constant necessity' to disclose or prove age in a variety of contexts, as well as the compulsory registration of births, deaths, and marriages.

Confronted by the fact that their 1911 figures showed that 80 per cent of all reported cases of deaf mutism were aged 10 to 14, rather than in the earliest age groups as would be expected for a congenital condition, Knibbs and Wickens sought the explanation in understatement by parents hoping that their children would recover or anxious about losing them to educational institutions. The group aged 10 to 14 would be thoroughly enumerated because they were likely to be receiving specialised education and their teachers would provide the census information. Ten years later the discovery that the age group 20 to 24 had the most deaf mutes made it clear that an epidemic of some sort must have affected this particular cohort. Later medical research, drawing heavily on the 1911 and 1921 Census results, established a convincing link between deaf mutism and rubella.

Knibbs justified the inclusion of a question about race as 'important for the Commonwealth Representation Act, which expresses the determination of the people of the Commonwealth to preserve their country as a white Australia'. While the racial question was principally concerned with European and non-European origins, full blooded Aboriginals in accordance with section 127 of the Constitution were not included in reckoning the numbers of the people. Not until 1933 were collectors instructed to gather as much information as they could about Aboriginals 'in employment or living in proximity to settlements'. Only after the repeal of section 127 of the Constitution in 1967, did the focus shift to identifying for policy purposes an 'Aboriginal/Torres Strait Islander' population rather than a

European one. Seventy years after Knibbs introduced the race question, the discredited concept of a 'European race' was dropped. Information sought thereafter about country of birth, citizenship, and language use reflected the concerns of a multi-cultural society; and the large number of persons identifying themselves as Aboriginal (40 per cent more in 1976 than in 1971) demonstrated a radical shift in attitudes.57

One of the most controversial aspects of the 1911 Census was the Statistician's calculation of the population of the States which showed that both federal and State inter-censal estimates had consistently overstated each State's population. Bickering over the reasons for the discrepancies did not disguise the real cause of concern—every head less was 25 shillings less in a State's coffers from federal contributions. The Commonwealth steadfastly resisted a call for a statisticians' conference to re-examine methods of calculating population. Believing themselves to be 'men competent to discuss the matter, and who have had the practical handling of Australian Statistics for many years', the State statisticians convened in Sydney in March 1912 and agreed on recommendations for compilation of overland migration figures. They also urged the Commonwealth to resume collection of interstate trade statistics and passed a ritual resolution in favour of a quinquennial census limited to 'sex and locality'. Incensed by a press statement by King O'Malley, Minister for Home Affairs, blaming the States for the 'dilatory supply of statistics', and threatening the establishment of 'Common-wealth Statistical Bureaus' in each State, they wrote to Knibbs asking if he was in sympathy with this view. They could not have been appeased by a reply suggesting the impropriety of asking for a comment from an official about a Minister. 'The facts will, of course, speak for themselves' Knibbs concluded.58

From its earliest days, the Bureau published regular bulletins on finance, population and vital statistics, production, transport and communication, and social statistics. From 1910 onwards, in a political environment increasingly concerned with inflation and employment issues, substantial effort was devoted to studies of employment, wages, prices, and the cost of living. Data from a household budget survey, in which only 222 out of 'approximately 1,500' account books dispatched were returned, were subjected to exhaustive manipulation. Knibbs expressed his regret that only 9.4 per cent of the families who embarked on the exercise 'persevered' throughout the twelve month period required. He compared Australians unfavourably with 'the masses of the community' in the United States and Germany whose performance on similar projects had demonstrated their understanding that 'sociological knowledge can contribute to national success'. Optimistically, Knibbs tried again in November 1913, inviting volunteers to fill in a detailed record of income and expenditure for a month. Of 7,000 sets of papers distributed only 392 useable budgets were returned. Although the sample left much to be desired, the analysis was suggestive, and once again included calculations of average weekly expenditure on food weighted for age and sex which were comparable with the most advanced contemporary overseas methodology. Nearly 50 years elapsed before the Bureau's next social survey venture-the labour force survey.59

In a report on Social Insurance written after his European trip of 1909, Knibbs noted the need for more information about unemployment before the impact of a scheme of insurance could be assessed.60 Fired by the 'entirely new development' represented by Winston Churchill's plans for national labour exchanges and compulsory unemployment insurance, Knibbs devised a new Department of Labour and Statistics 'to co-ordinate and centralise the Commonwealth agencies dealing with labour, industrial and statistical matters'. The Statistician envisaged detaching this Bureau from the Department of Home Affairs, adding responsibility for the administration of the Conciliation and Arbitration Acts from the Attorney-General's Department, and establishing a network of labour exchanges.61

Early in 1911, the Labour Minister for Home Affairs, King O'Malley, had directed his permanent head, David Miller, 'to eliminate the red-tape circumvention, the needless multiplication of records, the grave waste of time and the most useless expense' which allegedly characterised the 'ptolemaic business system' of his department.62 But, while he was emphatically in favour of more autonomy for the 'sub-departments' of his Ministry responsible for electoral, meteorological, and statistical matters, O'Malley's low standing in the government made Knibbs' ambition unattainable. Even the Statistician's more modest wish to establish the Bureau alone as an independent department with himself as a 'permanent head' with 'the necessary powers, as to organisation, control, and discipline' was, as it turned out, some 60 years premature.63

Within the Bureau a Labour and Industrial Branch was set up in 1911 and was responsible for reports on Prices, Price Indexes and Cost of Living in Australia, 1891 to 1912 and Trade Unionism, Unemployment, Wages, Prices, and Cost of Living in Australia 1891 to 1912. A Labour Bulletin began publication in 1913 covering industrial conditions and disputes, unemployment, retail prices, house rent, and cost of living, wholesale prices, and wage rates. Although much criticised by later officials and scholars, this was pioneering work providing information where previously there had been none and authoritative data for the Arbitration Court's deliberations on wages.64

In taking stock of the progress of official statistical endeavour by 1914, Knibbs commented that the compilation and computation of statistics relating to production, including agricultural, pastoral, dairying, mining, manufacturing, forestry and fisheries, remained the province of the States. He lamented the absence of a single centre where 'all the details are available for systematic study' and opined that 'the latent powers of the Commonwealth might need to be exercised to secure uniformity, efficiency, and reductions in cost. Another handicap to be overcome was the difficulty in recruiting, housing, and retaining staff with 'considerable powers of analysis, aptitude for original research, and the special ability to penetrate the hidden significance of statistical data'.65 The staff difficulty was shortly to be compounded by the enlistment of Bureau personnel and the transfer of others to wartime duties in other spheres. By 2 November 1916, only 15 of the staff of 27 remained, and the 44 year old Wickens who was married with children, had to be restrained by the Minister from joining the infantry following the failure of the conscription referendum.66

Shortly after the outbreak of war in 1914, Knibbs circulated an 'urgent' letter to his State colleagues recommending that production and trade statistics should hence-forth be compiled on a fiscal year basis rather than from calendar years or agricultural years (which ended either on February 28 or March 31). J.B. Trivett of New South Wales was the first to respond favourably. South Australia's new Statist, W.L. Johnston, advised in July

1916 that he had agreed with his predecessor that the statistical year should in future end on June 30. 'I have little doubt', Knibbs wrote, 'that . . . all will eventually fall into line'.67

One way of ensuring uniformity was for the Commonwealth to take over the State bureaus. King O'Malley, once again Minister for Home Affairs, was able to persuade the Acting Prime Minister, George Pearce, to propose that the Commonwealth 'should assume the duty of compiling and publishing all Australian statistics'.68 But the States proved uniformly unenthusiastic. R.M. Johnston of Tasmania advised his Premier that 'such a scheme of transfer and monopoly, of the right of publishing all statistics would be detrimental to State interests.69 In South Australia, where all statistics were collected under the authority of the Commonwealth Census and Statistics Act and little was collected beyond what the Commonwealth required, there had been a deliberate avoidance of duplication in tabulation, compilation, and publication. The South Australian statisticians believed that continued compliance with Commonwealth requirements, together with discontinuance of the vital statistics operations of the Registrar General of Births, Deaths and Marriages, would make a transfer of control unnecessary.70 In Victoria, the Chief Secretary warned that the discontinuance of State statistical endeavour would be 'crippling' to Parliament and Royal Commissions and inconsistent with the State's dignity.71

A motion in favour of amalgamating the statistical bureaus of the Commonwealth and the States was actually carried at a conference of Ministers in Adelaide in May 1916. But, after two years of desultory deliberation, the States announced via a memorandum from the Premier of New South Wales on 2 July 1918 that 'under the circumstances it is not proposed to take any further steps to give effect to the resolution passed at the Conference'. Although 'many manifest disabilities' were cited as more than counterbalancing any advantages that might accrue from amalgamation, no specific 'disabilities' were identified by the States. R.M. Johnston had once complained to Knibbs of 'frequent changes made by your central bureau without previous warning, and the gradual growth of details under various categories from year to year'. Clearly, while Johnston and other statists might continue to co-operate and to espouse a doctrine of uniformity, they remained unwilling to surrender the autonomy which they and their predecessors had enjoyed for so long.72

While State statisticians were resolute in maintaining their freedom of action, the exigencies of war—the need for what Prime Minister Hughes called a 'great scheme of organisation'—produced a War Census Act in July 1915 that imposed significant duties of disclosure and compliance on the Australian public. The onus to obtain, complete, and return the schedules was placed on respondents who were required to provide information not only about the present occupations of males aged eighteen to 59 but about other occupations they were capable of undertaking. The 'personal' card also asked questions of direct concern to military and security authorities—about health, military training, possession of firearms and ammunition, birthplace, and citizenship. A 'wealth and income' card sought details from all persons over eighteen not only of 'income' and 'property' but also about ownership of motor cars, motor cycles, other motor vehicles, and traction engines, and 'the kind and number of any other vehicles'. Information was also required on horses and foals (by sex and use), cattle (including working bullocks), mules, camels, sheep and pigs.

Using lists derived from their card indexes, the war census staff were able to facilitate the issue of recruiting appeals to all males other than the enemy subjects aged between eighteen and 45; and war loan appeals and prospectuses were dispatched to persons who had disclosed that they were 'in possession of £1,000 or upwards'. Complete lists of those born in enemy countries or whose parents were enemy aliens were 'prepared for the information of the military authorities'.73

Suspicion that the census of income and wealth was a prelude to fresh taxation imports led to 'conservative' estimates. There was evidence that some parents omitted to record the property of children under eighteen, and some older pensioners may not have filed. Nevertheless, in spite of the problems caused by those whom the South Australian Statist described as 'the simple minds of the community', the inquiry was a uniquely revealing exercise which, as the 1925 Year Book candidly admitted, was unlikely to be repeated in 'normal' times because of its 'inquisitorial character'.74

While conscious of the deficiencies of the war emergency census, Knibbs urged the desirability of distributing wealth and income forms with each decennial population census. The Statistician suggested:

In those cases in which there is an objection to disclosing the particulars, in respect of wealth and income to a local resident (the collector) even though under an oath of secrecy, arrangements could be made for the collector to furnish an envelope for the transmission of the form post free to the Commonwealth Statistician, and could, by a note to this effect in his record book, ensure that the person to whom the envelope was issued would not be overlooked in the event of default.75

Following several months in England in 1919 as the Australian representative on the double taxation sub-committee of the Royal Commission on the income tax, Knibbs had concluded that it would be desirable to collect more statistics on taxation of income and land. He reported to Stonham that there was a growing feeling in Britain that: there will have to be a heavy wealth tax, and that the nation's well-being will nor allow the War Debt to be a perpetual charge on the nation's productive activity . . . I am hoping, that in these, as in other matters, we shall be able to set the pace in Australia.76

But in the debates on the legislation required for the 1921 Census, the Labor leader, Frank Tudor, quoted correspondence in which Knibbs resiled from his support for a contemporary income and wealth survey which he now said was unnecessary, inconvenient, and impracticable. Reliance would be placed henceforth on inventory estimates of wealth, Knibbs having already advised the government that 'any estimate of wealth based on probate returns must take into account at least five, or still better, ten years experience.77

Early in 1920 Knibbs attended the first Empire Statistical Conference in London. In preparing for the Australian submission to the conference, Knibbs had compiled a comprehensive memorandum which advanced the case for an Imperial Statistical Bureau. Reflecting his experience at the head of a federal agency, Knibbs argued that the prestige of an imperial bureau would be 'a more potent factor in the introduction of uniformity that any number of Statistical Conferences'. Continuity would also provide regular analysis not available from the intermittent conference method of control' or a 'mere summarising agency'. Among Knibbs' observations was a condemnation of existing statistics on unemployment as 'meagre and unsatisfactory'. He emphasised the need to measure the 'efficiency' of labour and of manufacturing on a common basis, and saw an urgent need for better data on industrial disputes.78

In a letter to Stonham from London, Knibbs foreshadowed that 'we shall have to enlarge Industrial Section's work, and in a way which will take account of the industrial drift . . . 79 Knibbs had been developing his thinking on the social issues of race hygiene and migration. His changing interests, and the challenge of a new task, led Knibbs to accept the invitation of the Prime Minister to take up the directorship of the newly created Bureau of Science and Industries in 1921.80 In the fundamentally unpropitious environment of an emergent Commonwealth, Knibbs had built an organisation that was respected by those whose judgment was not impaired by jealousy or political and institutional antagonism. He had coped with a dizzying succession of Ministers, creating and maintaining a high reputation for professional competence and integrity. Occasional controversy and collisions of personality did not detract from basic achievement and growing authority of what had become a secure element of the federal administration. The New Zealand Government Statistician, Malcolm Fraser, had written to his Australian colleague in 1919:

I know that on account of your experience and pioneer work in Australia you would bring more initiative and influence to the Conference (of Empire statisticians) than any other Representative, and without your assistance the work of the Conference would suffer. I freely acknowledge New Zealand's indebtedness to you; your work in Australia has been a constant help and inspiration to us here. I notice also the Director of the new Statistical Office, established in South Africa, in his Year Book, which is so closely modelled on the Commonwealth Year Book, makes particular acknowledgment of your help and advice. No other Statistician in the Empire is so well known nor is there any whose views carry more weight—but your reputation is not confined to the Empire; it is world-wide.81

These unsolicited remarks, prompted neither by a valedictory occasion nor the hope of preferment, were a fitting tribute to the work of the first Australian statistician to bear national responsibilities.

PART IV: THE PATH TO UNIFICATION

THE WICKENS DECADE

CHARLES WICKENS had not disguised his ambition to succeed Knibbs and he was indisputably the most able professional statistician on the Bureau's staff. As Supervisor of the Census since 1912, he was by the end of 1918 being paid a salary of £606. On the basis of merit reflected in a salary differential of £66 and his status as a 'professional' rather than a 'clerical' officer, Wickens had argued unsuccessfully late in 1918 that he rather than John Stonham, the 'Chief Compiler', should act as Commonwealth Statistician during Knibbs' absence overseas.

Atlee Hunt, Secretary of the Department of Home and Territories, formally advised the rivals at that time:

... this decision in no way limits my complete freedom of recommendation in case a vacancy should occur in the office of Statistician, as in my judgment, the principles which should guide selection for acting and for permanent appointments are quite different.82

Wickens' appointment as the second Commonwealth Statistician in August 1922 (and the addition of the title 'Actuary' in 1924) was emphatic recognition of the outstanding place he already held in the Australian statistical community. His selection, from a field of seven, brought to the helm of the Bureau a man not only widely respected for his professional attainments, but with gifts of personality which his predecessor had lacked. Fortunately for Wickens, the passage of years had removed some of those State officials whose resistance to change had so frustrated Knibbs. By 1922 the Bureau's role was established and Federal-State co-operation was a habit rather than a novelty. But Wickens' own warmth and tact were now to be key elements in the greater harmony which characterised the 1920s.

A new mood was quickly sensed. As the delighted South Australian Statist put it after meeting Wickens for the first time at a conference in Melbourne in October 1923:

. . . . the atmosphere . . . and the results arrived at were an agreeable surprise to myself and I think also to the other delegates judging by after conversations. Whatever the ultimate decision of the States be [on unification] it is quite certain that the Conference was very effective in creating a much clearer and favourable understanding of the proposals of the Commonwealth, thanks largely to the genial personality of the Chairman and his lucid statements and sympathetic recognition of the local points of view.83

Within the Bureau, Wickens moved swiftly to fill consequential vacancies and clarify duties. To his previous position of Supervisor of Census he promoted E. T. McPhee. However, in a reversal of the classification he had argued for a decade earlier when seeking to have his own status made comparable to two of his 'professional' colleagues, Gerald Lightfoot and F. W. Barford, the Supervisor was now graded Clerical (Class 1) rather than professional (Class B). 'As the duties of the position are neither more nor less professional than those of the other senior positions in the Bureau,' Wickens contended, 'the distinction at present existing is undesirable'. For the disappointed Stonham there was the compensation of a new title as Editor, Official Year Book, and a salary increase of £24 a year. Stonham's position was to be placed in the special 'A' class of the Clerical Division, and he was to be responsible for editing the Quarterly Summary and the Pocket Compendium as well as the Year Book, and for 'general supervision over all matters involving printing and publishing'. With Wickens' own salary £250 less than Knibbs', and McPhee's lower by £158 than his predecessor's the new Statistician was able to show net savings on Bureau salaries of £484.84

Before his promotion, Wickens had already embarked on a campaign to enlarge the Bureau's role as a central tabulating agency for the government. There had been public talk of reducing the cost of the census by £10,000 to £12,000 by the use of leased tabulating equipment. As The Age commented on 4 August 1919, 'machines are now in existence that can automatically count, sort, and add, and do other wonderful things, seemingly bordering on the miraculous'. For the analysis of the 1921 Census data, collected by a team of 11 deputy supervisors, 75 enumerators, 979 sub-enumerators) and 9,500 collectors, electrical machinery and 'Hollerith' cards were supplied by the British Tabulating Machine Company. The Commonwealth signed a five year agreement under which, for £1,580 a year, it had the use of three counting machines, three sorting machines, and a counter tabulating machine. A company mechanic was made available for an additional £1,600 a year. So impressed was he with this equipment, and evidence of economies from overseas experience, that Wickens urged its wider use in a series of minutes to his departmental head. Having established the value of machine tabulation on census data, he pointed to trade and customs, and labour and industrial branch activities as promising areas for development. By November 1922 'dual' cards had been produced on which vital statistics could be recorded in the State registration offices both in writing and in punched form. But overtures to other departments and authorities—Postmaster-General's, Railways, Treasury, Trade and Customs, and the Commissioner for Taxation—were all rebuffed.

Wickens restated his case in July 1923 in the hope that the newly created Public Service Board might be moved to act under Section 17 (1) (a) of the Public Service Act which empowered it to 'advise means for effecting economies and promoting efficiency in the management and working of Departments'. 'I am convinced,' he pronounced: that any one who has had practical experience of the efficiency, economy, and adaptability of' the tabulating machinery would as little decline to use it as he would decline to use a typewriter or a comptometer after having become acquainted with their respective capabilities . . . .

The following are the principal advantages of a central tabulating bureau as compared with a number of small installations:

(i) Regular supply of data; ensuring continuous working.
(ii) Continuous running; enabling expert staff of operators to be organised.
(iii) Concentration of plant, facilitating effective and economical supervision of operators and plant.

(iv) Derangement of work due to temporary incapacitation of a machine minimised when other machines are on the spot to take up the running.

Notwithstanding the cogency of this classic argument for the centralised provision of tabulating services, Wickens met the resistance to be expected from public service barons jealously patrolling their ramparts. In the U.S.A., South Africa, and Egypt, staff savings of at least one-third had been made in tabulating trade and customs data, the statistician reported enticingly. 'The machinery method is as far ahead of the hand method as the motor car is ahead of the bullock dray' he affirmed unavailingly for those of his colleagues who were better at images than figures. Two years later, after an experiment on Victorian trade for February 1925, E. T. McPhee submitted a comprehensive proposal for centralisation of all machine processes of purchasing and tabulating trade statistics which Wickens estimated would produce cost savings of 15 per cent within three months. Trade and Customs was predictably unmoved. In a somewhat mischievous re-opening of the dialogue in 1927, the Comptroller-General of Customs passed on a suggestion from the Tasmanian Collector of Customs that if State statistical organisations were progressively to come under the aegis of the federal government there might be salary savings if the State organisations were placed 'under the control of the Customs Department'. It was the Bureau's turn to repel boarders. Responding to the Customs proposal on the basis of briefing from the Deputy Statistician, L. F. Giblin,—and the Acting Statistician, McPhee, the Secretary of Home and Territories returned a chilly reply on 26 May 1927:

. . . I am directed to state that it does not appear that any appreciable saving in money or staffs would be effected . . . However, if definite evidence of overlapping or duplication in specific cases is supplied, consideration will be given to the best means of obviating such overlapping or duplication.85

What had given some plausibility to the Customs gambit was the successful negotiation of arrangements for the transfer of the Tasmanian statistical bureau to the Commonwealth. The Prime Minister, Stanley Bruce, had persuaded a conference of Premiers and Ministers in May 1923 that it was 'desirable that one statistical authority shall be established' and that a statisticians' conference should be convened to make recommendations.

Under Wickens' chairmanship, a conference was held in October 1923 and produced a scheme designed to lead to 'the greatest attainable uniformity, efficiency, and economy in whatever arrangements might be made eventually by the several Governments'. Although Queensland showed some inclinations towards unification, and Victoria entered into comprehensive negotiations, it was Tasmania which took the lead. Realising that there was no prospect of the State ever being able to provide adequately for the necessary statistical work, L. F. Giblin (who had succeeded R. M. Johnston late in 1919 and had the confidence of his government) was a strong advocate of a federal takeover. 'At present,' Giblin had confided to Wickens early in 1924, 'we have three [temporary staff] . . . and at that can barely keep up—and are in fact all the time behind hand in most things'. Supplying agricultural statistics was a particular problem in Tasmania, Giblin noted, because:

> (1) The farmers supplying the statistics are often without education and indifferent or hostile to giving the facts.
> (2) The data are not given direct but are collected by Police Officers who may be indifferent or careless . . . collection of these statistics can be a pure farce, and has been in many cases.86

Unification of the Tasmanian and Commonwealth bureaus would assist in bringing down the curtain on the farce. It would also end the undesirable necessity to vote 'considerable sums' to enable the compilation of Tasmanian statistics to be, as Wickens put it to J. G. McLaren, his departmental head, brought up 'to the level required for Commonwealth purposes'. It took only a day of discussions between Wickens and Giblin to reach an understanding that proved acceptable to their respective governments. The agreement, which had been reached before the 1923 conference of statisticians, was embodied in legislation by both the federal and State parliaments and came into effect from 13 November 1924.87

In addition to the formidable Major Giblin, soldier, sportsman, adventurer, politician, and adviser to the Tasmanian Premier, J. A. Lyons—the merger of the two bureaus brought into the Commonwealth service a team of talented and uniquely qualified young men. Giblin had encouraged and supervised the Commerce degree courses of four Class 5 officers: C. L. Steele, K. F. Andrews, S. E. Solomon, and K. M. Archer. The agreement with the

Commonwealth incorporated provisions under which each could continue his studies and receive a refund of fees in return for undertaking to remain in the public service for five years after graduation. The indentured junior officers were a precious resource, and Giblin and Wickens subsequently pressed for financial incentives (through reclassification of positions) to retain their services. As Giblin commented in 1927:

The experiment in the appointing and training of officers for the Statistical Service has, in my considered opinion, abundantly justified itself. They have all four reached a high degree of competence for difficult statistical work—a very high degree considering the comparatively few years they have been engaged in it. This competence is combined with a keen interest in the work, and the growth of a strong professional spirit which has made this office the very antithesis of the popular conception of a Government Department.88

Wickens needed no convincing. He had himself lamented to Giblin some years earlier: 'Here in Victoria the entrance to the Commonwealth Service is still choked with returned soldiers who passed a relatively light examination in 1920 and have not yet been all absorbed'. While particularly solicitous for the four young men whom Giblin commended for having 'equipped themselves by a long and severe University training, undergone at great sacrifice of their leisure and recreations, . . showing daily an exceptional capacity to deal with problems which the ordinary clerical officer could not touch', Wickens was also a strong advocate of the claims of the Bureau clerical staff generally for a review of their status and salaries. The staff themselves drew attention to the growing complexity and wider scope of their duties resulting in part from the removal of their headquarters to Canberra in 1928:

Since the transfer of the Bureau to Canberra it has been brought into closer official proximity to other Departments than was formerly the case in Melbourne, with the result that the central staffs are now availing themselves more and more of the services of the Bureau. In fact there are very few questions of political or of other importance which arise without the Bureau being asked to prepare and submit some matter on the subject.89

In a memorandum to the Secretary of the Department of Home Affairs in January 1930 supporting renewed representations by his staff, Wickens alluded incidentally to the progress towards unification of statistics under his stewardship:

. . . it cannot be too strongly stressed that this Bureau, being recognised universally as the coordinating, interpreting and publishing authority in respect of statistics for the whole of Australia, the responsibility for accurate and comparable information is very great. It is in this regard that the work of the Annual Statistical Conferences has its origin, the Bureau in the majority of cases taking the initiative towards securing uniformity in collection and presentation. 90

In regularly bringing together the statistical fraternity, Wickens reversed the practice of Knibbs who eschewed conferences after 1906. Those statisticians who were most resistant to what they saw as Commonwealth incursions believed, as H. A. Smith of New South Wales advised his government, that 'All desirable uniformity can be obtained readily through periodic conferences of Statisticians'. While conceding that there was some apparent duplication in the collection of vital statistics, and information on wages, prices, banking, and insurance, the overlap was more nominal than real, Smith contended.91 In the event, a succession of annual conferences (interrupted in 1927 by several overseas absences) had brought increasing co-operation and rationalisation.92 Although the Victorian Government offered to transfer its bureau to the Commonwealth in 1925, Treasury insisted that the federal financial program made it impossible for the Victorian offer to be accepted. Wickens had to admit by February 1930 that, notwithstanding the stalling of unification, the conferences had been 'effective in greatly improving the statistical work of Australia and in bringing about certain of the improvements aimed at in the proposals for unification'. He remained convinced of the desirability of unification but realised that there was no prospect of a national government voluntarily assuming the additional £40,000 a year he estimated as the cost of performing the work being done by the States.93

Forty permanent officers of the Bureau and four temporary staff were transferred from the Rialto Building in Collins Street, Melbourne to Canberra in July and August 1928. Accommodated initially in the

Commonwealth offices at 'West Block', they made detailed plans to move to the Hotel Acton only to be informed at the end of June 1930 that this supposedly cost-saving relocation could not proceed because of 'the present financial situation'.94 A more serious problem was the scarcity of housing for single officers of whom 23 were placed in boarding houses or private billets. Wickens was particularly concerned about the female staff. It was desirable, he submitted that they be housed together:

. . . so that the elder girls may be able to look after the younger girls to some extent, and in the majority of cases the parents have made it a condition of the girls coming to Canberra that Miss Paterson or Miss Miller will look after them. If they are to be housed in different hostels this will be impossible . . . There is also a strong objection by all the girls to sharing a room, and this condition may preclude some from coming to Canberra. It will be seen, therefore, that apart from the wishes of the girls, the position in its effect on the work of the Bureau may be very serious as trained Hollerith Machine Operators are extremely difficult to get owing to the limited use of the machines in Australia.95

Anticipating further difficulties in assembling in Canberra the army of temporary staff that would be needed for the 1931 Census, Wickens had warned in March 1928 that it might be necessary to establish a census branch in either Melbourne or Sydney. The prospect of additional expense as well as the practical problems of attracting and housing an influx of census workers to the bush capital contributed to the misgivings of the Scullin Government about with the 1931 Census. As the financial situation deteriorated, fears that the Ministry contemplated abandoning Canberra altogether were reflected in a special written article in the 1931 Year Book on 'Canberra, Past and Present', a plea for the viability of the national capital.

Planning for the Census had begun in 1928 and Wickens recommended that the date be set by proclamation for midnight, 30 June 1931. In advice to his permanent head, he outlined the additional questions which had been agreed at a conference of statisticians in September 1929:

(i) Race, (particularly whether of European race or not).
(ii) Whether on active service abroad during the war of 1914-18.

(iii) Income group in the case of persons with annual incomes of £300 or less.
(iv) Unemployment, time lost and cause.
(v) Number of dependent children.
(vi) Number of horses and poultry.

The question on income was modelled upon one included in the New Zealand censuses of 1921 and 1926. Because information was already available on incomes greater than £300 through income tax statistics—which Wickens argued should be tabulated annually by the Bureau—the question was limited to income of £300 and below. Nevertheless, the introduction of any inquiry into income in an ordinary census was, Wickens believed, unique 'in any part of the world except New Zealand'.

Compared with Britain and most of the Dominions, however, Australia was deficient in orphanhood data. The draft 1931 schedule therefore required all persons under fifteen years old to state whether their parents were living or dead. This useful additional information was, to the chagrin of later generations of demographers, gained in substitution for fertility data—the question on children from existing or previous marriages being dropped 'owing to the labour and expense involved'. One of Wickens' major preoccupations after the 1921 Census had been classification of industry, occupation, and grade of labour. Paying tribute to what Wickens (and his successors) had achieved, Giblin concluded in 1936:

We shall henceforward be able . . . to compute accurate birth rates, death rates, and marriage rates by industries and occupations, and so get for the first time information about different fertility and reproduction rates in respect to occupation.

Unfortunately, the wording of the relevant question blurred the intended sharpness of distinction between industry and occupation. Nevertheless the Census was to yield fuller information on economic condition and status by industry and occupation than ever before.

For the administration of the census it was intended to follow the practice introduced in 1921 of using electoral office staff as collectors. In order to ensure proper supervision, Wickens first proposed that 'the whole work of coding, punching and tabulating the data' should be carried out in Canberra. But the realisation that sufficient temporary staff could not be found in Canberra, combined with the knowledge that the whole census exercise was expected to cost £316,000, was enough to convince the government that postponement of the census had to be considered. With the financial crisis deepening, the Minister for Home Affairs, Arthur Blakely broke the news personally to Wickens on 6 February 1930. 'I very greatly regret the necessity which has arisen for even considering such a proposal,' Wickens responded, 'but I realise that when a position arises which is as serious as the present every possible sacrifice must be made to balance our budget'. (On the same day, the Prime Minister and Treasurer issued a joint statement denying rumours that Australia was about to postpone interest payments on its overseas loans.)

Amending legislation was passed in time to allow for a later census. While sharing the sentiments of his State colleagues, who moved a mild remonstrance at their meeting in Brisbane in May 1930, Wickens admitted to being impressed with the view expressed by the Prime Minister 'that the owner of starving stock would be better advised to spend existing funds in feeding them than in counting them'.96 It was the newly elected Lyons Government which perceived that it was possible to feed at least some of the starving stock by counting the others. On 1 July 1931, the Labour Ministry had decided to further defer the census from 1933 to 1935. But in January 1932, Archdale Parkhill took the question to Cabinet with the strong recommendation of the Acting Commonwealth Statistician in favour of the earlier date. Revised estimates suggested a total expenditure of £275,000 mostly over the period 1932-36, with the possibility of off-setting revenue from 'advertising on the census schedules'. A more compelling argument was that 'approximately 80% or £220,000 would be disbursed directly as wages'. When the statisticians met in conference in Sydney in August 1932, they pressed in addition for the allocation of some unemployment relief funds to 'the employment of clerical workers for working up valuable material which lies unused in the offices of Statisticians'. The statisticians did, however, agree to omit questions on loss of limb or eye, ability to read and write English, materials of roof, and horses and poultry (except in Victoria).

In inviting the federal government to be represented at the Sydney conference, the New South Wales Premier, J. T. Lang, had written:

As no conference has been held since May, 1930, the need for a general meeting has become urgent since, in addition to the old problems which are awaiting a definite decision, and consequent action, a great variety of new difficulties now confront the statistician owing to the great divergence of the Australian pound from the pound sterling and of sterling from gold.

In 1930, it had been resolved that each State would supply the Commonwealth with as much information as possible 'in respect of the existence of unemployment and of the results of efforts to relieve it'. By August 1930, it was agreed that monthly reports 'embodying any information available from State sources on unemployment' should be circulated. But, in resigned recognition of the inadequacy of their statistical endeavours in the face of the economic catastrophe, it was noted that 'unemployment registrations were of very doubtful significance, but that expenditure on unemployed relief would often give useful information'.97

Pressure to hold the census in 1933 came from a variety of groups including the Australian Association for the Advancement of Science and the Federated Clerks' Union, the latter sending a deputation to the Minister on 14 April 1932. The clerks pointed out that their members were often the first to be laid off in hard times. They were also unsuited for the manual labour available under the State governments' relief schemes. With '10,000 unemployed clerks' awaiting his decision, the Minister capitulated. In spite of early hopes to employ cheaper female staff, the Bureau was bound by government policy to give preference to returned servicemen. Of the many applications and recommendations none is more poignant than the war historian C. E. W. Bean's letter on behalf of a former captain of his old school, Clifton College ('also the school of Haig and of Birdwood'):

He is at present getting one day a week's employment as tally clerk on the Brisbane wharfs [sic]. He fought with the A.I.F.—not in any cosy capacity either but, as you would expect of a first class cricketer and footballer, in the thick of it . . . he is unmarried, but I do hope that he will have a chance of employment in Canberra.98

The recruitment of temporary staff (and their eventual return by rail at Commonwealth expense to the capital city nearest their home) absorbed considerable energy at senior levels of the Bureau.99 But of more lasting significance were the promotions and appointments that followed the prolonged sick leave and eventual retirement of Wickens. For some time following the move to Canberra, Wickens had begun to show signs of strain. In mid-1929 he was forced to take two months' leave. 'My illness has been variously described in the press as a seizure and a stroke', he told A. W. Flux of the British Board of Trade on 8 July 1929, 'but if it was either the one or the other, the seizing or the striking, whichever it be, was done very gently . . . 100A year later he was absent for a fortnight with 'nervous dyspepsia'. These gentle warnings came in the midst of a cycle of ever more demanding activities. In addition to the ordinary work of the Bureau, and the progressive practical and conceptual refinements that accompanied the regular conferences with the States, Wickens was personally involved in a series of tasks for which his expertise made him the government's logical choice. He was frequently called on to advise the Royal Commission on National Insurance from 1924 onwards. In 1927 he represented Australia in England at a conference of actuaries and made extensive investigations in Geneva, Berne, and Berlin into social insurance leading to the preparation of the national insurance legislation presented to Parliament by Dr Earle Page in September 1928. Subsequently, Wickens took the leading role in investigating for the federal Cabinet the possibility of applying national insurance to workers' compensation, child endowment, widows' pensions, and government superannuation schemes. These complex matters were on the agenda of a conference of Commonwealth and State Ministers in May 1929 but were set aside after the defeat of the Bruce-Page Government and the onset of the economic depression.

Wickens gave evidence on statistics to the Royal Commission on the Constitution (1927) forcefully criticising Australia's failure to supplement production statistics with interstate trade statistics. He prepared statistics and gave evidence to the Royal Commission on South Australian Finance (1928), and supplied both data and personal assistance to the

British Economic Mission (1928). In collaboration with J. B. Brigden, Douglas Copland, E. C. Dyason, and L. F. Giblin (now a Professor at the University of Melbourne) he produced at the request of Prime Minister Bruce the important study, The Australian Tariff An Economic Enquiry in 1929. During 1928 and 1929 he also assisted the Attorney-General's Department in drafting a life insurance Bill. In the following year he was called on to furnish material and appear as a witness before both the Coal Commission and the Parliamentary Accounts Committee (on 'Tasmanian disabilities'). He was a special crown witness before the Commonwealth Arbitration Court in the Basic Wage case and was subjected to lengthy cross-examination by all parties. Other matters claiming his attention included a wrangle with Trade and Customs over adherence to a League of Nations convention on trade statistics and the additional burden of organising the supply of information for the world agricultural census sponsored by the International Institute of Agriculture.101

So overwhelmed was Wickens that in December 1929, hardly the most favourable time, he petitioned for the creation of a new position of Assistant Statistician. The appointment was warranted, he said: by the growth of the functions of the Bureau, and the extent to which the services of the Statistician are requisitioned by various departments in respect of statistical and actuarial matters. In addition . . . there are at present under consideration certain proposals for extending the tabulation . . . of trade statistics and of statistics of taxation. Any such development will necessarily create heavier responsibilities for staff organisation and control and will warrant a corresponding strengthening of the administrative section of the Bureau.

The requested relief was not forthcoming. Instead, apparently without comprehension of the magnitude of their request, the government added still further to the Bureau's work by seeking answers to 29 questions on the cost of living, national dividend, wages, taxation, housing finance, exchange rates, costs of production, and unemployment. Had the Labour Government proceeded with a proposal of their predecessors to create a Bureau of Economic Research, the burden of these wide-ranging inquiries would not have fallen on the Statistician. But, although the legislation had been passed, Labour shelved a project which was suspected by some as a device for subverting the Arbitration Court's independence in wage fixation. Worn out by his endeavours, culminating in the preparation of a statement for the Prime Minister's Department on the advantages to the secession-minded Western Australia of remaining in the federation, Wickens succumbed to a cerebral seizure on the afternoon of 2 February 1931. When it became clear that he was unlikely to return to duty the government took the opportunity to invite Giblin to act as Statistician on the understanding, as Giblin recorded, 'that I should be sufficiently relieved from administrative routine to be able to give the greater part of my time to special investigations required by the Minister'.102 Giblin's special position was demonstrated by his additional title of Chief Economic Adviser.

The advent of Giblin, who remained Acting Commonwealth Statistician until the end of 1932, accelerated a change in the role of the Bureau which had been gathering momentum under Wickens. Although Wickens, a self taught actuary, was best known for his demographic work, he was also highly respected in the small fraternity of Australian economists. He corresponded with Giblin over fluctuations in exchange rates, exchanged views on Keynes' Tract on Monetary Reform ('involves a good deal of unlearning of other theories which regard gold or similar basis as a sine qua non'), and joined with Copland, Giblin, and others in forming the Economic Society of Australia and New Zealand. In the Economic Society's journal, The Economic Record, he published articles on public debt statistics, 'productive efficiency', the 'relative significance of primary and secondary production', the statistics of factory output and Australian industry, and comparative costs of living. In October 1930 he reported to the Acting Prime Minister on 'stability of currency'. The report was leaked, then released, precipitating criticism of its reflationary recommendations. His responsibility for price indexes also brought Wickens into the centre of the political controversy surrounding the Arbitration Court's basic wage hearings and eventual decision in January 1931 for an emergency ten per cent reduction in wage rates. Having initiated revision of the wholesale price index regimen and the introduction of indices for all capital cities to complement the Melbourne index, he renovated the retail price index by shifting its base from 1911 to the average of the years 1923-27, 'a period in which there was relative stability of prices, and from which there is no evidence of a prospect of marked deviation in the near future'. He then turned to other problems including the collection of information on new capital issues and 'the difficult matter of securing reliable data as to the so-called invisible imports and exports" '103

In all of these activities, Wickens and the Bureau were drawn ineluctably into public prominence, a development which was discomfiting to his principal subordinate, Stonham. When the statistician begins to 'meddle with economics', Stonham wrote a little later:

. . . he is liable to incur political odium and to have his standing as a Statistician impugned. (Mr Wickens had an unfortunate experience in this respect as regards currency inflation, the disabilities of Tasmania under federation, and so on) . . . it is unwise for the statistician to enter the arena of public controversy. The late Sir George Knibbs resolutely set his face against it, and, in fact was opposed to appearing in the Arbitration Court.104

In reality, Knibbs had never shied from publicity, although he preferred to expose the labour branch head Gerald Lightfoot to cross-examination in the basic wage cases.

Stonham's fundamental objection was not so much to the public profile of his former chief who was an eminent and professionally qualified statistician. Nor was he objecting to the close involvement of Giblin, whose standing both as a statistician and as an economist placed him in a category of his own, in the government. (As Chief Economic Adviser, Giblin attended the Premiers' Conference in May 1931 where he came in conflict with J. T. Lang.) By 1933, the issue was different: what should be the role of an economist with no traditional statistical background in the senior management of the Bureau?

FROM WILSON TO CARVER

The economist in question was Dr Roland Wilson, a protege of Giblin's who had acquired doctorates from Oxford and Chicago and lectured for eighteen months at the University of Tasmania before being installed at a desk in the Statistician's room in February 1932 to assist Giblin on his policy assignments. Wilson has recalled:

It was L. F., as we used to know him, who brought me to Canberra as a back room boy in the Treasury, allegedly for six months. Those were the days when the only graduates in the Public Service were doctors or lawyers, or a few who did part-time courses after they were appointed . I had to be disguised by being put into the Stats. office as a clerk. But on my first day, lo and behold, there was a stop work meeting. They didn't like the idea of this graduate coming in and threatening their futures . . .

Not withstanding Giblin's assurance to the staff that Wilson's appointment was only for six months, in December 1932 Wilson was gazetted into a newly created post of Economist at a salary of £970 a year (nearly £300 a year more than the Editor, Stonham, and the Deputy Statistician in Tasmania, H. J. Exley). Wilson's promotion coincided with the return of Giblin to the University of Melbourne, and the appointment of E. T. McPhee to succeed him. McPhee, a Bureau veteran recruited from Tasmania in 1906, had returned from Melbourne to Hobart as Deputy Statistician when Giblin originally left for Melbourne University. He was already 63 in 1932 and apparently accepted the promotion to Canberra on the basis that Wilson was to be groomed as his successor. Wilson himself was not immediately aware of this plan and, in view of the resentment that had greeted his arrival, he could have been forgiven for not foreseeing that five days after his 29th birthday, McPhee would recommend that 'during future absences of the Commonwealth Statistician, the Bureau shall be under the control of Dr Roland Wilson, if he is present'. In explaining the recommendation (and the protest from Stonham which it provoked), McPhee wrote to his permanent head on 12 April 1933:

I understand that when Dr. Wilson joined the Bureau he did not wish to identify himself with the compilation of the statistics, and did not anticipate that he would be called upon to direct this work in a large measure. From his experience in the Bureau, however, Dr. Wilson has formed the opinion that an intimate knowledge of the various branches of statistics is essential to their proper economic interpretation and he is no longer averse from taking a part in this work.

It is also, I think obvious that as economic opinions must rest largely on statistical evidence, some knowledge of economics is essential to the proper selection of statistical data which should be compiled for the guidance of publicists, and to the direction of analyses which should be made of that data by the statistical staff. I feel that statistics and economics are so closely associated that in practice they are inseparable.

Dr. Wilson during his association with the Bureau, has had frequent conferences with heads of sections or departments of the Bureau work and is almost daily in consultation with one or other of these officers. Consequently Dr. Wilson has acquired a knowledge of the fundamental details of much of the work, and has contact with the daily affairs of the Bureau. The members of the stair readily seek his assistance when they feel the need of it. 105

Quite apart from Wilson's outstanding ability and training, which put him in a class apart from his talented Tasmanian near contemporaries, Archer and Solomon, what McPhee was testifying to was a basic rethinking of the Bureau's purpose and orientation. The new era was signalled in the Year Book for 1932. Issued by McPhee under instructions from the Treasurer, to whom the Bureau now reported, the Year Book acknowledged the contribution of Giblin as 'consultant economist.' Publication had been delayed so that the latest statistics relevant to the financial and economic crisis could be incorporated, and the preface pointed out that current conditions had created a demand for 'new information' on trade, production, and industry.

The demand, of course, was for understanding as well as knowledge, for policy prescription as well as diagnosis. From the mid-1920s onwards the Bureau operated in a disconcertingly evolving institutional landscape. A succession of temporary and permanent commissions and inquiries jostled for territory with emerging academic and bureaucratic rivals: the Tariff Board, the Development and Migration Commission, The Royal Commissions on National Insurance and Child Endowment, the British Economic Mission, the Loan Council, Premiers' Conferences, and always the Arbitration Court. The Economic Society, the Australian Institute of Political Science, and the Institute of Pacific Relations provided forums for informed exposition and debate. The Commonwealth Bank occupied much of the policy domain which was increasingly contested by the federal Treasury after the appointment of H. J. Sheehan as Secretary in 1932; and the Bank, stimulated by the visit of Sir Otto Niemeyer and Professor T. E.

Gregory in 1930, began to tabulate a range of banking, price, trade, railway, building, assurance, postal, bankruptcy and electrical power consumption statistics to indicate business conditions. A further sign of the times which Wickens had brought to Scullin's attention in February 1930, was the establishment in Queensland of a Bureau of Economics and Statistics under J. B. Brigden. By mid-1931, Brigden was producing an innovative Queensland business index.106 Arriving at the Bureau in Canberra when the trauma of depression had placed a high premium on the advice, albeit often contradictory, of economists, Roland Wilson found a fertile field for reform and expansion. The new Secretary to the Treasury, H. J. Sheehan, was inclined to take a more active part than his predecessor in economic policy-making but he lacked the resources and expertise that were directly at Wilson's disposal. Within two years, McPhee and his political masters were convinced that the Bureau could confidently be passed into Wilson's hands. The Assistant Treasurer, R. G. Casey, had at first been inclined to look to England for McPhee's successor; but Giblin persuaded him that British statisticians were too specialised and 'would take several years to learn the job in Australia'. Giblin convinced Casey that:

Wilson is the obvious man for the job, but that we should keep McPhee on as long as possible in order to give Wilson as much opportunity as possible of picking up the multitudinous threads of the job.

McPhee had been effectively deprived of 'three or four of his best men away on the Census job'. But Giblin believed that 'if Wilson has a good economic offsider, he should be able to give a fair amount of attention to specific Treasury problems'. In a parting public statement, the retiring Statistician confessed 'I have had enough of it':

The last three years have been very strenuous . . . The extensions of the functions of government and the continually increasing complexity of the social structure demand a continual expansion of the field of statistical inquiry. There is now an army of economists confident that, given sufficient bricks of the right type and quality, a way can be cleared to heaven. It is the statistician's job to provide the bricks.107

It was unnecessary for Wilson—whose inclination for a policy role was no secret—to proclaim that he had every intention of building the path as well as making the bricks.

Writing in the first issue of The Economic Record, in November 1925, Professor Douglas Copland had lamented that 'Economic research and advice is not recognised as necessary for good government . . . The neglect of economic research could partly be explained, Copland suggested, by 'the excellent service rendered by the extensive statistical bureaux of the Governments'. The early volumes of The Economic Record gave glimpses of the professional quality and interests of several of the Commonwealth Bureau's staff. E. T. McPhee reviewed books on tariffs and trade, and H. J. Exley, J. F. Barry, W. T. Murphy all contributed articles. J. T. Sutcliffe, already the author of books on Australian trade union history and 'The National Dividend', the latter a pioneering work on national income estimation, defended the Bureau's popularly misnamed 'cost-of-living' index and its unemployment statistics.

But, while the incomparable Giblin remained a regular contributor, even while he was directing the work of the Bureau, the significant initial participation of Bureau staff was not sustained. By the time young Dr Wilson was making tart comments in footnotes in 1931 ('A little more consistency in official statistics relating to such a comparatively simple matter [interest and dividend payments abroad] would not be amiss.') no one emerged to reply108 A new generation of economists had seized the intellectual initiative by the early 1930s. Copland's students, E. K. Heath and J. Polglaze, for example, set out in 1932 to prepare an index of business activity and I found official statistics to be 'quite inadequate necessitating recourse to unofficial statistics'. In 1933, Dr F. R. E. Mauldon, Senior Lecturer in Economics at Melbourne University, in a pamphlet based on a series of broadcasts on 3AR, identified 'some gaps which have still to be covered in the whole field of Australian economic statistics', which might well have been listed on a reform agenda for the Bureau:

We need more frequent census-taking . . . especially in view of inter-state migration, and it would be of great value to have enquiries made concerning wealth and income at the same time . . . In gathering statistics of the production of wealth in Australia the extent of crop failure areas in the total areas under crop in a season is a present serious omission . . . On the mining, manufacturing and building construction sides of production we need to know monthly values and /or quantity of output for all states. To clarify our knowledge of industrial and commercial structure . . . we ought to have data of the size of manufacturing establishments and of the character of ownership (individuals, registered companies, partnerships, co-operative societies, etc.) as distinct from numbers of establishments, or sections thereof, engaged in productive processes. We ought further to have enumeration and classification of wholesale and retail business, records of amalgamations, and records of the nature and membership of trade, primary producers' and industrial associations for mutual interest in business . . .

Mauldon added that statistics of interstate trade should be reviewed and that data on marketing costs, productivity, labour turnover, labour migration, employment, and prices needed to be assembled or augmented.109 For Wilson, however, the first priority had been the balance of payments. When his special chapter for the 1934 Year Book was circulated in advance, Giblin applauded 'this brilliant attack on one of the most important and difficult of statistical problems'. (Brilliant though it was, Wilson's treatment appalled Stonham who, as editor of the Year Book, found himself from 1932 onwards obliged to publish tables spattered with question marks where tradition dictated unambivalent precision.) The Conference of Statisticians in Canberra in March 1935 devoted its energies to Wilson's next major concern, production statistics, and agreed on new definitions and procedures covering agricultural, pastoral, and dairying production, mines and quarries. A start was made also on getting the States to prepare a 'key' plan to the statement of social services expenditure by 'functions with a dissection of all group or composite items. Although McPhee told a British correspondent in January 1935 that the greater part of Wilson's time had 'unfortunately . . . been claimed by the Treasury', Wilson had in fact found it hard to resist probing into most aspects of the Bureau's work. As he told the Secretary of the Treasury in supporting the case for his attendance at the Ottawa conference of Dominion statistical officers:

There are a number of subjects on the agenda on which I have been doing a great deal of work lately . . . (especially methods of compiling various indexes of prices, methods of calculating invisible items in the trade balance, and classification of commodities on a comparable basis in trade, production and price statistics).

In an interview in 1984, Wilson recalled:

. . . the more I poked into the compilation of statistics, the more disgusted I got. So it was one subject after another trying to find out just how the figures got put together . . . For instance, the retail price index . . . we were supposed to get returns from every state from a selected number of retailers, the price of a pair of curtains, otherwise undefined. When I looked at it I found the prices varied in some states from 6/lid, to 96/lid. There might be three or four quotes that were solemnly averaged, and that was the price of a pair of curtains.110

Wilson's appointment as Commonwealth Statistician and Economic Adviser to the Treasury was effective from 29 April 1936. On that day, a congratulatory deputation led by Horace Downing who had been to the fore in the office protest against Wilson's arrival in 1932, let their new chief know that they thought him the best man for the job. The next day, Wilson called on the Secretary to the Treasury to ask for substantial funds to 'reconstitute' the retail price indexes. 'It hasn't taken the new broom very long to sweep clean, has it?' Harry Sheehan remarked. But the money was found. So too, but more tardily, was approval eventually given for Wilson's scheme to create a new employment category—the research officer—to remedy the Bureau's shortage of staff versed in the economic and technical skills which a changing political environment made necessary. At first, however, he had to rely mainly on such advantage as he could derive from section 36A of the Public Service Act (a 1933 amendment) under which up to ten per cent of each year's appointments to the third division could be of university graduates aged up to 25. (He also contrived to appoint the first female librarian in the Commonwealth Public Service, by devising 'a set of qualifications with appropriate weighting' which ensured the selection of Miss Dora Whitelaw.) 111

During the overseas study tour that was planned around his visit to Ottawa, Wilson reported enviously to his political master, R. G. Casey, on the vast resources available to the various American statistical bureaus and New Deal organisations like the Works Progress Administration (WPA),

Agricultural Adjustment Administration (AAA), and National Recovery Administration (NRA). 'Doctors of philosophy are as common as sheep in Canberra, and young graduates from the universities simply infest Washington, especially in the new alphabetical agencies.' At Casey's side in Canberra at the time were the young Melbourne commerce graduate J. F. Nimmo, and Wilson's own if assistant economist, Arthur Smithies, whose career—from Hobart to Oxford to Harvard and thence via a teaching post at the University of Michigan to the Bureau as Assistant Economist in July 1935—had eerie echoes of Wilson's. With Smithies to understudy him on economic policy, Wilson had promoted H. C. Green from Supervisor of Census to Assistant Statistician at a salary 50 per cent higher than the next most senior officers (though less than half of Wilson's own salary).

In Casey, the Bureau found what no previous Commonwealth Statistician had enjoyed—a Minister who as Assistant Treasurer from September 1933 and Treasurer from October 1935 onwards, was intellectually engaged, influential and, above all, in office for long enough to establish rapport with his advisers. In Wilson, Casey found a mind he could respect and an undisguised expertise of which he was occasionally wilfully sceptical but more often in awe. Jocularly, Casey had sketched the basic problem for Wilson to address in August 1935:

I am more modest than most—all I want to know is what we should do within Australia to get things moving more quickly without unduly increasing the national debt, and the interest bill, without indulging in what might be described as inflation without risking an undue rise in the exchange rate with sterling.112

Fortunately for the Bureau, an economic revival, for which government could take only small credit, ensured that the reputation of its head was not prematurely jeopardised by questionable diagnoses and policy recommendations. By 1937, the Conference of Statisticians had clearly passed from a world of crisis to one in which it was possible to discuss without anxiety 'matters of statistical importance relating especially to factory output and retail prices'.113 There was time to reflect on such anomalies as the entirely different meanings of wholesale price indexes in Canada and Australia, and the impossibility of collecting in Australia the kind of data on private finance which was routinely gathered in New

Zealand. While for those who pressed the Bureau to publish an index of manufacturing production, Wilson confessed to the Economic Society in Melbourne his suspicion that 'the whole concept of the quantum of manufacturing production' might be 'a mere mirage which lures succeeding generations of statisticians to an untimely and unhonoured end'.114

A Monthly Review of Business Statistics was added to the Bureau's list of publications in 1937.115 The following year, the 'A' series retail price index, launched in 1912, was discontinued. The much renovated All Items ('C' series) index was to survive until 1960 when it was replaced by the Consumer Price Index. Wilson's substantial revision of the 'C' series regimen was agreed to in the 1936 Conference of Statisticians. To the Bureau's satisfaction, the Conciliation and Arbitration Commission adopted its own 'Court' series in 1937 primarily, as the Bureau's Labour Report explained in 1943, 'for the purpose of removing conditions which tended to engender the impression that the Commonwealth Statistician was in some way responsible for the fixation and adjustment of wage rates'.116

Averse as he was to bearing the imputed responsibility for wage rates, Wilson needed no convincing of the necessity for private enterprise to be 'subject to more conscious supervision and . . . more adequate guidance than has hitherto been available'. He had proclaimed in 1934 the need for 'a more vigorous and national control of the machinery for creating and distributing purchasing power'.117 As governments universally awakened to a similar need and potential for action, the publication of J.M.Keynes's General Theory of Employment, Interest and Money in 1936 crystallised a revolution in economic thinking. Keynesian analysis gave a new relevance to economic statistics, particularly to estimates of national income. A pioneer in national income studies, Colin Clark, was appointed to succeed J. B. Brigden as Director of the Queensland Bureau of Industry in 1938. Dr H. C. Coombs, who came to Canberra after the outbreak of war in 1939 as Economist to the Treasury to assist Wilson and Giblin, recalls that: with Clark's adventurous simplifications and estimations it became possible to produce estimates contemporaneously, and indeed, by judgment of current trends, events and policies, to produce forecasts some time ahead. For this process the relationships of the Keynesian model of the economic system provided a framework. Better data began to be assembled, techniques improved, and the estimates began to be used, not merely for historical purposes but for analysis; with results which appeared to justify their services.118

With preparations for war a growing preoccupation of the Lyons Government, the leader of the Country Party and Minister for Commerce, Dr Earle Page, asked the Statistician to prepare a comprehensive plan for industrial development and defence to be put to the State governments at the next Premiers' Conference. Wilson's submission to Page, on 1 November 1938, advocated the creation of a council for industrial development with an executive officer and secretariat linked to a network of specialist committees. Neither this visionary scheme, nor an alternative devised by Page and his permanent head, came to fruition.119

Concerned to strengthen the government's capacity to stimulate and steer the economy, Wilson had proposed as early as 1934 the creation of a central 'thinking agency'. With the coming of war in 1939, the climate was more propitious for a'central thinking committee'. An Advisory Committee on Financial and Economic Policy, set up late in 1938 to advise the Department of Defence and associated with the new Department of Supply and Development under R. G. Casey from April 1939, was now attached to the Treasury and rapidly granted a broader mandate. The Bureau undertook staff work for the 'F & E' Committee.

From his vantage point on the committee Wilson argued in July 1940 for the establishment of a Department of Labour and National Service with responsibility for vital manpower and labour issues.120 On his appointment late in 1940 as Secretary of the department he had proposed, Wilson successfully recommended S. R. Carver, Government Statistician of New South Wales since 1938, to lead the Commonwealth Bureau during his absence. 'It is intended that Dr Wilson should resume duty as Commonwealth Statistician as soon as the new Department is satisfactorily established, which I hope may be in six to nine months' time,' Prime Minister Menzies assured the New South Wales Premier. Carver was expected to pend only four days a week in Canberra and his duties would not extend to any of the committee work or the role of Economic Adviser played by Wilson. 121

Stan Carver, a highly respected statistician, had begun to make his mark in the late 1920s and was appointed Assistant Government Statistician in 1933. In 1936 he visited Britain with the Premier of New South Wales where he called on J. M. Keynes and met the young lecturer in statistics, Colin Clark. His 'extensive unpublished research' on the distribution of income in New South Wales had been prominently used by Colin Clark and J. G. Crawford in The National Income of Australia (1938). Outstandingly able as he was, he faced enormous problems in a poorly co-ordinated and rapidly evolving wartime administration. The six months transfer he had accepted was to stretch to the end of the war and beyond. The 'censorship complexity, new income tax data, casualty data and the half dozen other special matters' which he had expected to 'represent a fairly heavy addition to the usual flow' of Bureau work were swept up in a torrent of unanticipated demands. In January 1942, for example, Carver 'became extremely busy on the organisation of the War Statistics Section, which required me to spend a considerable time in Melbourne'. Immediately thereafter he was 'still more heavily occupied in assisting the Director-General of Manpower in the preliminary stages of organising the Civilian Register'. During 1942 and 1943 an 'army census' was carried out and a ten per cent sample was tabulated. 122

By mid-1943 it had become necessary to reorganise the management of the Bureau to provide more effective support for the Acting Statistican. The Public Service Board approved the temporary elevation of S. E. Solomon from Chief Research Officer to Assistant Statistician (War Statistics) and J. Barry from Senior Clerk and Supervisor of Census to Assistant Statistician (Administrative). J.C Stephen and K. Archer were also reclassified to handle production and food statistics, and State liaison and 'emergency statistics' respectively. Simultaneously, a brilliant young clerk, H. P. Brown, was promoted to Research Officer. The Secretary to the Treasury had expressed the 'fear that Mr Carver has been endeavouring to handle personally too many of the new problems which have arisen with war-time conditions . . . Although Carver was, and remained, an inveterate perfectionist, necessity imposed a greater degree of delegation than he was able to concede in less demanding times. A further reorganisation in September 1944, consequent on Solomon's return to Queensland, saw Barry promoted to Assistant Statistician, and 'second in charge of Bureau'.123

The official histories of Australia in World War II have provided authoritative accounts of major statistical endeavours on manpower, production, price control, rationing, and other problems of war. It is clear that the Bureau was overwhelmed by a range of tasks for which it was unprepared and under-staffed. 'Our pool of officers is about dry,' Carver confided to O. Gawler, the Victorian Statist on 9 February 1943, 'we have "diluted" to and beyond safe limits . . . Statistical units sprang up to meet the pressing needs of particular departments, but their work was usually narrowly focussed and of transient value. The Bureau itself lent officers to liaise with military authorities or to assist other organisations such as Food Control, S. J. Butlin, himself the Director of the Economic and Statistical Division of the Department of War Organisation of Industry from December 1941 to January 1943, concluded in retrospect:

Perhaps the worst result of all was that a 'particularly scarce form of skill was dispersed in isolated sections which it proved impossible to integrate into a single statistical service. The most remarkable achievement, later in the war, of the Acting Statistician was his high degree of success as a peripatetic diplomat in informal coordination of the work of these scattered workers.124

THE POST-WAR AGENDA

In January 1944, the Director-General of the Department of Post-War Reconstruction, H. C. Coombs, pronounced:

The fatalism which regarded the fluctuations of economic activity as something we must take for granted, and the miseries which attended them as inevitable burdens which we must patiently bear, was the first casualty of the war.125

The government's commitment to a 'full employment' policy, embodied in a White Paper published in 1945, had great significance for the future scope of the Bureau's role. Stan Carver presciently warned that 'to encourage the belief that it is within the Government's power to maintain a long-term high level of employment was to manufacture political dynamite'. It was also to manufacture a formidable burden for the Bureau. As early as November 1944 Carver commented that 'the post-war deluge of statistical development has begun and we are in no position to meet it with so much personnel away'.126

In a memorandum to Carver on 30 October 1945, Coombs sketched the improvements in the range and timeliness of statistics that were essential to full employment planning. Monthly or 'preferably weekly' information on employment, expenditure, and stocks, necessarily compiled on a sample basis, were required. The National Register of July 1939 had revealed unemployment considerably exceeding estimates based on trade union and other customary sources. More frequent censuses or occupational surveys were 'the only means of checking the validity of estimates of total employment, based [since 1941] on Pay Roll Tax and other miscellaneous data, of the number of employed and workers on their own account and of the number unemployed'. Unemployment statistics were now to be tabulated from the records of applicants under the Unemployment and Sickness Benefits Act. (The responsibility for compiling uniform unemployment statistics passed to the Commonwealth Employment Service in 1946.)

For information on past and prospective private capital expenditure, Coombs recommended twice yearly returns from manufacturers, large pastoral and mining companies, construction contractors, private utilities, transport companies, banks, insurance offices, wholesalers, large retailers, 'chain' hotels, restaurants, and theatres. Monthly output statistics for capital goods—the value of output and the volume of production where available—were also to be collected. Motor vehicle, building, and consumer durable expenditure information were desirable as were data on stock volumes. Believing that variations in public capital expenditure would be 'the most important means of affecting fluctuations in other types of expenditure in order to maintain full employment,' Coombs emphasised the necessity both of historical data and forecasts of expenditure and employment on public capital works. The era of national income and expenditure estimates had begun.

Summarising his paper in seventeen recommendations, Coombs concluded that 'as far as practicable, all important statistical information should be tabulated according to the regions determined by each State for purposes of regional planning'.127 (This visionary proposal, far beyond the resources or the political will of the mid-1940s, was to be revived in the 'urban and regional budget' project undertaken collaboratively by the Bureau and the Department of Urban and Regional Development under the Whitlam Government.) The Department of Post-War Reconstruction participated in a sub-committee of the Conference of Statisticians held in November 1945 which reported on the statistics needed in connection with employment policy. Papers from Post-War Reconstruction and the Commonwealth Bank amplified the outline of 'Essential Information' which had been incorporated in the White Paper on 'Full Employment'. The conference agreed on the desirability of a revised approach to the presentation of public finance and public works data, the subdivision of pay-roll tax statistics into all relevant industry classifications rather than classification according to the 'predominating' industry of the employer, an urgent census of distribution, and more comprehensive building statistics, as well as most of Coombs other requirements. To meet these needs, it would be necessary, Carver and his State colleagues concluded, to enlarge the trained staff of all of the bureaus 'to a level greatly beyond that of pre-war years'. Recalling this resolution four years later, the assembled statisticians again noted that 'the resources of Australian statistical bureaus are insufficient to meet in full either urgent national demands or international obligations . . . ' 128

In fact the pre-war Commonwealth Bureau permanent staff of about 80 had already doubled by 1948 (with a further 436 temporary staff), and in the next decade would double again. While in some States the resources devoted to statistical work did not keep pace with the tasks to be accomplished, it became increasingly clear that only a unified national organisation could satisfy modern demands. Even unification, however, could not be expected to overcome genuine conflicts of interest between the Commonwealth and the States. The Chairman of the Commonwealth Grants Commission, A. A. Fitzgerald, reminded the Prime Minister 21 August 1946 of the difficulties posed by 'the lack of uniformity in the financial practices and accounting methods and in the manner of presentation of the public accounts of the several States'. But, as a meeting of Grants Commission, Treasury, Commonwealth Bank, Post-War Reconstruction and Bureau of Statistics officials concluded on 12 December 1946, the possibility of persuading all States to publish supplementary tabulations was remote. The practice of transferring moneys to or from extra-budgetary funds was unlikely to be abandoned by governments wishing 'to arrive at the surplus or deficit which is considered politically desirable'.

The Bureau continued to argue for an economic classification of 'the true relationship of public finance to the private sector of the economy'. But, although there were marginal improvements, a conference of federal and State finance officers in April and August 1955 still admitted that 'the present tabulations and publications were inadequate'. The potentially dramatic effect of adopting a new functional classification of consolidated revenue, trust and special funds, and the loan fund in Queensland was exposed by Stan Solomon who in a letter to Carver on 29 March 1956 compared the proposed method with that used in the Finance Bulletin. Using data for 1954-55, Solomon found that only in one item (railways) did the old system produce something approximating a 'true' figure. Solomon himself was willing to consider a more open approach to what later became known as 'hollow logs'129

During the 1930s, the Commonwealth had not actively pursued the goal of unification. But, as Menzies noted at the time, Carver's dual appointment from late 1940 had 'the further advantage of knitting the work of the Commonwealth and States in the statistical field more closely together. 130 Although Wilson returned to the Bureau in March 1946, he was increasingly preoccupied with his economic advisory tasks. A planned six months' overseas assignment early in 1948 turned into an absence of fifteen months during which Carver was once again placed in command of the federal as well as the New South Wales bureau. In seeking Carver's services, Prime Minister Chifley was at pains to point out the prospective mutual benefits:

There may perhaps be a number of ways in which the Commonwealth Bureau of Census and Statistics could be of assistance in helping Mr. Carver to carry out his State responsibilities . . . I am hopeful that, if you consent to this proposal, it will enable a closer coordination of Commonwealth and State statistical activities to be achieved. All Governments today are in urgent need of fuller and more up-to-date statistics, and it is believed that this can be realised only by developing the closest possible relationships between the Commonwealth and State statistical agencies.131

James McGirr's warm endorsement the objective of 'closer co-ordination' Was the crucial turning point on the path to unification. In June 1949, McGirr agreed to the Commonwealth's proposal to house the New South Wales bureau and the three sections of the Commonwealth Bureau operating in Sydney together in Dymock's Building. The Premier endorsed action already initiated 'to unite in joint statistical ranches the Commonwealth and State staffs dealing with statistics of factories, building and employment in N.S.W'. To set the seal on these developments he also agreed to Chifley's suggestion that he unification process should continue towards 'some form of comprehensive statistical organisation which would serve the needs of both Commonwealth and State'. To this end, Carver was to be appointed Deputy Commonwealth Statistician (N.S.W.) concurrently with his State position, and the Commonwealth was to reimburse Carver's State salary as well as pay additional allowances. When Wilson finally became head of the Treasury in March 1951, Carver was his logical successor. But the New South Wales Government trembled on the brink of a final decision for integration with the Commonwealth. As a compromise, Carver was appointed Acting Commonwealth Statistician, the status he was to retain until August 1957 when, with integration about to be consummated, it was at last possible for him to enjoy the style and title of Commonwealth statistician.132

The War had caused the suspension of s me statistical collections from January 1942 onwards. The census due in 1941 was also deferred. As the War drew to a close, Carver discussed with Colin Clark the timing of the postponed census. Clark was eager to hold an early census and suggested that a family schedule could be collected when ration books were issued in June 1946 (an occupational survey had been taken in association with the issue of ration books in 1945).

But Carver saw insurmountable problems in the shortcake of skilled staff and the political sensitivity in 'anything that looks like saying "Fill in this big form before you get a Ration Book" '. Moreover: those who have to be convinced do not yet realise that information is essential to the type of future policy to which they are committed. Therefore there is an unwillingness to do unconventional or enterprising things to get information . . .

Carver's preference was for an 'intermediate census' in 1947. He agreed with H. C. Coombs that the occupational survey of all civilians aged fourteen and over taken in June 1945 would provide most of the data obtainable from a personal census. As Coombs advised the Minister for Post-War Reconstruction in 19 October 1945:

The only important information normally sought in a complete census, which will not be available, is data in respect of dwelling accommodation. As it is already known that there is a widespread and serious shortage of houses and that this is likely to be acute in the winter of 1946 when many demobilised Servicemen will still be looking for homes, questions on dwelling accommodation at that time might arouse public antagonism.

Contrary to Clark, who contended that there was little to be gained by delay as 'nothing really ever settles down properly these days', Coombs and Carver believed that 'population and conditions generally would be too unsettled' to justify a census before 1947.133 The 1945 Conference of Statisticians had concurred, and taken the opportunity to re-affirm their support for quinquennial censuses, recommending that 'the first post-war quinquennial census be held on 30 June 1947'. (Clark was successful in securing agreement to his proposal to reinstate a question about the issue of marriages which had been omitted in 1933. There were also new questions agreed with the Director of Housing on whether dwellings were built before 30 June 1933, materials of roof, availability of gas, electricity, and the running water, existence of bathroom, flush toilet, laundry, cooking facilities, and means of cooking.) The statisticians enjoyed the sympathy of the federal Prime Minister and Treasurer, J. B. Chifley, who nevertheless remitted their proposal for a permanent and substantial nucleus census organisation 'for future consideration by the Commonwealth Statistician, the Treasury and the Public Service Board, with a view to a further submission to Cabinet'. The Treasury alone was to consider the quinquennial census issue before Cabinet was invited to make a decision.134

In arguing in 1950 against taking a census in 1951, mainly because of difficulties in assembling the staff of collectors, compilers, tabulators, and draftsmen (for mapping and collectors' diagrams), Roland Wilson pointed out that a census in 1954 'would provide equal inter-censal interval of seven years between the Censuses of 1947, 1954 and (presumably) 1961'. This, he suggested, 'might turn out to be a reasonable first step towards the practice of taking Censuses quinquennially rather than decennially—an objective which we have long had in mind'. In the meantime, data from 1947 and ongoing collections were adequate for most purposes, and postponement to the later 1950s would allow for large numbers of immigrants, both received and projected, to he 'absorbed permanently into the Australian economy'.135 The case for censuses 'or at least dissected population counts, at short intervals of a few years' was again pressed by Carver in 1959. In a draft Cabinet paper he argued:

Overall population increase in the seven years 1947 to 1954, an important factor influencing the choice of 1954 as a Census year, was 1,407,172 persons, a number far in excess of any previous intercensal increase during this century. By comparison, the increase in the seven years 1954 to 1961 may exceed this number, bringing the population of Australia at mid 1961 to possibly over 10.4 millions. This recoded expansion will render the Census information currently available quite out-of-date.

There was a further difficulty in measuring the interstate movement of population because of the rapid development of travel by air and road. A Ministerial conference in June 1958 had drawn attention to the effect of increasingly inaccurate population estimates on tax reimbursements grants. Within the Bureau there was also growing dissatisfaction with the decreasingly dependable estimates of employment, unemployment, and work force projected forward from 1954 on the uncertain basis of pay roll tax returns. Heeding these concerns successive governments consented to a census every five years from 1961. The Census and Statistics Act 1977 made a quinquennial census mandatory, a fresh impetus having been imparted by a High Court decision of 1976 requiring an electoral redistribution within the life of every Parliament.136

The expanding post-war demand from administrative authorities and representatives of primary, secondary, and tertiary industry for innovatory and more comprehensive statistical collections, strained the Bureau's regulatory and organisational framework. All forms, other than those relating to 'factories, mines and productive industries generally' had to be prescribed by statutory rules and gazetted. Only prescribed persons were obliged to complete forms. Experience with the collection of building statistics demonstrated the inconvenience and embarrassment which this cumbersome process entailed. For the fifteen quarterly collectors of building statistics from September 1945 to the first half of 1949, new forms had to be prescribed six times. When Carver sought further changes in 1949 to implement 'a hard won agreement to collect building statistics on behalf of the Victorian Minister or Housing, he learned that it would be at least six months before the necessary rules could be prepared and gazetted. The only alternative to proceeding without legal authority was to change the legislation. Carver convinced Chifley, who in turn carried the Cabinet, to remove the requirement to prescribe both forms and persons.

As a later Bureau commentator saw it:

No longer would the work of statistical collection be bogged down through the threat, or the fact, of recalcitrant and litigious respondents challenging prescriptive wording on individual collection forms. The fact of being sent a form by the Statistician was to be sufficient to oblige a person to comply with the requirements of the Act, in a stroke "prescribing" both the respondent and the schedule to be completed.

Simultaneously, the Bureau obtained an extension of the secrecy obligations of section 24 of the Census and Statistics Act to cover information supplied voluntarily as well as 'furnished in pursuance' of the Act. The second reading speech explained that statutory authority was now given to the unwritten and inviolable law concerning the privacy of information, about individual persons and individual businesses, obtained for statistical purposes by the Statistician'. Henceforth that secrecy could not be violated by regulation or by administrative action. Confidentiality was extended not only to returns supplied to the Statistician (by State statisticians as well as by individuals and organisations) but to copies of returns held by respondents themselves.137

In parallel with these regulatory developments came strains on human resources and a re-orientation of the Bureau's function. During the War, the Commonwealth Government had assumed responsibility for national economic management. The High Commonwealth Court's legitimisation of uniform taxation and State reimbursement laid the foundation for a greatly expanded role in the peacetime economy. State government interest in developing the capacity for long term planning was interrupted, and buoyant post-war conditions diminished the imperative to monitor and moderate economic fluctuations. As post-war reconstruction lost its momentum, federal policy initiative was grasped by the Treasury whose ascendancy was both symbolised and assured by Wilson's appointment as Secretary in 1951. Treasury annexed the economic domain (contesting some parts of it successively with the Departments of Prime Minister and Cabinet, Commerce and Agriculture, and Trade). The Bureau's fusion of statistical and economic advisory roles embodied most notably in Giblin and Wilson was irrevocably terminated with Wilson's departure and Treasury's rapid recruitment of a team of economists.138

When the Commonwealth decided the time was ripe to re-open negotiations towards integration of State and federal statistical bureaus, they were to find themselves embracing what one official was subsequently to describe as 'generally depleted statistical capacities'. In a personal letter to the Western Australian Under Treasurer, Carver noted in September 1953 that 'at least three of the States, without recognising it, have been abandoning their statistical organisations and automatically throwing more and more on to us to do in Canberra'. Nevertheless, Carver was hopeful because 'statistical coordination has come actively to life in both Brisbane and Melbourne, where joint premises and other joint arrangements contingent on the Census are being made'. Meanwhile, in Canberra, the Public Service Board had 'provided career jobs which will now enable us to continue the development of Australian statistics towards the levels attained in the United Kingdom, Canada and the United States'. One of the key jobs created was that of Assistant Statistician (Administrative), a position specially approved in 1949 to regularise Wilson's refusal to allow Archer to take up a promotion in the Department of Health.139

With the encouragement of Archer and O'Neill, a frustrated H.P. Brown produced for Carver early in 1950 a list of the Bureau's 'general deficiencies', and 'specific items' which required action. Brown found fault with uncoordinated publication policy, 'inadequate thinking' about 'general statistical policy' as well as a lack of experimental work on questionnaires, insufficient attention to seasonal variations in monthly collections, and the narrowness of the range of monthly statistics. Delays in compilation and publication, and the 'very summary fashion' in which the inquiries of private persons were dealt with were linked directly with staff shortages, as, by implication, were 60 neglected categories of statistics. Remedying all of the inadequacies nominated by Brown was beyond the resources of even a rapidly growing organisation. But significant progress was made in some important areas. With D.V. Youngman, Brown himself had already pioneered social accounting and had developed sampling techniques for business surveys. Further important analytical work was done on national accounts during the 1950s, but greater emphasis was placed on compiling statistics. In 1950, quarterly surveys of retail establishments began, complementing a Census taken in 1948 and 1949 after strong requests from the business sector. A survey of wage and salary taxpayers introduced in 1952 resulted in a saving of 80 staff who had previously compiled taxation statistics by complete enumeration. The creation in 1953 of a sampling section under I.G.Jones in the Development Branch saw the new techniques established, although a sceptical Carver was tempted to discontinue all sampling operations when the 1954 Census of retail establishments could not at first be reconciled with the surveys for the corresponding quarters. From the mid-1950s onwards, in spite of resistance from some informants who queried the Statistician's authority to use sampling techniques, sample surveys embraced some elements of monthly production, wool clip estimates, stocks, capital expenditure, local government employment, company tax and award occupations, as well as special assignments for the Reserve Bank and various government departments, town planning authorities, and academic institutions. Developmental work on a household expenditure survey was undertaken by Dr F.B. Homer and G.R. Palmer but the dispersal of senior staff to State offices (and the beginning in 1958 of studies related to the introduction of computers) led to the suspension of household expenditure work and other new projects. Meanwhile, however, E.K. Foreman prepared the groundwork for a labour force survey and the extension of sampling into census quality control. Foreman became the driving force behind a core sampling organisation that progressively, and not without friction with some other 'line' managers, undertook responsibility for innovation in a variety of applications of mathematical statistics.140

UNIFICATION AND A NEW WORLD

It fell to Archer, at Carver's behest, to usher in the era of the computer. A sympathetic response from Roland Wilson and Lenox Hewitt of the Treasury ensured that funds were available for the purchase of computers (a Control Data 3600 in Canberra and satellite CD 3200s in State capital offices), the programming staff having been recruited from Britain in 1962. Archer and Dr John Ovenstone, a Weapons Research Establishment and subsequently Defence Department expert, had been entrusted by a 'quite terrified' Carver with defining the Bureau's needs and overseeing the installation. The new world which the Bureau was attempting to cope with using advanced techniques and vastly enhanced computational power, was de-scribed some years later in a memorandum arguing the case for major statutory changes:

The pressures which were being exerted on the Commonwealth Bureau during the post-War years reflected not only the increase in the volume of statistics being sought, but also a fundamental change in the manner in which official statistics were being used. Whereas in pre-War years, statistics were used primarily as a measure of past performance, since the War they have been used increasingly as a means of evaluating current trends and as a basis for anticipating future economic trends for planning, both in Government and in private industry.141

The management problems of the 1960s and beyond were to be problems of an expanding organisation, still conscious of a mismatch between resources and commitments, where overlapping, duplication, lack of coordination, and excessive subject-matter specialisation are endemic. With 3,100 staff by 1969 and 2,000 publications (550 titles) released each year, it was an organisation whose work could be strategically directed but no longer given the degree of personal oversight to which Carver had aspired.142 As the scope of activities widened, Bureau officers in the State capitals found themselves responding to media inquiries on 'sensitive areas of public opinion (income, expenditure patterns, pension sources, types of illness or infirmity)'.143 As academic, business, and government researchers widened the ambit of their concerns, anxieties about the erosion of privacy were more frequently expressed in Parliament and the community. While economic statistics remained central to the Bureau s mission—and were radically enhanced by the introduction in 1969 of an integrated census of mining, manufacturing, electricity, gas, wholesale and retail trade, and certain services—there was a growing emphasis on social statistics. Statistics of house-hold expenditure and the use of motor vehicles had acknowledged policy relevance. In line with overseas practice, seasonal adjustment of a wide range of series became accepted procedure; input-output tables and econometric models were produced; and attention was even turned to the long resisted but pressingly demanded indexes of production and productivity.144

While the Bureau's leading officers were anything but complacent, particularly as other federal departments developed independent and sometimes incompatible data systems, they had rightfully recognised that the achievement of unification agreements with all States laid the essential foundation for a re-invigorated and extended national statistical enterprise. Negotiations towards an integrated statistical service were re-opened by the Commonwealth in 1953. Discussions with Victoria were promising but inconclusive. The Queensland Labour Government decided to 'retain its own Statistical office to meet all State Governmental, Local Authority and State Industrial requirements' a stance that was promptly reversed by the Country Party-Liberal Party coalition in 1957.145 But all States consented to a transitional step of housing their statistical officers in the same premises as Commonwealth officers. Even this move was delayed, as Carver explained to Wilson, by 'the messing about of various Commonwealth intrumentalities, even involving the fundamental question as to whether a State Statistical office could be housed in the Commonwealth space'. Carver proceeded cautiously until mid-1953, feeling that he was 'a bit out of step' with Wilson with whom he insufficient opportunity to confer. But having been assured that he was not 'running contra' to Wilson's views, he proceeded 'actively but guardedly with suasion' to the point of having the Treasurer ready by October 1953 to recommend a simple amendment to the Census and Statistics Act to facilitate the negotiation of agreements with individual States. It was to take another three years, however, before legislation was in place.

By early August 1954, Carver had distilled his thinking eleven 'principles' which he discussed first privately with well in New South Wales, South Australia and Western Australia. A draft agreement on integration, with special reference to Western Australia, was prepared by the Crown Solicitor in January 1955. The following month, Carver advised the Chairman of the New South Wales Public Service Board that an enabling Bill and a draft or staff reorganisation were also ready.146 Agreement in principle with the governments of Western Australia, New South Wales, and South Australia proved less difficult than had been feared. The draft agreement with Western Australia became the prototype of arrangements to be made with each State following enactment of the Statistics (Arrangements with States) Bill, authority for which was finally sought from the Cabinet by Arthur Fadden in February 1956. Fadden advised Cabinet that the proposed arrangements entailed the creation of:

an integrated statistical service operated by Commonwealth officers under the immediate direction of each State of a Statistician who would hold office under both the Commonwealth and the State . . . No State would be required to surrender its sovereign powers in the field of statistics. It would agree to exercise them in a special way through an integrated service.147

In a series of agreements, beginning with South Australia in March 1957 and ending with Victoria in June 1958, the vision that had fired a succession of statisticians from Coghlan to Carver at last became a reality. Of all the benefits predicted to flow from integration, one of immeasurable practical and symbolic significance was identified by the compiler of 'Preliminary Notes on the Provisional Agenda' for the 1958 Statisticians' Conference: 'The Central Bureau can now, for the first time in history, make a firm printing timetable with the Commonwealth Printer.148 While the completion of unification was Carver's greatest achievement, he also influenced the future course of the Bureau by his nurturing of the careers of Keith Archer and Jack O'Neill. Archer had been made responsible for 'the main statistical work and general administration of the office' under Carver.149 He was created Deputy Commonwealth Statistician in 1958 and regularly acted for Carver when the Statistician was absent. He succeeded Carver in February 1962. O'Neill, Archer's close colleague for three decades, followed him as Deputy and ultimately as Statistician in 1972. With the departure of O'Neill in 1975, a half century of continuity was ended. The re-christening of the organisation as the Australian Bureau of Statistics, its statutory autonomy, the appointment of its head from outside, and its headquarters consolidation in concrete isolation eight kilometres from the centre of Canberra at Belconnen, all heralded a new era that awaits its historians.

Notes pertaining to Parts 3 & 4

1. Report on the Proposed Establishment of a Central Bureau of Statistics', T. A. Coghlan to Sir William Lyne, 21 April 1903, Sir Edmund Barton MSS, NLA 51/1/1112-14.
2. E. C. Fry, 'T. A. Coghlan as an Historian', paper presented to Section E, ANZAAS Congress, Aug.1965, p. 9.
3. National Australasian Convention, Sydney, 1891, Votes and Proceedings, p. clxxvi; John Quick and Robert Garran, Annotated Constitution of the Australian Commonwealth Sydney, 1901, p. 572.
4. Census of Australasia 1901, Conference of Statisticians' Report, Legislative Assembly, New South Wales, 1900, p. 1.
5. ibid., p. 3.
6. Correspondence Register, Department of Home Affairs, AA A100.
7. Conference of Statisticians, Hobart, Jan. 1902, Parliament of Tasmania, No. 25, 1902, Appendix III, pp. 32-3.
8. ibid., p. 33.
9. ibid., p.7.
10. Unification of Australian Statistical Methods and Co-ordination of the Work of the Commonwealth and State Bureaux, Conference or Statisticians of the Commonwealth and States of Australia and Colony of New Zealand, Melbourne, 1906, p. 24.
11. Conference of Statisticians . . . 1902, pp. 8-9.
12. Sir Edmund Barton's Diary, 6 March 1903, Barton MSS, NLA 51/2/951; Coghlan to Lyne, 21 April 1903, Barton MSS, NLA 51/1/1118-25.
13. Joan M. Cordell, T. A. Coghlan Government Statist of New South Wales 1888-1905, unpublished ts.,n.d., p. 99; Commonwealth Statistician and Actuary to Secretary, Department of Home Affairs, 8 Feb. 1930, AA A571, 32/2037, refers to Johnston's letter.
14. Cordell, p. 119. For Coghlan's work on the organisation or export and import statistics see his correspondence with the Commonwealth Treasurer, Sir George Turner, Nov-Dec. 1904, AA A571, 05/ 3601.
15. Cordell, p. 100; Coghlan to W. McLeod, 11 April 1906, Cordell p. 101; and letters to Deakin urging that the Commonwealth take over

the work of the state agents general, 6 Sept. and 27 Oct. 1905, Alfred Deakin MSS, NLA 1540/15/2430, 2446.

16. 'Appointment of Commonwealth Statistician', Department of Home Affairs office memorandum, 12 Feb.1906; Prime Minister (Deakin) to Premier of New South Wales (Carruthers), 6 Feb. 1906, AA A 100, 1906/1258; Coghlan to Deakin,

15 Feb. 1906, Deakin MSS, NLA 1540/1/1334. For an interpretation showing Carruthers in a bad light' see D. I. Wright, Shadow of Dispute, Aspects of Commonwealth—State Relations, 1901-1910, Canberra, 1970, pp. 78-9; cf David Carment, Australian Liberal: A Political Biography of Sir Littleton Groom 1867-1936, Ph.D. Thesis, A.N.U., 1975, pp. 46-9.

17. Secretary, Department of Home Affairs for Minister for Home Affairs, 21 Dec. 1905; T. T. Ewing to L.E. Groom, 27 Dec. 1905; Secretary, Department of Home Affairs to Minister, 12 Jan. 1906, Sir Littleton Groom MSS, NLA 236/1/398, 403, 413; Coghlan to Deakin, 28 Dec. 1905, Deakin MSS, NLA 1540/1/1280—2; Commonwealth Gazette 24 Feb. 1906, p. 150; Nation Building in Australia The Life and Work of Sir Littleton Ernest Groom, Sydney, 1941, pp. 44-5, 50-1, 118.

18. Report of the Proceedings of the Conference between the Commonwealth and State Ministers, Hobart, 1905, pp. 87, 90.

19. Commonwealth of Australia Parliamentary Debates (CPD), vol. XXXII, House of Representatives, 23 Aug. 1905, pp. 1384-5.

20. The secrecy provisions inadvertently inhibited State statisticians from using information obtained under the Commonwealth Act for State purposes until a regulation remedied the unintended consequence in 1909. (ABS 06/200.) Four Tasmanian businessmen earned the distinction of being the first people to be prosecuted for failure to furnish information. Convictions were recorded and more serious penalties threatened for future delinquents (The Mercury, 16 June 1910, ABS Box R8 903/09.) It was not until 1935 that all States had legislative authority for their own statistical collection: Tasmania (Statistical Returns Act 1877); Queensland (Statistical Returns Act 1896); New South Wales (Census Act 1901); Western Australia (Statistics Act 1907); Victoria (Statistics Act 1928); South Australia (Statistics Act 1935). An amending Act in 1920 explicitly empowered

the Statistician to publish census results and abstracts 'as the Minister directs, with observations thereon'.

21. CS (C. H. Wickens) to Secretary, Department of Home Affairs, 8 Feb. 1930, AA A571, 32/2037; Coghlan to Deakin, 28 Dec. 1905, Deakin MSS, NLA 1540/1/1280-2.
22. Cordell, p. 112; Susan Bambrick, 'The First Commonwealth Statistician: Sir George Knibbs', Journal and Proceedings, Royal Society of New South Wales, vol. 102, 1969, pp. 127, 132-3. Knibbs' appointment as Acting Professor of Physics at Sydney University is mentioned in various obituaries but there is no official record of it at the university.
23. Lyne to Groom, 11 May 1906, Groom MSS, NLA 236/1/449. When more prominent statisticians like Victoria's William McLean and Coghlan's deputy and successor, J. B. Trivett, had recently been subjected to public dissection of their methods and social philosophies in the inquiries of the Mackellar Commission into the birth rate, the advantage of having nothing known against him was a considerable assets to Knibbs. (Neville Hicks, 'This Sin and Scandal' Australia's Population Debate 1891-1911, Canberra, 1978, ch. 7; W. D. Borrie, Population Trends and Policies: A Study in Australian and World Demography, Sydney, 1948, Ch. IV.) Fortuitously, Knibbs was on the platform with Deakin, Groom and the Labour Leader, J. C. Watson, at the launching of the Immigration League of Australia in October 1905. (Michael Roe, Nine Australian Progressives: Vitalism in Bourgeois Social Thought 1890-1960, St Lucia, 1984, pg.162.)
24. Coghlan to ID. C. Mc Lachlan, 29 June 1906, Cordell, p. 102.
25. Coghlan to Deakin, 29 June 1906, Deakin MSS, NLA 1540/1/1449.
26. Coghlan to Ewing, 26 Oct. 1906, Cordell. p. 102.
27. J.Stonham to Secretary of the Treasury, 3 May 1933, ABS 57/1530.
28. George Handley Knibbs, 'The History and Development of the Statistical System of Australia', in John Koren (ed), The history of Statistics, Their Development and Progress in Many Countries New York, 1918, P. 60; Commonwealth Bureau of Census and Statistics (CBCS), Official Year Book of the Commonwealth Australia . . . , No. 1, 1908, Melbourne, 1908. p. 12.
29. Conference of Statistician . . . 1906, p. 4.
30. ABS 140/08

31. Conference of Statisticians . . . 1906, pp. 15—17,8.
32. ibid., p. 6. For the shrewd observations and suggestions of an experienced South Australian mounted police constable, see Leo Dingle to Government Statist, 19 June 1922, ABS (Adelaide), 141/1916.
33. ibid., pp 7.23; Knibbs argued vigorously for quinquennial enumeration in a memorandum to the Secretary, Department of Home Affairs, 1 Feb. 1907, AA A100, 7/861.
34. ibid., pp 12-13; Ian vanden Driesen. 'Demographic Grumbles: Some Problems with Population Data in Western Australia 1850—1900', Australian historical Statistics, No. 6, Jan. 1983, p.23.
35. Conference of Statisticians . . . 1906, pp. 20-1, 6.
36. G.H. Knibbs, Local Government in Australia, Melbourne, 1919, preface; for an early attempt to minimise unwarrantable and misleading' divergences in defining metropolitan areas, see CS (Knibbs) to South Australian Government Statist, 21 June 1911, ABS (Adelaide), 91/1911.
37. Conference of statisticians . . . 1906, pp. 20—1.
38. ibid., p 21; CBCS, Year Book 1917, p. 197.
39. Coghlan to Deakin, 10 July 1905, Cordell, p. 41; Coghlan to Deakin, 20 July 1906, CS (Knibbs) to Secretary, Department of Home Affairs, 12 July 1907, AA A100, 07/4753; CPD, vol. XLV, House of Representatives, 31 March 1908, p. 9875. Knibbs was also riled by the unauthorised description of Coghlan in Who's Who in Australia 1907 as 'Statistician to the Federal Government since 1906' (CS Knibbs to Secretary, Department of Home Affairs, 5 Feb. 1907, AA A100, 7/938.)
40. CS (Knibbs) to Secretary, Department of Home Affairs, 21 March 1908, ABS 45/26.
41. Memo by CS (Knibbs), 24 March 1908, ABS 45/26; CPD, vol. XLIV, Senate, 24 March 1908, p. 9422; in a memorandum to the Secretary, Department of Home Affairs on 15 Jan. 1907, Knibbs had foreshadowed the annual publication of a 1,500 page Commonwealth statistical register and a quinquennial 1,500 page 'Statistical Account of the Development of the Commonwealth of Australia' as well as the Year Book. (AA AI00, 07/666.)
42. CS (Knibbs) to Secretary, Department of Home Affairs, 21 Oct. 1907; 9 April 1908 (approved by Minister, 23 April 1908), ABS 45/26.
43. ABS 45/26.

44. CS (Knibbs) to Secretary, Department of Home Affairs, 4 March 1908, ABS 45/26; L. H. Sholl, the South Australian Government Statist, was particularly dismayed by his State's inability to collect and publish production statistics as promptly as Victoria and New South Wales (Government Statist, South Australia to Victorian and New South Wales Government Statists, 21 June 1911, and replies 12 July 1911 and 28 June 1911, ABS, Adelaide, 95/1911).
45. CS (Knibbs) to Secretary, Department of Home Affairs, 5 Nov. 1908, minuted by Hugh Mahon, 18 Nov. 1908, ABS 45/26.
46. CS (Knibbs) to Secretary, Department of Home Affairs, 9 May 1908, ABS 45/26. The similarity between some sections of the Year Book and corresponding portions of earlier works by Coghlan gave a particular piquancy to the denigration of Knibbs' prose style. Mr B. D. Haig kindly drew my attention to some parallel passages in the works of Coghlan and the Year Book.
47. Coghlan to N. C. Lockyer, 8 Jan. 1909, Cordell, p. 48.
48. Coghlan to Deakin, n.d. (ca Oct. 1908), Deakin MSS, NLA 1540/1/2126; Coghlan to MacLachlan, 19 March 1909, Cordell, p.48
49. Year Book 1908, pp. 760-1, 767, 516-22.
50. ibid., p. 7.
51. G. H. Knibbs, The Problems of Statistics, Brisbane, 1910, passim. For an assessment of Knibbs' social and economic thinking see Craufurd D. W. Goodwin, Economic Enquiry in Australia, Durham N. C., 1966, pp 261-2, 349-50, 448-52, 487-91.
52. Hughes to Mahon, 15 April 1909, Mahon MSS, NLA 937/129.
53. Coghlan to Lockyer, 18 March 1908; to Macleod, 21 Oct. 1910, Cordell, pp. 103, 102; Coghlan to Deakin, 25 March 1909, Deakin MSS, NLA 1540/1/2336.
54. AA A 100, 07/5356; Groom's opinion, 5 Aug. 1907, is published in Patrick Brazil and Bevan Mitchell (eds), Opinions of the Attorneys-General of the Commonwealth of Australia, with opinions of Solicitors-General and the Attorney-General's Department, vol. 1, 1901-14, A.G.P.S., Canberra, 1981, pp. 345-6;of Robert Garran's comment, 11 Aug. 1908, in Brazil and Mitchell (eds), p. 402.
55. CS (Knibbs) to Secretary, Department of Home Affairs, 26 Nov. 1909; Prime Minister to Premier of Western Australia, 20 Nov. 1908, ABS 06/200; CS (Knibbs) to Secretary, Department of Home

Affairs, 5 Jan. 1909, ABS Box R24, 140/08; CS (Knibbs) to Secretary, Department of Home Affairs, 16 Dec.1909, ABS 200/06. The limits on Knibbs' authority were clearly illustrated by his failure to persuade Queensland and New South Wales to continue the costly compilation of the particulars relating to 'distinct persons' convicted at magistrates' courts which facilitated comparisons of data on lower and higher courts. (CS to Government Statistician, Queensland, 3 Nov. 1910, ABS Box R15, 200/06; cf Satyanshu K. Mukherjee et al., Crime Trends in Twentieth Century Australia, Sydney, 1981, pp. 13-15)

56. F. B. Homer, 'The Evolution of the Census', Address given to the N.S.W. branch of the Economic Society of Australia and New Zealand, 23 April 1954, p. 11; David Tait, 'Respectability, Property and Fertility: The Development of Official Statistics about Families in Australia', Labour History, No. 49, Nov. 1985, p. 92; G. H. Knibbs, The First Commonwealth Census, 3 April 1911, Notes, Bureau of the Census team as consisting of 400 enumerators, 7,000 collectors, a maximum of 280 tabulators, and Census and Statistics, Melbourne, 1911; in Koren (ed.), The history of Statistics, p.64, Knibbs spoke of the Census team as consisting of 400 enumerators, 7,000 collectors, a maximum of 280 tabulators, and an expenditure of £170,000. British developments are noted in Richard Lawton (ed.), The Census and Social Structure: An Interpretative Guide to Nineteenth Century Censuses for England and Wales, London, 1978, p. 20.

57. A. Adrian, 'Trends in Social Statistics: The Australian Census 1911-1981', Working Paper No. C10, 1981 Census of Population and Housing, Development Programme, ABS Canberra, [1982], pp. 3-4, 5-9; ABS evaluation of the 1976 Census race question indicated that 'the quality of the data is suspect'. (Brian Doyle and Raymond Chambers, 'Census Evaluation in Australia', Working Paper No. C4, 1981 Census of Population and Housing, Development Programme, ABS, Canberra, [1980], Appendix 2.) On the deaf-mute problem, see H. O. Lancaster, An Introduction to Medical Statistics, New York, 1975, pp. 1-4.

58. Press cuttings, Dec. 1910 to July 1911, ABS (Adelaide), 161/1909; CS (Knibbs) to South Australian Government Statist, 13 May 1912, ABS (Adelaide), 96/1912; Conference of Statisticians of the States of Australia, Sydney, March 1912, pp. 17, 8, 10, 13. Within weeks of the conference the Commonwealth had moved to arrange for daily

reports on interstate rail migration to be supplied by railway officers at border towns. (Minister for Home Affairs, Schedule No. 8, 30 April 1912, AA A742.)

59. Year Book 1912, pp. 1167-84; G. H. Knibbs, Inquiry into the Cost of Living in Australia 1910-11, CBCS, Melbourne, Dec. 1911; G. H. Knibbs, Expenditure on Living in the Commonwealth, November 1913, Labour and Industrial Branch Report No. 4, CBCS, Melbourne, Aug. 1914.
60. G. H. Knibbs, Social Insurance, Report by the Commonwealth Statistician . . . , CBCS, Melbourne, Sept. 1910, pp. 83, 92.
61. An undated draft 'Labour and Statistics Department Bill', Regulations, and Explanatory Memorandum are in King O'Malley MSS, NLA 460/3046-58.
62. Minister for Home Affairs to Secretary, Department of Home Affairs, 13 March 1911, 24 Jan. 1911,13 Feb. 1911, (copies), O'Malley MSS, NLA 460/40-3, 1, 25-8.
63. Minute by Minister for Home Affairs, 24 March 1911, (copy); CS (Knibbs) to Minister for Home Affairs, 30 Sept. 1912, O'Malley MSS, NLA 460/44, 3059-60. It was not until 1975 that the Commonwealth Statistician had the full powers of a departmental head.
64. Year Book 1913, pp. 1123-55; CPD, vol. LXII, House of Representatives, 24 November 1911, p. 3165; C.Forster, 'Australian Unemployment, 1900—1940', The Economic Record, vol. 41, no. 95, Sept. 1965, pp. 426-50 and 'Indexation and the Commonwealth Basic Wage 1907-22', Australian Economic History Review, vol. XX, no. 2, Sept. 1980, pp. 99—118; the early development of the Labour and Industrial Branch can be traced in 'schedules' of current work circulated to parliamentarians by King O'Malley, Oct. 1911 to May 1913 (AA A742).
65. Knibbs in Koren (ed.), The History of Statistics, pp. 65-8. By December 1912, Wickens had accumulated 54 days untaken leave 'through pressure of exceptional official duties'. (Wickens to CS, 30 Dec. 1912, ABS W/65)
66. CS (Knibbs) to Minister for Home Affairs, 2 Nov. 1916, annotated by O'Malley, 6 Nov. 1916, ABS W/65. In answer to a question on notice, the Senate had been told on 14 September 1916 that there were 24 permanent staff and 28 temporaries employed on the usual

work of the Bureau, with an additional 107 temporary staff on war census work. (CPD, vol. LXXXIX, Senate, 14 Sept. 1916, p. 8534).

67. CS (Knibbs) to South Australian Government Statist, 4 Sept. 1914; New South Wales Government Statistician to CS, 1 Oct. 1914, (copy); R. M. Johnston to G. H. Knibbs, 23 Sept. 1914, (copy), ABS (Adelaide), 159/1914; Memorandum, Government Statist to Chief Secretary, 26 July 1916, ABS (Adelaide), 144/1916; South Australian Government Statist to CS (Knibbs), 13 July and 18 Aug. 1916; CS (Knibbs) to Government Statist, 17 July and 22 Aug. 1916, ABS (Adelaide), 136/1916. As early as 24 Sept. 1908, Knibbs had commented that production statistics could be improved and issued earlier if the State bureaus 'were relieved of effort in connection with Vital Statistics'. (ABS Box 24, 140/08.)
68. G. F. Pearce to Premier, South Australia, 3 June 1916; 'Report Upon the Work of the State Statistical Department and the Proposal for Transfer to the Commonwealth Government'. Government Statist, 30 June 1916, ABS (Adelaide), 118/1916 (CPD, vol. XCIV, Senate, 24 Nov. 1920, p. 6871).
69. R. M. Johnston to Premier, 17 July 1916, (Tasmanian Premier's Department 1.269) quoted in D. N. Allen, The Development of Official Statistics in Tasmania, Diploma of Public Administration thesis, University of Tasmania, 1965, p. 81.
70. Report . . . 30 June 1916', ABS (Adelaide), 118/1916; the Registration of Births, Deaths, and Marriages Department was amalgamated with the Statistics Department in 1928, bringing South Australia into harmony with Victoria, Queensland, and Western Australia, with Tasmania and New South Wales the exceptions. (CS [Wickens] to Secretary Department of Home Affairs, 8 Feb. 1930, AA A571, 32/2037.)
71. The Age 13 Dec. 1916. As a war economy, Victoria had, ceased publishing its Statistical Register, shortened its Year Book, and reduced the print run. (Unsigned and undated memorandum ca 1920, ABS Melbourne; Erle Bourke, Victorian Year Book 7986, Melbourne, 1986, pp. 18-19.)
72. CS (Wickens) to Secretary, Department of Home Affairs, 8 Feb. 1930, AA A571; Johnston to Knibbo, 23 Sept. 1914, (copy), ABS (Adelaide), 159/1914.

73. G. H. Knibbs, The Private Wealth of Australia and its Growth as ascertained by various methods, together with A Report of The War Census of 1915, CBCS, Melbourne, 1918, pp. 8-13, 19; Knibbs to G. Pitt-Rivers, 17 March 1921, (copy), AA A1606, BS/1 Part 3.
74. ibid., pp. 36-7; Government Statist, South Australia to CS (Knibbs), 8 Sept. 1915, ABS (Adelaide), 129/1915; Colin Clark and J. G. Crawford, The National Income of Australia, Sydney, 1938, p. 7; L. Soltow, 'The Censuses of Wealth of Men in Australia in 1915 and in the United States in 1860 and 1870', Australian Economic History Review, vol. XII, no. 2, Sept. 1972, pp. 125-6; F. Lancaster Jones, 'The Changing Shape of the Australian Income Distribution, 1914-15, and 1968-69', Australian Economic History Review, vol. XV, no. 1, March 1975, pp. 21-34. Understatement was also evident in responses to the voluntary questions on income in the 1933 Census. (Clark and Crawford op. cit., pp. 7-22.)
75. Knibbs, Private Wealth, p. 178.
76. Knibbs to Stonham, 23 Dec. 1919, ABS 26 19/579. Knibbs had admitted to an inquirer in 1919 that not all information about the sources of personal income had been tabulated at the war census. (CPD, vol. XCL, House of Representatives, 4 March 1920, p. 201.)
77. CPD, vol. XCIV, House of Representatives, 6 Oct. 1920, p. 5364; Knibbs to Sholl, 29 Jan. 1915, ABS (Adelaide) 23/1914.
78. CS (Knibbs') to Minister for Home and Territories, 25 Feb. 1918, AA A461, D320/1/3; ABS R12 18/ 169. Knibbs' comprehensive treatment of the proposed imperial bureau, including a floor plan for the offices and library, suggests a personal as well as an official interest in the outcome. While in London, Knibbs pointed out that the British had no central bureau of statistics. The Commonwealth government was unenthusiastic about committing funds to an organisation that might necessarily have to undertake tasks more properly the responsibility of the British alone. With the British themselves bent on economy the scheme languished. (R. R. Garran to Prime Minister, 25 Jan. 1924, AA A461, D320/1/3.)
79. Knibbs to Stonham, 23 Dec. 1919, ABS 26 19/579.
80. G.H. Knibbs, 'Statistics and National Destiny', United Empire, vol. Xl (New Series), No. 1, Jan. 1920, pp. 14-25; 'The Problems of Population, Food Supply and Migration', Scientia, vol. XXVI, Dec. 1919, pp. 485-95.

81. Fraser to Knibbs, 9 May 1919, ABS 26 19/579.
82. Secretary, Home and Territories Department to CS (Knibbs), 28 July 1919; CS (Knibbs) to Secretary, Home and Territories Department, 23 July 1919 (copy), ABS R26 19/579. Wickens had not been one of Knibbs' original choices for the Bureau but had successfully applied when his more senior Perth colleague W. Siebenhaar had declined an offer of appointment. (C. F. Wilson, Colonial Treasurer, to CS [Knibbs], telegram, 24 Oct. 1906, ABS 53/06.)
83. J. G. McLaren (Secretary, Home and Territories Department) to Knibbs, 19 May 1921, CSIRO Archives 1/175 Pt 1; H. O. Lancaster, 'Charles Henry Wickens 1872-1939', Australian Journal of Statistics, vol. 16, no. 2, 1974, pp. 71-82 for Wickens' life and an assessment of his contributions to demography and vital statistics in particular. Sir Roland Wilson, recalling a view expressed in the Bureau in the early 1930s, credits Wickens with authorship of The Mathematical Theory of Population, the major work published over Knibbs' name. Wickens himself, in an obituary of Knibbs, described the study as Knibbs' 'most ambitious effort'. Professor C. C. Heyde concludes from a study of this and earlier works that Wickens would have had a claim to recognition as co-author (private communication, 15 Feb. 1988). ('An address by Sir Roland Wilson to mark the 50th anniversary of his appointment as Commonwealth Statistician', ABS, Canberra, 29 April 1986, pp. 1-2; C. H. Wickens, 'Sir George Knibbs'. The Economic Record, vol. v, no. 9, Nov. 1929, p. 335.) George Pearce saw the deaths of several State officials as affording 'a splendid opportunity' for reform. (CPD, XCIV, Senate, 24 Nov. 1920, p. 6871.) W. L. Johnston to Wickens, 22 Oct. 1923, ABS 08/140.
84. CS (Wickens) to Secretary, Home and Territories Department, 9 Aug. 1922, AA A571, 32/2030; CS (Knibbs) to Secretary, Department of Home Affairs, 18 March 1911, (copy), ABS Box W165 53/06. Barford, who was to be principal assistant to Stonham, also found himself reclassified from professional to clerical.
85. Year Book 1922, pp. 1084-5. The machine tabulation saga is documented in AA A571, 32/2034-5. In the mid 1920s, the New South Wales and Victorian bureaus were each using two Powers Automatic Key Punches and a Powers Automatic Counting Sorter which could sort about 18,000 cards an hour. (ABS, Adelaide, 49/1926.)

86. Extract from Report of Conference between Prime Minister, State Premiers and Ministers . . . Melbourne, May, 1923', ABS (Melbourne); Conference of Statisticians, Melbourne 2/10/'23 to 5/10/23, typescript report to Prime Minister and Premiers, 5 Oct. 1923; Giblin to Wickens 12 March and 4 April 1924. ABS 08/140.
87. CS (Wickens) to Secretary, Home and Territories Department, 10 Sept. 1924, ABS 08/140. Correspondence, memoranda, and copies of legislation relating to the takeover of the Tasmanian operation are in AA A571, 32/2028, ABS 08/140 and 39/1/1. (The property transferred to the Commonwealth by the Tasmanian Act included three revolving chairs, five mats, a waste paper basket, three Fuller slide rules, and an arithmometer. The South Australian Bureau's copy of the Act has a marginal query about the last two items: 'What are these? Wd they help the office'. [ABS, Adelaide 215/1924].)
88. Giblin to CS (Wickens), 18 March 1927 (copy), and subsequent exchanges with the Public Service Board, AA A571, 32/2041. K. A. Archer, Commonwealth Statistician 1962-70, was paid personally by Giblin for his first nine months in the Hobart office until his appointment was formalised retrospectively when Giblin's friend, Lyons, became Premier in 1924. As the other juniors were 'town-bred', Archer's farming background led to his assignment to understudy the 63 year old J. R. Green on 'stock and crop' statistics (NLA, TRC C12/38). J. P. O'Neill was another Commonwealth Statistician to benefit from Giblin's guidance and support in obtaining a free place for university study in 1929 (ABS 30/57). In his enthusiasm for youth, Giblin apparently did not sense the frustration of his principal assistant. In a protest over his treatment since 1924, the 64 year old W. T. Murphy obliquely indicated a suspicion that neither merit nor age was the crucial factor. 'I understand that the laws of Italy now provide that no member of the Public Service shall be at the same time a member of any Secret Society. Such a law cannot possibly be an injustice to any one; and would, undoubtedly, have the effect of considerable saving to the taxpayers, of greater efficiency in the Service, and of inspiring confidence in the administration.' (W. T. Murphy to Chairman, Public Service Board of Commissioners, 6 Jan. 1929, ABS 30/57.)
89. CS (Wickens) to Tasmanian Government Statistician, 10 April 1924, ABS 08/140; CS (Wickens) to Assistant Secretary, Department of

Home Affairs, 24 Oct. 1924; J. Stonham et al to CS (Wickens) 16 Sept. 1929, and subsequent correspondence between CS, PSB, and Home Affairs Department, AA A571, 32/2030. In the harsh economic climate of 1929-30, Wickens' advocacy on behalf of his staff, and his request for the creation of a position of Assistant Statistician fell on deaf ears.

90. CS (Wickens) to Secretary, Department of Home Affairs, 22 Jan. 1930, AA A571, 32/2030.
91. H.A. Smith, 'Report upon Scheme for Unification of Australian Statistics . . . 11 May 1923, ABS (Melbourne).
92. The conferences attended by Wickens were held in Adelaide (1924), Sydney (1925), Perth (1926), Hobart (1928), Canberra (1929), and Brisbane (1930). The agenda usually embraced population and vital statistics, finance, transport and communication, trade and commerce, local government, production, labour and industrial, with production statistics usually a major item. The 1924 conference, for example was urged by the Western Australian Statist to review various categories affected by the rapid growth of the automobile industry. 'The fact that motor chassis manufacture has not yet been undertaken Australia does not preclude the intelligent anticipation of the likelihood of such a possibility.' (Brief notes for CS [Aug. 1924], Treasury 69/1975.)
93. The Victorian deliberations are documented in ABS (Melbourne) files. The history of unification effort from 1906 was summarised in CS (Wickens) to Secretary, Department of Home Affairs, 8 Feb. 1930, AA A571, 32/2037; cf 'Uniformity in Statistics', paper for meeting of Commonwealth and State Ministers, 20 Feb. 1930, AA A571, 30/1011.
94. Wickens had speculated hopefully on 29 March 1928 that it was 'unlikely that a move will take place at midwinter'. (AA A571, 32/1587 Pt 1); for the proposed move to the Hotel Acton see ABS 30/328.
95. CS (Wickens) to C. Laverty, 23 June 1928, ABS 45/1486. The Public Service Board had decided February 1924 that machine tabulation 'is routine work and particularly suitable for the employment female officers of the Fourth Division with duties embracing coding statistical information, punchi cards according to the code, and general routine work of machine tabulation . . . in addition to economy which will be thus effected, it may be anticipated that there will be a gain in

efficiency by establishment of a nucleus of trained staff . . . (AA A571, 32/2030.)

96. CS (Wickens) to Secretary, Home and Territories Department, 29 March 1928, 8 Oct. 1929; Memoranda by Wickens 4 Nov., 2 and 7 Dec. 1929; CS (Wickens) to Minister for Home Affairs, 6 Feb. 1930; CS (Wickens) to Secretary, Department of Home Affairs, 27 June 1930, AA A571, 32/1587 Pt 1. For political background see John Robertson, J. H. Scullin, A Political Biography, Perth, 1974, chapters 11-22. For E. G. Theodore's interest in the income question and Wickens' explanation see CS (Wickens) Secretary, Department of Home Affairs, 14 March 1930; H. J. Sheehan (Assistant Secretary, Treasury to Minister for Home Affairs, 21 March 1930, AA A571, 32/2046. As the income question was recommended by the statisticians' conference in September 1929 it could not have been, as has been accepted on the authority of the Statistician's Report on the 1933 Census, 'actuated in part . . . by special interest in the effects upon the pattern of distribution produced by three years of severe depression' (Adrian, 'Trends in Social Statistics . . . p. 14; Ian McLean and Sue Richardson, 'More or Less Equal? Australian Income Distribution Since 1933', The Economic Record, vol. 62, March 1986, p. 7. On orphans and fertility see Report, Resolutions, and Agenda of the Conference of Statisticians Australia . . . Canberra, 9 to 13 September 1929, Canberra, 1929, pp.4-5; Adrian, 'Trends in Social Statistics . . . ', pp. 12-13. Occupational data are discussed in L. F. Giblin, 'The Census and Occupation Trends', G. V. Portus (ed.), What the Census Reveals, Adelaide, 1936, pp. 55-80; Roland Wilson Census of the Commonwealth wealth of Australia 30th June 1933, Statistician's Report, Canberra, 1940, chapter xxii-xxiv. Wilson does not appear to have pursued Giblin's vision of fertility and reproduction rates occupation.

97. Parkhill's Cabinet submission, 28 Jan. 1932, AA A571, 32/1587 Pt 1; Report, Resolutions, and Agenda of the Conference of Statisticians of Australia . . . Sydney, 10 to 17 August, 1932, Sydney, 1932, p.10 Acting CS (Giblin) to Secretary Treasury, 30 Sept. 1932, AA A571, 1932/1587 Pt 2. Premier of New South Wales to Prime Minister, 9 March 1932, AA A571, 32/1781; Report, Resolutions, and Agenda of the Conference of Statisticians of Australia . . . Brisbane, 22 to 27 May, 1930, Brisbane, 1930, p. 8. The Bureau's declining public commitment

to its trade union figures as an indicator of unemployment charted in Forster, 'Australian Unemployment . . . pp. 433-6. Cf. J. L. K. Gifford, Economic; Statistics for Australian Arbitration Courts, Explanation of their Uses, Criticisms of Existing Statist and Suggestions for their Improvement, Melbourne, 1928, ch. II.

98. CS (Wickens) to Secretary, Department of Home and Territories, 29 March 1928; Bean to Perkins (Treasury), 26 April 1933, AA A571, 32/1587 Pts 1-3.

99. For lobbying by the R.S.S I L. and the government's response see AA A461, L320/1/1 and M320/1/1 Preference was given to returned soldiers as sub-enumerators, and only ex-soldiers were eligible for appointment to the Canberra temporary clerical staff. The Statistician instructed the Deputy Supervisor of Census to select suitable unemployed persons as collectors. These positions were exempted by order-in-council from the returned soldiers' preference section of the Public Service Act but the Public Service Commissioners still supported the general policy of preference.

100. ABS 27/646.

101. On Wickens' health and activities in 1927-31, see ABS W165, 27/646 (trade statistics), 24/873 (world agricultural census), Royal Commission on the Constitution, Vol. 1, Minutes of Evidence, Pt III, Melbourne, 1927, pp. 378-81 29/429 (social insurance), T. H. Kewley, Social Security in Australia 1900-72, Sydney, 1974, pp. 143-54. In his first discussion on tariffs with Wickens, Giblin and Dyason, Bruce was relieved to discover 'they were equally fogged with myself as to what had actually been the effect from the economic standpoint of Australia's policy of protection', (Bruce to F. L. McDougall 29 Sept. 1927, quoted in W. H. Richmond, 'S. M. Bruce and Australian Economic Policy 1923-29 Australian Economic History Review, vol. XXIII, no. 2, Sept. 1983, p. 251).

102. CS (Wickens) to Secretary, Department of Home Affairs, 16 Dec. 1929, AA A571, 32/2030; Minister for Home Affairs to Minister for Defence, 4 Nov. 1931, AA A571, 34/2633; CPD, CXX, Senate, 20 March 1929, pp. 1495-1518; J. Buckley-Moran, 'Australian Science and Industry Between the Wars', Prometheus, vol. 5, no. 1, June 1987, pp. 12-13; Acting CS (Giblin) to Secretary, Department of Home Affairs, 24 April 1931, ABS W165; Neville Cain, 'Lyndhurst Falkiner Giblin', in Bede Nairn and Geoffrey Serle (eds), Australian

Dictionary of Biography, vol. 8: 1891-1939, CI-Gib, Melbourne, 1981, pp. 646-8.

103. Wickens to Giblin, (copy), 4 Feb. 1924, ABS 08/140; Notes on agenda, Conference of Statisticians, Perth, Aug. 1926, Treasury 69/1974; Wickens, 'Some of the Problems of Index Numbers', typescript [1929], ABS 19/2; CS (Wickens) to B. Latham (Commonwealth Bank), 18 and 28 Nov. 1930, ABS 30/1357; Neville Cain, 'The Economists and Controversy over Policy in 1930-31', Economic History Joint Seminar paper, A.N.U. 1 May 1987, pp. 5-6, 17-18.

104. Stonham to Secretary to the Treasury, 3 May 1933,(copy), ABS 57/1530. In 1930 Wickens had crossed swords publicly with Giblin over Tasmania's claim for additional financial allocations from the Commonwealth.

105. An address by Sir Roland Wilson . . . p. 3; Giblin to (E. M. Giblin), 8 Feb. 1932, L. F. Giblin MSS, NLA 366, Ser. 5,1-88-CS, (McPhee) to Secretary to the Treasury, 12 April 1933, AA A571, 33/1625. The joint Parliamentary Committee on Public Accounts had recommended in its Report on the General Question of Tasmania's Disabilities, the creation of a permanent body to study federal-state financial relations with 'a qualified economist' under the control of the Commonwealth Statistician.

106. C. B. Schedvin, Australia and the Great Depression, Sydney, 1970, ch. IV; Neville Cain, 'Economics Between the Wars: A Tall Poppy as Seedling', Australian Cultural Of History no. 3, 1984, pp. 74-86; ABS 39/1/1 and 30/1357 for the Queensland Bureau of Economics and Statistics and the Commonwealth Bank. The Queensland Bureau of Economics and Statistics was reconstituted as a Bureau of Industry in late 1932, shorn of one of its original functions of assisting the Industrial Court (B. H. Molesworth, 'The Bureau of Industry in Queensland', The Economic Record, vol. ix, no. 16, June 1933, pp. 105-8). For Development and Migration Commission and Royal Commission on National Insurance interest in unemployment, see Colin Forster, 'An Economic Consequence of Mr Justice Higgins', Australian Economic history Review, vol. XXV, no. 2, Sept. 1985, pp. 103-9.

107. Casey to Sheehan, 26 Jan. 1935, (copy), Lord Casey MSS, AA CP503/1 Bundle 3; The Argus, 26 Feb. 1936.

108. D. B. Copland. 'The Economic Society—Its Origin and Constitution', The Economic Record, vol. 1, no. 1, Nov. 1925, p. 140; Roland Wilson, 'Australian Capital Imports, 187 1-1930', ibid., vol. vii, no.12, May 1931, p. 53 fn 1; 'Australian Monetary Policy Reviewed', ibid., vol. vii, no. 13, Nov. 1931, pp. 195-215.
109. E. K. Heath and J. Polglaze, 'A Business Index for Australia', The Economic Record, vol. ix, no. 17, Dec. 1933, p. 215; F. R. E. Mauldon, The Use and Abuse of Statistics, With Special Reference to Australian Economic Statistics, Melbourne, 1933, pp. 21-2. Mauldon, by then Professor of Economics in Tasmania, was appointed Economist and Research Director in the Bureau in 1939 but left two years later. Other economists calling for new approaches to statistics included E. R. Walker and G. L. Wood. The Economic Record, vol. XII, no. 2, Dec. 1936, pp. 290-1. For contemporary developments in the United States, see Wilson Gee (ed.), Research in the Social Sciences, Its Fundamental Methods and Objectives, New York, 1929; A. Ross Eckler, The Bureau of the Census, New York, 1972; Joseph W. Duncan and William C. Shelton, Revolution in United States Government Statistics 1926-1976, U.S. Department of Commerce, Washington, 1978.
110. The Economic Record, vol. ix, no. 17, Dec. 1933, p. 297; Report, Agenda and Resolutions of the Conference of Statisticians of Australia . . . Canberra, 6 to 8 March 1935, Canberra, 1935; MePhee to H. Leak, 15 Jan. 1935, ABS 34/1195; Wilson to Secretary, Treasury, 2 April 1935, Sir Roland Wilson MSS (ABS); Interview, Sir Roland Wilson, NLA TRC 1612/1. At the 1936 statisticians' conference agreement was reached on extensive revision of the 'C' Series Index and the appointment of six field officers to collect and check retail price and rent data. (Report and Resolutions of the Conference of Statisticians of Australia . . . Canberra, 16 April to 22 April, 1936, Canberra, 1936, pp. 4-8; correspondence with Premiers June-July 1936, AA A461, C320/1/2).
111. An address by Sir Roland Wilson . . . pp. 5-6; Robert S. Parker, Public Service Recruitment in Australia, Melbourne, 1942, pp. 109-10; Wilson Interview . . . NLA TRC 1612/1. Under the previous librarian, Wilson recalled, 'if you wanted a book . . . you had to tell him what size it was, how thick, what colour the binding was, then he'd bring you three or four to pick from!'.

112. Wilson to Casey, 6 Dec. 1935, (copy); Casey to Wilson, 13 Aug. 1935, Wilson MSS (ABS). Wilson's promotion to Economic Adviser was accelerated by Casey's intervention on learning that Wilson was contemplating an invitation to become Professor of Economics at the University of Tasmania. (W. J. Hudson, Casey, Melbourne 1986, p. 99.) Schedvin
113. (Australia and the Great Depression, p. 316) dismisses Casey as energetic but uninspired in his successive Treasury positions; but see for example Casey's analysis of Australia's balance of payments position utilising Wilson's figures in a letter to S. M. Bruce, 19 Oct. 1936 (AAA1963/391/ [50]).
114. W. V. Lancaster (Treasury) to Secretary, Prime Minister's Department, 10 Feb. 1937, AA A461, B320/ 1/3. The conclusions of a secret conclave of economists and bank officials on the causes, prospects, and policies for economic recovery were conveyed by Giblin to Wilson on 14 Oct. 1935 (Wilson MSS, ABS).
115. Acting CS (Giblin) to Secretary, Department of Home Affairs, 20 Nov. 1931, (copy), Wilson MSS (ABS): Wilson, 'Price, Quantities and Values', 24 Sept. 1937, H. P. Brown MSS, 36, H. P. Brown Library, Australian National University.
116. The next general publication issued by the Bureau, the Digest of Current Economic Statistics, did not appear until 22 years later. (W.H.D. Morris, 'Australian Statistics and Commonwealth Bureau of Census and Statistics Publications', Legislative Research Service, Commonwealth Parliamentary Library, [Feb. 1970]. p. 23.)
117. Labour Report, 1943, No. 33, p. 34.
118. Roland Wilson, 'The Economic Implications of Planning', in W.G.K. Duncan (ed.), National Economic Planning, Sydney, 1934, pp. 74-5; Greg Whitwell, 'The Social Philosophy of the F & E Economists', Australian Ecomonic History Review, vol. xxv, no. 1. March 1985 pp. 2-6.
119. H.C. Coombs, Trial Balance: Issues of My Working Life, Melbourne, 1983, p. 3. Giblin had been told by Sir Otto Niemeyer of the Bank of England on 19 Oct. 1932 that 'Keynes (of all people) has recently been saying that economists are apt to reason far too much from statistics, to which they attach a degree of dogmatic verity which is hardly deserved by the closeness with which abstract and general statistics fit the varying and individual manifestations of actual

business', (Giblin MSS, NLA 366, Ser. 5, 1-88). R I. Downing saw Clark's work as part of an older tradition rather than as the precursor of the social accounts' approach. ('Current Problems of the Australian Economy', in Business and Economic Policy. Third Summer School of Business Administration 1958, University of Adelaide. Adelaide, 1958, pp.5-6.)

120. Paul Hasluck, The Government and the People 1939-1941, Canberra 1965 (1st edn. 1952), pp. 130-1.

121. Wilson, 'The Economic Implications of Planning', pp. 68-9; Wilson, A Note on Economic Policy and Organization for War, 12 Sept. 1939, AA A571, 39/3251; Hasluck, op. cit., pp. 451-3; S.J. Butlin, War Economy 1939-1942, Canberra 1961.

122. (1st edn. 1955), pp. 21-3; Rodney Maddock and Janet Penny, Economists at War: The Financial and Economic Committee 1939-44', Australian Economic History Review vol. xxiii, no. 1, March 1983, pp. 28-47.

123. R.G. Menzies to A. Mair, 21 Nov. 1940, (copy), ABS 57/1530.

124. Colin Clark to Cameron Hazlehurst, 4 Mar. 1987; Colin Clark and J.G. Crawford, The National Income of Australia, Sydney, 1938, pp. 14-18; A/g CS to Secretary, Treasury, 8 April 1942, ABS 35/5 (J.C. Stephen file). For the Bureau's collaboration with the military authorities see ABS 62/1983, 67/5938, and AA CP200, Box 3. On censorship, ABS 62/1984 reveals Carver's differences with the navy and Defence department.

125. Secretary to Treasury to Chairman, Public Service Board 24 July 1943, and reply 27 July 1943, ABS 35/5. Stephen had been flown to Britain in 1942 to study production statistics methods. (E.K. Foreman, 'State Government Statistical Requirements—Historical Perspective', typescript, 30 May 1980, ABS Library.) Another recruit in 1943 was P.H. Karmel. 'He has performed several pieces of original statistical research of a high order,' Carver told the Secretary to the Treasury on 28 Sept. 1944, 'and 24 shows real capacity for the work'. (ABS 35/S.)

126. ABS 67/5938; S.J. Butlin, War Economy 1939-1942, Canberra, 1955, p. 354. Compare U.S. experience in Aryness Joy Wickens, 'Statistics and the Public Interest', Journal of the American Statistical Association, vol 48, no. 261, March 1983, p.3.

127. H.C. Coombs, 'The Economic Aftermath of War', in D.A.S. Campbell (ed.), Post-War Reconstruction in Australia Sydney, 1944, p.85.
128. Coombs, Trial Balance, p. 51; Selwyn Cornish, Full Employment in Australia: The Genesis of a White Paper, Research Paper in Economic History, No. 1, 1981, Department of Economic History, Faculty of Economics, Australian National University, pp. 78-9; Carver to H.C. Green, 1 Nov. 1944, ABS 67/5938. On the emerging post-war agenda, see Robert Watts, The Foundations of the National Welfare State, Sydney, 1987.
129. Director-General, Post-War Reconstruction to A/g CS (Carver), 30 Oct. 1945; 31 Oct., 5/6, 7 Nov. 1945, ABS 53/682.
130. A/g CS (Carver), to Secretary, Treasury, 5 Dec. 1945, ABS 45/79; Report and Resolutions of the Thirteenth Conference of Statisticians of Australia . . . 19 November to 23 November, 1945, Canberra, 1945, pp. 11-12, 4; Report and Resolutions of the Fifteenth Conference of Statisticians . . . 31 October to 4 November, 1949, Canberra, 1949, p. 2. The importance of professional judgment in forecasting was implicitly acknowledged in a report by the Department of Post-War Reconstruction for the I.L.O. in 1948: 'The general method is to study critically the trend in individual statistical series and to use general impressions combined with historical precedents in order to assess the imminence of any downward tendency in effective demand'. (United Nations, Department of Economic Affairs, The Maintenance of Full Employment . . . U.N., New York, 1949, Appendix: No. 3 Reply from Australia, p 77.)
131. ABS 53/682 covers public finance correspondence and reports 1946 to 1956. On the 1954-55 roads expenditure Solomon revealed 'an error of £10,000,000' in the old system figures.
132. Prime Minister to Premier, N.S.W., 21 Nov. 1940, (copy), ABS 57/1 530.
133. Prime Minister to Premier, N.S.W., 2 Feb. 1948, 27 June 1949; Premier, N.S.W. to Prime Minister, 13 Feb. 1948, 15 July 1949, (copies), ABS 57/1530.
134. Secretary, Treasury to Treasurer, 20 July 1951, (copy), ABS 57/1530. Curiously, Carver's appointment did not make him either an officer of the Public Service or of the Parliament. (Minute by R. Whalen, 15 Aug. 1958, ABS 57/1530.) Early in 1971 it was realised that there was

no legislative basis on which an 'Acting Commonwealth Statistician' could be appointed when the office of Commonwealth Statistician was vacant. Carver therefore could not validly have been 'Acting Commonwealth Statistician' between 1951 and 1957 although he was properly empowered to perform the duties of the Statistician. The similar situation which occurred after Archer's retirement was expounded in a memorandum from E. Smith (Attorney-General's Department) to Secretary, Treasury, 25 Feb. 1971, ABS 57/1530.

135. P.C. Spender. 'Proposed Census of 1941', Cabinet Paper, 11 April 1940, AA A461, N 320/1/1; 'Proposals for Effecting Economic Operation Bureau Section 1939-45 War', ABS 62/1982; Clark to Carver 14 May 1945: Carver to Clark

18 May 1945; Director-General, Post War Reconstruction to Minister, 19 Oct. 1945; A/g CS (Carver) to A.P. Elkin, 11 Dec. 1945, ABS 45/79. The refusal of rationing authorities to withhold ration books from applicants who failed to produce occupational survey cards had undermined the comprehensiveness of the occupational survey. (ABS CR8.)

136. For details of the professional discussions on the 1947 Census, including the decision to drop questions on 'sickness or infirmity' and 'education' see ABS (Treasury) 62/2055, 60/1404, and J.B. Chifley, 'Proposed Census 1947', draft Cabinet submission, 1 Feb. 1946, ABS 45/79. Cabinet rejected the option of deleting all specified categories of census questions from the Act and providing that the contents of the census schedule should be prescribed by regulation. This approach was eventually adopted in 1979. For R.S.L. urging of a census of 'alien immigrants' and queries from the Jewish Council to Combat Fascism and Anti-Semitism about the concept of 'race' embodied in the census schedule see AA A461, p 320/1/1.

137. CS (Wilson) to Treasurer, 21 June 1950, ABS (Treasury) 62/2055.

138. CS (Carver) to Secretary, Treasury enclosing 'Date of Next Census', draft Cabinet submission, 20 April 1959, ABS 59/694. With Treasurer Harold Holt's encouragement the Bureau successfully resisted Cabinet pressure to bring forward the 1961 Census so as to facilitate an electoral redistribution before the next Commonwealth election. (J.F. Nimmo to Secretary, Treasury and CS, 28 May 1959, ABS 59/694.) For 1970s see Brian Doyle, 'The Politics of Census Taking', Working Paper No. C2, 1981 Census of Population and Housing,

Development Programme, ABS, Canberra, [1979]. By 1973 senior Bureau officers were unconvinced about legislating for quinquennial censuses. 'I wonder about the wisdom of quinquennial Censuses or even the necessity. The decision to do the 1966 one related to Commonwealth Grants & Queensland's population. Our part in the Grants is peculiar. I would rather use the resources on filling up some gaps.' (Minute by C.S. [O'Neill] on K.S. Watson to J.G. Miller, 9 Jan. 1973, ABS 70/2447.)

139. Memorandum for Secretary, Treasury: draft amendments, Cabinet submission, and associated documents, May-June 1949, ABS (Treasury) 60/1404; S. Horn to D. Trewin, 'History of Legislation', 7 Nov. 1983, ABS. Horn noted that the considerable importance which the changes represented in 'balance of authority' for collecting statistics was 'downplayed in favour of efficiency arguments' in the Cabinet submission. The extension of confidentiality to voluntary returns was made discretionary thirty years later.

140. Michael Howard, The Growth in the Domestic Economic and Social Role of the Commonwealth Government in Australia, from the late 1930s to the early Post-war Period: Some Aspects, Ph. D. thesis, University of Sydney, 1978. Sir Claus Moser, former head of the British Government Statistical Service, noted a hardening of boundaries between economists and statisticians in the mid-1950s. ('Statistics and Public Policy', Journal of the Royal Statistical Society, A, vol. 143, 1980, Pt 1, p. 23; cf R. Petridis, 'Australia: Economists in a federal system', in W.A. Coats (ed.), Economists in Government: An international comparative study, Durham, N.C., 1981, pp. 71-3); Greg Whitwell, The Treasury Line, Sydney, 1986, ch. 1.

141. Foreman, 'State Government Statistical Requirements Carver to A.J. Reid, 10 Sept. 1953, (copy), Sir Stanley Carver MSS, ABS; Archer interview, NLA TRC 12/38.

142. Brown to Carver, Feb. 1950, Brown MSS, 49; Brown was appointed Reader in Economic Statistics at the Australian National University in 1950 and published his criticisms in 'Australian Statistics-A Programme', Institute of Public Affairs Review, May-June 1952, pp. 90-6. E.K. Foreman, 'Development and Co-ordination Division—Historical Note,' 31 March 1977, ABS Library, is a valuable chronicle. Cf K.A. Archer interview, NLA TRC 12/38; Dr F. B. Homer interview, NLA TRC 1594/1; J.P. O'Neill interview, NLA TRC 1613/1; B.D. Haig

and S.S. MeBurney, The Interpretation of National Income Estimates, Canberra, 1968. On the census of retail establishments see 'Census of Distribution in Australia', Papers Presented at the Conference of British Commonwealth Statisticians 1951 . . . Canberra, [1951]. pp. 111-13. On challenges to legality of sampling, see 'Proposals for Revision of the Census and Statistics Act'. March 1967, ABS 64/1537; Secretary, Attorney-General's Department (K.H. Bailey), memorandum for A/g CS, 8 Oct. 1954, ABS 70/2447. Nearly two years after a Bureau officer had first raised the matter, a judge of the N.S.W. Supreme Court, whose Wahroonga home was in the sample for the quarterly population survey in May 1964, prompted urgent review (and an amendment to the Census and Statistics Act) by advising a senior compiler that in his opinion the act did not authorise the 'statistician to obtain information by interview at private dwellings. (Dep. CS [N.S.W.] to CS, 21 May 1964. and minute, O'Neill to AW. Mumme 27 May 1964, ABS 64/1537; Mumme to I.G. Jones 21 Nov. 1963 and minute 12 June 1962. ABS 70/2447.)

143. Archer interview, NLA TRC 12/38; unsigned and undated memorandum, [April 1969], ABS 71/3155 Pt 1 The Dominion Bureau of Statistics in Canada had an IBM 705 Model III operational from 1961. The U.S. Bureau of the Census had UNIVAC 1 in service in 1951 but card-to-tape converters were not satisfactory until 1953, and a 'high speed' printer (120 character lines at 600 lines per minute) was not available until 1955. (Marjorie Tucker, 'Recent Developments in the Work of the Dominion Bureau of Statistics Canadian Journal of Economics and Political Science, vol. xxv, no. 4, Nov. 1959, p. 501;) Duncan and Shelton, Revolution in United States Government Statistics . . . , pp. 126-8.) Between 1964 and 1971 a network of eleven medium to large scale and four small scale computers costing $12m had placed the Bureau's mechanical tabulation equipment and associated electronic calculators. Over 800 staff were employed in a computer service centre. (F.N. Bennett, 'Computers and the User of Australian Economic Statistics', paper presented to Section 24, ANZAAS Congress, May 1971; 'Automating Australian Statistics', symposium paper, Statistical Society of Australia, N.S.W. Branch, 24/25 Aug. 1972.)

144. A.W. Mumme, 'A Case for Functional Specialisation in the Bureau of Census and Statistics', Nov. 1970; P.A.A Kaufmann, 'Towards

a Socio-Demographic Statistics Organisation', 1 Feb. 1972, ABS Library.

145. Extended scope of duties is outlined in a series of submissions to the Public Service Board in 1974 (ABS, Adelaide Z/402/2 Pt III).
146. A/g CS (O'Neill), 'Work Programme and Staff Requirements 1970-72', 9 June 1970, ABS 70/2080; B.D Haig, 'Indexes of Australian Factory Production, 1949-50 to 1962-63', The Economic Record, vol. 41 no. 95, Sept. 1965, pp. 451-2.
147. Premier, Queensland (Gair) to Prime Minister (Menzies), 16 Dec. 1953; Treasurer (A.W. Fadden), Note for file, 16 Sept. 1957, AA A571, 61/1058.
148. Carver to Wallace Wurth, 6 Aug. 1954; to A.W. Bowden, 10 Aug. 1954; to F.W. Sayer 15 Sept. 1954; to L. L. Chapman, 6 Oct 1954; to SA. Taylor, 20 Jan. 1955, to Wurth, 22 Feb. 1955, Carver MSS, ABS.
149. Fadden Statistics (Arrangements with States) Bill', Cabinet submission, annexure A, 1 Feb. 1956, AA A571, 563/2351 Pt I.
150. AA A571 53/2351.
151. A/g CS (Carver) to Secretary, Treasury, 25 March 1954, ABS 57/1530.

Related links Back to top

Main Features Time Series Spreadsheets Catalogue Companion Data

Australia Now Publications Media Releases 2001 Census Data

Data Sources Statistical Concepts Library Other Related Articles

Australian Statisticians and the development of official statistics

(Year Book Australia, 1988)

Article reproduced from Year Book Australia, 1988 (ABS Catalogue No. 1301.0) Written by Colin Forster and Cameron Hazlehurst.

Contents

PART I: IMPERIAL STATISTICS 1788-1855

THE EARLY YEARS 1788-1822

Arthur Phillip was the first Australian statistician. In 1787 he was appointed Captain-General and Governor-in-Chief of New South Wales and its dependencies with the widest powers: powers necessary to transport a fleet of convicts and establish and maintain a settlement far beyond immediate supervision from London. With this freedom of action however went accountability. The settlement was seen as an economic means of disposing of felons, but only time and comprehensive accounting records would show whether the experiment was a success. More than economics was involved, with the British authorities requiring reports on social and legal matters. Accountability is implicit throughout the Instructions given to Phillip in April 1787, and this involved the collecting and collating of information in numerical form. Some tasks were specified. He was required to issue tools and utensils and use every proper degree of economy, and be careful that the Commissary so transmits an account of the issues from time to time to the Commissioners of our Treasury, to enable them to judge of the propriety or expediency of granting further supplies. The clothing of the convicts and the provisions issued to them, and the civil and military establishments, must be accounted for in the same manner. 1.

To the appropriate Secretary of State had to go 'an account of the numbers inhabiting the neighbourhood of the intended settlement'. Land grants could be made to emancipated convicts, in which case 'you will cause copies of such grants as may to passed to be preserved, and make a regular return of the said grants', not only to Treasury but also to the Committee for Trade and Plantations.

The type of statistical material produced by Phillip can be seen in his early reports on 9 July 1788 in his fourth dispatch to Lord Sydney at the Home Office, Phillip included, along with an account of population numbers, tables relating to livestock in the settlement, to a general return on the four companies of marines and to a return on the sick and the dead since the landing. The following day, reporting to the Admiralty, he referred to the inclusion with his dispatch of 'the weekly accounts'. On

28 September a Commissariat return was sent to the Home Office on the state of stores and the number of persons being victualled at Sydney and Norfolk Island. A detailed return of the whole population was included in Phillip's dispatch dated

25 July 1790; it was signed by the Commissary and numbered the population in categories of men, women and children classified as military, civil or convict. Phillip's first return with details of land grants was dated 5 November 1791; it listed the names of 87 settlers who had been granted land in New South Wales and Norfolk Island with details of their status, marital situation, date of settling, size and location of grant and area in actual cultivation.8 The following year on 16 October the return was able to indicate what crops were being grown on the cleared ground.

On Phillip's departure in December 1792, Lieutenant-Governor Grose administered the settlement, and he was informed on 15 November 1793 that his duties included 'a yearly return . . . signed by the Governor of the settlement . . . of all births and deaths within the settlement'. Grose was also reminded of the detail reacquired in the Commissariat returns:

A like return should be transmitted of all provisions, clothing, and stores, annually received for the use of the settlement . . . [and] returns of their distribution, under separate heads, of clothing, stores, and provisions. The distribution of the provisions should appear in a victualling-book, which should be kept by the Commissary, in like manner as is usual with pursers in the Navy, bearing the persons on separate lists, where their rations differ, the title of each list expressing the ration; and the ready-made clothing should be distributed in the manner above mentioned; and a regular account, both as to the time and the numbers, mentioning their names to whom it is distributed, should appear in a yearly return of clothing.

In the years that followed, a flow of statistics was sent from New South Wales to Britain, while for their part the British colonial authorities, with varying success, ordered more types of information, more accurate information and more regular information. The Governors not only had the duty of reporting on the state of the colony, they had actually to administer the colony: a colony established as a large gaol in a wilderness, which grew rapidly and in which free settlement soon became important. For their own use the Governors required detailed information, and the very nature of the colony, the fact that it was under firm government control, meant that from its beginning the statistics created were basically official statistics. Four areas of statistics are now considered.

Population

A gaol requires the careful counting and identification of prisoners. This requirement was reinforced in New South Wales because prisoners were not only the workforce of the settlement but had to be supplied from the public stores, which themselves were wholly imported and were at critically low levels in the first years of settlement. Phillip's first report on population was in his dispatch of 9 July 1788:

Of the convicts, 36 men and 4 women died on the passage, 20 men and 8 women since landing—eleven men and one woman absconded; four have been executed, and three killed by the natives. The number of convicts now employed in erecting the necessary buildings and cultivating the lands only amounts to 320—and the whole number of people victualled amounts to 966—consequently we have only the labour of a part to provide for the whole.

Convicts then were constantly being counted and often as part of the total population. These counts took the form of 'musters', actual assemblies of the population, which were commonly supervised by the Governor or his deputy. Records of population musters exist for almost every year between

1790 and 1825. The method of mustering took many forms and was clearly much easier to organise when the population was small, wholly dependent on government stores and the area of settlement was limited. An early form of general muster is suggested by an order of 23 September 1795:

"A General Muster will be held on Saturday next, the 26th instant, at Sydney; on Thursday, the 1st of October, at Parramatta and Toongabbic; and on Saturday, the 3rd of October, at the settlement at the Hawkesbury,—at which places the Commissary will attend for the purpose of obtaining a correct account of the numbers and distribution of all persons (the military excepted) in the different aforementioned settlements, whether victualled or not victualled from the public stores.

With the order went the threat that those who failed to attend would 'be either confined to the cells, put to hard labour, or corporally punished'.

For administrative convenience this muster took place over several days, but Governor Hunter ordered a simultaneous muster because the previous method

" . . . gave good time for impostors and other villains to practise their tricks and ingenuity by answering the first call at Sydney, where they have received provisions and slops as one resident in that district; on the day of call at Parramatta they have appeared there, have been entered in the muster list of that place, and have been again victualled and sometimes clothed; the attempt has sometimes been made (and not always unsuccessfully) at the third muster.

And in December 1796 in order to protect property when the population assembled at a muster, Hunter found it necessary to order that servants and labourers assemble one day and settlers the next.16 In 1801 Governor King summed up what he thought an unsatisfactory situation:

I have used every means to ascertain the numbers of every description of persons in the colony, which has not been done without much difficulty, owing to the scattered state they were in, the numbers who had obtained false certificates of their times being expired, and their being no general list whatever of the inhabitants.

By 1809 the muster extended over a fortnight with different classes of people assigned different muster days.18 By 1812 the period of muster had extended to almost one month19, and in 1819 it took from 27 September to 12 November 20. In 1820 expansion of settlement necessitated new methods: three new muster centres were added to the existing four and supervision was conducted by magistrates rather than the Governor and the Deputy Commissary-General.21 In 1823 there were sixteen muster-stations22 and 1825, twenty.23 The accuracy of the picture of the population presented by the musters must vary between individual years, but in general they appear to be in significant error. The change to the counting by magistrates in 1820 was a failure. Governor Macquarie found the returns so inaccurate that he felt unable to send them to England24, and even a second attempt by the magistrates was no more satisfactory.25 As a result, in 1821, Macquarie reverted to his method of personal supervision of the muster. Not that his method would guarantee satisfactory results: In 1823 and 1825 the official Population figures of 29,692 and 38,217 were made up partly from those who actually attended the musters, but also from an estimated 4,853 in 1823 and 5,203 in 1825 who were 'unaccounted for'.

The Commissariat

The key economic institution in the settlement was the Commissariat. It was established to provide the supply of stores for the penal colony. From the beginning the task was a demanding one. In 1796 Commissary Palmer complained that he had been required to keep accounts in the same manner as the 'purser of a man-of-war',

. But when the numbers to be accounted for are from three to four thousand persons, the books then required to be kept become very extensive, particularly those of the slop and victualling accounts.

Moreover, he went on, his duties were more than those of a purser since he was

Obliged to keep a particular account of all kinds of stores received and expended in the colony, and to transmit accounts of all ordnance, naval, victualling, and hospital stores, that may be received and issued to the different Boards.

And he foresaw great difficulties as both the numbers in the colony and the area of settlement expanded.

Already, by 1796, the Commissariat had expanded beyond its original purpose of a store of issue. It developed as the main market for local produce and the main retail outlet for supplies. Goods were sometimes bartered, but were more often sold on cash or credit. It was the most important source of foreign currency for the colony. It has been called 'Australia's first bank'. 29 The activities of the Commissariat were under the control of the Governors until 1813. Concern over misconduct in its administration then led to it being made directly responsible to the office of the Commissary General in London, itself a sub-department of the Treasury.

The activities of this institution were central to the functioning of the colony's economy for at least the first thirty or forty years. Its accounts and reports are the main source of economic statistics. These records would arise naturally in the circumstances of the operation of the business, but their extent, form and regularity of appearance were strongly influenced by a stream of complaints and instructions from London. The early Governors' dispatches regularly included such information as the stock of stores, rate of consumption, numbers and quantity of rations of those victualled at the store. The quarterly returns by the Commissariat of its accounts to the Treasury for auditing have been preserved.

Vital Statistics

Governors were required to report annually on the numbers of births and deaths. these reports, however, although headed births and deaths, record only some baptisms and burials. The position was summed up by the surgeon responsible for the returns in 1801:

The state of births and deaths in this report is accurate as far as comes within our knowledge, but people die and children are born without our being made acquainted herewith.

The various authorities debuted to record vital statistics—clergy, surgeons and magistrates—don't appear to have taken their duties very seriously, and difficulties became more pronounced as settlement spread. Moreover, the absence of Roman Catholic clergy until 1820 (except for 1803-08) seems to have meant the virtual exclusion of members of this sect from the returns. Indeed official figures for Roman Catholics do not appear until 1831.

Agricultural Statistics

Providing statistics of stock owned by the government in the early years of settlement was relatively straightforward. As agriculture expanded and increasingly was conducted in private hands, the collection of accurate statistics became much more difficult. One early method required military officers to put in a return on their own agricultural activities and constables to collect the information from settlers. Later, and more systematically, the collection of agricultural information was combined with the population musters. For example, a return in 1800 based on musters of 18 July and 15 August gave numbers for sheep, cattle, horses, goats, hogs, and acres in wheat and acres of maize to be planted, according to ownership by government or individuals.

This discussion of types of statistics transmitted to Britain is not meant to be exhaustive. Returns on other areas such as customs revenue and land grants were also made. It is obvious that the reliability of the statistics varied greatly, as did the punctuality and regularity of their appearance; for instance, in 1821 the Colonial Office drew Macquarie's attention to the fact that there had been no land grant returns since 1812. All these statistical reports may be regarded as official, but the relationship between the colonial and the British authorities meant that they were of the nature of documents reporting and accounting within government departments. Although the contents of some would find occasional publication in a British parliamentary paper, they were never published on any regular basis.

There has been no discussion so far of the colony in Van Dieman's Land. Obviously it has its own story, but in terms of the nature, problems and significance of official statistics, it is broadly similar to that of New South Wales. After 1822 and to 1855 this type of statistical reporting by New South Wales and Van Dieman's Land continued, and they were joined by other Australian colonies, Western Australia, South Australia and Victoria, as they were established. Although these returns continued, their importance in representing Australian official statistics was greatly diminished when they were largely incorporated in a single, annual volume.

THE BLUE BOOKS 1822-1855

The mainstream of official statistics in Australia begins with the Blue Books, the annual statistical returns of the Australian colonies to the Colonial Office. When self-government was obtained in 1855, the Blue Books were transformed into the Statistical Registers of the second half of the nineteenth century. Blue Books were not limited to Australia: all British colonies had to make the same type of statistical returns. Their emergence reflected the new imperial situation following the loss of the American colonies and the end of the Napoleonic wars.

In 1788 colonial affairs centred in the hands of the Home Office, but were administered simply as part of the general business of that department. Moreover, other departments such as Treasury, Admiralty, Ordnance and Customs had their own officials in the colonies that were responsible directly to them. A significant change took place in 1801 when colonial administration was turned over to the recently created office of Secretary of State for War. War precluded much attention being given to the colonies, until the appointment of Lord Bathurst in 1812 heralded a sustained period of reorganisation. Continuity in the office was maintained, since Bathurst retained his post until 1827 and his Under-Secretary, Goulburn, stayed with him until 1822. Their achievements have been highly rated:

[They] unquestionably created a Colonial Office where none existed before, and in so doing they performed a task, which was essential if the British Empire was to survive. To build central machinery, which could furnish information for the ministry and parliament on colonial affairs, was the first step toward the reorganisation of the empire in the nineteenth century.

The continuing war probably delayed Bathurst from giving his full attention to the colonies until 1815, when the long-run overhaul of colonial administration began. Legal, economic, financial, social, military matters, all needed revision. Central to change and to efficient administration was the systematic gathering of information. Initially, the Blue Books were seen by Bathurst as supplying the financial data.

He first introduced the preparation of what were called the 'Blue Books', which name is now even adopted in Parliamentary documents; and when in my evidence before the Canada Committee in 1828 I stated my opinion 'that it was expedient that the most unqualified publicity should be given both in the Colonies and the mother country to all pecuniary accounts, appropriations and matters of finance,' I only stated the opinion which had led to the adoption of this Blue Book system, which system as far as I have been able to ascertain, has been approved by the most rigid economists.

The origin of the term 'Blue Book' appears to lie simply in the colour of the report cover. It was sufficiently institutionalised by 1829, that when, in a dispatch Governor Darling referred to the 'Crown Book' Under-Secretary Hay replied that this had been noticed by the Secretary of State, and that 'I am directed to acquaint you that the original name given to this compilation, that of the "Blue Book", is preferred'. An early reference to the term was in 1817 when returns were made to a House of Commons Select Committee on Finances. The Committee had requested information from the responsible government departments concerning office holders in the colonies: office, possession or reversion, salary, name and date of appointment. Some departments were unable to provide this information in full. In its reply the Colonial Office named only fourteen officers in New South Wales (headed by the Governor) and four in Van Dieman's Land. It was probably this request from the Finance Committee, which brought home to the Colonial Office its lack of information. In the same month it dispatched to the colonies forms, which were to be filled in by all office-holders, and collected by the Governor.

The annual system of reporting by Blue Book was initiated with its dispatch from London in March 1822 to the Governors of the colonies. It was accompanied by a circular from Bathurst, which began with a formal explanation:

I have had occasion to remark that a want of a regular form of transmission of detailed information respecting the financial resources of His Majesty's Colonies, and the several branches of their expenditure, is a deficiency, which creates much inconvenience to the public Service.

Bathurst went on to list the five main divisions of the book and to discuss the sort of information required. The topics reflected British preoccupation with the cost of the colonies: 'Abstract of the Net Revenue and Expenditure'; 'Schedule of Taxes, Duties, etc.'; 'Military Expenditure'; 'Establishment'; and 'Schedule of the Fees, etc.' The Governors were informed that in future the books should be returned 'as soon as possible to this department after the close of every year'. Further, more general, information was required in a circular of April 1823, relating to 'Population' 'Exports and Imports' and 'Currency'. In the event, the first Blue Book for New South Wales was completed for the year 1822.

The table of contents of the first Blue Book consisted of the eight subjects listed above and at the bottom of this page was printed 'This Book and the Duplicate of it must be returned to the Colonial Office'. The inside pages had printed headings indicating in more detail what contents were required; the entries made in New South Wales were entirely hand-written. In length it was made up of 77 folios, not all of them with entries, with almost a half being given over to 'Establishment'; details were there required relating to each office holder, beginning with the Governor. The importance of the West Indian Colonies at this time is suggested by the population section, which has headings referring to 'Free Blacks' and 'Slaves'. In New South Wales these pages were ignored and there are later entries for the civil and military populations.

The birth of the Blue Book in New South Wales was difficult. Governor Brisbane was unable to complete a return for 1821, and in May 1823 was sent a reproof from the Colonial Office urging him to 'lose no time' sending a return for 1822[42], for which fresh forms were enclosed. The timing was already late for 1822, because, as the Colonial Office later admitted, 'unfortunately, in consequence of accident, [they] were not sent to you as soon as to the other Colonies'. In January 1824 Brisbane could reply only with a summary statement of finance, pleading that this 'altogether new' form of presentation of information was 'attended with so much labour'.

He was not able to dispatch the 1822 Blue Book until March 1825. He believed it 'to be as accurate as the time and the nature of so complicated an undertaking will admit of, for a first attempt'. For its part, the Colonial Office had continued to be laggardly: it did not send the 1823 Book to New South Wales until April 1824.

There was no Book from New South Wales for 1824. After 1824 this annual report was always presented, but delays, recriminations and explanations continued. In June 1828 the Secretary of State wrote firmly to Governor Darling:

It is impossible for me to imagine why so little care seems hitherto to have been taken to send home the Blue Book regularly and in due time . . . I anxiously hope that you will not render it necessary for me to remind you again of His Majesty's Pleasure upon this subject.

He went on to order that the New South Wales Colonial Secretary should take responsibility for the Blue Book. The Colonial Secretary's problem, apart from overwork, was that of obtaining satisfactory accounts on time from the various officers responsible. For the past three years, although the Blue Book was compiled in his office, 'I did not consider that I was answerable for the financial Statements which it contained, any further than as to the correctness of the transcription'. Now that he was to be held personally responsible for their 'correctness', an immense amount of work was involved to 'put them into an intelligible form'. As a result, and because the 1828 Blue Book had to be printed, he could send only one incomplete copy in July 1829.

The complete book was dispatched ultimately in October, and on the last page the Colonial Secretary cautiously wrote:

I certify that this Book has been compiled under my immediate inspection, and that the several Statements and returns contained in it are as accurate as the means in my power have enabled me to make them.

Delays continued, the 1829 Blue Book was not sent from New South Wales until February 1831. Again the Colonial Office had been late in sending the blank Book; again there was pressure of work on the Colonial Secretary; but on this occasion he also pointed out:

That the printed Books, which are sent to us to be filled up, are, in most of the Forms, not applicable to this Colony, and that our Returns must therefore be less perfect than they otherwise would have been.

1833 brought copies of two circulars dispatched on the same date from the Colonial Office. One was a reminder of an increasing need for punctuality because of parliamentary interest; the other more positively made a contribution to punctuality since it was accompanied by six blank copies of Blue Books as a contingency reserve.52 However, in March 1840 the Colonial Office had still not received the 1838 Blue Book and the Secretary of State firmly reminded Governor Gipps of 'Chapter 5 of the Printed Book of Regulations, Page 51' which forbade him to pay 'the first Quarter of the year's Salary to the Colonial Secretary unless he shall have delivered the Blue Book for the previous year to the Governor for transmission to this Office'.53 The Governor responded promptly but shifted the blame from the Colonial Secretary:

. . . Finding every exertion which I have hitherto used ineffectual to expedite returns from the different Heads of Departments, which are required for the compilation of this Book, I have this day given an order that no salary shall be issued to any person whom so ever, from whom returns for the Blue Book may be due on the 1st of March in every year.

In January 1841, Lord Russell heartily commended Gipps' action, but several months later came the order that the Colonial Secretary should not escape the penalty if he was laggardly; it other public officers had not punctually submitted their returns then the Colonial Secretary, as a stopgap, should submit an incomplete Blue Book on time. Punctuality was now even more pressing because henceforth the Blue Book and the

Governor's Annual Report accompanying it were to be submitted together to Parliament. To assist in meeting this timetable the accounting period was changed from the calendar year to the year ending 30 September, and a tight schedule was imposed on Governors to transmit the Blue Book by 30 November.

The Annual Report now put the Governor in the firing line. He was strongly reprimanded for not sending a report for 1839.58 His 1840 report was 'not' of the character required:

The Report now before me describes merely the political and judicial constitution of the Colony, whereas it was the object of the instruction to produce a review, retrospective and prospective, of the state and condition of the Colony, under each of the heads into which the Blue Book is divided.

Gipps may have drawn some solace from a significant rider to this criticism: 'At the same time, I have pleasure in acknowledging the very satisfactory manner in which the Blue Book itself is prepared'. What the Colonial Office required in the Annual Report involved the presentation of a variety of statistical information, and a later Secretary of State (Earl Grey) was to refer to it as 'the Statistical report on the State of the Colony'.

The change to the year ending 30 September was short-lived. Governors complained of difficulties and strict comparability with earlier returns was lost. From 1844 the calendar year was again used and three months grace was allowed for preparation and dispatch. This appears to have begun a period when the New South Wales returns were regarded as satisfactory. The fact that they were not dispatched until May rather than by 31 March was accepted apparently without comment by the Colonial Office.

New South Wales Blue Book: Size, Scope, Distribution and Accuracy

The changing size and composition of the New South Wales Blue Book between 1822 and 1855 reflects the increasing size and complexity of the New South Wales Government and economy, the changing British interest in New South Wales, and the production of statistics in response to local developments as well as British needs.

The 1822 Book consisted of 154 pages; it was 218 pages in 1830, 410 in 1840 and 803 in 1850. The inclusion of the census in the 1856 volume raised it to its peak of 1,020 pages.

The instruction for the contents of the 1821 Blue Book referred only to the establishment and to government financial matters. A broader coverage was indicated for 1822 with the addition of the topics of population, trade and currency. The 1825 Book had an appendix written in with results of the 1825 muster and some miscellaneous statistics.

In 1828 a wider range of subject matter was introduced into the Blue Book. Additional topics added to the printed table of contents, on which reports were required, included: Education; Agriculture; Manufactures; Mines and Fisheries; Grants of Land; and Gaols and Prisoners. These changes appear to stem from a new emphasis being given to the purpose of the compilation. In late 1828, the Secretary for State sent a circular to all Governors in which he made a very good case for the annual production of a wide range of official statistics. After referring to the importance of the Blue Book, he stated that an 'additional measure' would be for Governors to use their annual address to the legislature as a fit occasion for exhibiting in detail a view of the existing state of the Colony, and of exhibiting in a clear and methodical form such statistical information as is most important to a correct understanding of its past progress and future prospects.

To this end he suggested a number of topics on which information should be gathered. The statement would then 'lead the mind of the governor himself to an exact scrutiny into all those circumstances which most affect the welfare' of his settlement. For the Colonial Office, knowledge of this material would permit 'good government', because 'an exact summary of facts with a careful though brief enquiry into their causes and probable results will supply a deficiency which is daily felt'. In 1836 a printed abstract of the 1836 census was included. What might be regarded, as the first move towards the format of the Statistical Register was the inclusion in the 1841 Blue Book of a section headed 'Printed returns' (pp. 384-395) which presented economic and demographic statistics over a period, often from the 1820s, to 1840. In 1843 this became a section of 13 pages headed 'New South Wales: Statistical Returns: From 1822 to 1842', and it was in fact a paper printed for the Legislative Council. These returns, normally covering ten years were included in each subsequent Blue Book, and by 1855 had reached 44 pages. They normally arose from annual figures entered in earlier Blue Books. Other printed matter entered the Blue Book: returns of New South Wales banks, exports and imports; in 1855 the large section relating to Taxes, Fees, avenue and Expenditure was mainly printed. It should be emphasised that overwhelmingly the largest section of the Blue Book remained the civil establishment, which in 1851, for example, made up 274 pages, almost one-third of the total.

The Blue Book began, and essentially remained, a hand-written document. Initially the Colonial office appears to have envisaged a production run of two. On the cover of the New South Wales hook for 1822 was printed: 'This Book and the Duplicate of it must be returned to the colonial Office'. But another copy was made and retained by the Governor. Following representation from colonial legislatures the Secretary for the Colonies agreed they should retain a copy. In the case of New South Wales he instructed Governor Bourke in January 1837 to lay [a copy] annually before the Legislative Council . . . It is highly proper that the Council should have access to these Returns, and the knowledge that they will be subjected to the scrutiny of that Body will serve as an additional motive to correctness, to those officers in the various Departments, to whom you must look for the details of which the Blue Book is composed.

At the bottom of the contents page of the 1836 Book was the additional statement: 'Triplicate to be retained for the Governor's information'. And added to this distribution in 1839 was: 'One for the Council, and the other for the Assembly'. An exception to the usual hand-written Book was the 1828 production. The Colonial Office wanted 30 printed copies to be prepared in New South Wales for a Parliamentary Committee. Printing posed problems and these were advanced by the Colonial Secretary as one reason for the lateness of the return:

I shall only observe on this subject that those, who have experienced the expedition with which such things are done in London, can form no idea of the difficulty of getting any printing containing what is called Ruled-work, or any thing out of the common way done in this Colony.

New South Wales had considerable difficulty in arranging its financial accounts in the manner required for the Blue Book. This reflects both the casual accounting, which existed, and the lack of trained and experienced officials to introduce and operate the new system. Specific areas like the Commissariat and customs required overhaul. But pressure from Britain, auditing requirements and the growth of experience meant that by the beginning of the 1830s the accounts appear to have been in reasonable shape. Giving evidence to a Select Committee on Colonial Accounts in 1837, G. R. Porter, head of the newly-formed Statistical Department of the Board of Trade, said of the Blue Books in general: 'at first they were found to be exceedingly inaccurate, but later he emphasised 'great and progressive improvement' especially over the last two or three years. Among the returns, which were 'very good', he included those of New South Wales and Van Dieman's Land.

In two areas the New South Wales returns were admitted to be in significant error. One was vital statistics where no attempt for complete coverage was made until the middle 1850s. The other was agriculture. There are numerous warnings as to the usefulness of the agricultural statistics; a very strong assessment was made as late as 1859:

It is much to be regretted that information of so much importance . . . should be left to the casual and unchecked collection of the constabulary . . . It would be a mere waste of time to enter upon an analysis of figures in which no one believes.

<u>Blue Book: Other Colonies</u>

Van Dieman's Land produced its first Book for 1822, the same year as New South Wales, and maintained annual delivery without a break. Two other colonies began completing their Books once they had overcome early settlement problems. Western Australia began in 1834 and South Australia in 1840. Victoria began in 1851, immediately after separation from New South Wales. As with New South Wales, these Blue Books reflected growing local concern with statistics, and small volumes of official statistical returns began to appear semi-independently of the Blue Book themselves. Possibly the earliest such volume was in Van Dieman's Land. In response to a request from Governor Arthur for a statistical coverage of his period of office, the Colonial Secretary produced the Statistical Return of Van Dieman's Land for the Years 1824 to 1835. It contained forty-six tables.

CENSUSES

New South Wales

The first formal census of the modern type in Australia was held in New South Wales in 1828. It had been recognised that the previous proclamations by the Governor calling free citizens to muster had no legal force, and this census was authorised by Act of the New South Wales Legislative Council (9 Geo. IV, No. 4) dated 30 June 1828. It was described as 'An Act for ascertaining the number, names, and conditions of the Inhabitants of the Colony of New South Wales; and the number of Cattle; and the quantities of located, cleared, and cultivated Land within the said Colony'. In framing their first census New South Wales administrators were of course aware of the English model of 1821, but in fact they appear to have been more influenced by Australian conditions and to have followed in the tradition of the musters. Information was obtained for New South Wales relating to age, sex, occupation and religion and for housing in Sydney. Details of 'class' were also required.

The Column for the 'Class' is to be filled up with one of the following Abbreviations, according to the Circumstances, viz., B.C., for Born in the Colony; C.F., for Came Free; F.S., for Free by Servitude; A.P., for Holding an Absolute Pardon; C.P. for holding a Conditional Pardon; T.L., for Holding a Ticket of Leave; C., for Convict; C.S., for Colonial Sentence; and G.S., for Government (or Assigned) Servant.

This concern with civil status reflected the continuing penal aspect of the colony: of a civil population of 30,827 over 12 years of age registered at the census, roughly three quarters had been or were convicts. Other information obtained in the census related to numbers of stock and the area of cultivated land.

What was distinctively new in this census was the distribution of printed forms by responsible persons 'by whom, as well as by the respective Householders, who can write, each Form is to be signed when duly filled up'.

How accurate was this first census? One observation in 1836 noted that all population enumerations in New South Wales 'are considered very inaccurate by those who know the colony well, especially that of 1828, when the settlers were apprehensive of the establishment of a poll tax'. This assessment of the 1828 census was repeated, perhaps not independently, in a paper read to the Statistical Society of London in 1849.76 An official recognition of inaccuracy in the total count is in a note appended to the 1828 return in the Blue Book. It declared that account should be taken of Runaway Convicts in the Bush', 'Persons who have no fixed Place of Residence' and 'Omissions that may have occurred', but that in total these 'do not exceed 2,000 persons.

Censuses in New South Wales were carried out in 1833 and then after only three years in 1836, presumably to adapt planned five-year periods to the British decennial census dates, which began in 1801. The five-year interval was maintained in New South Wales from 1836 to 1861. After 1828 the agricultural section of the census was dropped, and in 1833 and 1836, possibly because the Governor was sympathetic to public sensitivity, civil condition was simply distinguished as free or convict. Between 1841 and 1851, when the question was put for the last time, ex-convicts were identified. The census of 1841 was said by a contemporary to have been 'taken from the principle laid down in the former Census Acts of England, with such alterations as the nature of our society and our circumstances rendered expedient'. Supervised by the Colonial Secretary, E. Deas-Thomson, this census showed 'a marked advance over all preceding enumerations'. 'As well as a more detailed population census there was an enumeration of housing in New South Wales. In the 1846 census two new lines of inquiry, education and birthplace, were added to the seven of 1841; results were now presented in fifty-six tables instead of five.80 The 1851 and 1856 censuses were very similar to that of 1846; the 1856 census, the first after self-government, was introduced by a report analysing the returns.

Other Colonies

Beginning in 1841 the Port Phillip district was distinguished in the New South Wales censuses; by then the population was 11,738 compared with the 224 of 1836. Legal separation from New South Wales was accomplished in 1851, and the only census conducted by the Victorian authorities before self-government was in 1854—in the middle of a population explosion brought on by the gold discoveries. Formally it was in the hands of the Registrar General, and the British example was drawn upon heavily. British schedules were adapted by W. H. Archer, the Assistant Registrar General, 'to the circumstances and requirements of the Colonial Census'81, and the information was published in the British form 'to comply with the expressed desire of scientific men at home, that the statistics of every part of the Empire should be drawn up on one uniform plan'. There was little time for preparation for this census, and the Registrar General emphasised the difficulties he faced.83 In the event, the census showed a growth of population from 77,345 in 1851 to 236,798 in 1854. There is further discussion of this census in a later section.

There were censuses in 1841, 1844, 1846 and 1851 in South Australia. The 1841 census appears to have classified the population by age and district only. The later censuses added conjugal condition, religion, occupation and housing.

In this period the population of Western Australia was very small. The Registrar General in 1848 claimed that the count of that year was the first 'systematic census', although earlier, almost annual enumerations existed. In 1848 the total non-Aboriginal population was 4,622 and was classified in districts by age, conjugal condition, religion and occupation. Agricultural information was also obtained. By the next census in 1854, convicts had been introduced and the population was 11,976. At both censuses some information was collected on Aboriginal numbers.

Censuses began in Van Dieman's Land at a date considerably later than in New South Wales. They were held in 1842, 1843, 1848 and 1851. In 1842 the population of 57,420 was classified for each district by age, conjugal condition, civil condition, religion, occupation and housing. There was little change in the schedule over the four censuses. Like New

South Wales, Tasmania was a convict colony and 'civil condition' specified whether 'free' or 'bond', and within the free group ex-convicts were distinguished. An assessment of these censuses describes them as being 'of doubtful accuracy'.

CONCLUSION

Three main vehicles of official statistics have been identified for the period from the foundation of Australia to 1855. Up to 1822 attention was directed to a wide range of reports for the British authorities, a large proportion of which came directly from the Governor's office. From 1822 annual Blue Books of statistical information, designed by the Colonial Office, were the most important means of reporting. Local influences increasingly affected the character of these books, and the practice developed of retaining copies in the colonies for local use. The Governor remained formally responsible for their production, but the actual statistical collating devolved on to a public servant, usually the Colonial Secretary. The third type of official statistic was the census, the first being held in 1828 in New South Wales. The form and the timing of the censuses were decided in the colonies.

What was achieved in the Australian colonies must be seen in the context of developments in British official statistics. Although decennial population censuses began in 1801, it was not until the 1830s that attention was directed towards making some general use of the statistical material generated by individual government departments. Forth is purpose the Statistical Department of the Board of Trade was formed in 1832. Its head was G. R. Porter, a distinguished statistician, and it is claimed that under him 'the incoherent mass of periodical tables then prepared was for the first time reduced to orderly and comprehensive returns, accompanied by lucid explanations of the meaning and limitations of the figures . . . and giving to it a comparative character by including the figures for a series of years'. Further evidence of the growing interest in the social usefulness of statistics was the formation of the Statistical Society of London (later Royal Statistical Society) in 1834, the function of which, according to its prospectus, was to 'procure, arrange and publish facts calculated to illustrate the condition and prospects of society'.

It was easier to impose the collection of such statistics on the colonies, than to negotiate their introduction into Britain. The annual production of statistical material in some thirty colonies throughout the world, required by the Blue Book, was a significant statistical achievement. Colonial practice was ahead of Britain's. Not until 1854 was the first Statistical Abstract produced for the United Kingdom: it covered the years 1840 to 1853 and was a mere 27 pages in length. The Statistical Returns prepared for the Legislative Council in New South Wales in the 1840s stand comparison with it.

At the beginning of the 1850s the five small Australian colonies, with a total population of some 400,000, were producing statistics relating to their societies, which were impressive in quality and range. Their small bureaucracies had become accustomed to the discipline of the annual production of statistical material to meet the standards of an outside authority. The impact of self-government remained to be seen.

Quoted from the Terms of Reference of the House of Commons Select Committee

The Charter created two Courts—the Governor's Court and the Supreme Court
The Epitome of Official History of NSW—page 30
Extract from the Official Account of the Trip to Governor Macquarie
The Epitome of Official History of NSW—page 29
The Epitome of Official History of NSW—Page 31
The Diaries and Letters of G.T.W.B. Boyes Volume 1 1820-1832
Bathurst to Bigge—Letter of appointment and terms of reference, 1819
Macquarie to Bathurst HRA 1:20:653
Summary prepared by this author from quarterly reports of Police & Orphan Fund revenues and expenditures printed in the *Sydney Gazettes*
Taken from Ginswick MS as reported by N.G. Butlin in 'The Economy before 1850'
'William Lithgow – Biography' by G.W. Beckett

BIBLIOGRAPHY AND FURTHER READING

FURTHER READING

On population growth in NSW

1. Historical Records of Australia, Series I, Vol I, pp. 11-12.
2. HRA: I:I; 14.
3. HRA: I:I; 15.
4. HRA: I:I; 52—4
5. HRA: I:I; 63.
6. HRA: I:I; 80.
7. HRA: I:I; 203.
8. HRA: I:I; 279-82.
9. HRA: I:I; 401-2.
10. HRA: I:I: 456.
11. HRA 1:1:456
12. HRA: I:I: 51.
13. HRA: I:I: 678.
14. HRA 1:1:678
15. HRA: I; 2: 17.
16. HRA: 1:2:69
17. HRA: 1:3:8
18. T.A Coghlan General Report on the Eleventh Census of New South Wales, 1894, p. 48.
19. Coghlan, p. 51.
20. Coghlan, p. 60.
21. Coghlan, p. 62.
22. Coghlan, p. 68.
23. Coghlan, p. 69.
24. HRA: I, X, 380.

25. HRA: I, X, 533.
26. Coghlan, pp. 68-9 and N.S.W, Blue Book, 1828, p. 146.
27. HRA: 1:1:651
28. HRA1: 1:651.
29. S.J. Butlin, Foundation of the Australian Monetary System 1788-1851, Melbourne, 1953 p. 48
30. HRA: 1:3:55
31. See, e.g. HRA: 1:2:208-9.
32. HRA: 1:2:632
33. HRA: I, X, 408.
34. H.T. Manning, British Colonial Government After the American Revolution 1782-1820, New Haven, 1935, p. 483.
35. R.W. Horton, Exposition and Defence of Earl Bathurst's Administration of the Affairs of Canada when Colonial Secretary during the years 1822 to 1827, Inclusive, London, 1838 p. 40. Horton was Under-secretary of the department 1822-1827.
36. HRA: 1:15:239
37. HRA: 1:15:441
38. British Parliamentary Papers (H.C), XVII (129), 231-42.
39. Colonial Office, 324/104, Feb. 24, 1817.
40. HRA: 1:14:223
41. C.O. 954/1, 113.
42. HRA: 1:11:83
43. HRA: 1:11:244
44. HRA: 1:11:206
45. HRA: 1:11:552
46. HRA: 1:11:252
47. HRA: 1:14:222-3
48. HRA: 1:15:69
49. HRA 1:15:69.
50. N.S.W. Blue Book, 1828.
51. HRA: 1:16:99
52. HRA: I: XVII: 194-5.
53. HRA: I: XX: 579-80.
54. HRA: I: XX: 753-4.
55. HRA: I: XXI: 188.
56. HRA: I: XXI: 316-7.
57. ibid.

58. HRA: I: XXI: 436.
59. HRA: I: XXII: 36.
60. HRA: I: XXII: 98.
61. HRA: I: XXVI: 701.
62. HRA: I: XXIII: 22-3.
63. C.O. 323/208, 72.
64. C.O, 323/208, 73.
65. C.O. 323/208, 74.
66. HRA:, I, XVIII, 656-7.
67. HRA: I, XV, 69.
68. H.C. 1837, VII (516) p. 100.
69. ibid, p. 194.
70. ibid, p. 100.
71. Statistical Register of N.S.W. from 1850 to 1859, Registrar General's Report, p. 8.
72. N.S.W. Legislative Council, Votes and Proceedings, 1828, p. 43.
73. Government Notice: Census for the year 1828', reprinted in Coghlan, p. 71.
74. ibid.
75. R. Montgomery Martin F. S. S., History of Australasia Comprising New South Wales, Van Diemen's island, Swan River, South Australia, etc., London, 1836, p. 134.
76. J.T. Danson, 'Some particulars of the Commercial Progress of the Colonial Dependencies of the United Kingdom, during the Twenty years, 1827-46', Quarterly Journal of the Statistical Society of London, November, 1849.
77. N.S.W Blue Book, 1828, p. 147.
78. Ralph Mansfield, Analytical View of the Census of New South Wales for the Year 1841; With Tables Showing the Progress of the Population during the previous Twenty Years, Sydney, 1841, p. 3.
79. Coghlan, p. 81.
80. ibid., p. 85.
81. Census of Victoria, 1854, Population Tables, Report, p. vi.
82. ibid. p, iii.
83. ibid. p, v.
84. Government Gazette of Western Australia, Dec. 19, 1848, p. 1.

85. D. N. Allen, The Development of Official Statistics in Tasmania (Dissertation for Diploma of Public Administration, University of Tasmania, 1965), p. 46.
86. J. Koren (ed.), The History of Statistics: Their Development and Progress in many Countries, New York, 1918, Chapter by A. Baines, 'Great Britain and Ireland', p. 374.
87. ibid., p. 385.
88. Statistical Abstract for the United Kingdom in each Year from 1840 to 1853: First Number (1854).
89. For a listing of the official publications, see Jennifer Finlayson, Historical Statistics of Australia: A Select List of Official Sources, Canberra, 1970.

BIBLIOGRAPHY

Shann, E. O. 'Economic History of Australia'

Yarwood, A. T. - Samuel Marsden (1977)

Collins, David 'An Account of the English colony in NSW' (1798)

Steven, Margaret 'Merchant Campbell 1769-1846)

Bigge, John Thomas 'Report of Commissioner of Inquiry, on the State of Agriculture and Trade in New South Wales' (1823)

Palmer, L.H. 'Our John's Adventures' (1988)

Carter, W. E. R. 'John Palmer: Father of the Colony' (1986)

Collins, David ' An Account of the English Colony in NSW' (1798)

Beckett, G. W. 'The Development of Public Finance in the Colony'

Crawley, Frank 'Colonial Australia ' Vol 1

The Sydney Gazette 1803-1809-1816-1821

The Australian Chronicle

H.R.A. series 1 vol 1 -10 (10-p651)

HRNSW Vols 1-IV

Marjorie Barnard - "A History of Australia"

Foster, Josephine "John Palmer' Journal Royal Aust Hist, Soc Vol 11 (1925)

Mackaness, G. 'The Life of William Bligh'

Coghlan, T. A. 'Labour & Industry in Australia Vol 1-IV (1918) '

Butlin, N. G. 'Forming a Colonial Economy'

Report of the Committee of Inquiry into Transportation - Evidence by John Palmer 1812

The Late John Palmer. An article in "New South Wales Magazine -vol 1834"

Lea-Scarlett, Errol 'Queanbeyan - The District & Its People.

Evatt, H. V. 'The Rum Rebellion'(1938)

Crowley, F -'Colonial Australia' Vol 1

Illustrated History of Australia

Collins, David -'An Account of the English Colony in N SW'

Flannery, T (Ed) - 'The Birth of Sydney'

The Oxford History of Australia

Hughes, R - 'The Fatal Shore'

Historical Records of NSW

Macquarie Publishing ' A Colonial Time-Line'